# Trade Policy and Global Poverty

CENTER FOR GLOBAL DEVELOPMENT
INSTITUTE FOR INTERNATIONAL ECONOMICS

# Trade Policy and

# Global Poverty

WILLIAM R. CLINE

Washington, DC
June 2004

**William R. Cline** is a senior fellow jointly at the Institute for International Economics and the Center for Global Development. He has been a senior fellow at the Institute since its inception in 1981. During 1996–2001, while on leave from the Institute, he was deputy managing director and chief economist at the Institute of International Finance. He was a senior fellow at the Brookings Institution (1973–81); deputy director of development and trade research, office of the assistant secretary for international affairs, US Treasury Department (1971–73); Ford Foundation visiting professor in Brazil (1970–71); and lecturer and assistant professor of economics at Princeton University (1967–70). His publications include *International Debt: Systemic Risk and Policy Response* (1984), *Exports of Manufactures from Developing Countries* (1984), *The US-Japan Economic Problem* (1985), *Mobilizing Bank Lending to Debtor Countries* (1987), *The Future of World Trade in Textiles and Apparel* (1987), *United States External Adjustment and the World Economy* (1989), *The Economics of Global Warming* (1992), *International Economic Policy in the 1990s* (1994), *International Debt Reexamined* (1995), and *Trade and Income Distribution* (1997).

**CENTER FOR GLOBAL DEVELOPMENT**
1776 Massachusetts Avenue, NW, Suite 301
Washington, DC 20036
(202) 416-0700    FAX: (202) 416-0750
www.cgdev.org

Nancy Birdsall, *President*

**INSTITUTE FOR INTERNATIONAL ECONOMICS**
1750 Massachusetts Avenue, NW
Washington, DC 20036-1903
(202) 328-9000    FAX: (202) 659-3225
www.iie.com

C. Fred Bergsten, *Director*
Valerie Norville, *Director of Publications and Web Development*
Edward Tureen, *Director of Marketing*

*Typesetting by BMWW*
*Printing by Kirby Lithographic Company, Inc.*

Printed in the United States of America
06 05 04    5 4 3 2 1

**Library of Congress Cataloging-in-Publication Data**

Cline, William R.
   Trade policy and global poverty /
   William R. Cline.
      p. cm.
   Includes bibliographical references and
   index.
   ISBN 0-88132-365-9
   1. Commercial policy.  2. Tariff preferences.  3. Protectionism.  4. Free trade—Economic aspects—Developing countries.  5. Poverty—Developing countries.  6. Income distribution—Developing countries.  7. Developing countries—Commercial policy.  I. Institute for International Economics (U.S.)  II. Center for Global Development.  III. Title.

HF1411.C4355  2004
339.4'6—dc22                    2003065584

The views expressed in this publication are those of the author. This publication is part of the overall program of the Center and the Institute, as endorsed by their respective Boards of Directors, but does not necessarily reflect the views of individual members of their Boards or Advisory Committees.

# Contents

**Figures**

# Preface

Would freer trade free more of the world's poor from the misery their poverty represents? Though few would argue anymore that globalization has only winners and no losers, this book answers the question with a resounding yes. Though successive rounds of postwar multilateral trade negotiations have reduced the costs of protection and increased trade and its benefits, there is much more still to be gained, especially for the developing countries. And much of those gains for developing countries could come from further reductions in protection in the richest countries.

The recent Uruguay Round of negotiations, completed in 1994, continued the pattern of progress toward sharp reductions in protection in industrial countries for most manufactures but only meager advances in liberalizing high protection in sectors with politically important domestic constituencies, especially agriculture and textiles and apparel. Yet these are the sectors in which the developing countries have a comparative advantage. The Uruguay Round left tariffs largely unchanged in these sectors, although it converted agricultural quotas to tariffs and promised the removal of textile and apparel quotas by 2005. The effective postponement of liberalization meant that developing countries gained much less from the round than they might have. Stiff resistance in Europe to cutting its large farm subsidies and an increase in these subsidies within the United States have recently deepened this impression. So has the increasing attention paid to the rules developing countries agreed to on intellectual property rights, which became closely associated in the public mind with the high costs of medicines to fight the AIDS pandemic in the poorest countries.

The current Doha Round was therefore designated the "Development Round" to show international commitment to a stronger realization of potential benefits for developing countries from the new round. The implication is that the Doha Round is designed to go beyond the traditional commercial deal-making whereby countries place import liberalization offers on the table solely to obtain reciprocal offers from trading partners. To live up to its title, the round will have to make special efforts to ensure the opening of new opportunities for developing countries.

William R. Cline, a joint senior fellow at the Center for Global Development and the Institute for International Economics, has written extensively on both trade and development issues. This study seeks to provide a comprehensive analysis of the potential for trade liberalization to spur growth and reduce poverty in developing countries. It provides specific analysis of how much impact liberalization by industrial countries, along with liberalization by the developing countries themselves, can have on global poverty.

Cline finds that the global poverty stakes in trade policy are large. Global free trade would convey long-term economic benefits of about $200 billion annually to the developing countries. Half or more of these gains would be attributable to the removal of industrial-country protection against developing-country exports. By removing their trade barriers, the industrial countries could thereby convey economic benefits to developing countries worth about twice the amount of their annual development assistance. Helping developing countries grow through trade, moreover, would be accompanied by economic benefits for the industrial countries themselves in the form of lower consumer costs for imports and other increased economic efficiencies from opening trade.

The study further estimates that free trade could reduce the number of people in global poverty (earning less than $2 per day) by about 500 million over 15 years. This would cut the world poverty level by an additional 25 percent. Agricultural liberalization alone contributes about half of these gains. Cline thus judges that the developing countries were right to risk collapse of the Doha Round at the Cancún ministerial meeting in September 2003 by insisting on much deeper liberalization of agriculture than the industrial countries were then willing to offer.

The study calls for a two-track strategy. The first track is deep multilateral liberalization involving phased but complete elimination of protection by industrial countries and deep reduction of protection by at least the middle-income developing countries, albeit on a more gradual schedule. The second track is immediate free entry for imports from "high risk" low-income countries (heavily indebted poor countries, least developed countries, and sub-Saharan Africa), coupled with a 10-year tax holiday for direct investment in these countries. The "poverty intensity" of imports from these countries is far higher than the average for imports from other developing countries, and the head start from immediate free entry would provide an important boost to the pace of global poverty reduction.

Political leadership is required to realize the poverty-reduction potential of global free trade. As this book goes to press there are some signs that this leadership is emerging and can begin to overcome the powerful resistance from such interests as the recipients of agricultural subsidies. If this new momentum can build, the Doha Round may yet prove worthy of being recorded as the Development Round.

* * *

The Center for Global Development is a nonprofit, nonpartisan institution dedicated to reducing global poverty and inequality through policy-oriented research and active engagement on development issues with the policy community and the public. A principal focus of the Center's work is policies of the United States and other industrialized countries that affect development prospects in poor countries and policies of the international institutions such as the World Bank and the IMF that are central to the world's development architecture.

The Center's Board of Directors bears overall responsibility for the Center and includes distinguished leaders of nongovernmental organizations, former officials, business executives, and some of the world's leading scholars of development. The Center receives advice on its research and policy programs from the Board and from an Advisory Committee that comprises respected development specialists and advocates. The Center's president works with the Board, the Advisory Committee, and the Center's senior staff in setting the research and program priorities, and approves all formal publications. The Center is supported by an initial significant financial contribution from Edward W. Scott Jr. and by funding from philanthropic and other organizations.

The Institute for International Economics is a private, nonprofit institution for the study and discussion of international economic policy. Its purpose is to analyze important issues in that area and to develop and communicate practical new approaches for dealing with them. The Institute is completely nonpartisan.

The Institute is funded largely by philanthropic foundations. Major institutional grants are now being received from the William M. Keck, Jr. Foundation and the Starr Foundation. A number of other foundations and private corporations contribute to the highly diversified financial resources of the Institute. About 18 percent of the Institute's resources in its latest fiscal year were provided by contributors outside the United States, including about 8 percent from Japan.

The Board of Directors bears overall responsibility for the Institute and gives general guidance and approval to its research program, including the identification of topics that are likely to become important over the medium run (one to three years), and which should be addressed by the Institute. The director, working closely with the staff and outside Advisory Committee, is responsible for the development of particular projects and makes the final decision to publish an individual study.

The Center and the Institute hope that their studies and other activities will contribute to building a stronger foundation for international economic policy around the world. We invite readers of these publications to let us know how they think we can best accomplish this objective.

NANCY BIRDSALL
President
Center for Global
  Development
May 2004

C. FRED BERGSTEN
Director
Institute for
International Economics
May 2004

# Acknowledgments

I thank Ceren Ozer for inspired and tireless research assistance, including implementation of the general equilibrium model. Robert Johnson provided detailed research on protection for an early draft of chapter 3. I am indebted to Ethan Kapstein and an anonymous reviewer for comments on the final manuscript. For fruitful dialogues on key sections of the study, I am especially grateful to Angus Deaton, Thomas Rutherford, David Tarr, and Dominique Van der Mensbrugghe. Helpful comments on various parts of the study were also given by Barry Bosworth, Scott Bradford, Mac Destler, Kimberly Elliott, Charles Gore, Thomas Hertel, Bernard Hoekman, Gary Hufbauer, Douglas Lippoldt, Will Martin, Branko Milanovic, Richard Newfarmer, David Orden, Howard Pack, Steven Radelet, Sherman Robinson, Dani Rodrik, David Roodman, Andrew Warner, and John Williamson. Important suggestions and feedback were provided by participants in study groups hosted by the Center for Global Development and Institute for International Economics in April 2002 and September 2003 and in seminars presented in October-December 2003 at the Centre d'Etudes Prospectives et d'Informations Internationales, UNCTAD, WTO, Centre for International Trade and Sustainable Development, and World Bank. I particularly thank Nancy Birdsall and C. Fred Bergsten for their sustained encouragement and guidance in this project. This book is dedicated to my grandchildren: Kathryn, Joseph Harwood, Joseph William, and Annemarie.

# Summary

Global poverty remains at a remarkably high level. Half of the world's population lives in poverty today if one uses the definition of $2 per day (at purchasing power parity, which takes into account the lower local cost of living in poor countries). One-fourth of the world's population has an income of $1 per day or less. The proportion in poverty has gradually declined during the past decade, but the absolute number has remained about the same after taking into account population growth.

Global concessional assistance from rich to poor countries amounts to about $50 billion a year, which works out to about $17 a year per poor person globally. This assistance can make a critical difference, especially when focused on the poorest countries and linked to sound governance and economic policies. Even with potential increases, however, aid alone can make only modest inroads in reducing global poverty.

There is a second policy instrument that can make a powerful contribution to the fight against global poverty: trade policy. The opportunity to boost economic growth through increased exports to more open markets may be the most valuable benefit that policies in rich countries can give to the poor in developing countries. Moreover, opening markets would give gains to the industrial countries themselves in the form of lower prices for consumers.

The estimates of this study suggest that global free trade would confer income gains of at least about $90 billion annually in developing countries for traditional "static" effects, and total long-term gains including dynamic effects would be about $200 billion annually (chapter 5).[1] This

---

1. This is at 1997 prices and economic scale.

study, moreover, estimates that at least half of these gains would arise from removing protection against developing-country products in industrial-country markets, especially in agricultural goods and textiles and apparel. On this basis, it can be estimated that the elimination of industrial-country protection would provide long-term gains to developing countries of about $100 billion annually, or about twice as much as annual concessional assistance.

Chapter 1 sets the stage for this study by reviewing the evidence on trends in global poverty and delineating the principal relationships of trade policy to economic growth and poverty reduction. A poverty mapping locates about half of the world's poor in China and India alone, and places another one-seventh in just four countries with more than 100 million poor people each—Indonesia, Pakistan, Nigeria, and Bangladesh. About one-fourth of the world's poor are located in what may be called "at-risk" countries already identified in special international groupings: the least developed countries (LDCs), heavily indebted poor countries (HIPCs), and sub-Saharan Africa (SSA).

Chapter 1 proposes the concept of the "poverty intensity of trade" as useful for gauging the potential impact of trade policy in industrial countries on the global poor. This measure would be 100 percent for imports coming from a country with an entirely poor population, and zero for imports from a country with no poor people (at the $2 level). It turns out that industrial-country imports from all developing countries have an average poverty intensity of 33 percent on a headcount basis and only 7 percent on an income-share basis (figure S.1). In contrast, imports are much more poverty intensive from the at-risk countries (LDCs, HIPCs, and SSA), at a range of 60 to 70 percent on a headcount basis and 40 to 50 percent on an income-share basis.

Considering the poverty intensity of trade leads quickly to thinking about a two-track strategy for international trade policy. In the first track, there would be phased reduction or elimination of protection on a multilateral basis by all countries. In a parallel second track, there would be immediate free market access for imports from the at-risk countries, where the potential impact on the poor would be the greatest. Both tracks would be pursued in the current Doha Round of multilateral negotiations within the World Trade Organization (WTO). Ideally, middle-income countries would participate in the liberalization offered on both tracks. Because the base of imports from the at-risk countries is small (ranging from 4 percent of imports from developing countries for Japan and 6 percent for the United States to 8 percent for the European Union), any special adjustment problems in industrial-country markets from the deepening of existing special-access arrangements to immediate complete free access would be minimal, as would any likely trade diversion away from other developing countries.

The background analysis in chapter 1 considers various controversies about global poverty. One is whether the World Bank, the key source for

**Figure S.1  Poverty intensity of industrial-country imports from developing countries**

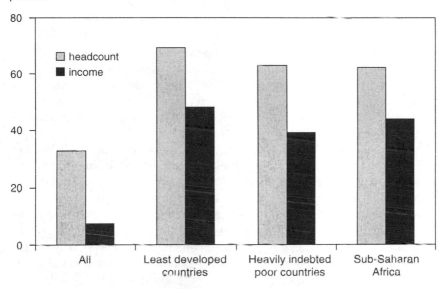

percent

Note: Weighted average: Canada, European Union, Japan, and United States.

*Source:* See table 1.4.

global poverty estimates, has underreported the pace of poverty reduction. It relies on household surveys, and over time these have increasingly tended to understate average consumption relative to levels reported in national accounts. Although Bhalla (2002) uses this divergence to estimate much more rapid poverty reduction than estimated by the World Bank, a review of the debate suggests that his view is too optimistic. A second controversy is whether there has been a "convergence" of income levels in international growth experience. Appendix 1C to chapter 1 presents data showing that if growth is weighted by population, convergence has in fact been occurring during the past four decades.

Finally, chapter 1 presents summary data strongly suggesting that the pace of GDP growth has been correlated with export growth. GDP growth, in turn, is the underlying force providing the potential for reducing poverty. On average, 1 percentage point of additional growth translates into a 2 percent reduction in the number of poor people. Appendix 1A shows that in a mathematical function for income distribution (lognormal), this "growth elasticity" of poverty is higher when the ratio of average per capita income to the poverty threshold is higher, and lower when the degree of income concentration is higher. Country estimates of poverty elasticities taking these influences into account are used in the subsequent estimates of poverty reduction effects from trade liberalization.

In part as a basis for better understanding the potential of the "two-track" policy strategy set forth above, chapter 2 reviews past experience with regimes of preferential market access. It finds that whereas the Generalized System of Preferences (GSP) has tended to have little effect because of product and country exclusions, more intensive special regimes have had more positive effects on developing-country exports. These include the EU's Lomé Convention and the United States' Caribbean Basin Initiative and Andean Trade Preference Act. The chapter also reviews the initial evidence on the impact of the US African Growth and Opportunity Act and makes suggestions for its enhancement.

Chapter 3 then sets forth the empirical landscape for industrial-country protection against imports from developing countries. In manufactures, textiles and apparel are confirmed to be the main locus of substantial protection and tariff peaks, while other manufactures face relatively low protection. Protection tends to be high in agriculture. Agricultural tariffs (including specific tariffs and high above-quota tariffs of "tariff-rate quota" protection) are high in Canada, the European Union, and especially Japan. Ironically, much of the public attention has instead focused on agricultural subsidies. The chapter develops a method for translating subsidies into tariff equivalents, which tend to be lower (e.g., at about 10 percent for subsidies vs. 33 percent for agricultural tariffs in the European Union).

The elimination of agricultural protection and subsidies in industrial countries would tend to boost world agricultural prices, because production would decline in these countries. Appendix 3C presents a simple model that calculates the impact of higher world prices on global poverty, which depends on whether the poor are mainly in the rural or urban sector, and on the share of food in the household budget of the poor. Because about three-fourths of the world's poor are located in the rural sector and would enjoy income gains from higher agricultural prices, global poverty would tend to decline from the elimination of industrial-country agricultural protection and subsidies. Using reasonable assumptions, the reduction could be large, at a central estimate of 200 million lifted out of poverty globally.

It turns out, moreover, that concerns about losses for food-importing developing countries have been exaggerated. Most of the world's poor live in countries that are net agricultural exporters. Even most of the least developed countries (with the notable exception of Bangladesh) have a comparative advantage in agricultural goods, and so should benefit rather than lose from a rise in world agricultural prices following industrial-country liberalization.

Chapter 3 combines the protection estimates for textiles and apparel, other manufactures, and agriculture to arrive at an Aggregate Measure of Protection against developing countries. This turns out to be relatively low at 4 percent for the United States, significant at 10 percent for the European Union, and relatively high at 16 percent for Japan. Although these levels are not high by historical standards, they remain substantial, and the removal of protection could make a major difference for export opportunities for developing countries. Moreover, the aggregate protection levels, which are based on most-favored-nation (MFN) protection weighted by imports from developing countries, are unlikely to be overstated by much because of duty-free entry for LDCs and SSA. As noted, the shares of these countries in total imports from developing countries are simply too small to affect the aggregates by much.

As background for the subsequent estimates of this study, chapter 3 then surveys existing computable general equilibrium (CGE) model estimates of the potential impact of global trade liberalization for developing countries. The chapter concludes with a brief consideration of protection in the services sectors. While acknowledging that this could potentially be large, the discussion suggests that the existing estimates in this area tend to be highly speculative and may be overstated.

Chapter 4 applies a leading CGE model and the most widely applied database for trade and protection to estimate the impact of international trade liberalization on global poverty[2] The PEHRT model developed in this study divides the world into 24 developing and 6 industrial countries or regions and 22 product categories.[3] The model first replicates existing production and trade flows, and then it estimates how they would change as a consequence of reduction or removal of protection. An important output of the model is the change in the "factor prices" for unskilled labor, skilled labor, capital, and land. The impact of trade liberalization on the wages of unskilled labor is then used as the main basis for calculating the rise in income for poor households after liberalization. This increase is applied to the "poverty elasticity" and initial number of people in poverty, for each region, to compute the impact of multilateral liberalization on global poverty.

Alternative runs of the model show three important patterns. First, agriculture is crucial to potential welfare gains from free trade, accounting for about half of the total for both industrial and developing countries. This confirms that agricultural liberalization is crucial if the Doha Round is to fulfill its potential.

Second, between one-half and two-thirds of developing countries' gains from free trade arise from the removal of protection in industrial countries. This is lower than the fraction identified in a recent study by the Organization for Economic Cooperation and Development (OECD 2003c) but higher than estimated in a corresponding study by the World

---

2. The model is that of Harrison, Rutherford, and Tarr (1996), or HRT. The database is the Global Trade Policy Analysis compilation (GTAP5; Dimaranan and McDougall 2002).

3. PEHRT is an abbreviation for the "Poverty Effects" version of the HRT model.

Bank (2002a). The technical reasons for the differing attribution of gains are set forth in chapter 4, but for policy purposes a key point is that the findings here tend to refute the view that the developing countries are themselves to blame for the vast bulk of the losses they experience from protection (e.g., see *The Economist*, September 6, 2003).

Third, the developing countries achieve a surprisingly high fraction of their total potential gains in a scenario in which the industrial countries fully eliminate protection but the developing countries cut protection only by half (but eliminate protection against each other). This result lends some credence to a somewhat differentiated Doha Round outcome providing for substantial but not complete liberalization by developing countries accompanied by complete liberalization by industrial countries.

The "static" estimates of the model estimate global poverty reduction of about 110 million people as a result of global free trade. In light of the alternative estimate of 200 million for agriculture alone in the simpler model of chapter 3, this estimate may be seen as conservative. In a longer-term "Steady State" version of the PEHRT model, in which additional capital investment induced by new trade opportunities is taken into account, poverty reduction rises to as much as 535 million people.

Chapter 5 then examines dynamic productivity effects. It begins with a critical review of the econometric literature relating growth to trade and trade policy. This review leads to a summary estimate that for each 1 percent increase in the ratio of trade to GDP, long-term output per capita rises by 0.5 percent. After reducing this estimate to avoid double counting the influence of induced investment, this "productivity elasticity" amounts to 0.4. Because the CGE model estimates that global free trade would raise developing-country trade by about 5 percent, the estimate for long-term productivity gain amounts on average to $0.4 \times 5 = 2$ percent above the baseline. When applied to country-specific trade increases, poverty elasticities, and poverty populations, this approach yields an estimated 200 million people lifted out of poverty globally from the long-term productivity effect of global free trade.

When the static poverty reduction estimates are added to the dynamic productivity estimates, and conservatively one-half of the additional contribution from the induced investment (steady state) effect is added, the central estimate for total poverty reduction from global free trade amounts to 540 million people lifted out of poverty over 10 to 15 years as a consequence of global free trade.[4] The stakes in international trade policy are thus large. The move to free trade could reduce global poverty by about one-fifth of today's total, and by about one-fourth of the total projected by 2015.

---

4. Note that the corresponding estimate in World Bank (2002a) is 320 million. The difference is essentially the addition of (half of) the incremental effect from taking induced investment into account, a component not included in the World Bank estimates.

Although this estimate is large, from one important standpoint, it may be understated: It does not include the impact of liberalizing trade in services. Some estimates place these gains at considerably more than the gains from liberalizing merchandise trade, suggesting that there is an ample cushion against overstatement in the poverty-impact estimates of this study.

Chapter 6 concludes by first recapitulating in greater detail the principal findings of this study, and then considering the implications for the Doha Round. The temporary breakdown of the round at Cancún in September 2003 may best be seen as a legitimate forcing move by the developing countries to obtain a more meaningful offer of agricultural liberalization from the industrial countries. A compromise between the United States and the European Union shortly before the Cancún ministerial meeting had produced a minimalist proposal for liberalizing agriculture, yet this is the sector most highly protected by the industrial countries and most important for developing countries in terms of blocked market access.

A blueprint for successfully concluding the Doha Round set forth in chapter 6 includes the following main components. First, the industrial countries would commit to deep reductions in tariffs, including in agriculture and in textiles and apparel. Second, they would also commit to "decouple" agricultural subsidies from production and exports. Third, at least the middle-income developing countries would commit to major cuts in their own protection (e.g., by at least 50 to 60 percent). These liberalization commitments would all be phased in over several years. Fourth, the "second track" of trade policy would also be mobilized by the granting of immediate free access to imports from the at-risk countries (LDCs, HIPCs, and SSA). Fifth, also in this second track, the industrial countries would adopt tax incentives for direct investment in these countries.

The second-track measures would not only serve to focus early liberalization where it would have the most potential to reduce poverty but could also help address one of the potential obstacles to a successful outcome: the concern of LDCs and some other poor countries that they stand to lose more from the erosion of their existing trade preferences than they stand to gain from further multilateral liberalization. A tailored run of the PEHRT model suggests that this concern is misplaced. These countries would tend to gain from liberalizing their own markets, and from new market access in countries not currently granting free access (including middle-income countries), by enough to offset the erosion of the preference margin from existing special-access regimes in the US and EU markets.

Nevertheless, the least developed countries' concern about preference erosion appears to be strong, and the new "single-undertaking" structure of WTO negotiations could make it tempting for them to block an overall agreement. The second track of immediate deepening of special access would serve as a positive incentive for the least developed countries to support an overall Doha Round agreement for moving decisively toward global free trade.

# Sizing Up the Issues

**1**

This study examines the impact of trade policy on global poverty, with an emphasis on how changes in policies in the United States and other industrial countries could help reduce poverty in developing countries. To gauge the problem, this chapter first reviews the extent of global poverty and its trends over time. A key concept, analyzed more formally in appendix 1B below, is the "elasticity of poverty" with respect to growth. The underlying notion is that ultimately it is economic growth that will be the major engine that lifts hundreds of millions out of poverty, and it is important to understand the influences that determine how responsive poverty reduction is to growth. The chapter then develops a concept of "poverty intensity of trade" to identify the potential antipoverty leverage of industrial-country trade policy vis-à-vis different groupings of countries and differing product categories. The final section sets the stage for the subsequent chapters by outlining the broad features of the relationship of growth to trade, a subject that is analyzed more fully in chapter 5.

## The Extent and Location of Global Poverty

The World Bank has compiled increasingly comprehensive data on income distribution and poverty by country. This chapter uses this information, in combination with certain procedures to fill in the gaps in the data (see appendix 1A), to arrive at an enumeration of the poor by country, using the definition of $2 per day (1999 purchasing power parity, or

PPP) as the threshold for headcount poverty. Mapping global poverty in this way reveals several important patterns:

- About 2.9 billion people, or about half of the world's population, live below the international poverty line of $2 (PPP) per day.

- Only about 260 million people live in those developing countries that have *average* per capita income at or below this poverty line, so about 90 percent of global poverty reflects inequality *within* the other developing countries.

- An estimated 715 million of the world's poor are located in either the least developed countries (476 million poor), the heavily indebted poor countries (418 million), or sub-Saharan Africa (470 million), three largely overlapping country groupings.

- This in turn means that three-fourths of the world's poor live in countries considered too developed to qualify for any of the special regimes oriented toward benefiting countries in these groupings.

- Just two countries, India and China, account for 1.5 billion of the world's poor, or about half of the total. This number drops to 975 million if a cross-country poverty regression line is used to estimate the two countries' poverty rates, rather than applying the rates reported by the World Bank.

- Together with India and China, another 29 countries with at least 10 million people living in poverty cumulate to 90 percent of the global poor. Four of these have approximately 100 million poor people each (Indonesia, Pakistan, Nigeria, and Bangladesh).

The trend in global poverty is toward slow improvement in relative terms but stagnation in absolute numbers. The World Bank (2001, 21) calculates that the fraction of developing-country (including transition country) population in extreme poverty defined as $1 per day or less (1993 PPP) has fallen, but only slowly, from 28.3 percent in 1987 to 24.0 percent in 1998. This 15 percent reduction in the proportionate share of population in extreme poverty over a decade is encouraging. However, it was almost exactly offset by an 18.1 percent rise in global population during the same period.[1] As a result, the absolute number of people in extreme poverty remained virtually unchanged at 1.4 billion from 1987 to 1998. Although the World Bank does not report a comparable estimate for the trend in poverty under the $2 definition, a similar moderate decline in relative incidence and stagnation in absolute number seems likely.

---

1. World population may be calculated at 4.99 billion in 1987 and 5.89 billion in 1998 from UNDP (2001).

The two alternative threshold estimates provide a basis for a rough estimate of the first half of a global Lorenz curve (relating cumulative percent of income on the vertical axis to cumulative percent of population on the horizontal axis). Global GDP in 1999 (PPP) amounted to $40.1 trillion (calculated from table 1A.1 and corresponding World Bank estimates for industrial countries). With a corresponding aggregate population of 5.9 billion, global average per capita income in 1999 was $6,800 (1999 PPP).[2] The bottom one-fourth of global population receives $365 per year or less, and the next quartile less than $730. Even overstating their income by imputing all population in the first group at $365 and in the second at $730, the first quartile of global population receives only 1.4 percent of global income, and the next quartile, only 2.7 percent.[3] The upper half of the global income distribution thus receives 95.9 percent of global income, at an average level of $13,000 per capita or 24 times the average for the bottom half.

## Poverty Location by Size Groups

On the basis of the full set of country estimates reported in appendix 1A, table 1.1 reports the poverty estimates for 31 large developing countries, each of which accounts for at least 10 million poor by the global definition ($2 per day threshold). In the top tier, India and China have about 860 million and 670 million poor respectively (but see the special estimates below for these two countries). In a second tier, four countries have approximately 100 million in poverty each (Indonesia, Pakistan, Nigeria, and Bangladesh). There then begins a spectrum of another 25 countries with the number of poor declining relatively smoothly from about 50 million in Ethiopia to 10 million in Peru. Together, the 31 countries account for 2.57 billion of the global poor, or 90 percent.

This array of large agglomerations of poor people includes instances of moderate population with very high poverty rates (e.g., Madagascar, with a population of 15 million and 13 million in poverty) as well as large populations with more modest poverty rates (e.g., Brazil, with a population of 168 million and 29 million in poverty). The latter combination means that several upper-middle income economies account for somewhere between 10 and 40 million poor each, despite their relatively high per capita incomes. These include Mexico, Russia, Brazil, South Africa, Thailand, and Turkey (all with PPP per capita income of about $6,000 or more).

---

2. For this estimate, it is assumed that average per capita income is $1 per day for Afghanistan, North Korea, Myanmar, Somalia, and Sudan, and $2 per day for Cuba and Iraq; direct estimates are not available for these countries.

3. This assumes that 1.5 billion people receive $365 per year and another 1.5 billion $730 per year, with the remaining 3 billion receiving the rest.

## Table 1.1　Countries with more than 10 million people living in poverty ($2 per day basis)

| Country | Population (millions) | Per capita income[a] (dollars) | Millions living in poverty | Poverty rate[b] (percent) | Gini coefficient |
|---|---|---|---|---|---|
| India | 997.5 | 2,230 | 859.9 | 86.2 | 0.378 |
| China | 1,253.6 | 3,550 | 673.2 | 53.7 | 0.403 |
| Indonesia | 207.0 | 2,660 | 136.8 | 66.1 | 0.365 |
| Pakistan | 134.8 | 1,860 | 114.2 | 84.7 | 0.312 |
| Nigeria | 123.9 | 770 | 112.5 | 90.8 | 0.506 |
| Bangladesh | 127.7 | 1,530 | 99.3 | 77.8 | 0.336 |
| Ethiopia | 62.8 | 620 | 48.0 | 76.4 | 0.400 |
| Vietnam | 77.5 | 1,860 | 41.4 | 53.4[c] | 0.361 |
| Mexico | 96.6 | 8,070 | 41.0 | 42.5 | 0.537 |
| Russia | 146.2 | 6,990 | 36.7 | 25.1 | 0.487 |
| Congo, Democratic Republic of | 49.8 | 800 | 36.2 | 76.8[d] | n.a. |
| Egypt | 62.7 | 3,460 | 33.0 | 52.7 | 0.289 |
| Myanmar | 45.0 | n.a. | 32.8 | 72.8[e] | |
| Philippines | 74.3 | 3,990 | 29.2 | 39.4[c] | 0.462 |
| Brazil | 168.0 | 6,840 | 29.2 | 17.4 | 0.600 |
| Sudan | 29.0 | n.a. | 21.1 | 72.8[e] | n.a. |
| Tanzania | 32.9 | 500 | 19.7 | 59.7 | 0.382 |
| Afghanistan | 26.6 | n.a. | 19.3 | 72.8[e] | n.a. |
| Nepal | 23.4 | 1,280 | 19.3 | 82.5 | 0.367 |
| Kenya | 29.4 | 1,010 | 18.3 | 62.3 | 0.445 |
| Thailand | 60.2 | 5,950 | 17.0 | 28.2 | 0.414 |
| Iran | 63.0 | 5,520 | 16.8 | 26.8[c] | 0.380 |
| Uganda | 21.5 | 1,160 | 16.6 | 77.2 | 0.392 |
| South Africa | 42.1 | 8,710 | 15.1 | 35.8 | 0.593 |
| Mozambique | 17.3 | 810 | 13.6 | 78.4 | 0.396 |
| Madagascar | 15.1 | 790 | 13.4 | 88.8 | 0.460 |
| Colombia | 41.5 | 5,580 | 11.9 | 28.7 | 0.571 |
| Ukraine | 50.0 | 3,360 | 11.8 | 23.7 | 0.325 |
| Turkey | 64.4 | 6,440 | 11.6 | 18.0 | 0.415 |
| Uzbekistan | 24.4 | 2,230 | 11.6 | 47.4[c] | 0.333 |
| Peru | 25.2 | 4,480 | 10.4 | 41.4 | 0.462 |

n.a. = not available

a. In 1999 purchasing power parity dollars per capita.
b. World Bank (2001) poverty rate estimate, unless otherwise noted.
c. Poverty rate calculated from actual Gini and per capita income.
d. Poverty rate calculated from regional Gini and per capita income.
e. Average least developed country poverty rate applied.

*Source:* World Development Indicators (World Bank 2001).

Table 1.2 reports the poverty estimates for four other groupings of developing countries arrayed by the absolute number of poor people in each. Fifteen countries each having 7 to 10 million poor together have 135 million in poverty. Twenty countries each having 3 to 7 million poor together have 96 million in poverty. And 22 countries each having 1 to 3 million poor together have 47 million in poverty. At the tail of the poverty-

**Table 1.2   Economies with number of people living in poverty by range** (millions)

| Number In poverty | Economies | Total population | Total in poverty |
|---|---|---|---|
| More than 10 | See table 1.1 | 4,193.2 | 2,570.9 |
| 7–10 | Ghana, Mali, Burkina Faso, Malawi, Zambia, Cameroon, Niger, Venezuela, Sri Lanka, Angola, Côte d'Ivoire, Zimbabwe, Cambodia, Guatemala, Somalia, Rwanda | 209.6 | 134.7 |
| 3–7 | Ecuador, Senegal, Romania, Syria, Yemen, Chad, Malaysia, Burundi, Argentina, Haiti, Algeria, Benin, Honduras, Poland, Guinea, Sierra Leone, Azerbaijan, El Salvador, Bolivia, Chile | 288.7 | 96.4 |
| 1–3 | Central African Republic, Laos, Togo, Nicaragua, Turkmenistan, Eritrea, Papua New Guinea, Congo Republic, Georgia, Kyrgyzstan, Kazakhstan, Liberia, Morocco, Paraguay, Saudi Arabia, Armenia, Lesotho, Moldova, Dominican Republic, Albania, Mongolia, Tunisia | 150.4 | 47.1 |
| 0.1–3 | See note a | 154.0 | 15.2 |
| Industrial economies[b] | | 841.0 | 0 |
| Excluded developing economies[c] | | 103.6 | |
| **Total** | | **5,941.0** | **2,864.4** |

a. Guinea-Bissau, Botswana, Namibia, Costa Rica, South Korea, Gambia, Panama, Jamaica, Bulgaria, Croatia, Macedonia, Mauritania, Latvia, Bhutan, Hungary, Gabon, Jordan, Comoros, Trinidad and Tobago, Lithuania, Estonia, Solomon Islands, Uruguay, Czech Republic, Belarus, Portugal, Mauritius, Equatorial Guinea, Cape Verde, São Tomé and Príncipe, Slovak Republic, Vanuatu, Maldives, Kiribati, Samoa, New Zealand, and Slovenia.
b. Includes Hong Kong and Singapore.
c. Bosnia-Herzegovina, Cuba, Iraq, North Korea, Libya, Oman, Tajikistan, West Bank and Gaza, Yugoslavia (Serbia), Israel, United Arab Emirates, Lebanon, and Kuwait.

*Source:* World Development Indicators (World Bank 2001).

count distribution, 37 small countries account for an aggregate of 15 million poor.

Table 1.2 also imputes zero incidence of global-scale poverty (i.e., $2 per day or less) to the 840 million people living in industrial countries. Poverty as defined in these economies is at a far higher standard of living (e.g., in the United States the poverty line is set at household income of

$18,000 for a family of four, or $4,500 per capita). It might be considered that the homeless in industrial countries are good candidates for inclusion in the category of under $2 per day. However, the homeless population in these countries is relatively small (one recent estimate for the United States places the figure at 0.8 million; Burt et al. 2001). A more fundamental question, perhaps, is whether the PPP threshold of $2 per day used internationally is really comparable to $2 per day in an industrial country.

It may be that the PPP conversions that are designed to capture the full range of consumption are misleading for a subsistence basket of goods, because it is difficult to envision survival on $2 per day in the United States, for example.[4] In broad terms, nonetheless, the assumption of zero "world-scale" poverty within industrial countries seems appropriate, in part because of their public and charitable infrastructures available to assist the poorest.

## Least Developed, Heavily Indebted Poor, and sub-Saharan African Countries

Despite the large share of the world's poor that is located in India, China, and a number of large intermediate-income countries, the most explicit international regimes oriented toward dealing with the poor tend to concentrate on subsets of the poorer countries that exclude many or even most of the global poor. Three regimes in particular have been prominent: the United Nations' list of the least developed countries (LDCs), the heavily indebted poor countries (HIPCs), and the sub-Saharan African countries (SSA). Thus, the European Union's Everything But Arms regime of duty-free imports has been made available to the LDCs; the US African Growth and Opportunity Act (AGOA) has provided preferential entry for SSA; and the Paris Club's forgiveness of bilateral debt and associated forgiveness of multilateral debt have been oriented toward the HIPCs.

Because of their importance for international policies toward poverty alleviation, these three country groupings are examined in table 1.3. The table's first panel reports population and this chapter's poverty estimate for the United Nations' list of LDCs (UNCTAD 2002b). This group of 49 countries accounts for approximately 644 million people, of which approximately 476 million are in poverty by the international ($2) definition.

The second panel of table 1.3 examines the corresponding population and poverty estimates for the HIPCs. Several important poverty concen-

---

4. A classic linear-programming problem is to identify the least-cost diet subject to nutritional constraints. One recent study using this approach places the minimum-cost diet in the United States at $650 annually for men and $535 for women in 1998 prices (Informs Online 2002). If valid, this would leave only 38 cents per person per day to pay for lodging and clothing after purchasing the minimum-cost diet, subject to a $2 per day ceiling.

## Table 1.3  Poverty in least developed, heavily indebted poor, and sub-Saharan African countries

| Country and group | Number of countries | Population (millions) | In poverty (millions) |
|---|---|---|---|
| **I. Least developed countries (LDCs)[a]** | 48 | 644.1 | 476.1 |
| Of which[b] | | | |
| Bangladesh | | 127.67 | 99.33 |
| Ethiopia | | 62.78 | 47.97 |
| Congo, Democratic Republic of | | 49.78 | 36.24 |
| Myanmar | | 45.03 | 32.78 |
| Sudan | | 28.99 | 21.11 |
| Tanzania | | 32.92 | 19.65 |
| Afghanistan | | 26.55 | 19.33 |
| Nepal | | 23.38 | 19.29 |
| Uganda | | 21.48 | 16.58 |
| Mozambique | | 17.30 | 13.56 |
| Madagascar | | 15.05 | 13.36 |
| Mali | | 10.58 | 9.59 |
| Burkina Faso | | 11.00 | 9.43 |
| Malawi | | 10.79 | 9.18 |
| Zambia | | 9.88 | 9.06 |
| Niger | | 10.50 | 8.95 |
| Angola | | 12.36 | 8.51 |
| Cambodia | | 11.76 | 7.47 |
| Somalia | | 9.71 | 7.07 |
| Rwanda | | 8.31 | 7.03 |
| Senegal | | 9.29 | 6.30 |
| Yemen | | 17.05 | 6.05 |
| Chad | | 7.49 | 5.66 |
| Burundi | | 6.68 | 5.50 |
| Haiti | | 7.80 | 5.16 |
| Benin | | 6.11 | 4.49 |
| Guinea | | 7.25 | 4.01 |
| Sierra Leone | | 4.95 | 3.69 |
| **II. Heavily indebted poor countries (HIPCs)[c]** | 41 | 615.5 | 418.5 |
| Of which, not included in LDCs[b] | | | |
| Vietnam | | 77.52 | 41.37 |
| Kenya | | 29.41 | 18.32 |
| Ghana | | 18.78 | 9.74 |
| Cameroon | | 14.69 | 9.00 |
| Niger | | 10.50 | 8.95 |
| Angola | | 12.36 | 8.51 |
| Côte d'Ivoire | | 15.55 | 7.68 |
| Somalia | | 9.71 | 7.07 |
| Honduras | | 6.32 | 4.35 |
| Guinea | | 7.25 | 4.01 |
| Bolivia | | 8.14 | 3.14 |
| **III. Sub-Saharan Africa (SSA)** | 46 | 642.7 | 469.7 |
| Of which, not included in LDC or HIPC[b] | | | |
| Nigeria | | 123.90 | 112.50 |
| South Africa | | 42.11 | 15.07 |
| Zimbabwe | | 11.90 | 7.64 |
| **IV. Countries in LDCs, HIPCs, or SSA** | | 1,005.90 | 714.70 |

a. Excludes Tuvalu.
b. Countries with 3 million or more living in poverty.
c. Excludes Guyana.

*Source:* World Bank (2001) and author's calculations.

trations are to be found in the HIPCs that are omitted from the LDC list, including Vietnam (41 million poor) and Kenya (18 million poor). Conversely, a number of LDCs with sizable poor populations are excluded from the HIPC grouping (in large part because their external borrowing in the past has been insufficient to place them under an unsustainable debt burden), including Afghanistan (19 million poor), Bangladesh (99 million poor), and Nepal (19 million poor). The total for the HIPC group is an aggregate population of 616 million, of which 418 million are in poverty.

The third panel of table 1.3 shows the corresponding aggregates for SSA, at an aggregate population of 643 million and with 470 million in poverty. Three large concentrations of poverty are in the SSA group but are in countries not designated as either an LDC or HIPC: Nigeria, with 112 million poor people; South Africa, 15 million; and Zimbabwe, 8 million.

Because the three groupings have considerable overlap (see table 1A.1), the combined total of the poor for all countries that are members of at least one of the three groupings is 715 million, almost exactly half of the simple sum of the poor for the three groupings individually (1.36 billion). This means, in turn, that the countries that belong to at least one of the three groupings for which the principal international regimes for poverty reduction tend to be oriented account for only 25 percent of the global total of those in poverty (715 million out of 2.86 billion).

## India and China

Because of their overwhelming importance for the global total, the poverty estimates for India and China warrant a closer look. The estimates reported in table 1.1 apply the poverty rates reported by the World Bank (2001) to the country populations. Nonetheless, these poverty rates might be seen as on the high side, especially in China, whose per capita income stands at $3,550. Not only is this almost 5 times the $2 per day benchmark, but it is surprisingly close to the $4,500 per capita definition of poverty in the United States.

The World Bank reports the headcount fraction of population in poverty ($2) at 53.7 percent for China and 86.2 percent for India. As a gauge of the possible bias in these estimates, it is useful to apply the cross-country equation A.1 given in appendix 1A relating the poverty rate to per capita income and the Gini coefficient. This equation yields an estimated poverty rate of 39.2 percent for China and 48.4 percent for India. The Indian estimate especially is lower than the World Bank figure. For the two countries combined, substituting these equation-estimated poverty rates reduces the number of the poor from 1.53 billion to 975 million. This alternative estimate also places the number of the poor at almost identical levels for these two largest cases: at 492 million for China and 483 million for India. If these alternative estimates for China and India are applied, the global poverty total is reduced to 2.41 billion, or 16 percent below the main estimate of 2.86 billion.

## Implications

The most sobering estimate here is that half of the world's population is in poverty using a $2 per day threshold. This is relatively well known from previous World Bank estimates (World Bank 2001, 3). A less obvious finding, however, is that only about one-fourth of the global poor are to be found in countries that are typically included in the special trade or aid regimes, the LDCs, HIPCs, and SSA.

Another little-known pattern is that by far the great majority (90 percent) of global poverty is to be found in countries whose *average* per capita income is above, and sometimes far above, the international poverty line. This fact indeed contains a hint of why the international special regimes tend to leave out the bulk of the poor: Because donor countries sense that the moderately well-to-do developing countries should be expected to address at least a considerable portion of their own internal problems of poverty rather than expecting the global community to do so.

A more positive reformulation of the same basic point would be that countries with per capita income above the lowest ranges include important cases where growth has been relatively strong, so they enjoy favorable prospects of reducing poverty over time on their own. This implicit perception, for example, would judge that China, whose annual per capita consumption growth has been recorded at 7 percent during the past two decades (World Bank 2001, 276), can deal relatively well on its own with its poor population (whether the figure is about 500 or 675 million).

An alternative prism that could help explain the international policy focus on only about one-fourth of the world's poor is a concern about an implicit "transfer leakage." In the sizable number of countries with intermediate per capita income levels alongside substantial poverty, the strong implication is that the bulk of income goes to the nonpoor. Consider Mexico. The World Bank estimate is that 42.5 percent of its population is in ($2) poverty (table 1.1). Even if all of them were just exactly at this threshold rather than being distributed at and below it, this would imply that whereas Mexico's poor have an average income of $730 annually, the other 57.5 percent of Mexicans enjoy an average income of $13,495, or 18.5 times that of the poor. Moreover, the upper 57.5 percent would account for at least 96 percent of total income.[5] Rich-country policymakers could thus reasonably be concerned that for each dollar of special benefit conveyed generally to Mexico, less than 10 cents would reach those who are

---

5. On the first calculation: $0.425 \times 730 + 0.575 \times 13,495 = 8,070$. The second calculation is $(0.575 \times 13,495)/8,070$. An alternative estimate is that the top 60 percent receive 89 percent of income (World Bank 2001, 283).

at or below the international poverty line. This leakage would typically be considerably lower for a low-income country that is, for example, in the HIPC group.[6] Even so, the leakage could remain relatively large.

## Trade Patterns in Relation to Poverty

If industrial-country imports of goods produced by the poor are to serve as a vehicle for the alleviation of global poverty, these imports must come from countries where the poor are located. It is thus germane to examine the pattern relating industrial countries' imports to poverty incidence in their developing-country trading partners. Moreover, as just noted, a particular developing country may have a high incidence of poverty by the headcount measure but have a low share of its national income going to the poor, and hence a high degree of "leakage" to the nonpoor for any countrywide economic variable such as trade.

To explore the trade-poverty relationship, it is useful to measure what may heuristically be called the "poverty intensity of trade." If the entire population of a country is poor, then imports from this country may be said to have 100 percent poverty intensity. Conversely, imports from a nation with zero (world-scale) poverty may be said to have zero poverty intensity. The measure can be calculated first with reference simply to the headcount incidence of poverty. To take account of leakage to the nonpoor, however, a more meaningful measure can be calculated using instead the share of national income accruing to the poor in the supplying developing country. Both measures are only initial approximations meant to give a rough idea of whether the trade flows in question have a potential impact on the poor. A more complete analysis, for example, might seek to consider whether the poor are actually employed as factors of production in the goods traded.

Appendix table 1A.1 reports the percent of population in poverty (by the $2 PPP definition) for 127 developing countries. The table also includes an estimate of the percent of total national income accruing to the poor in each country.[7] These two alternative measures are then multiplied by the

---

6. By way of illustration, for Uganda, a calculation along the lines of the Mexican example finds that the above-poverty-line population has an income averaging only 3.7 times that of the poor (vs. 18.5 in Mexico), and that the "leakage" share of total income accruing to the nonpoor amounts to 53 percent rather than 96 percent.

7. The estimate is an upper bound because it treats all of the poor as having the full $2 per day income. Thus, the income share of the poor, $S_p$, is estimated as $S_p = (730H)/y^*$, where $H$ is the headcount fraction of population in poverty and $y^*$ is the average PPP per capita income, subject to a ceiling of $S_p = 1.0$. This follows from the fact that total income of the poor is $NH \times 730$, where $N$ is total population, while total income is $Ny^*$.

fraction of industrial countries' imports from developing countries as a group that comes from each of the individual developing countries, to obtain a weighted average "poverty intensity of imports" from developing countries for each of the major industrial-country groupings (table 1.4).[8]

Table 1.4 is first useful in highlighting the principal developing-country exporters. China, South Korea, Mexico, Russia, and Malaysia alone account for 46 percent of developing-country exports to world markets. In contrast, the aggregates for the three special-regime poor-country groupings are striking in revealing how little trade is actually involved. Thus, in 2000 total exports of the LDCs stood at a meager $35 billion, only 2.1 percent of the developing-country total. Of total imports from developing countries, those from LDCs accounted for only 1.8 percent for the United States and 2.4 percent for the European Union. Although the HIPC totals are somewhat larger and the SSA totals even larger, both remain small. Imports from SSA made up only 4.5 percent of total imports from developing countries into the United States, and 6.7 percent for the European Union.

Finally, the aggregates also reveal that only about 60 percent of developing-country exports goes to industrial-country markets, and the rest goes to developing countries.[9] The 40 percent developing-country market share for developing-country exports significantly exceeds these countries' share in global GDP, at market prices (not PPP), reflecting the typically higher shares of trade in GDP for developing countries than in especially the largest industrial countries (the United States, Japan, and the European Union as a unit).[10] This suggests that in the search for international trade as a vehicle for alleviating global poverty, it should be kept in mind that increased market opportunities in developing countries' own markets, especially those of middle-income economies, have a potentially important role to play.

---

8. The poverty-intensity indexes are thus, for each importing area: $P_{Ii} = 100 \times [(\Sigma_i M_i H_i)/M]$, for the headcount weighting, and $P_s = 100 \times [(\Sigma_i M_i S_{pi})/M]$, for the income-share weighting, where $M_i$ is imports from country $i$ and $M$ is total imports from developing countries.

9. The IMF (2001a, 10) similarly reports that 57.0 percent of developing-county exports go to industrial-country markets. Note, however, that the substantially larger magnitude for "developing-country" exports in the DOTS total ($2.34 trillion in 2000, vs. $1.72 trillion in table 1.4) reflects the exclusion in the present study of Hong Kong, Singapore, and Taiwan from the "developing country" set, as well as such high-income oil-exporting economies as Kuwait and United Arab Emirates. Exports in 2000 of the three largest omitted exports amounted to $202 billion for Hong Kong, $138 billion for Singapore, and $135 billion for Taiwan; IMF (2001a) and Central Bank of China (Taiwan), www.cbc.gov.tw.

10. The South-South trade share is about the same as the 43 percent share of developing and transition economies in global purchasing parity GDP (IMF 2001b, 187). However, it is nominal market GDP, not PPP GDP, that matters for world trade markets.

## Table 1.4  Imports from developing countries, 2000

| Country or group | World | United States | Canada | Japan | European Union |
|---|---|---|---|---|---|
| **Amount** (billions of dollars) | 1,717.7 | 434.0 | 18.5 | 143.5 | 416.6 |
| Of which: | | | | | |
| Argentina | 26.6 | 3.0 | 0.2 | 0.4 | 4.6 |
| Brazil | 56.1 | 13.4 | 0.6 | 2.5 | 15.0 |
| China | 249.2 | 52.2 | 3.2 | 41.7 | 38.2 |
| Czech Republic | 28.9 | 0.8 | 0.1 | 0.1 | 19.9 |
| Hungary | 28.1 | 1.5 | 0.0 | 0.2 | 21.1 |
| India | 44.2 | 10.0 | 0.8 | 2.4 | 10.5 |
| Indonesia | 62.1 | 8.5 | 0.4 | 14.4 | 8.7 |
| Iran | 27.5 | 0.2 | 0.1 | 4.9 | 7.1 |
| South Korea | 171.8 | 37.8 | 2.4 | 20.5 | 23.5 |
| Malaysia | 98.2 | 20.2 | 0.8 | 12.8 | 13.4 |
| Mexico | 166.5 | 147.7 | 3.4 | 0.9 | 5.6 |
| Philippines | 38.2 | 11.4 | 0.3 | 5.6 | 6.8 |
| Poland | 31.6 | 1.0 | 0.2 | 0.1 | 22.2 |
| Russia | 103.0 | 8.0 | 0.1 | 2.8 | 36.9 |
| Saudi Arabia | 75.2 | 13.0 | 0.6 | 12.9 | 13.2 |
| Thailand | 69.1 | 14.7 | 0.8 | 10.2 | 10.9 |
| Turkey | 27.8 | 3.1 | 0.2 | 0.1 | 14.5 |
| Venezuela | 34.0 | 17.3 | 0.4 | 0.2 | 1.6 |
| | | | | | |
| Least developed countries (LDCs) | 35.4 | 8.0 | 0.2 | 1.0 | 10.0 |
| Heavily indebted poor countries (HIPCs) | 57.1 | 10.3 | 0.4 | 3.4 | 15.5 |
| Sub-Saharan Africa (SSA) | 83.3 | 19.6 | 0.7 | 2.5 | 28.1 |
| | | | | | |
| **Total, relative to importing area** | | | | | |
| GDP (percent) | | 4.4 | 2.7 | 3.1 | 5.0 |
| Total imports[a] (percent) | | 35.1 | 7.7 | 38.0 | 40.9 |
| | | | | | |
| **Poverty intensity**[b] | | | | | |
| Total | | | | | |
| Headcount weighting | 32.21 | 38.11 | 35.98 | 35.74 | 26.07 |
| Income-share weighting | 7.77 | 8.16 | 8.41 | 7.82 | 6.88 |
| Least developed countries | | | | | |
| Headcount weighting | 66.2 | 69.2 | 73.8 | 64.6 | 69.7 |
| Income-share weighting | 49.0 | 44.1 | 49.7 | 58.0 | 50.3 |
| Heavily indebted poor countries | | | | | |
| Headcount weighting | 61.7 | 66.1 | 61.6 | 56.7 | 62.3 |
| Income-share weighting | 41.4 | 38.7 | 34.6 | 31.7 | 41.2 |
| Sub-Saharan Africa | | | | | |
| Headcount weighting | 62.1 | 70.3 | 66.8 | 50.7 | 57.5 |
| Income-share weighting | 43.8 | 55.8 | 49.2 | 27.8 | 36.9 |

a. For the European Union, this refers to imports from non-EU countries.
b. Maximum possible: 100 percent; see the text.

*Sources:* Country exports to market in question, as reported in IMF (2002a); this study, table 1A.1.

The final panel in table 1.4 indicates that, weighting by supplier-country headcount poverty shares, 32 percent of worldwide imports from developing countries come from the global poor. This poverty intensity is the highest for the United States, at 38 percent. It is approximately the same level for Canada and Japan, but lower at 26 percent for the European Union. The explanation for the EU figure is that a larger share of EU imports comes from Central and Eastern European economies, such as Russia, Poland, Hungary, and the Czech Republic, which tend to have relatively low poverty headcount ratios (25, 10, 4, and 2 percent, respectively).

The income-share poverty weighting, in contrast, places the percent of imports from the poor considerably lower: at about 8 percent for all the importing areas except the European Union, where it stands at about 7 percent. The difference between the poverty headcount weighting and the income-share weighting is the largest for the United States (38.1 percent vs. 8.2 percent), reflecting the large share of US imports coming from Mexico and China, in combination with the relatively low ratios of the poverty group's income share to headcount share in both of these key economies.

For the three poor-country regime groupings (LDCs, HIPCs, and SSA), the poverty-intensity estimates are considerably higher. The headcount-weighted measures show a range of 60 to 70 percent of imports from these countries as being from the poor, almost twice the rate for developing countries as a whole. The increase is even greater for poverty-intensity weighting by income shares of the poor. By this measure, about half of the imports from the three special regime groupings come from the poor, or about seven times the rate for developing countries as a whole.

This contrast to the large leakage to the nonpoor in imports from major developing-country exporters such as China, Mexico, and South Korea seems likely to be an important explanation for why the special-treatment regimes have been limited to these economies, even though they account for only about one-fourth of the world's poor. Namely, special opportunities granted to the LDCs, HIPCs, and SSA are much more heavily focused on the poor than would be the case for such access to developing countries generally. Of course, another and perhaps more important reason is that, as suggested by their extremely small shares in total trade, these economies' exports are not large enough to induce much disruption or reaction in industrial-country markets.

The differences among the four industrial-country groupings in import poverty intensity are somewhat greater for the three special-regime group ings than for developing countries overall. In particular, the income-share-weighted poverty intensity for US imports from SSA, at 56 percent, is considerably above the 37 percent for the European Union. The high US figure reflects especially the high share of Nigeria in US imports from SSA (48 percent, compared with 19 percent for the European Union), coupled with the high estimated income share of the poor in Nigeria (86 percent). This pattern in turn reflects lesser concentration in oil for EU imports from SSA, and greater imports from such economies as South Africa and Côte d'Ivoire where the income share of the poor is considerably lower.[11]

For developing countries as a whole, the estimates in table 1.4 suggest that there are not large differences among the major industrial-country groupings in the extent to which their imports are oriented toward the poor, especially when the measurement is on an income-share basis. A noteworthy nuance is that the low poverty incidence of Eastern Europe more than offsets the high poverty incidence of Africa in yielding a somewhat lower poverty intensity of imports into the European Union than into the other major industrial-country areas, but again this difference is not large when the income-share weights are applied.

Another basis for identifying differences among the industrial-country importers is to simply compare the magnitude of imports from developing countries relative to GDP or total imports of each major industrial-country area. These ratios are reported in the middle panel of table 1.4. Here the pattern is somewhat the reverse, because imports from developing countries are a moderately higher share of total imports (from nonmembers) for the European Union than for the United States (40.9 vs. 35.1 percent), and the same holds true for imports relative to GDP (5.0 and 4.4 percent of GDP, respectively). The comparisons are ambiguous for Japan, because at 38 percent, the developing-country share of total imports stands intermediate between the US and EU ratios, whereas at 3.1 percent imports from developing countries are considerably lower as a share of GDP. The latter thus reflects the relatively low overall ratio of imports to GDP for Japan, rather than a low share for developing countries in Japan's imports. Canada is the outlier of the industrial countries, because its imports from developing countries are far smaller relative to total imports (at 7.7 percent) than is true for the other industrial-country areas; and even relative to GDP, Canada's imports from developing countries are the lowest among the industrial-country areas. This likely reflects Canada's greater similarity to many developing countries in its role as a natural resource–exporting economy.

Finally, the poverty intensity of trade can also be examined with respect to product sectors, again measuring by the poverty characteristics of the supplying countries rather than the factor composition of production or other measures. Table 1.5 reports these estimates for US imports from developing countries in 2001. The estimates identify the top 23 product categories for these imports, using variously 2- and 3-digit Standard Inter-

---

11. Note, however, that the imputation method, whereby all the poor are attributed the threshold income of $730, compared with the relatively low per capita income in Nigeria, probably understates the income share of the nonpoor, because many of the poor could be receiving well below the $730 threshold.

## Table 1.5 Poverty intensity of principal US imports from developing countries, 2001

| Import category | Imports (billions of dollars) | Poverty intensity By number | Poverty intensity By income share |
|---|---|---|---|
| Petroleum (33) | 64.7 | 39.13 | 17.47 |
| Apparel (84) | 49.8 | 47.16 | 12.38 |
| Computers (752) | 26.9 | 35.09 | 5.09 |
| Telecommunications (764) | 22.6 | 32.96 | 4.42 |
| Motor vehicles (781) | 21.9 | 29.37 | 2.64 |
| Semiconductors (776) | 15.5 | 26.18 | 3.75 |
| Toys (894) | 14.9 | 50.75 | 10.24 |
| Footwear (85) | 13.1 | 48.60 | 10.08 |
| Office machinery (759) | 11.5 | 36.70 | 5.92 |
| Furniture (821) | 10.7 | 46.17 | 8.14 |
| Textiles (65) | 8.7 | 47.74 | 12.28 |
| Vehicle parts (784) | 6.6 | 39.24 | 4.57 |
| Electrical goods (773) | 6.6 | 41.84 | 4.95 |
| Televisions (761) | 6.6 | 38.68 | 3.98 |
| Iron and steel (67) | 5.8 | 27.84 | 4.03 |
| Radios (762) | 5.8 | 42.74 | 6.86 |
| Electrical appliances (772) | 5.5 | 40.74 | 5.34 |
| Pearls (667) | 3.1 | 68.80 | 21.03 |
| Copper (682) | 2.3 | 31.62 | 3.95 |
| Coffee (071) | 1.4 | 41.33 | 9.76 |
| Tobacco (12) | 1.0 | 29.14 | 9.71 |
| Cocoa (072) | 0.6 | 49.22 | 16.80 |
| Sugar (061) | 0.6 | 35.30 | 7.96 |
| Subtotal | 306.2 | 39.81 | 9.60 |
| All others | 164.8 | 39.47 | 6.74 |
| Total | 471.0 | 39.69 | 8.60 |

Note: The number in parentheses following the import category is the Standard International Trade Classification category.

Source: Import values are from USITC (2002).

national Trade Classification (SITC) categories. These products account for 65 percent of total US imports from developing countries.

The table shows that the largest import value from these economies is in petroleum, at $65 billion. Next is apparel, at $50 billion. The next four categories reflect the dramatic change in import composition during the past several years, because these goods are far from the traditional stereotypes of products in which developing countries have a comparative advantage: computers, telecommunications goods, motor vehicles, and semiconductors, summing to $87 billion. The next two categories revert to more traditional developing-country specialties—toys and footwear. Close behind is another familiar category, textiles. Somewhat surprisingly, the classical developing-country commodity products do not appear in the ranking until the bottom of the list, where copper, coffee, tobacco, cocoa, and sugar are found to total only $6 billion.

The table then applies the headcount and income-share poverty measures by supplying country (from table 1A.1) to calculate the corresponding poverty-intensity estimates by product. The most poverty-intensive product is "pearls, precious and semiprecious stones" (SITC 667). These are heavily concentrated in imports from India (66 percent of US imports from developing countries) and South Africa (15 percent). Both countries have a high poverty headcount incidence, and India has a relatively high share of income going to the poor.

A more important surprise in the table is that the next most poverty-intensive good is also the import with the largest value: petroleum. This result reflects the fact that except for Saudi Arabia (which accounts for 19 percent of US oil imports from developing countries), the principal oil exporters have high poverty headcount incidence (Algeria, Colombia, Mexico, and Venezuela) and, in the case of Angola and Nigeria, relatively high poverty income shares.

The finding that oil is a relatively poverty-intensive product is perhaps counterintuitive and warrants certain caveats. The control of oil (and other natural-resource) rents may be more highly concentrated than the general distribution of income. In particular, unskilled labor is the main factor endowment of poor households, and unskilled labor will tend to have a smaller share in value added from oil than in agriculture and most manufacturing sectors. In some countries such as Nigeria, moreover, a high incidence of corruption may concentrate oil income, although in other countries such as Mexico and Venezuela the state ownership of oil probably tends to make the distribution of its income more in line with the general distributional incidence of public spending.

In principle, any special cooptation of oil income by the rich should already have been taken account of in the poverty share estimate. In practice, however, as noted above, this is an upper-bound estimate that assumes all of the poor receive a full $2 per day. The resulting potential overstatement of the share of the poor in national income could be particularly problematical in some of the oil-producing economies (e.g., Nigeria, where this estimation approach yields 86 percent as the share of the poor in national income). Despite these limitations, the relatively high poverty-intensity estimate for oil serves as a reminder that oil imports do tend to come disproportionately from poor countries.

The other product categories with relatively high poverty intensity are goods more intuitively expected: cocoa, apparel, textiles, toys, and footwear, all of which have a poverty-income-share intensity of 10 percent or above. Conversely, and as also would be expected, the high-technology complex of goods that bulks large in the dollar totals tends to have very low poverty intensity, in the range of 3 to 5 percent on the income-share measure. This reflects the characteristics of the principal suppliers. Thus, in

**Table 1.6  Poverty intensity of principal developing-country exports to the world, 2000** (percent)

| | Exports (billions of dollars) | Poverty intensity | |
|---|---|---|---|
| Export category | | By number | By income share |
| Wheat (041) | 2.17 | 15.68 | 1.73 |
| Rice (042) | 3.41 | 47.21 | 13.04 |
| Maize (044) | 2.58 | 32.44 | 6.22 |
| Sugar (061) | 4.34 | 31.40 | 7.45 |
| Coffee (071) | 9.43 | 44.05 | 15.47 |
| Cocoa (072) | 3.19 | 51.42 | 22.73 |
| Cotton textile fibers (263) | 4.01 | 50.09 | 22.82 |
| Jute textile fibers (264) | 0.06 | 74.76 | 35.59 |
| Electrical appliances (772) | 0.00 | 35.73 | 6.14 |
| Pearls (667) | 16.41 | 62.01 | 21.84 |
| Copper (682) | 14.97 | 25.94 | 5.74 |
| Computers (752) | 70.58 | 30.91 | 5.04 |
| Office machinery (759) | 48.31 | 33.84 | 5.68 |
| Televisions (761) | 25.18 | 34.71 | 5.34 |
| Radios (762) | 16.52 | 41.06 | 7.41 |
| Telecommunications (764) | 60.39 | 33.48 | 5.53 |
| Electrical goods (773) | 18.80 | 33.70 | 5.11 |
| Semiconductors (776) | 93.33 | 23.36 | 3.47 |
| Motor vehicles (781) | 45.71 | 21.56 | 2.18 |
| Vehicle parts (784) | 16.76 | 26.17 | 3.30 |
| Furniture (821) | 25.59 | 38.18 | 7.23 |
| Toys (894) | 36.81 | 51.02 | 10.52 |
| Tobacco (12) | 5.23 | 35.43 | 13.67 |
| Oil seeds (22) | 6.11 | 27.65 | 8.45 |
| Petroleum (33) | 289.33 | 32.30 | 13.63 |
| Textiles (65) | 61.00 | 41.01 | 10.66 |
| Iron and steel (67) | 52.04 | 25.04 | 4.25 |
| Apparel (84) | 144.10 | 43.80 | 11.00 |
| Footwear (85) | 32.53 | 48.27 | 10.49 |

Note. The number in parentheses following the export category is the Standard International Trade Classification category.

Source: Export values from United Nations (2002).

semiconductors, 29 percent of US imports from developing countries is from Malaysia, 23 percent from South Korea, 23 percent from the Philippines, and 9 percent from Mexico, all countries with low poverty income shares (although Mexico and the Philippines boost the headcount measure).

Table 1.6 reports the headcount and income-share poverty intensities by product category, weighting by developing-country exports to all markets. These are generally close to the corresponding estimates for US imports from developing countries.

There are two major implications of these poverty-intensity estimates. The first is that trade policy in industrial countries is likely to be most efficiently directed toward reducing global poverty when it is specifically tailored to encourage imports from poor countries. For poor countries that have already been identified in special international regimes (i.e., the

LDCs, HIPCs, SSA), about 50 percent of import value is associated with people who are poor at the global threshold of $2 per day, weighting by income shares of the poor (rather than their higher "headcount" shares). In contrast, for imports from all developing countries, this share is only about 8 percent, because the bulk of these imports is from middle-income countries where the income share of the poor is low even if the headcount incidence of poverty is not. This contrast suggests that whatever their past shortcomings, regimes of special trade access for poor countries warrant renewed consideration for enhancement as a means of addressing global poverty. These programs are reviewed in chapter 2.

At the same time, the considerably lower poverty intensity for imports from those middle-income and other developing countries that are not members of the three major low-income groupings should not be interpreted as implying that opening markets to their exports holds little scope for reducing poverty. On the contrary, it will be shown in chapters 4 and 5 that global trade liberalization could reduce global poverty substantially. Similarly, it should be kept in mind that three-fourths of the world's poor live in countries not included in the LDC, HIPC, or SSA groupings.

The second major area for policy implications concerns the product category estimates of poverty intensity. These provide a guide to the sectors in which changes in industrial-country protection could be most effective in alleviating (liberalization) or aggravating (heightened protection) global poverty. As expected, apparel, textiles, light manufactures such as toys and footwear, and some tropical products (cocoa) have a relatively high poverty intensity. About 10 to 20 percent of trade value is associated with the globally poor in these products, given the income shares of the poor in the countries of origin. A crucial and surprising poverty-intensive product is petroleum, which not only has a high intensity (17 percent on the income-share basis) but is also the largest product by value in industrial-country imports from developing countries ($65 billion).

One product serves to illustrate the relevance of taking product-sector poverty intensity into account in policy decisions. One of the high-profile issues at the September 2003 meeting of the World Trade Organization's trade ministers in Cancún, Mexico, was the request by several African countries for the elimination of US subsidies for cotton production (and interim compensation pending such elimination). As indicated in table 1.6, "cotton textile fibers" are one of the most poverty-intensive products exported by developing countries, at about 23 percent, weighting by the income share of the poor. There was thus a good case on the grounds of fighting global poverty for beginning the attack on farm subsidies with cotton.[12]

---

12. US negotiators instead suggested the integration of cotton into the textiles-apparel arrangements. As discussed in chapter 5, however, the Cancún talks broke down, primarily over the issue of agricultural subsidies and protection more generally and the question of extension of World Trade Organization rules to new areas (the "Singapore issues" concerning investment, competition, trade facilitation, and government procurement).

It is appropriate, nonetheless, to conclude this section on the "poverty intensity of trade" with the reminder that this concept is essentially indicative rather than rigorous. The concept could be fleshed out more fully with empirical estimates of the factor shares for factors of production involved in export products, by country and by sector, and/or with a more complete analysis of the actual shares of the poor in national incomes. A more detailed analysis could reduce the estimate of the poverty intensity of oil, for example, by capturing a disproportionate share of the rich in resource rents. Conversely, for some products (e.g., perhaps cocoa), a more accurate estimate might boost the measured poverty intensity. The main purpose of the concept, however, is merely to shed light on the potential for trade to affect global poverty directly. For this purpose, even the broad-brush calculations here would seem to provide a relatively reliable basis for refocusing attention on the approach of giving special trade opportunities to poor countries. It is partly on the basis of the concept of poverty intensity of trade that this study suggests a two-track policy strategy, with immediate free market access for imports from the "at-risk" poor countries, and phased multilateral free trade for all other countries (chapter 6).

## Poverty, Growth, and Trade

The ultimate source of global poverty reduction is sustained economic growth. To complete this initial review of the principal issues involved in the trade-poverty relationship, it is thus important to highlight the basic interrelationships in, and analytical controversies surrounding, the trade-growth-poverty nexus.

### Does Growth Reduce Poverty?

There is relatively widespread agreement that sustained economic growth in developing countries is essential to the reduction of global poverty. The World Bank (2001, 47, 54) has synthesized numerous household survey studies to arrive at the following general relationship: A 1 percent increase in real per capita income reduces the incidence of poverty by 2 percent. This "growth elasticity of poverty" is higher (in absolute terms) where the degree of income equality is greater, and lower where it is lower (with the central elasticity reaching about 3 where the Gini coefficient of concentration is as low as 0.2, and only about 1.5 where the Gini is as high as 0.6).[13]

---

13. The intuition on this point is that an equal income distribution means the households are tightly bunched, so more of them will pass over a given poverty threshold for a given percentage increase in income. (I am indebted to François Bourguignon for this perception.)

Growth might not lead to poverty alleviation if it were typically associated with an ever-increasing inequality of income. Although for a long time development economists feared that this was exactly the pattern for growth in the early stages of development, by the late 1990s the stylized fact had emerged that sustained growth has tended to be neutral with respect to the resulting distribution of income.[14] Thus, in their prominent compilation of data on income inequality, Deininger and Squire (1996, 566) found that "for the ninety-five growth spells for which we have information on income shares, we find no systematic link between growth and inequality, but we do find a strong positive relationship between growth and poverty reduction." Dollar and Kraay (2001a, 1) found that "the share of income accruing to the bottom quintile does not vary systematically with average income." As discussed below, however, subsequent research has suggested that although within-country distribution has tended to be stable on the scale of several decades, it showed a trend toward equalization in the first part of the postwar period, followed by a return toward greater inequality in the period 1980–2000.

## The Paradox of Persistent Global Poverty

There does appear to be a major paradox to be explained, either by a renewed trend toward inequality or otherwise. The paradox is that *the main estimates of global poverty show a smaller decline during the 1990s than would be predicted by the growth-poverty relationship.* As discussed above, the central estimate of the elasticity of poverty incidence with respect to growth is –2. The decline in the World Bank's measure of the incidence of poverty in developing and transition economies (at the $1 per day threshold) is from 28.3 percent in 1987 to 24.0 percent in 1998. But this decline was too small to match the observed growth combined with the central poverty elasticity.

From 1990 to 2000, real gross domestic product in the low- and middle-income economies grew at an annual average rate of 3.6 percent, while their population grew at an average rate of 1.6 percent (World Bank 2002e, 233, 237). Real per capita income growth averaged 2.0 percent. With a poverty elasticity of 2, this pace would be expected to reduce the inci-

---

14. The well-known "Kuznets curve" postulated that income distribution first becomes more unequal and then reverts to greater equality as development proceeds (Kuznets 1955). The argument was that in the absence of a significant surplus, poor economies necessarily start from relatively equal distributions; that as urbanization and modern-sector development occur, the shift in the share of population and the economy to the urban sector increases the weight of the more unequal part of the economy; but that eventually incomes are high enough to facilitate political interventions to alleviate poverty (and increasing capital boosts the marginal product and thus pay of labor). Development experience, however, has shown that, especially in some of the Asian economies where early land reform helped equalize assets, sustained growth has not necessarily been accompanied by rising inequality.

dence of poverty by 4 percent a year. But at this pace, the poverty inci-dence fraction should have fallen by 35 percent, or from 28.3 to 18.4 per-cent (instead of 24.0 percent), during the 11-year period 1987–98.[15] So the incidence of severe global poverty fell less than half as much as should have been expected in the 1990s.[16]

This is the *time-series* paradox of persistent poverty. A further analysis suggests there is also a *cross-section* paradox, because most middle-income countries have more poverty than would be expected under the most common statistical form (i.e., lognormal) for income distribution, as de-veloped below.

At least two possibilities could help explain the time-series paradox. First, perhaps the World Bank's estimates have a time trend bias that in-creasingly overstates poverty. Second, perhaps the usual postwar con-stancy of within-country income concentration has changed into a trend toward rising inequality.

## Misleading Data?

Bhalla (2002) has carried out a major empirical study concluding that the World Bank's poverty data have failed to capture the actual pace of poverty reduction. The core of his argument is that the World Bank ac-cepts the average incomes reported in household surveys, but that this in-come has increasingly fallen below the average income implied by na-tional accounts data. He does not have an explanation for this generalized pattern, but he is confident enough that the national accounts are right and the sample means are wrong to conclude that in fact the incidence of severe poverty in developing countries fell from his estimated 30 percent (vs. the World Bank's 28.3 percent) in 1987 to 13 percent in 2000 (vs. the World Bank's 24 percent) (Bhalla 2002, 3). If he is right, the time-series paradox disappears.

Attempting to resolve whether Bhalla or the World Bank is right, and more generally the extent to which sample survey data as opposed to na-tional accounts data should be relied upon, would unduly detain the pres-ent study.[17] A few thoughts, however, are nonetheless worth mention-ing.[18] On the one side, the seeming overstatement of estimated poverty in

---

15. That is, $28.3/(1.04)^{11} = 18.4$.

16. Or by only 43 percent. $(28.3 - 24.0)/(28.3 - 18.4) = 0.43$.

17. The principal author on the World Bank side of the debate, Martin Ravallion, has pro-vided a detailed critique of the Bhalla method (Ravallion 2002). Bhalla (2003) has provided a rejoinder. The dispute turns on such arcane issues as whether or not Bhalla has sufficiently taken into account the 1993 change in the official Indian national accounts statistics raising consumption estimates (and resultingly reducing the ratio of the sample survey to national accounts).

18. This is in addition to the key points made by Deaton (2003), as discussed below.

India and China when compared with international patterns, as analyzed earlier in this chapter, is suggestive of important problems in the key data for global poverty, although it does not address the question of the trend bias.[19] Also on this side, there are certainly reasons why sample surveys might be expected to report a declining share of national accounts income over time. Thus, rising shares of national income spent by governments on education and health, for example, would not tend to show up in household" surveys of income and consumption.[20] In addition, the practice of "top coding" income brackets in surveys, so that the highest-income families report only that they receive more than a given threshold (rather than the actual income level), means that an increasing share of income may go to households in the top bracket and that imputation of their income increasingly falls short of the actual total.[21]

On the other side of the debate, it is unclear whether Bhalla sufficiently addresses the likely concentration of sample income understatement in the higher income brackets. If not, his approach of using the sample survey distributions but applying them to the mean income levels from national accounts would tend to bias upward the income levels of the lower-income households, biasing downward measured poverty.

Deaton (2003) has examined this controversy, in part on the basis of data from some 550 surveys of industrial and developing countries during the period 1980–2000. His most striking finding is that the ratio of mean survey consumption to mean national accounts consumption systematically falls as income rises. The ratio actually exceeds unity in SSA, where nonmarket consumption is often captured less fully in national accounts than in surveys. For all countries, however, the average ratio of survey to national accounts consumption is 0.86 unweighted and 0.77 weighting by country population; and for the Organization for Economic Cooperation and Development (OECD), the ratio is only three-fourths. The gap is even wider for income, for which the ratio is only 60 percent, but for which there is no systematic pattern as income rises. In the United States, the trend in the consumption gap is pronounced; the ratio of the survey to national accounts fell from 80 percent in 1984 to 64 percent in 2001. For all non-OECD countries, population-weighted PPP consumption from surveys has grown at only half the rate reported in the Penn World Tables for national accounts.

---

19. Indeed, removing China decreases rather than increases the pace of poverty reduction (leaving it at a decline from 28.5 percent in 1987 to 26.2 percent in 1998; World Bank 2001, 23).

20. Note that this is not offset by simply excluding government consumption from household income in Bhalla's method, in which "household income has to be approximated by per capita GDP" (Bhalla 2002, 104–05).

21. I am indebted to Gary Burtless for these observations. Note, however, that top coding may not be a frequent practice in surveys for developing countries.

The UN Conference on Trade and Development (UNCTAD 2002a, 48) similarly shows that national accounts consumption data yield a higher incidence of poverty than survey consumption data at very low per capita income levels (below $500 PPP at 1985 prices) but a lower incidence of poverty than the survey data at higher income levels. In these data, which apparently combine time-series and cross-section information, a central regression curve relating poverty incidence to PPP per capita income places $1 per day poverty incidence at 80 percent for $300 PPP income using national accounts data but only at 50 percent using survey data. Conversely, at $900 PPP income, the national accounts place this poverty at 10 percent, while survey data place it at 33 percent.[22] UNCTAD prefers the national accounts basis, which yields a higher incidence of poverty for the LDCs than the levels normally reported on the basis of surveys.[23]

For his part, Deaton judges that "there can be no general presumption in favor of one or other of the surveys and the national accounts" (2003, 17).[24] He also judges that "it would be incorrect to apply inequality or distributional measures, which are derived from surveys which measure one thing, to means that are derived from the national accounts, which measure another" (p. 35), a critique that applies to Bhalla's method. In particular, national accounts include the imputed rental value of owned housing, as well as financial services that are indirectly imputed. Both of these are income-elastic and so constitute a larger fraction of the consumption of the rich than of the poor, so this would seem to be a specific source of bias that would overstate the income and consumption of the poor if means from national accounts were applied to survey income distributions.

Deaton's bottom line is that "the downward bias in survey measures of consumption almost certainly bias upward the World Bank's estimates [of poverty, such that] the rate of decline is probably downward biased. Yet there is essentially no choice but to use the surveys, because only the surveys provide direct measures of the living standards of the poor" (p. 37).

Overall, it would seem reasonable to judge that the World Bank estimates understate the pace of decline in global poverty, but it seems unlikely that they do so by as much as Bhalla in particular argues. Indeed, the simplest assumption about the nonreporting of consumption and income in surveys would seem to be along the following lines. Households at the poverty line and below report relatively accurately, because they

---

22. For $2 per day poverty, the crossover is at about $600 PPP per capita. At $1,350 per capita, e.g., national accounts place this poverty at 25 percent, whereas surveys place it at 45 percent.

23. Choice of the national accounts would seem, however, to provide a substantial overstatement of poverty at very low income levels because of the problem of failure to capture nonmarket consumption, as noted above.

24. One implication, which Deaton notes but does not emphasize, is that global economic growth may have been considerably slower than the national accounts data indicate.

have little to hide. Households above the poverty line have a greater incentive to understate (e.g., because of fear of taxation), and the degree of underreporting rises monotonically with income. Under these circumstances, the sample will unambiguously understate inequality.[25]

If this simple model of reporting is accurate, then Bhalla has it backwards: National accounts data should be used to obtain the missing income in surveys, and this missing income should be allocated to the nonpoor, especially the higher brackets, rather than using national accounts means and applying unchanged survey distributional data. This model also implies that true inequality has tended to rise, and that the constancy of survey-based inequality is misleading.

In sum, Bhalla has usefully alerted researchers to the possibility of a bias in the time trend of the World Bank poverty data. Deaton has provided additional evidence that suggests systematic decline in survey consumption relative to national accounts consumption as income rises. The implication is that at least some of the time-series paradox of persistent poverty may be attributable to misleading data. Nonetheless, and as implied by Deaton, on balance it seems likely that in making adjustments to the survey estimates, Bhalla has overstated the pace of decline in global poverty.

## Rising Inequality?

Another explanation of the time-series paradox may be simply that within-country inequality increased during the 1990s when the World Bank data showed so little poverty reduction, such that a simple application of growth data to the usual poverty elasticity (which assumes a constant degree of inequality) would overstate expected poverty reduction. It

---

25. In contrast, where all households accurately report income but there is a higher incidence of absence from the sample by higher-income households (rising nonresponse), the sample measure of inequality need not be biased downward. Mistiaen and Ravallion (2003) show that if nonresponse rises monotonically with income, the sample Lorenz curve will cross the population Lorenz curve, making inequality comparisons ambiguous. (Nonetheless, empirically they find for the United States that nonresponse does rise monotonically with income, and that "correcting for selective compliance appreciably increases mean income and inequality" [p. 1].) Deaton (2003) shows that for the lognormal income distribution, under the restrictive assumption that, above a threshold income, the logarithm of the probability of nonresponse rises linearly with the logarithm of income, the sample has the same variance (and hence inequality) as the population but the sample mean is biased downward.

A stronger statement can be made about the Pareto distribution, which has the form: $N = Ay^{-b}$, where $N$ is the number of households with income of $y$ or greater. The Gini coefficient for this distribution is $G = 1/[2b - 1]$ (Cline 1972, 227). Because neither $N$ nor $y$ appears in the Gini coefficient, it can be said that this distribution is fractal: A sample from any portion of it will yield the same Gini coefficient as a sample from any other portion. So a monotonic rise of nonresponse with income would not bias the sample measure of the Gini if the distribution is Pareto.

does indeed appear that, in contrast to the earlier stylized fact of constant within-country distribution, more recent research has tended to identify a trend of rising inequality in the 1980s and 1990s. Cornia and Kiiski (2001, 1) find that, for 73 developing, industrial, and transition economies constituting four-fifths of world population, "over the past two decades inequality rose in two-thirds of these 73 countries . . . [in] a clear departure from . . . trends recorded since the end of World War II." The authors suggest, but do not test, the hypothesis that the upturn in inequality was associated with market-oriented "Washington Consensus" policies.[26]

New statistical tests using the World Institute for Development Economics Research (WIDER) database on inequality confirm these more recent findings, that there have been two subperiods of first declining and then rising within-country inequality. A simple ordinary-least-squares regression of the following form may be estimated:

$$G_{it} = a + bt + c_i D_i + dt D_{EE} \qquad (1.1)$$

where $G_{it}$ is the Gini coefficient for country $i$ in year $t$; $a$ is a constant; $b$ is the overall coefficient relating the Gini coefficient to time; $D_i$ is a separate dummy variable for each country; and $D_{EE}$ is a dummy variable if the country is an Eastern European or former Soviet Union economy. If there is a trend toward rising within-country inequality, the regression coefficient $b$ will be positive. The inclusion of an Eastern European dummy allows for divergence in these economies from the general trends, in view of the strong indications that the transition process was associated with a rise in inequality.

Table 1.7 reports the results of applying this regression equation to 526 observations on country-year Gini coefficients (expressed in percentage form), spanning the period 1950 through 2000 and including observations for 76 countries.[27] In the upper panel, the unweighted regression for the full period finds a small but statistically significant negative coefficient on time (where $t = 1$ for 1950, rising to 51 for 2000). Approximately the same coefficient is found for the period 1950–79. This result supports the proposition of stable or slightly declining inequality in this period.

In contrast, for the period 1980–2000, the coefficient of the Gini on time turns positive, and it is again statistically significant. In this period, each additional year is associated with a rise in the Gini coefficient of 0.118. For

26. Galbraith and Kum (2002) use United Nations Industrial Development Organization data on average wages in industry to estimate that there was a declining trend in within-country inequality in the 1960s and 1970s, followed by a rising trend in the 1980s and 1990s. However, it would seem questionable to place much weight on the industrial wage data, given the small share of industry in employment in most countries and the paucity of detail available from the two or three dozen industrial category averages available.

27. The data are from WIDER (2000).

**Table 1.7    Regression results: Time trend of Gini coefficients**

| Period | Constant | Time | | Eastern Europe dummy | | Adjusted $R^2$ | Number of observations |
|---|---|---|---|---|---|---|---|
| **Unweighted** | | | | | | | |
| 1950–2000 | 39.4 | –0.075 | (–3.8) | 0.316 | (7.0) | 0.86 | 526 |
| 1950–79 | 52.0 | –0.076 | (–1.6) | –0.069 | (–0.5) | 0.92 | 168 |
| 1980–2000 | 13.7 | 0.118 | (2.0) | 0.426 | (5.7) | 0.87 | 358 |
| | | | | | | | |
| **Weighted** | | | | | | | |
| 1950–2000 | 45.8 | –0.013 | (–11.9) | 0.394 | (53.5) | 0.79 | [126,609] |
| 1950–79 | 31.5 | –0.181 | (–103.9) | –0.049 | (–1.8) | 0.94 | [38,609] |
| 1980–2000 | 19.7 | 0.467 | (189.8) | 0.266 | (35.8) | 0.83 | [88,000] |

Note: *t*-statistics are in parentheses. Individual country dummy variables are not shown.

example, during the 20 years, a country starting with a Gini coefficient of 40.0 (percent) would be expected to experience a rise to 42.36. The upper panel also confirms the impression that the transition process for socialist economies was unequalizing. In the period 1980–2000, these economies had a large positive coefficient on the time variable.[28] The regressions achieve a high degree of explanation ($R^2$), although likely primarily due to the country dummy variables, which capture the large and typically persistent differences among countries in inequality levels.

The lower panel of table 1.7 reports results for weighted regressions, in which each country's weight is proportional to its population and inversely proportional to its number of observations.[29] These population-weighted results find an even more dramatic reversal from equalizing trends through 1979 to unequalizing trends thereafter (the *b* coefficient is a larger negative value in the first period and a larger positive value in the second period than in the unweighted regressions). The coefficient for the period 1980–2000 implies a rise of a remarkable 9 points on the Gini coefficient over the 20-year span (e.g., from 40.0 to 49.3).[30]

Figure 1.1 displays the time trends for the Gini coefficients of eight major developing countries with large poor populations. The figure shows

28. In the regression equation, an Eastern European economy has a time coefficient equal to $b + d$.

29. The latter weight adjusts for the fact that for some countries sample survey data are available for nearly every year, whereas for others only a few years are available; the absence of the weights would tend to overstate the experience of the country with more observations, which might be useful for some purposes but not for the purpose of a population-weighted result seeking overall representativeness.

30. Note that the *t*-statistics for the weighted regressions are not reliable indicators of statistical significance. Because each observation is multiplied by the ratio of the country's population to the population of the smallest country, there is an artificial ballooning of the "number" of observations (hence the brackets on the number of observations in this panel of the table), overstating the usual *t*-statistic measure.

**Figure 1.1   Time path of the Gini coefficient for selected economies, 1950–98**

Gini coefficient

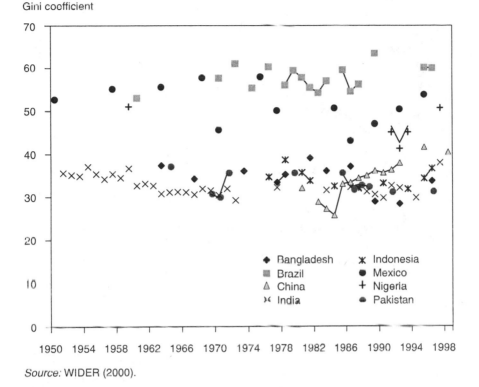

*Source:* WIDER (2000).

that each country's Gini tends to remain relatively close to its particular plateau. It also shows important increases in the Gini coefficient in recent years for a number of key economies, however, including Brazil, China, Indonesia, Mexico, and Nigeria. These countries bulk large enough in the global poverty totals for their rising inequality to have played a substantial role in explaining the time-series paradox of persistent poverty despite the achievement of global growth.

## Cross-Section Paradox

Even if the time-series paradox can be partly or fully explained by trend bias in the measured poverty data and/or a trend of rising within-country inequality after 1980, there remains a strong cross-section paradox of persistent poverty as well. As developed in appendix 1B, the incidence of poverty in many middle-income countries seems to be persistently higher than one might expect from certain standard distributional analytics. In particular, if it is assumed that the underlying income distribution is normal in terms of the logarithm of income (the "lognormal" distribution),

**Figure 1.2  Actual versus lognormal-predicted poverty** (percent)

percent

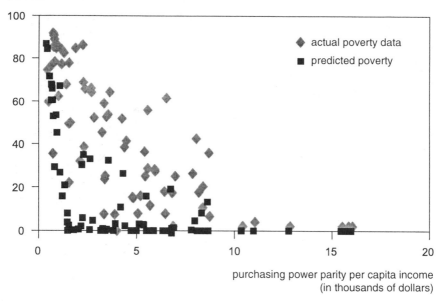

purchasing power parity per capita income
(in thousands of dollars)

*Source:* Author's calculations.

the poverty incidence fraction can be predicted from the average per capita income, poverty threshold, and Gini coefficient (see appendix 1B). The predicted headcount poverty fraction will be lower as the average per capita income rises (for a constant global poverty threshold, in this case the $730 annual PPP income international line), but will be higher if the Gini coefficient is higher.

Figure 1.2 displays the actual and predicted poverty percentages for those countries in appendix table 1A.1 for which World Bank estimates are available on both poverty and Gini coefficients. In the figure, the actual poverty data are indicated by a diamond. In comparison, for each country, the corresponding predicted poverty percentage is shown by a square. As the figure shows, in the range of PPP per capita incomes of about $400 to $1,200, predicted poverty tends to be in the same range as actual poverty. Thus, of the 15 observations in this range, the median actual poverty incidence is 84 percent, and the median predicted incidence is 66 percent. In contrast, at higher income ranges, the lognormal-predicted poverty rate falls further and further below the actual rate. For example, for 16 observations in the range of $5,000 to $8,000 PPP per capita, the median actual poverty rate is 25 percent, while the median pre-

**Table 1.8  Actual and predicted poverty rates for selected countries**

| Country | PPP per capita income (1990 dollars) | Gini coefficient (ratio) | Actual poverty incidence (percent) | Lognormal predicted poverty (percent) |
|---|---|---|---|---|
| Tanzania | 500 | 0.38 | 59.7 | 84.4 |
| Ethiopia | 620 | 0.40 | 76.4 | 71.6 |
| Nigeria | 770 | 0.51 | 90.8 | 65.9 |
| Senegal | 1,400 | 0.41 | 67.8 | 20.9 |
| India | 2,230 | 0.38 | 86.2 | 2.0 |
| China | 3,550 | 0.40 | 53.7 | 0.5 |
| Colombia | 5,580 | 0.57 | 28.7 | 15.9 |
| Brazil | 6,840 | 0.60 | 17.4 | 19.2 |
| Mexico | 8,070 | 0.54 | 42.5 | 4.5 |

PPP = purchasing power parity

*Sources:* Tables 1A.1 and 1B.1 in the appendices.

dicted rate is 0.1 percent. The underprediction is acute for the countries with relatively greater equality.[31]

To illustrate these points, table 1.8 reports actual and predicted poverty rates for selected economies. The illustrative cases in table 1.8 show the strong influence of the degree of inequality (Gini coefficient) in determining whether the lognormal distribution increasingly overpredicts poverty incidence as real per capita income rises. Brazil, which has the highest Gini (0.60), is the only middle-income country for which the predicted poverty incidence exceeds the actual incidence. In contrast, even for Mexico and Colombia, which both have relatively high income concentration but not as high as that of Brazil, the predicted poverty level is lower than the actual level. For Mexico, which has a substantially higher per capita income than Colombia, the underprediction is severe.

In short, the cross-section paradox of persistent poverty poses a caveat to the reliance on growth to reduce poverty. Poverty incidence remains stubbornly higher, as per capita income rises, than would be expected under at least one of the main theoretical distributional functions (the lognormal), except for countries with very high inequality. If this pattern is combined with the proposition that there is no systematic rise in inequality as per capita income rises (i.e., no Kuznets curve), in other words the stylized facts as of the late 1990s, an implication would seem to be that as

---

31. Underprediction is substantial even at intermediate inequality. Thus, the high ratio of average per capita income to the poverty threshold in China (about fivefold), combined with an intermediate inequality (Gini = 0.4), gives a lognormal-predicted poverty incidence of only 0.5 percent, far below the actual 53.7 percent. In contrast, for Brazil, where per capita income is even higher relative to the poverty threshold (ninefold), the high degree of inequality (Gini = 0.6) yields a predicted poverty rate of 19.2 percent, which is close to the actual 17.4 percent, suggesting high sensitivity to the Gini coefficient.

per capita income rises, the contribution of low-percentile components of the distribution to overall inequality rises while that of high-percentile components decreases, relative to the composition that would be expected from the lognormal distribution. In this way, overall inequality might not be rising, but that associated with the poverty group could be.[32] Some such effect would also seem likely to be required to harmonize the cross-section paradox even with the most recent stylized fact of rising inequality after 1980, simply because for most countries the most recent Gini coefficient levels are still far too low to generate lognormal-predicted poverty incidence anywhere near as high as actual poverty incidence (except for the lowest-income economies).

## Population Growth Offset

Finally, there is one much more obvious reason why economic growth may reduce poverty only slowly over time: Even without any rise in within-country inequality, the *absolute number* of the poor globally can remain stubbornly high despite a falling poverty incidence because of a rise in total population and hence in the absolute number of the poor for any given headcount poverty ratio.

Suppose within-country distribution remained constant, the developing (and transition) economies grew at 2 percent per capita annually, and the poverty elasticity is 2. Suppose population growth continues at 1.6 percent. Then the absolute number of the poor would decline at only 2.4 percent a year, composed of a 4 percent annual decline from growth (2 percent × poverty elasticity of 2) minus the 1.6 percent population growth rate. At this rate—which is optimistic in light of the experience of at least 1980–2000—*it would take 29 years to cut the absolute number of people in extreme poverty in half*, or about twice as long as the 15-year target set forth in the United Nations Millennium Development Goals adopted in 2000 (United Nations 2002).[33] The influence of population growth in boosting the absolute number of the poor and hence slowing its reduction from economic growth is no great surprise, nor does it pose a paradox, but it is important to keep in mind in thinking realistically about the scope

---

32. Consider an example. The poor 60 percent of the population receive 20 percent of income, the middle-class 30 percent receive 25 percent, and the rich 10 percent receive 55 percent of income. The Gini coefficient is 0.55. After, say, two decades, per capita income doubles, but the poor 60 percent have no increase in income at all. Their share of income drops to 10 percent. Say the middle class share rises to 50 percent, and the rich share eases to 40 percent. The Gini coefficient remains unchanged at 0.55, but the composition of inequality has been redistributed, with a greater share of total inequality at the bottom of the distribution and a lesser share in the middle and upper classes. The second Lorenz curve lies below the first to the left (the poor 60 percent) and above it to the right (the top 40 percent).

33. That is, $1/(1.024)^{29} = 0.5$. For the United Nations Millennium Development Goals, see www.un.org/millenn:ungoals.

of the challenge involved in reducing by half the absolute number of those in severe poverty globally.

## The Issue of Convergence

Despite the caveats, the central principle remains valid that the most certain way to reduce poverty is to achieve sustained growth. The question then becomes whether growth can be expected in the developing countries. This question in turn is related to the issue of whether there has been convergence or divergence in income levels between industrial and developing countries.

Much of the recent rhetoric in the policy and even research arenas seems to maintain that in economic terms the populations of poor countries have fallen farther behind the rich during the past several decades. Thus, in September 2000, World Bank president James D. Wolfensohn stated in a speech: "Something is wrong when the average income for the richest 20 countries is 37 times the average for the poorest 20—a gap that has more than doubled in the past 40 years." Similarly, the economist Paul Romer (1994) has developed "endogenous growth" theory to explain why diminishing returns to capital do not cause growth in industrial countries to slow down and why poor countries did not grow faster than rich countries in the decades after 1960.

The problem with this "nonconvergence" analysis is that it is built on an optical illusion that gives a misleading diagnosis. It focuses on "countries" instead of "people." It is true that many small countries have had slow growth, but it turns out that they are not representative of the experience of the majority of people who live in poor countries.

As shown in appendix 1C, when attention is focused on 75 countries with a population of 1 million or more, accounting for 83 percent of global population, it turns out that there was significant convergence in income levels in the period 1960–2000. The average real per capita growth rates for those countries that at the beginning of the period accounted for the bottom 60 percent of global population in PPP per capita income rankings amounted to 4 percent annually. In contrast, the corresponding rate for the initial fourth quintile was 2.34 percent, and for the top quintile, 2.23 percent. By 1999, the (population-weighted) per capita income of countries accounting for the poorest 60 percent in 1960 had doubled relative to that for the world's richest 20 percent in 1960.

The principal meaningful area of nonconvergence has been in the growth experience of sub-Saharan Africa. A statistical test in appendix 1C finds that per capita growth in this region in the past four decades has been 3 percent lower than in other developing regions, after taking account of the starting per capita income level. This result, however, suggests the need for special approaches toward this region, rather than blanket pessimism about developing countries' growth potential.

The more general pattern of convergence is not surprising, given the well-known growth successes of such economies as China, India, and South Korea, all of which were in the bottom 60 percent in 1960. What is surprising is that much of the convergence debate seems to have lost track of the forest by focusing on the individual trees, without considering the appropriate weight of each one. In short, the concern about nonconvergence is largely a red herring when it comes to its applicability to the question of whether global growth can or cannot be expected to help lift the world's poor out of poverty. Growth has been doing just that in a number of key countries that account for the bulk of the world's poor.

## Does Trade Increase Growth?

If we accept that growth is instrumental to reducing poverty, and that despite concerns about nonconvergence the postwar growth record for the bulk of the population in developing countries has been relatively favorable, a central issue for this study then becomes: How can trade policy affect growth? This question in turn has two components: How does a developing country's own trade policy affect its growth? And how do industrial countries' trade policies affect developing countries' growth?

Much has been written on the first of these two questions. It is probably fair to say that there is a weak consensus that open trade policies, including low protection on imports, help foster growth. Although there is a recognition that industrialization in such economies as South Korea and Brazil developed with the aid of infant-industry protection, there is also a recognition that the highly inward-oriented development strategies of the Latin American economies in the 1960s and 1970s eventually led to serious inefficiencies and weak export bases, especially as these strategies entered their later phases of expansion into the production of capital goods. The alternative strategy of a strong emphasis on export expansion and participation in world markets in Korea is usually seen as having proved to be superior.

As discussed in chapter 5, there is nonetheless division among economists on the extent to which open strategies, and especially simple import liberalization, have contributed to growth. This has been the dominant conceptual framework in the international official organizations since at least the 1980s, premised in part on important empirical work on major country case studies (Little, Scitovsky, and Scott 1970; Balassa 1971; Krueger 1978). More recent work finding similarly that "trade is good for growth" includes in particular that by Edwards (1993) and Dollar and Kraay (2001b). This work, however, is not without critics. In particular, Rodriguez and Rodrik (2000) have questioned the results of the statistical work relating growth to open trade policies, on such grounds as the absence of good measures of the extent of protection. Similarly, Birdsall and

**Figure 1.3  Average GDP and export growth, 1980s and 1990s**

average annual GDP growth

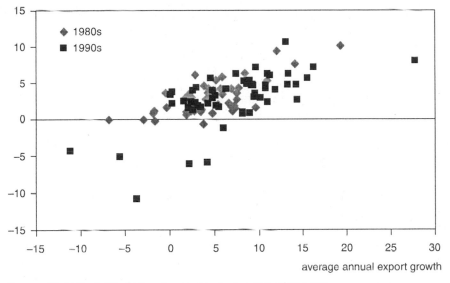

Source: World Bank, World Development Indicators CD-ROM, 2001.

Hamoudi (2002) have shown that the "increase in openness" variable used by Dollar and Kraay (2001b) is subject to bias from capturing primarily the erosion of world prices for raw materials exports rather than any failure to open trade.

There is far more consensus, in contrast, that open trade policies for *industrial* countries are favorable to the growth prospects of developing countries. There has been little if any empirical work on this issue, probably because it would be difficult to formulate a conceptual basis for arguing the contrary (whereas the infant-industry and other arguments can be marshaled to question the free trade position for developing countries' own policies). At the very least, the elimination of import barriers in industrial countries to exports from developing countries should raise the terms of trade for the latter. In practice, the more important dynamics probably have to do with the growing integration of production in developing countries with more open industrial-country markets, which is often coordinated by multinational firms. The explosion of Mexico's exports to the United States during the past decade thanks to free trade under the North American Free Trade Agreement is a prime example.

The evidence does show that higher export growth is associated with higher GDP growth. Thus, figure 1.3 displays, for 64 developing countries with populations over 10 million in 1999, the rate of real growth of GDP on the y-axis and that of exports of goods and services on the x-axis. The diamonds refer to the period 1980–90; the squares, to 1990–99. There is a clear positive relationship between export growth and GDP growth in both periods.[34] A simple (ordinary-least-squares) regression of GDP growth on export growth for this set of data yields the following results:

$$g_Y = 1.58 + 0.153 \, g_X \, ; \text{Adj. } R^2 = 0.13 \qquad (1.2)$$
$$\quad (6.8) \quad (6.1)$$

where growth rates are in real annual average percentage terms, and the $t$-statistics are shown in parentheses. The export growth term is highly significant, and its coefficient indicates that each percentage point of additional export growth has been associated with a rise of 0.15 percentage point in GDP growth.

Even after taking account of such considerations as ambiguity in causality because exports are part of the national accounts identity for GDP, it seems highly likely that the inference would remain valid that faster export growth spurs economic growth in developing countries. One reason is that exports provide financing for imports of key intermediate inputs, capital goods, and technologies not available domestically. Another is that export orientation tends to impose the discipline of international competitiveness on domestic production.

It should be recognized, moreover, that a strong correlation between export growth and GDP growth implies, other things being equal, that lower protection in developing countries is likely to help rather than hinder growth. The reason is that high protection tends to act as a tax on exports, by creating a distorted incentive for producing for the domestic rather than the international market. Indeed, there is a formal proposition (the Lerner symmetry theorem; Lerner 1936) that maintains that an import tariff has an effect equivalent to an export tax.

In turn, through the successive removal of trade barriers, industrial countries should be able to help spur the exports of developing countries by increasing their export opportunities. Although it is difficult to quantify how much faster developing countries' exports can be expected to grow under alternative scenarios of industrial-country import liberalization, increasing market access would seem to be a central way in which industrial countries contribute to growth and hence poverty reduction in the developing world.

## Conclusion

The task of reducing global poverty is enormous: Fully half of the world's population lives in poverty at the $2 per day threshold. Because trade is

---

34. The data are from the World Bank's World Development Indicators CD-ROM for 2001.

the most natural economic relationship between industrial and develop-ing countries, it is important to consider how changes in trade policy could serve as a means by which industrial countries could help reduce global poverty.

Special market access for poor countries has so far been the main pol-icy oriented toward this end. These regimes are potentially important and relatively efficient at reaching the poor. The reason is that the "poverty in-tensity of trade" with these countries is higher than that for imports from developing countries more generally, especially when considering the share of the poor in national income rather than in number of households. This chapter develops this concept and finds that whereas industrial-country imports from developing countries overall have a poverty inten-sity of 32 percent weighting by headcount and only 8 percent by income share, imports from the LDCs, HIPCs, and SSA have a poverty intensity of 60 to 70 percent on a headcount basis and about 50 percent on an income-share basis. Chapter 2 examines the experience with special-access regimes.

The poverty-intensity concept can also be used to highlight the products most important for reducing poverty. These include the well-known cases of apparel and textiles, toys, and footwear; and certain agricultural goods (e.g., cocoa and cotton); but also less immediately obvious products such as precious stones and, arguably, the key case of petroleum (where the large weight of such suppliers as Nigeria, Angola, Algeria, and Venezuela means relatively high poverty intensity). By implication, high protection on poverty-intensive products is more onerous for global poverty than that on other goods such as semiconductors and motor vehicles.

Although the poverty intensity focus suggests that trade and other gen-eral economic instruments may reach the global poor more efficiently if they are concentrated on the LDCs, HIPCs, and SSA, it turns out that these recognized groupings account for only one-fourth of the global poor. Only two of the countries with poverty populations in excess of 100 million (Bangladesh and Nigeria) are in one of these groupings. Trade policy will thus have to provide new opportunities for a much wider range of developing countries if it is to help address the other three-fourths of the global poor. These include the two largest national concen-trations of poverty: India (with 860 million poor) and China (670 million). Two other countries with more than 100 million poor people each (In-donesia and Pakistan) are also outside the normal poor-country group-ings, as are numerous countries with 30 to 50 million poor people each, comprising middle-population poor countries (e.g., Ethiopia, Vietnam, and Egypt) as well as large-population middle-income countries with substantial inequality (e.g., Mexico, Russia, and Brazil). As developed in chapters 4 and 5, global trade liberalization could provide major inroads in reducing poverty in these countries as well. In short, the strategy for using trade policy to help reduce global poverty should involve both an "intensive" track of prompt free access for the special regime candidates and an "extensive" track of general multilateral liberalization for the other developing countries where in aggregate many more of the world's poor are to be found.

The analysis of this chapter suggests that growth reduces poverty, but that the pace of decline has been below what might have been expected, and higher poverty persists than might be expected in many middle-income countries. Appendix 1B sets forth the analytics relating poverty incidence to per capita income and the degree of inequality using the log-normal income distribution. Where income inequality is moderate, the "poverty elasticity" is 2 to 3 or higher, meaning that a 1 percent rise in per capita income reduces the number in poverty by 2 to 3 percent. Where income is highly unequally distributed, or where per capita income is very low, this elasticity is closer to unity.

Given the expected range for this elasticity, however, the pace of poverty reduction has been disappointing. World Bank estimates indicate that extreme poverty ($1 per day) fell only from 28 percent of global population in 1987 to 24 percent in 1998, whereas the application of a central poverty elasticity of 2 to the rise in per capita income should have reduced this incidence to about 18 percent during this period. An intense debate has developed between Bhalla (2002) and World Bank experts, in which Bhalla has argued that the survey data used by the World Bank have increasingly understated the incomes of the poor, as demonstrated by the shortfall of survey averages from those national accounts data. After considering the analysis and data brought to bear on this issue by Deaton (2003), this chapter suggests that although World Bank estimates may understate the pace of poverty reduction, Bhalla likely overstates it considerably.

Even so, the central judgment remains valid that growth should reduce poverty, even if the pace has been slower than might have been expected. The more recent data suggest that the discrepancy may partly be explained by rising within-country inequality in the past two decades, a new pattern following the previous "stylized fact" that within-country distributions have remained constant over long periods. New regression estimates in this chapter show that whereas there was virtually no statistical time trend for Gini coefficients in the period 1950–80, in the period 1980–2000 there was a statistically significant if moderate increase (and the size is much larger weighting by population).

Whether growth reduces poverty also depends on whether developing countries achieve growth. Appendix 1C examines the "convergence" controversy. It finds that the popular notion that there has been a failure of convergence between rich and poor countries in global growth experience is based on a statistical illusion because it fails to take account of the importance of each country in global population. When this is done, it is demonstrated that for the period 1960–2000, global growth showed convergence rather than divergence. Moreover, this was not a "China only" story. The list of major economies that started out in the bottom 80 percent of world population arrayed by per capita income in 1960 and achieved faster per capita growth than the top 20 percent includes not only China but also India, Indonesia, Pakistan, Thailand, Egypt, Sri Lanka, Korea, Turkey, Malaysia, Brazil, Hong Kong, Chile, and several other developing economies, as well as now-developed Portugal, Japan, Greece, and Spain.

If growth is ultimately the main source of reducing poverty, then the link to trade policy turns importantly on whether trade policy reforms can help achieve greater growth. Cross-country evidence shows a close correlation between export growth and GDP growth. Each 1 percentage point of additional export growth is associated with 0.15 percentage point of faster GDP growth, although more sophisticated econometric techniques would be required to take account of endogeneity (exports are part of GDP in national income accounting). The evidence over the past four decades is nonetheless suggestive enough to provide support for the idea that improved trade opportunities for developing countries resulting from global trade policy reform could make an important contribution to growth and hence poverty reduction over time. The trade-growth-poverty relationship is analyzed further, and quantitative estimates are summarized, in chapter 5.

# Appendix 1A
## Estimating Poverty Rates

The World Bank (2001) provides direct estimates for the percentage of the population of each country living under the $2 per day poverty threshold, or the "headcount ratio" measure of poverty.[35] There are, however, numerous countries for which these estimates are not available. To obtain working estimates for these countries, it is possible to estimate a statistical regression of the poverty fraction on PPP per capita income and the Gini coefficient of income concentration using data on those countries for which poverty rates are available. A higher average income should reduce the fraction of the population below the international poverty line, whereas a higher income concentration should leave a larger fraction of the population in poverty than would otherwise be expected.

Figure 1A.1 shows the expected downward-sloping relationship for the percent of population in poverty (vertical axis) to the average PPP per capita income (horizontal axis). The concave relationship also suggests the logarithm of income, rather than absolute level, as the appropriate specification. As for the influence of income concentration, the expected effect would be for the slope of the poverty-income curve to be steeper for a more equal income distribution (lower Gini) and gentler for a less equal distribution (higher Gini). In effect, at very low average per capita income, the headcount poverty fraction will start out close to 100 percent, but otherwise the poverty-income curve will swivel upward or downward depending on the degree of concentration. The estimation form $\Phi_p = a + b \ln y^* + c (G \ln y^*)$ captures this relationship, where $\Phi_p$ is the percent of population below the poverty line, $y^*$ is 1999 PPP per capita income, and $G$ is the Gini coefficient (from 0 to 1, typically in the range 0.35–0.55). With $b$ negative and $c$ positive, the effect is to make the slope of the regression line equal to $-[b - cG]$, accomplishing the swivel of the curve associated with varying concentration.

For a set of 69 countries with World Bank data available for both poverty incidence and the Gini coefficient (World Bank 2001, 280–83), an ordinary-least-squares regression yields ($t$-statistics in parentheses):

$$\Phi_p = 245.0 - 27.8 \ln y^* + 6.48 (G \ln y^*); \text{Adj. } R^2 = 0.74 \qquad (A.1)$$
$$\quad (15.1) (-13.8) \qquad (2.96)$$

For 14 countries with estimates available for $y^*$ and $G$ but not $\Phi_p$, equation A.1 may be applied directly to estimate the percent of population below the international poverty line. For another 33 countries with $y^*$

---

35. This appendix uses the data available on the CD-ROM for *World Development Report 2001*.

**Figure 1A.1  Poverty incidence and per capita income**

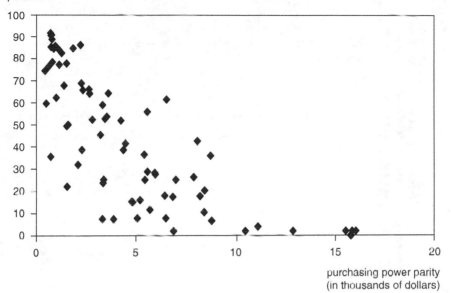

percent

*Sources:* World Bank (1982, 2001).

available but no available estimate of the Gini coefficient, applying the median Gini for the region in question also permits the use of equation A.1 to estimate the poverty headcount.[36] Finally, for 8 LDCs for which no estimate of per capita income is available, it is assumed that the poverty rate is equal to the average for 18 LDCs for which World Bank poverty estimates are available (72.8 percent). The resulting poverty estimates for 127 individual developing countries are reported in appendix table 1A.1. These countries have a total population of 5.0 billion and account for all but about 100 million of the population of developing countries (see table 1.2).

---

36. For 73 countries with Gini coefficients available from the World Bank, the regional median values are Africa, 0.408; Asia-Pacific, 0.367; Latin America, 0.503; Middle East, 0.38; and emerging Europe, 0.327.

**Table 1A.1  Poverty in developing countries ($2 PPP per day definition)**

| Country | Population (millions) | Per capita income[a] | Number in poverty (millions) | Gini coefficient | Percent in poverty | Income share of poor | Least developed countries[c] | Heavily indebted poor countries[c] | Sub-Saharan Africa[c] |
|---|---|---|---|---|---|---|---|---|---|
| Afghanistan | 26.55 | | 19.33 | | 72.8 | 1.000 | 1 | 0 | 0 |
| Albania | 3.38 | 3,240 | 1.26 | 0.327 | 37.5 | 0.084 | 0 | 0 | 0 |
| Algeria | 29.95 | 4,840 | 4.52 | 0.353 | 15.1 | 0.023 | 0 | 0 | 0 |
| Angola | 12.36 | 1,100 | 8.51 | 0.408 | 68.9 | 0.457 | 1 | 1 | 1 |
| Argentina | 36.58 | 11,940 | 5.37 | 0.503 | 14.7 | 0.009 | 0 | 0 | 0 |
| Armenia | 3.81 | 2,360 | 1.74 | 0.327 | 45.6 | 0.141 | 0 | 0 | 0 |
| Azerbaijan | 7.98 | 2,450 | 3.56 | 0.327 | 44.6 | 0.133 | 0 | 0 | 0 |
| Bangladesh | 127.67 | 1,530 | 99.33 | 0.336 | 77.8 | 0.371 | 1 | 0 | 0 |
| Belarus | 10.03 | 6,880 | 0.20 | 0.217 | 2.0 | 0.002 | 0 | 0 | 0 |
| Benin | 6.11 | 920 | 4.49 | 0.408 | 73.4 | 0.582 | 1 | 1 | 1 |
| Bhutan | 0.80 | 1,350 | 0.49 | 0.367 | 61.8 | 0.334 | 1 | 0 | 0 |
| Bolivia | 8.14 | 2,300 | 3.14 | 0.420 | 38.6 | 0.123 | 0 | 1 | 0 |
| Botswana | 1.59 | 6,540 | 0.98 | 0.408 | 61.4 | 0.069 | 0 | 0 | 1 |
| Brazil | 167.97 | 6,840 | 29.23 | 0.600 | 17.4 | 0.019 | 0 | 0 | 0 |
| Bulgaria | 8.21 | 5,070 | 0.64 | 0.283 | 7.8 | 0.011 | 0 | 0 | 0 |
| Burkina Faso | 11.00 | 960 | 9.43 | 0.482 | 85.8 | 0.652 | 1 | 1 | 1 |
| Burundi | 6.68 | 570 | 5.50 | 0.333 | 82.3 | 1.000 | 1 | 1 | 1 |
| Cambodia | 11.76 | 1,350 | 7.47 | 0.404 | 63.5 | 0.344 | 1 | 0 | 0 |
| Cameroon | 14.69 | 1,490 | 9.00 | 0.408 | 61.2 | 0.300 | 0 | 1 | 1 |
| Cape Verde | 0.44 | 4,680 | 0.13 | 0.367 | 30.2 | 0.047 | 1 | 0 | 0 |
| Central African Republic | 3.54 | 1,150 | 2.97 | 0.613 | 84.0 | 0.533 | 1 | 1 | 1 |
| Chad | 7.49 | 840 | 5.66 | 0.408 | 75.7 | 0.657 | 1 | 1 | 1 |
| Chile | 15.02 | 8,410 | 3.05 | 0.565 | 20.3 | 0.018 | 0 | 0 | 0 |
| China | 1,253.60 | 3,550 | 673.18 | 0.403 | 53.7 | 0.110 | 0 | 0 | 0 |
| Colombia | 41.54 | 5,580 | 11.92 | 0.571 | 28.7 | 0.038 | 0 | 0 | 0 |
| Comoros | 0.56 | 1,490 | 0.33 | 0.367 | 59.3 | 0.291 | 1 | 1 | 1 |
| Congo, Democratic Republic of[b] | 49.78 | 800 | 38.23 | 0.408 | 76.8 | 0.701 | 1 | 1 | 1 |
| Congo, Republic of | 2.86 | 540 | 2.48 | 0.408 | 86.8 | 1.000 | 0 | 1 | 1 |
| Costa Rica | 3.59 | 7,880 | 0.94 | 0.470 | 26.3 | 0.024 | 0 | 0 | 0 |
| Côte d'Ivoire | 15.55 | 1,540 | 7.68 | 0.367 | 49.4 | 0.234 | 0 | 1 | 1 |
| Croatia | 4.46 | 7,260 | 0.60 | 0.268 | 13.4 | 0.013 | 0 | 0 | 0 |
| Czech Republic | 10.28 | 12,840 | 0.21 | 0.254 | 2.0 | 0.001 | 0 | 0 | 0 |

| | (1) | (2) | (3) | (4) | (5) | (6) | (7) | (8) |
|---|---|---|---|---|---|---|---|---|
| Djibouti | 0.66 | | 0.48 | | 72.8 | 1.000 | 0 | 1 |
| Dominican Republic | 8.40 | 5,210 | 1.34 | 0.487 | 16.0 | 0.022 | 0 | 0 |
| Ecuador | 12.41 | 2,820 | 3.40 | 0.437 | 52.3 | 0.135 | 0 | 0 |
| Egypt, Arab Republic | 62.65 | 3,460 | 33.02 | 0.289 | 52.7 | 0.111 | 0 | 0 |
| El Salvador | 6.15 | 4,260 | 3.19 | 0.523 | 51.9 | 0.089 | 0 | 1 |
| Equatorial Guinea | 0.45 | 4,770 | 0.14 | 0.408 | 32.0 | 0.049 | 0 | 1 |
| Eritrea | 3.99 | 1,040 | 2.31 | 0.408 | 70.3 | 0.493 | 1 | 0 |
| Estonia | 1.44 | 8,190 | 0.26 | 0.354 | 17.7 | 0.016 | 0 | 1 |
| Ethiopia | 62.78 | 620 | 47.97 | 0.400 | 76.4 | 0.900 | 1 | 0 |
| Gabon | 1.21 | 5,280 | 0.36 | 0.408 | 29.4 | 0.041 | 0 | 1 |
| Gambia, The | 1.25 | 1,550 | 0.75 | 0.408 | 60.3 | 0.284 | 0 | 1 |
| Georgia | 5.45 | 2,540 | 2.38 | 0.327 | 43.7 | 0.126 | 1 | 0 |
| Ghana | 18.78 | 1,850 | 9.74 | 0.327 | 51.9 | 0.205 | 0 | 1 |
| Greece | 10.54 | 15,800 | 0.00 | 0.327 | 0.0 | 0.000 | 0 | 0 |
| Guatemala | 11.09 | 3,630 | 7.13 | 0.596 | 64.3 | 0.129 | 0 | 0 |
| Guinea | 7.25 | 1,870 | 4.01 | 0.403 | 55.3 | 0.216 | 1 | 0 |
| Guinea-Bissau | 1.18 | 630 | 0.98 | 0.408 | 82.9 | 0.960 | 1 | 1 |
| Haiti | 7.80 | 1,470 | 5.16 | 0.503 | 66.1 | 0.328 | 0 | 1 |
| Honduras | 6.32 | 2,270 | 4.35 | 0.537 | 68.8 | 0.221 | 1 | 0 |
| Hungary | 10.07 | 11,050 | 0.40 | 0.308 | 4.0 | 0.003 | 0 | 0 |
| India | 997.52 | 2,230 | 859.86 | 0.378 | 86.2 | 0.282 | 0 | 0 |
| Indonesia | 207.02 | 2,660 | 136.84 | 0.365 | 66.1 | 0.181 | 0 | 0 |
| Iran, Islamic Republic | 62.98 | 5,520 | 16.85 | 0.380 | 26.8 | 0.035 | 0 | 0 |
| Jamaica | 2.60 | 3,390 | 0.65 | 0.364 | 25.2 | 0.054 | 0 | 0 |
| Jordan | 4.74 | 3,880 | 0.35 | 0.364 | 7.4 | 0.014 | 0 | 0 |
| Kazakhstan | 14.93 | 4,790 | 2.28 | 0.354 | 15.3 | 0.023 | 0 | 0 |
| Kenya | 29.41 | 1,010 | 18.32 | 0.445 | 62.3 | 0.450 | 0 | 1 |
| Kiribati | 0.09 | | 0.07 | | 72.8 | 1.000 | 1 | 0 |
| Korea, Republic of | 46.86 | 15,530 | 0.94 | 0.315 | 2.0 | 0.001 | 0 | 0 |
| Kyrgyz Republic | 4.86 | 2,420 | 2.38 | 0.405 | 48.9 | 0.147 | 0 | 0 |
| Laos | 5.10 | 1,430 | 2.92 | 0.304 | 57.4 | 0.293 | 1 | 1 |
| Latvia | 2.43 | 6,220 | 0.50 | 0.324 | 20.6 | 0.024 | 0 | 0 |
| Lesotho | 2.11 | 2,350 | 1.38 | 0.560 | 65.7 | 0.204 | 0 | 1 |
| Liberia | 3.13 | | 2.28 | | 72.8 | 1.000 | 1 | 1 |
| Lithuania | 3.70 | 6,490 | 0.29 | 0.324 | 7.8 | 0.009 | 0 | 0 |
| Macedonia | 2.02 | 4,590 | 0.58 | 0.327 | 28.5 | 0.045 | 0 | 0 |

(table continues next page)

49

**Table 1A.1  Poverty in developing countries ($2 PPP per day definition)** *(continued)*

| Country | Population (millions) | Per capita income[a] | Number in poverty (millions) | Gini coefficient | Percent in poverty | Income share of poor | Least developed countries[c] | Heavily indebted poor countries[c] | Sub-Saharan Africa[c] |
|---|---|---|---|---|---|---|---|---|---|
| Madagascar | 15.05 | 790 | 13.36 | 0.460 | 88.8 | 0.821 | 1 | 1 | 1 |
| Malawi | 10.79 | 570 | 9.18 | 0.400 | 85.1 | 1.000 | 1 | 1 | 1 |
| Malaysia | 22.71 | 7,640 | 5.59 | 0.485 | 24.6 | 0.024 | 0 | 0 | 0 |
| Maldives | 0.28 | 4,880 | 0.08 | 0.367 | 29.2 | 0.044 | 1 | 0 | 0 |
| Mali | 10.58 | 740 | 9.59 | 0.505 | 90.6 | 0.894 | 1 | 1 | 1 |
| Mauritania | 2.60 | 1,550 | 0.57 | 0.408 | 22.1 | 0.104 | 1 | 1 | 1 |
| Mauritius | 1.17 | 8,950 | 0.19 | 0.408 | 16.2 | 0.013 | 0 | 0 | 0 |
| Mexico | 96.59 | 8,070 | 41.05 | 0.537 | 42.5 | 0.038 | 0 | 0 | 0 |
| Moldova | 4.28 | 2,100 | 1.37 | 0.344 | 31.9 | 0.111 | 0 | 0 | 0 |
| Mongolia | 2.38 | 1,610 | 1.19 | 0.332 | 50.0 | 0.227 | 0 | 0 | 0 |
| Morocco | 28.24 | 3,320 | 2.12 | 0.395 | 7.5 | 0.016 | 0 | 0 | 0 |
| Mozambique | 17.30 | 810 | 13.56 | 0.396 | 78.4 | 0.707 | 1 | 1 | 1 |
| Myanmar | 45.03 |  | 32.78 |  | 72.8 | 1.000 | 1 | 1 | 0 |
| Namibia | 1.70 | 5,580 | 0.95 | 0.408 | 55.8 | 0.073 | 0 | 0 | 1 |
| Nepal | 23.38 | 1,280 | 19.29 | 0.367 | 82.5 | 0.471 | 1 | 0 | 0 |
| Nicaragua | 4.92 | 2,060 | 2.84 | 0.503 | 57.8 | 0.205 | 0 | 1 | 0 |
| Niger | 10.50 | 740 | 8.95 | 0.505 | 85.3 | 0.841 | 1 | 1 | 1 |
| Nigeria | 123.90 | 770 | 112.50 | 0.506 | 90.8 | 0.861 | 0 | 0 | 1 |
| Pakistan | 134.79 | 1,860 | 114.17 | 0.312 | 84.7 | 0.332 | 0 | 0 | 0 |
| Panama | 2.81 | 5,450 | 0.71 | 0.485 | 25.1 | 0.034 | 0 | 0 | 0 |
| Papua New Guinea | 4.70 | 2,260 | 2.63 | 0.509 | 55.8 | 0.180 | 0 | 0 | 0 |
| Paraguay | 5.36 | 4,380 | 2.06 | 0.591 | 38.5 | 0.064 | 0 | 0 | 0 |
| Peru | 25.23 | 4,480 | 10.45 | 0.462 | 41.4 | 0.067 | 0 | 0 | 0 |
| Philippines | 74.26 | 3,990 | 29.24 | 0.462 | 39.4 | 0.072 | 0 | 0 | 0 |
| Poland | 38.65 | 8,390 | 4.06 | 0.329 | 10.5 | 0.009 | 0 | 0 | 0 |
| Portugal | 9.99 | 15,860 | 0.20 | 0.356 | 2.0 | 0.001 | 0 | 0 | 0 |
| Romania | 22.46 | 5,970 | 6.18 | 0.282 | 27.5 | 0.034 | 0 | 0 | 0 |
| Russian Federation | 146.20 | 6,990 | 36.70 | 0.487 | 25.1 | 0.026 | 0 | 0 | 0 |
| Rwanda | 8.31 | 880 | 7.03 | 0.289 | 84.6 | 0.702 | 1 | 1 | 1 |

| | | | | | | | | | |
|---|---|---|---|---|---|---|---|---|---|
| Samoa | 0.17 | 5,090 | 0.367 | 0.05 | 28.1 | 0.040 | 1 | 0 | 0 |
| São Tomé and Príncipe | 0.15 | | | 0.11 | 72.8 | 1.000 | 1 | 1 | 1 |
| Saudi Arabia | 20.20 | 11,050 | 0.38 | 1.85 | 6?.2 | 0.006 | 0 | 0 | 0 |
| Senegal | 9.29 | 1,400 | 0.413 | 6.50 | 6?.8 | 0.354 | 1 | 1 | 1 |
| Sierra Leone | 4.95 | 440 | 0.629 | 3.69 | 74.5 | 1.000 | 1 | 1 | 1 |
| Slovak Republic | 5.40 | 10,430 | 0.195 | 0.11 | 2.0 | 0.001 | 0 | 0 | 0 |
| Slovenia | 1.99 | 16,050 | 0.268 | 0.04 | 2.0 | 0.001 | 0 | 0 | 0 |
| Solomon Islands | 0.44 | 1,730 | 0.367 | 0.24 | 55.5 | 0.234 | 1 | 1 | 1 |
| Somalia | 9.71 | | | 7.07 | 72.8 | 1.000 | 0 | 0 | 0 |
| South Africa | 42.11 | 8,710 | 0.593 | 15.07 | 35.8 | 0.030 | 1 | 0 | 0 |
| Sri Lanka | 18.99 | 3,230 | 0.344 | 8.62 | 45.4 | 0.103 | 0 | 0 | 0 |
| Sudan | 28.99 | | | 21.11 | 72.8 | 1.000 | 1 | 1 | 1 |
| Syrian Arab Republic | 15.71 | 3,450 | 0.380 | 6.07 | 38.7 | 0.082 | 0 | 0 | 0 |
| Tanzania | 32.92 | 500 | 0.382 | 19.65 | 59.7 | 0.872 | 1 | 1 | 1 |
| Thailand | 60.25 | 5,950 | 0.414 | 16.99 | 28.2 | 0.035 | 0 | 0 | 0 |
| Togo | 4.57 | 1,380 | 0.408 | 2.88 | 63.2 | 0.334 | 1 | 1 | 1 |
| Trinidad and Tobago | 1.29 | 7,690 | 0.503 | 0.33 | 25.5 | 0.024 | 0 | 0 | 0 |
| Tunisia | 9.46 | 5,700 | 0.402 | 1.10 | 11.6 | 0.015 | 0 | 0 | 0 |
| Turkey | 64.39 | 6,440 | 0.415 | 11.59 | 18.0 | 0.020 | 0 | 0 | 0 |
| Turkmenistan | 4.73 | 3,340 | 0.408 | 2.82 | 59.0 | 0.129 | 0 | 0 | 0 |
| Uganda | 21.43 | 1,160 | 0.392 | 16.58 | 77.2 | 0.486 | 1 | 1 | 1 |
| Ukraine | 49.55 | 3,360 | 0.325 | 11.84 | 23.7 | 0.051 | 0 | 0 | 0 |
| Uruguay | 3.31 | 8,750 | 0.423 | 0.22 | 6.6 | 0.006 | 0 | 0 | 0 |
| Uzbekistan | 24.41 | 2,230 | 0.333 | 11.56 | 47.4 | 0.155 | 0 | 0 | 0 |
| Vanuatu | 0.20 | 2,940 | 0.367 | 0.08 | 42.0 | 0.104 | 1 | 1 | 1 |
| Venezuela | 23.71 | 5,420 | 0.486 | 8.63 | 36.4 | 0.049 | 0 | 0 | 0 |
| Vietnam | 77.52 | 1,860 | 0.36? | 41.37 | 53.4 | 0.209 | 0 | 0 | 0 |
| Yemen, Republic of | 17.05 | 730 | 0.395 | 6.05 | 35.5 | 0.355 | 1 | 1 | 1 |
| Zambia | 9.88 | 720 | 0.498 | 9.06 | 91.7 | 0.930 | 1 | 1 | 1 |
| Zimbabwe | 11.90 | 2,690 | 0.568 | 7.64 | 64.2 | 0.174 | 0 | 0 | 0 |

a. 1999 purchasing power parity collars (World Bank 2001).
b. Per capita income from UNDP (2001).
c. 1 indicates applicable, 0 not applicable.

# Appendix 1B
## Poverty Incidence and Elasticity under the Lognormal Distribution

A functional form that has been found to be representative of income distributions is the lognormal distribution.[37] In this form (see Aitchison and Brown 1963, 8), the natural logarithm of income has a normal distribution. The probability distribution function of income $y$ is[38]

$$f(y) = \frac{1}{\sqrt{2\pi}\sigma y} e^{\frac{(\ln y - \delta)^2}{2\sigma^2}} \tag{B.1}$$

where the total integral of equation B.1 is unity, $e$ is the base of the natural logarithm, $\delta$ is the mean of $\ln y$, and $\sigma$ is the standard deviation of the logarithm of $y$. To normalize, divide income by the mean of income to get $x = y/\mu$. Following Bourguignon (2002), the lognormal distribution of this relative income may be expressed as a standard normal distribution $\psi$ with mean 0 and standard deviation of unity, as follows:

$$f(x) = \frac{1}{\sigma x} \psi\left(\frac{1}{\sigma}\ln x + \frac{\sigma}{2}\right). \tag{B.2}$$

Correspondingly, the cumulative density function, or cumulative probability that relative income is less than or equal to a given level $x$, is the integral of equation B.2 up to the given relative income level. Again, this may be expressed in terms of the cumulative distribution function of the standard normal, yielding

$$F(x) = \Pi\left(\frac{1}{\sigma}\ln x + \frac{\sigma}{2}\right) \tag{B.3}$$

The headcount fraction of population in poverty is the integral of the probability distribution function up to (or value of the cumulative density function at) the poverty income threshold $y_p$, or

$$w_p = F(x_p) \tag{B.4}$$

---

37. This appendix is adapted and extended from Cline (2002a).

38. As Aitchison and Brown (1963) begin with the cumulative distribution function, which is normal in $\ln y$ rather than $y$, and obtain the probability distribution function as the derivative of the cumulative function, the term $y$ in the denominator of B.1 results from taking the derivative of the logarithm of $y$. This term is absent from the more familiar normal probability distribution of $y$ rather than $\ln y$.

Equation B.4 provides a basis for estimating the incidence of headcount poverty if we are given the average per capita income ($\mu$), the poverty threshold income ($y_p$), and the distribution parameter of the lognormal function, $\sigma$. From Bourguignon (2002), the latter is

$$\sigma = 2\left\{\Pi^{-1}\left(\frac{G+1}{2}\right)\right\}^2$$  (B.5)

where $\Pi^{-1}$ is the inverse function of the cumulative density function, and $G$ is the Gini coefficient for the distribution. Equations B.3 through B.5 can then be used to calculate the headcount poverty fraction given the ratio of the poverty income threshold to the average income.

For its part, the elasticity of the poverty headcount with respect to distributionally neutral growth is given by the percent change in the headcount for a 1 percent change in mean income, or

$$\varepsilon_p^g = -\frac{dF(x_p)/d\mu}{F(x_p)/\mu}$$  (B.6)

By definition, the derivative of the cumulative density function $F(x)$ is the probability distribution function $f(x)$. By the chain rule,

$$\varepsilon_p^g = \frac{-f(x_p)[dx_p/d\mu]}{F(x_p)/\mu}$$  (B.7)

Using the transform to the standard normal, we have

$$\varepsilon_p^g = \frac{-\dfrac{1}{\sigma x_p}\psi\left(\dfrac{1}{\sigma}\ln x_p + \dfrac{\sigma}{2}\right)\left[-\dfrac{y_p}{\mu^2}\right]}{\Pi\left(\dfrac{1}{\sigma}\ln x_p + \dfrac{\sigma}{2}\right)/\mu} = \frac{\dfrac{1}{\sigma}\psi\left(\dfrac{1}{\sigma}\ln x_p + \dfrac{\sigma}{2}\right)}{\Pi\left(\dfrac{1}{\sigma}\ln x_p + \dfrac{\sigma}{2}\right)}$$  (B.8)

Using the "hazard ratio," defined as the ratio of the probability density function to the cumulative density function or $\lambda(..) = \psi(...)/\Pi(...)$, rewriting equation B.8 confirms Bourguignon's (2002) result that the poverty elasticity with respect to growth is

$$\varepsilon_p^g = \frac{1}{\sigma}\lambda\left(\frac{1}{\sigma}\ln\frac{y_p}{\mu} + \frac{\sigma}{2}\right)$$  (B.9)

Equation B.9 shows that in the lognormal distribution, the poverty elasticity is a function of the ratio of average income to poverty threshold in-

**Table 1B.1  Lognormal poverty elasticity[a] as a function of Gini coefficient and ratio of mean income to poverty threshold income**

| Gini | $\sigma$ | $\mu/y_p$ | | | | | |
|------|------|------|------|------|------|------|------|
| | | 10 | 5 | 3.33 | 2.5 | 2 | 1.67 |
| 0.3 | 0.3 | 25.3 | 18.0 | 13.6 | 10.6 | 8.4 | 6.6 |
| 0.35 | .041 | 13.6 | 9.7 | 7.4 | 5.8 | 4.7 | 3.8 |
| 0.4 | 0.56 | 7.3 | 5.2 | 4.0 | 3.2 | 2.7 | 2.2 |
| 0.45 | 0.72 | 4.4 | 3.1 | 2.5 | 2.0 | 1.7 | 1.4 |
| 0.5 | 0.91 | 2.7 | 2.0 | 1.6 | 1.3 | 1.1 | 0.95 |
| 0.55 | 1.15 | 1.6 | 1.2 | 0.97 | 0.82 | 0.71 | 0.62 |
| 0.6 | 1.4 | 1.1 | 0.79 | 0.64 | 0.55 | 0.48 | 0.43 |

a. Absolute value.

come ($\mu/y_p$) and the degree of inequality (which, as noted, is a function of the parameter $\sigma$). Table 1B.1 reports the corresponding calculated poverty elasticity from the lognormal distribution for alternative combinations of the ratio of mean income to poverty-threshold income and the inequality parameter $\sigma$, along with the corresponding Gini coefficient.

As shown in the table, for a given degree of inequality, a higher ratio of mean income to poverty threshold income leads to a higher poverty elasticity. Conversely, for a given mean/poverty income ratio, a higher degree of inequality leads to a lower poverty elasticity. When using a global threshold for poverty (e.g., $2 per day), this means that the elasticity will tend to be high in areas such as East Asia, where mean income is relatively high and inequality relatively low, but low in regions such as sub-Saharan Africa, where mean income is low, or Latin America, where inequality is high.

# Appendix 1C
# Convergence Versus Divergence in International Income Levels

It has become something of a stylized fact that income levels in poor countries have failed to converge toward those of industrial countries during the past several decades. However, the impressive growth of such key economies as China, South Korea, and even Brazil (with its 1970s "miracle" growth) suggests that in at least some important dimensions convergence has been taking place. This appendix finds that although nonconvergence holds if the frame of reference is the unweighted number of countries, progress toward convergence has indeed taken place for a majority of the global population. For many purposes, the latter concept would seem the more relevant.

The World Bank's annual *World Development Report* provides data on real GDP growth over decadal periods (World Bank 1982, 110–11; 2001, 294–95). It also provides PPP income levels (most recently, for 1999, in World Bank 2001, 274–75). Given population (from World Bank 2001, 274–75, for 1999; and from IMF 2002b for 1960), it is possible to calculate per capita growth rates and income levels to examine the course of convergence during the period 1960–99.

## Unweighted Country Observations

Figure 1C.1 displays the average real per capita GDP growth rate for this period for 75 countries. This group includes all countries with population of 5 million or more in 1999 for which the full set of data (GDP growth, PPP income levels in 1999, and population) is available. The resulting coverage accounts for 82.8 percent of total world population in 1999.[39]

The horizontal axis shows the real PPP income per capita in 1960 imputed as follows. First, the country's own national accounts estimates of real GDP growth and the end-point population levels are used to determine the average annualized growth rate for real per capita income during this 39-year period. Second, the 1999 PPP per capita incomes are combined with these per capita growth rates to impute the 1960 level of PPP per capita income in 1999 dollar terms. The latter is displayed on the horizontal axis (logarithmic scale), while the average real per capita growth rate is shown on the vertical axis.

---

39. Countries excluded for lack of data include several large economies (former Soviet Union, Poland, Bangladesh, Saudi Arabia, Tanzania, and Vietnam) as well as countries under 5 million population in 1999.

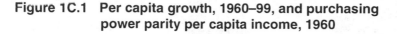

**Figure 1C.1   Per capita growth, 1960–99, and purchasing power parity per capita income, 1960**

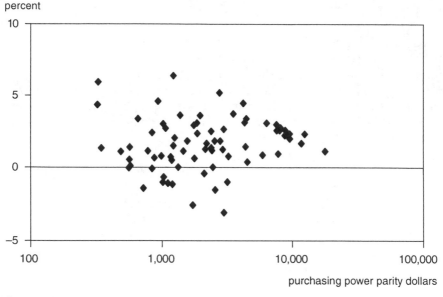

percent

*Sources:* World Bank (1982, 2001).

This scatter diagram supports the notion that when a simple test is made across all countries without taking population size into account, there is an absence of convergence. For convergence to be present, there would need to be a downward-sloping relationship in the figure, with systematically higher per capita growth rates at lower initial real per capita income levels. Instead, the scatter is random (and a simple linear regression shows a positive but infinitesimal and statistically insignificant coefficient of per capita growth rate on income level).

## Taking Population into Account

Once the actual countries behind the individual observations are taken into account, however, it turns out that there has been some significant convergence. Table 1C.1 examines the experience taking into account population size. It arrays the countries in ascending order of 1960 real per capita income (1999 PPP dollars per capita). It then separates the countries into three groups: those comprising the bottom 60 percent of total population in 1960, those in the next 20 percent, and those in the top 20 percent. Because of the large populations of China and India, the cutoff point for the bottom 60 percent of population is reached with the first 25 countries (cutoff: South Korea).[40] In contrast, the next quintile of 1960 population comprises 35 countries (cutoff: South Africa). The third and richest group comprises 15 countries, of which all are industrial economies except for Argentina (which just qualifies in the lower end of this income grouping in 1960).

The groupings in table 1C.1 are by base-period income position. There are important instances in which countries with rapid growth reach income levels that would classify them in higher groupings if arrayed by incomes at the end of the period. The most dramatic case is that of Japan, placed in the fourth quintile by the base-period ordering but with end-period per capita income right at the average for the fifth quintile. However, it is the base-period ordering that matters for the test of convergence, because the question is whether those countries starting out poor made relative progress.

The grouped data in table 1C.1 find that income levels did partially converge during the past four decades. This is evident, first, in the group average growth rates for real per capita income: 4 percent for the bottom 60 percent of world population, 2.34 percent for the quintile 60–80 percent, and 2.23 percent for the top 20 percent. (The individual country per capita growth rates are weighted by population to obtain the group weighted averages.) With higher growth rates in the poorest grouping, income levels must have been converging.[41]

This is borne out by comparing the ratios of group average per capita incomes at the beginning and end of the periods. Thus, at $567 in 1960, average per capita PPP income (in 1999 dollars) for the world's poorest 60 percent stood at 5.5 percent of the corresponding average income level for the top 20 percent. By 1999, in contrast, at $2,723, the average per capita income (PPP) had reached 10.9 percent of that for the top 20 percent

---

40. The actual cumulative population cutoffs for 1960 are 60.5 percent (at South Korea) and 80.6 percent (at South Africa).

41. I take it as self-evident that it is relative income levels, and hence higher per capita income growth rates for poorer countries, that define convergence, rather than absolute per capita income differences. This choice can be buttressed by, e.g., invoking logarithmic utility functions, but fundamentally reflects the intuition that, e.g., losing $100 in income is far more devastating to an urban slum dweller than to a millionaire. For its part, the absolute difference in per capita income will continue to diverge until the ratio of per capita income of rich to poor falls to no more than the ratio of per capita growth of poor to rich, at which point the absolute income levels will also begin to converge. Thus, e.g., the per capita growth differential between the poor 60 percent in table 1 and the upper 40 percent is about 2 percentage points. Considering that the median-country 1960 per capita income (in 1999 PPP dollars) was about $840 for the poorest 60 percent and $8,800 for the top 20 percent, the relative gap to be overcome is 10 to 1. If the 2-percentage-point growth differential were maintained, both the relative and absolute gap would be eliminated in about 150 years. Of this period, the absolute income gap would widen for the first 35 years before beginning to narrow.

## Table 1C.1   Initial per capita income and per capita growth performance, 1960–99

| Economy | y*60 | y*99 | gy*60–99 | Pop60 | Pop99 |
|---|---|---|---|---|---|
| Pakistan | 322 | 1,757 | 4.35 | 92.7 | 135 |
| China | 326 | 3,291 | 5.93 | 662.1 | 1,250 |
| Malawi | 345 | 581 | 1.34 | 3.4 | 11 |
| Nigeria | 484 | 744 | 1.10 | 51.6 | 124 |
| Burundi | 556 | 553 | −0.01 | 2.9 | 7 |
| Mali | 561 | 693 | 0.54 | 4.1 | 11 |
| Kenya | 564 | 975 | 1.40 | 8.1 | 29 |
| Ethiopia | 572 | 599 | 0.12 | 20.7 | 63 |
| Indonesia | 653 | 2,439 | 3.38 | 92.7 | 207 |
| Sierra Leone | 718 | 414 | −1.41 | 2.2 | 5 |
| Nepal | 780 | 1,219 | 1.15 | 9.2 | 23 |
| Chad | 839 | 816 | −0.07 | 3.0 | 7 |
| India | 839 | 2,149 | 2.41 | 429.0 | 998 |
| Uganda | 874 | 1,136 | 0.67 | 7.6 | 21 |
| Thailand | 931 | 5,599 | 4.60 | 26.4 | 62 |
| Togo | 987 | 1,346 | 0.79 | 1.5 | 5 |
| Zambia | 1,013 | 686 | −1.00 | 3.2 | 10 |
| Egypt | 1,019 | 3,303 | 3.02 | 25.9 | 62 |
| Mozambique | 1,027 | 797 | −0.65 | 6.6 | 17 |
| Sri Lanka | 1,062 | 3,056 | 2.71 | 9.9 | 19 |
| Niger | 1,106 | 727 | −1.08 | 3.1 | 10 |
| Côte d'Ivoire | 1,162 | 1,546 | 0.73 | 3.3 | 15 |
| Cameroon | 1,184 | 1,444 | 0.51 | 4.7 | 15 |
| Madagascar | 1,197 | 766 | −1.15 | 5.4 | 15 |
| South Korea | 1,218 | 14,637 | 6.38 | 24.7 | 47 |
| **Bottom 60 percent, weighted average** | **567** | **2,723** | **3.99** | **1,539.6** | **4,671.9** |
| | | | | | |
| Bolivia | 1,219 | 2,193 | 1.50 | 3.8 | 8 |
| Syria | 1,246 | 2,761 | 2.04 | 4.6 | 16 |
| Senegal | 1,327 | 1,341 | 0.03 | 3.1 | 9 |
| Romania | 1,375 | 5,647 | 3.62 | 18.4 | 22 |
| Papua New Guinea | 1,456 | 2,263 | 1.13 | 1.9 | 5 |
| Morocco | 1,562 | 3,190 | 1.83 | 11.6 | 28 |
| Angola | 1,715 | 632 | −2.56 | 4.8 | 12 |
| Tunisia | 1,752 | 5,478 | 2.92 | 4.2 | 9 |
| Honduras | 1,767 | 2,254 | 0.62 | 1.9 | 6 |
| Turkey | 1,847 | 6,126 | 3.07 | 27.5 | 64 |
| Dominican Republic | 1,862 | 4,653 | 2.35 | 3.0 | 8 |
| Malaysia | 1,954 | 7,963 | 3.60 | 8.1 | 23 |
| Ghana | 2,100 | 1,793 | −0.41 | 6.8 | 19 |
| Guatemala | 2,146 | 3,517 | 1.27 | 3.8 | 11 |
| Paraguay | 2,196 | 4,193 | 1.66 | 1.8 | 5 |
| Brazil | 2,379 | 6,317 | 2.50 | 69.7 | 168 |
| El Salvador | 2,383 | 4,048 | 1.36 | 2.5 | 6 |
| Philippines | 2,412 | 3,815 | 1.18 | 27.4 | 77 |
| Zimbabwe | 2,452 | 2,470 | 0.02 | 3.8 | 12 |
| Iran | 2,531 | 5,163 | 1.83 | 21.5 | 63 |
| Haiti | 2,551 | 1,407 | −1.53 | 3.6 | 8 |
| Hong Kong | 2,760 | 20,939 | 5.20 | 3.1 | 7 |
| Colombia | 2,794 | 5,709 | 1.83 | 15.4 | 42 |
| Algeria | 2,926 | 4,753 | 1.24 | 10.8 | 30 |
| Congo, Democratic Republic of | 2,977 | 897 | −3.08 | 14.6 | 50 |

*(table continues next page)*

**Table 1C.1** *(continued)*

| Economy | y*60 | y*99 | gy*60–99 | Pop60 | Pop99 |
|---|---|---|---|---|---|
| Chile | 2,982 | 8,370 | 2.65 | 7.6 | 15 |
| Nicaragua | 3,172 | 2,154 | −0.99 | 1.4 | 5 |
| Peru | 3,240 | 4,387 | 0.78 | 10.0 | 25 |
| Portugal | 3,538 | 15,147 | 3.73 | 8.8 | 10 |
| Japan | 4,220 | 24,041 | 4.46 | 94.1 | 127 |
| Greece | 4,329 | 14,595 | 3.12 | 8.3 | 11 |
| Mexico | 4,402 | 7,719 | 1.44 | 36.1 | 97 |
| Spain | 4,460 | 16,730 | 3.39 | 30.5 | 39 |
| Venezuela | 4,542 | 5,268 | 0.38 | 7.4 | 24 |
| South Africa | 5,944 | 8,318 | 0.86 | 17.1 | 42 |
| **Fourth quintile, weighted average** | **3,145** | **8,053** | **2.34** | **499.0** | **1,103.0** |
| | | | | | |
| Finland | 6,388 | 21,209 | 3.08 | 4.4 | 5 |
| Denmark | 7,604 | 24,280 | 2.98 | 4.6 | 5 |
| Italy | 7,627 | 20,751 | 2.57 | 49.6 | 58 |
| Argentina | 7,821 | 11,324 | 0.95 | 19.9 | 37 |
| France | 8,034 | 21,897 | 2.57 | 45.7 | 59 |
| Austria | 8,143 | 23,808 | 2.75 | 7.1 | 8 |
| United Kingdom | 8,790 | 20,883 | 2.22 | 52.4 | 59 |
| Belgium | 8,850 | 24,200 | 2.58 | 9.2 | 10 |
| Netherlands | 9,114 | 23,052 | 2.38 | 11.5 | 16 |
| Australia | 9,161 | 22,448 | 2.30 | 10.3 | 19 |
| Canada | 9,567 | 23,725 | 2.33 | 17.9 | 31 |
| Sweden | 9,588 | 20,824 | 1.99 | 7.5 | 9 |
| Germany | 11,728 | 22,404 | 1.66 | 55.4 | 82 |
| United States | 12,437 | 30,600 | 2.31 | 180.7 | 273 |
| Switzerland | 17,757 | 27,486 | 1.12 | 5.4 | 7 |
| **Top 20 percent, weighted average** | **10,380** | **24,938** | **2.23** | **481.4** | **678.0** |

y* = per capita purchasing power parity income in 1999 dollars
gy*60–99 = average annual growth rate of purchasing power parity per capita income, 1960–99
Pop60 = population, 1960 (millions)
Pop90 = population, 1990 (millions)

*Sources:* World Bank (1982, 2001); IMF (2002b).

grouping Thus, *by 1999 the per capita income of countries accounting for the world's poorest 60 percent of population in 1960 had doubled relative to that for the countries accounting for the world's richest 20 percent in 1960.*

However, the intuition that convergence was dominated by some superperformers such as China and South Korea is borne out in table 1C.1 as well. Thus, of the 25 countries in the bottom 60 percent of world population, only four countries had average per capita income growth rates that exceeded the population-weighted group average: Pakistan, China, Thailand, and Korea. The lopsided nature of growth for the poor countries is underscored by the fact that seven countries in this grouping had negative per capita growth rates (Burundi, Sierra Leone, Chad, Zambia, Mozambique, Niger, and Madagascar). This subset also highlights the apparently accurate stylized fact that, as analyzed further below, it is the African countries that have lagged behind the most and been the most pronounced exceptions to convergence.

There has also been little convergence for the world's middle-income countries. The 35 countries in the 60–80 percent group of the distribution in 1960 had only minimally higher per capita growth rates (weighted average) than those in the top 20 percent (2.34 vs. 2.23 percent). Moreover, there was far more uniformity of growth performance among the top 20 percent grouping of industrial economies than among the 60–80 percent distributional group. In the latter (middle-income) grouping, strong performers such as Hong Kong, Japan (over the four decades as a whole), Malaysia, Turkey, Portugal, Spain, and Greece dominated the overall increase in group per capita income. In contrast, several major middle-income economies experienced per capita growth that was well under 1 percent annually (including South Africa, Venezuela, and Peru), or even negative growth (Angola, Ghana, Haiti, Congo, and Nicaragua).

## Divergence: Sub-Saharan Africa

A casual inspection of table 1C.1 reveals that a number of countries with negative per capita growth in the period 1960–99 were in sub-Saharan Africa. There is the possibility, therefore, that even without taking population size into account, a simple relationship showing convergence can be found if the test is conducted excluding, or otherwise taking special account of, countries in this region. Figure 1C.2 does this by simply omitting country observations from SSA.

Figure 1C.2 shows a fairly clear pattern of lower growth per capita for countries that started the period with higher per capita incomes; in other words, convergence even before weighting for population. A statistical test using ordinary least squares confirms this result by isolating the influence of SSA using a dummy variable. Thus:

$$g_y = 6.23 - 0.484 \ln(y) - 3.01D; \text{ adj. } R^2 = 0.45 \qquad \text{(C.1)}$$
$$\quad (4.3) \quad\quad (-2.68) \quad\quad (-7.84)$$

where $g_y$ is average per capita growth in 1960–99, $\ln(y)$ is the natural logarithm of 1960 per capita income (PPP in 1999 dollars, as discussed above), $D$ is a dummy variable with value 1 if the country is in SSA and 0 otherwise, and the $t$-statistic is reported in parentheses. This result shows a statistically significant negative relationship between per capita growth and the starting per capita income level. In other words, there is statistical confirmation of the convergence hypothesis even without applying population weights, so long as the experience of SSA economies is specially taken into account.

**Figure 1C.2  Growth performance, excluding sub-Saharan Africa**

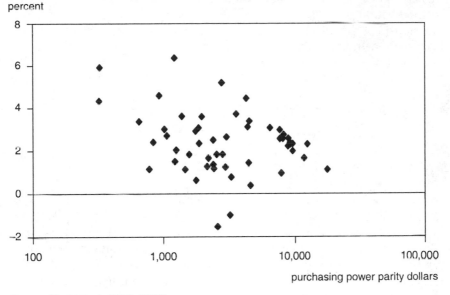

Source: World Bank (1982, 2001).

In particular, from equation C.1 a country with a per capita income of $400 in 1960 (at 1999 PPP) would have typically grown at an average per capita rate of 3.33 percent during the next four decades, whereas a coun try with a per capita income of $10,000 would have grown at an average per capita rate of only 1.77 percent. In contrast, a typical SSA country with the same starting per capita income of $400 would have grown almost none at all (0.02 percent annually per capita).

It may be noted that the examples just given yield a lower growth rate for the poorest countries than suggested by the results in table 1C.1, which shows average growth of per capita income at 3.99 percent for the initially poorest 60 percent of world population total. The higher rate in the table reflects the other key influence: Taking population size into account further intensifies the convergence relationship because of the greater relative importance of China in particular and also Pakistan and South Korea, all three of which grew at rates considerably faster than the weighted poor-group average.

## Accounting for Both Population Size and sub-Saharan Africa

Finally, the same regression test as presented in equation C.1 may be conducted using frequency weights that are proportional to country population. Thus, whereas Togo had a population of 1.4 million in 1960, China had a population of 662 million, so in the frequency-weighted test Togo is treated as one observation but China as $662/1.4 = 472$ observations. This method balloons the "sample" size and hence the observed $t$-statistics, but the statistical significance of the convergence relationship has already been demonstrated without the weighting in equation C.1, and the focus of attention is now the change in the steepness of the slope relating per capita growth to starting income level. The weighted regression results are

$$g_y = 10.1 - 0.901 \ln(y) - 3.75D; \text{adj. } R^2 = 0.597 \tag{C.2}$$

$$(62.3) \quad (-40.5) \quad (-32.9)$$

where all variables are as before.

In the weighted regression results, the large weight of China (26.6 percent of the total sample by population) combined with its high per capita growth (5.9 percent annually) causes a steeper relationship of per capita growth to the logarithm of income level, with the constant term rising to 10 percent and the coefficient on the logarithm of per capita income growing from $-0.48$ in the unweighted test to almost twice as large, $-0.9$, in the weighted results. The downward shift for SSA from the overall relationship is somewhat larger in this test (3.75 percentage points below the general growth line, versus 3.01 percentage points in the unweighted results).

## Conclusion

These results challenge the increasingly common view that the economic development record has been one of nonconvergence or even divergence between poor and rich countries. This impression may have arisen by a tendency to focus on the trees rather than the forest. Although it is true that if each country is treated as a single observation regardless of size, there is no relationship between per capita growth and the starting level of per capita income, once population size is taken into account, there is indeed a relationship of convergence. The countries accounting for the poorest 60 percent of global population in 1960 grew about twice as fast per capita in the period 1960–99 as the countries in the top 40 percent of global population. The finding of convergence is strengthened and verified statistically once the special experience of SSA is isolated and attention is focused on all other countries. Once the combined influences of population weighting and the special treatment of SSA are taken into account, the proconvergence finding is strengthened further.

Moreover, it is incorrect to characterize the growth experience as having shown convergence by "only China," as is sometimes suggested. Instead, there is a relatively long list of economies in the bottom 80 percent of global population in 1960 that achieved more rapid per capita growth during the next four decades than the average for the economies with the top 20 percent of population. This list includes (in order, from table 1C.1) Pakistan, China, Indonesia, India, Thailand, Egypt, Sri Lanka, South Korea, Romania, Tunisia, Turkey, the Dominican Republic, Malaysia, Brazil, Hong Kong, Chile, Portugal, Japan, Greece, and Spain.

The encouraging message in these results is that the development experience is far more successful at generating catch-up growth for the world's poor than much of the current international dialogue seems to recognize. The discouraging part of the findings, however, is the confirmation of another stylized fact: that SSA has been falling further and further behind. The statistical tests here suggest that with per capita growth about 3 percentage points below what has been the experience elsewhere over the past four decades, SSA has not even achieved nonconvergence (let alone convergence) but instead has followed a divergent growth path of falling relative income. An implication of these findings would seem to be that it is in Africa-specific causes and remedies (e.g., in the area of governance) that the specific problem of SSA's divergence must be addressed, rather than in global influences such as the international trade and monetary regimes.

# 2

# Arrangements for Preferential Access:
# Experience and Potential

The initial review of trade and global poverty in chapter 1 suggests a two-track strategy for using trade policy as an instrument for reducing poverty. One track, oriented toward about one-fourth of the world's poor, would grant early and deep preferential market access to imports from at-risk countries where the share of the poor in national income is relatively high, including in particular the least developed countries (LDCs), heavily indebted poor countries (HIPCs), and sub-Saharan Africa (SSA). The optic of the "poverty intensity of trade" developed in chapter 1 leads naturally to the inclusion of this approach in any overall strategy seeking to mobilize trade to help reduce global poverty.

The other track would address the other three-fourths of the world's poor by increasing opportunities for trade and growth in developing countries more generally. This would be done through the phased reduction and elimination of trade barriers, on a multilateral basis through World Trade Organization (WTO) negotiations. It will be argued in chapter 6 that the two tracks are complementary even in terms of building coalitions for multilateral liberalization, because without the positive inducement of prompt deepening of free access for poorer countries, some of them may be tempted to block the general consensus needed in the new "single-undertaking" structure of WTO negotiations. At the same time, the commitment to global free trade on a phased-in multilateral basis would ensure that the enhanced free entry for poor "at-risk" countries would be only a temporary preference, by virtue of eventual free market access for all countries.

The international trading system already has considerable experience with a two-track approach in the form of past preferential regimes for developing countries alongside steady progress toward multilateral liberalization. It thus behooves policymakers to take stock of what has already been accomplished under preferential arrangements in the past, in order to have a more informed view of the potentialities and pitfalls of deeper preferential access in the future. This chapter seeks to review the experience of preferential regimes and to draw relevant lessons for future policy. The subsequent chapters of this study then turn to the potential effects of multilateral liberalization for the reduction of global poverty.

There has been an important evolution in the emphasis in regimes of special market access for developing countries during the past four decades. The initial framework was one of a Generalized System of Preferences (GSP) granting duty-free entry for imports from developing countries, which were considered appropriately eligible for "special and differential" treatment that did not require reciprocal free entry on their part. The objective was to permit infant-industry protection in developing countries while addressing their seemingly weak prospects for earnings from traditional raw materials exports by encouraging the development of new export industries. The underpinnings of this framework increasingly eroded, however, as the implementation of the GSP in practice tended to be relatively restrictive.

At the same time, import-substituting industrialization increasingly fell out of favor as a development strategy, as the distortions and inefficiencies it encountered as some developing countries moved further into heavy industries unsuited for their comparative advantage began to become more apparent. The idea gained favor that unilateral liberalization of at least highly protected sectors, and especially by middle-income countries, was more likely to contribute to their development than was continued protection. There was a parallel growing sense that developing countries' emphasis on special and differential treatment in past trade negotiations had in the end been a bad bargain because it induced negotiating partners to leave off the table the products of particular importance to developing-country exporters given that the protection of the latter countries was off the table.

Within the past two decades or so, however, a second track of preferential access began to emerge even as the GSP approach increasingly seemed outdated. In part because of growing concern about the severe lag and often retrogression of economic conditions in low-income countries, and in part because of political motivations from former colonial ties or considerations of the Cold War or the drug war, the European Union and United States developed regimes much closer to free entry for goods from low-income countries. The EU's Lomé Convention and Everything But

Arms initiative and the United States' Caribbean Basin Initiative, Andean Trade Preference Act, and African Growth and Opportunity Act are the principal efforts in this second track. For middle-income countries, in contrast, the new trend was toward the negotiation of free trade arrangements based on at least phased reciprocity, as best illustrated by the North American Free Trade Agreement (NAFTA).

Economists have tended to view special-access regimes skeptically, some because the regimes do not work and others because they might work. The former can legitimately cite the restrictive application of the GSP in practice, while the latter worry that special regimes cause trade diversion. However, to the extent that the trade policy instrument is to be used as a vehicle to address global poverty, regimes of special access for poor countries would appear to hold considerable promise. Not only do they follow naturally from a focus on the "poverty intensity of trade," but they also tend to involve minimal trade diversion because the economic base of the beneficiaries is too small in the aggregate to have much impact in distorting global trading patterns.

This chapter begins with a review of the oldest of the special-access regimes, the GSP, and then turns to the evolving programs for enhanced special access for poor countries in EU and US trade policy. After an attempt to identify statistical evidence for the impact of these regimes on beneficiary-country export performance, the chapter concludes with an outline of directions for policy to make the regimes for poor-country market access more effective.

## The Generalized System of Preferences

The oldest preferential regime, the GSP, was designed to include all developing countries. The rapid rise of strong competitive pressures from some middle-income economies, most recently and notably China, helps explain why in practice the regime has been applied in a restrictive manner, and why the more recent preferential initiatives have increasingly focused on the poorer and weaker economies.

### Origins and Status

A Generalized System of Preferences for imports from developing countries was first proposed in 1964 by Raul Prebisch, then secretary general of the UN Conference on Trade and Development (UNCTAD). The proposal reflected the then-popular notion that the commodity exports of developing countries faced unfavorable demand elasticities, condemning their economies to falling terms of trade and slower growth than in industrial countries unless they industrialized themselves. Duty-free entry for exports from developing countries (particularly manufactured goods) was seen as one partial remedy (import-substituting industrialization behind high protective barriers was seen as another). Even though preferences were to be "generalized," from the outset there was a recognition of "graduation," in that less advanced developing countries should be granted special preferences, and that preferences for more advanced developing countries would "gradually have to disappear" after permitting a period of use "to prevent or rectify the structural imbalance in their trade" (UNCTAD 1964, Laird and Safadi 2001).

By 1968, the second UNCTAD adopted the principle of a "generalized, non-reciprocal, non-discriminatory system of preferences in favour of developing countries." In 1971, the General Agreement on Tariffs and Trade (GATT) granted a 10-year waiver to the most-favored nation (MFN) provisions to allow preferences, and in 1979 the Tokyo Round negotiations adopted an "Enabling Clause" providing a formal legal basis for preferences (Laird and Safadi 2001). All the major industrial countries, along with a handful of middle-income countries, currently have GSP regimes.[1]

Despite the prevalence of these regimes, few would disagree that the GSP has fallen short of the original hope that it could be a major vehicle for development. As will be shown, its benefits have been meager. In part, this has reflected restrictions (e.g., on sensitive products); in part, it has been a consequence of inherently diminishing scope as multilateral liberalization has reduced MFN tariffs, making the preferences less valuable. Many would also argue that developing countries have directed too much negotiating effort toward seeking preferences and too little to offering reciprocal liberalization in return for reductions in industrial-country protection of goods of special interest to them. Moreover, the true restraints on trade increasingly have not been tariffs, against which preferences could be of help, but nontariff barriers, including not only quotas in agriculture and textiles and apparel but also such "process-protection" mechanisms as antidumping and countervailing duty (antisubsidy) measures.

UNCTAD (1999) nonetheless argues that the GSP remains relevant today and for the future. It judges the scope of the program as significant, noting that in 1997 GSP programs granted preferential entry to about $100 billion in imports, or 18 percent of imports, from beneficiary nations into preference-granting countries. Moreover, it points out that the tariffication of agricultural quotas in the Uruguay Round has increased the potential benefit from tariff preferences in agriculture.

---

1. GSP programs are offered by Australia, Canada, the European Union, Japan, New Zealand, Norway, Switzerland, and the United States, as well as Belarus, Bulgaria, the Czech Republic, Hungary, Poland, Russia, and the Slovak Republic (Laird and Safadi 2001).

# The European Union

The European Union's GSP program is by far the most substantial.[2] Its product coverage is wide, and includes food and agricultural products, metal products and machinery, wood and paper, textiles and apparel, and leather goods. In 1997, the European Union (EU) granted tariff preferences covering $65 billion in imports and according $1.6 billion in forgone revenue.[3] These imports represented 56 percent of imports covered by the GSP, and 23 percent of total imports from 106 developing countries. In 1995, the European Union eliminated quota restrictions in the program and introduced "tariff modulation." The preference margin (i.e., the percent cut from MFN tariff) under this approach is 15 percent for "very sensitive" products, 30 percent for "sensitive" goods, 65 percent for "semi-sensitive" goods, and 100 percent (duty-free) for "nonsensitive" goods.[4] The resulting average duty in 1997 for GSP beneficiaries (excluding LDCs) was 3.4 percent, compared with the average MFN tariff of 6.0 percent.

For the 49 LDCs, the European Union's GSP prior to 2001 provided for duty- and quota-free entry of all but about 900 agricultural tariff-line items, out of the European Community's 10,500-line tariff nomenclature (Bora, Cernat, and Turrini 2002, 18; European Commission 2000, 3). As a result, in 1997 the overall average tariff on (MFN-dutiable) imports from LDCs was a minimal 0.2 percent (see table 2.1). Beginning in 2001, the European Union pushed free entry for LDCs further with its Everything But Arms initiative, which is discussed below.

The European Union has set $6,000 per capita (in 1991) as the income level for graduation from its GSP program, and in 1996 South Korea, Hong Kong, Singapore, Saudi Arabia, and a number of smaller oil-producing economies became ineligible on this basis.[5] The program also graduates a supplier to ineligibility in a particular product when its supply exceeds 25 percent of total EU imports of the good from GSP beneficiaries. Despite the provisions for product graduation, benefits under the program have been concentrated, with approximately 50 percent of preference-receiving imports provided by the top three countries (China, 31.8 percent; India, 10.3 percent; and Thailand, 6.5 percent). Product coverage

---

2. These descriptions of the EU, US, and Japanese GSP programs are primarily from UNCTAD (1999).

3. Note, however, that Laird and Safadi (2001) place the amount at only $38.2 billion in 1999, using WTO data.

4. From the resulting preferential tariffs, there are further cuts ranging from 10 to 35 percent for the first three categories respectively if the country meets labor and environmental standards.

5. Despite this, UNCTAD (1999) shows small remaining GSP-benefiting imports from these countries in 1997, and total imports from them are included in the base mentioned above.

**Table 2.1    Generalized System of Preferences (GSP) imports of the European Union, United States, and Japan, 1997**
(billions of dollars, percent)

| Measure | European Union | United States | Japan | Total or average |
|---|---|---|---|---|
| A Countries covered (number) | 106 | 123 | 170 | 133 |
| B Total imports from GSP countries | 279.6 | 101.3 | 173.1 | 554 |
| C Imports from all developing countries | 431.5 | 420.8 | 185.5 | 1,037.8 |
| D GSP country imports/total (B/C percent) | 64.8 | 24.1 | 93.3 | 53.4 |
| E Dutiable imports from GSP countries | 179.2 | 66.0 | 93.5 | 338.7 |
| F Of which: covered by GSP | 115.9 | 25.1 | 40.0 | 181.0 |
| G Imports receiving GSP | 64.8 | 15.3 | 17.0 | 97.1 |
| H Potential coverage ratio (F/E percent) | 64.7 | 38.0 | 42.8 | 53.4 |
| I Utilization rate (G/F percent) | 55.9 | 61.0 | 42.5 | 53.6 |
| J Utility rate (G/E percent) | 36.2 | 23.2 | 18.2 | 28.7 |
| K Tariff revenue forgone | 1.6 | 0.24 | 0.35 | 2.19 |
| L Percent GSP-receiving imports (K/G percent) | 2.5 | 1.6 | 2.1 | 2.3 |
| M Percent total imports from GSP countries (K/B percent) | 0.57 | 0.24 | 0.20 | 0.40 |
| Share of top 5 in GSP country Imports (percent) | 30.6 | 48.2 | 50.0 | 39.9 |
| Imports receiving GSP benefits (percent) | 64.4 | 62.5 | 74.0 | 65.8 |
| Share of LDCs in GSP country Imports receiving GSP benefits (percent) | 1.0 | 5.2 | n.a. | n.a. |
| Revenue forgone (percent) | n.a. | 10.0 | n.a. | n.a. |
| Tariff averages on GSP countries MFN rates (percent) | 6.0 | 6.7 | 5.9 | 6.1 |
| Incorporating preferences All but LDCs (percent) | 3.4 | 4.8 | 3.4 | n.a. |
| LDCs (percent) | 0.2 | 3.3 | 2.3 | n.a. |
| Tariff peak products, average tariff MFN (percent) | 40.3 | 20.8 | 27.8 | n.a. |
| GSP (percent) | 19.8 | 16.0 | 22.7 | n.a. |

LDCs = least developed countries
MFN = most-favored nation
n.a. = not available

*Sources:* UNCTAD (1999); IMF (2002a); IMF-World Bank (2001).

remains high at 70 percent for China. In contrast, LDCs have consistently accounted for only about 1 percent of preference-receiving imports from GSP beneficiaries.

Although the EU program is relatively large, the "utilization rate" is somewhat lower than might be expected: Imports receiving preferences were 56 percent of GSP-covered imports in 1997. The latter, in turn, were a relatively high 64.7 percent of total imports from the GSP countries, but the combination of nonuse and noncoverage reduced preference-receiving imports to only 36 percent of total imports from these countries. This, in turn, suggests that in a number of products for many GSP countries, even the relatively generous EU program provides too modest an incremental advantage to warrant utilization, reflecting low MFN tariffs and implying significant informational and administrative costs. Indeed, in the aggregate, the forgone tariff revenue amounts to only 0.9 percent of the value of total dutiable imports and 0.6 percent of total imports from GSP countries, suggesting only a marginal overall potential impact.

## The United States

The United States' GSP program has been considerably smaller than that of the European Union. In 1997, imports granted GSP preferences amounted to $15.3 billion, and the corresponding tariff revenue forgone was only $242 million (UNCTAD 1999).[6] The most conspicuous country absent from the US plan is China, in contrast to the EU scheme. Otherwise, the profile of concentration among principal beneficiaries is not unlike that of the European Union. Thus, countries that bulk large in the US program (Brazil, with 14.4 percent of US imports benefiting from GSP preferences; Thailand, 16.5 percent; Indonesia, 12.7 percent; the Philippines, 10.8 percent; and India, 8.2 percent) also tend to do so in the EU program (6.8, 6.5, 8.8, 1.5, and 10.3 percent, respectively).

The general list of products eligible for duty-free entry in the US program comprises 4,650 product categories out of the total of approximately 10,500 at the 8-digit level in the Harmonized Tariff System of the United States (HTSUS). In addition, beginning in 1997, another 1,770 categories were made eligible for 40 LDCs (USTR 1999). The US program has relatively greater participation by LDCs, which accounted for 5.2 percent of imports receiving preferences in 1997, than other industrial countries.[7] In contrast to the EU approach of conferring alternative depths of preferential cuts from MFN tariffs depending on the product and the country, the US program grants duty-free entry.

The US program excludes from eligibility countries that exceed competitive-need thresholds for the product in question. These are triggered by either of the following: (1) a country accounts for more than half of total US imports of the product category; or (2) the amount in question ex-

---

6. According to Laird and Safadi (2001), by 1999 the amount of imports receiving GSP was $16.7 billion.

7. For the LDCs, moreover, the average revenue forgone was 3.1 percent of import value benefiting from GSP, compared with 1.6 percent for the program as a whole. This conveyed 10 percent of total forgone revenue to the LDCs (calculated from UNCTAD 1999).

ceeds $100 million.[8] A list of 28 countries currently has such product inel-
igibilities, ranging from Belize, with a single restricted good, to numerous
restrictions for Brazil (64 products), Argentina (158), and especially India
(775) (USITC 2002). In addition to restrictions, the US GSP program has
been marked by uncertainty, because it has been subject to periodic expi-
rations and reinstatements only after a hiatus.

The overall effect of the program has been relatively restrictive. Thus,
in 1997, out of a total of $66 billion in imports from GSP-eligible devel-
oping countries dutiable at the MFN level, only $25 billion were GSP-
eligible (38 percent potential coverage ratio). As a result, despite a utilization rate (61 percent) approximately the same as in the European Union,
the overall ratio of imports receiving GSP treatment to GSP-eligible imports ("utility rate") was only 23.2 percent, or about two-thirds that of the
EU program (UNCTAD 1999). Total revenue forgone was a modest 1.6
percent of value even on imports actually benefiting, a slimmer 1.0 percent for potentially eligible imports, a still smaller 0.36 percent of the total
value of dutiable imports from GSP countries, and a thin 0.24 percent of
the value of all imports from these countries.

## Japan

In 1997, the total value of imports benefiting from the GSP in Japan was
$17 billion, and tariff revenue forgone was $353 million (UNCTAD 1999).
These amounts were modestly larger than those for the United States. A
key difference is that China is eligible for the GSP in Japan's program, and
in 1997 it accounted for 33 percent of total GSP benefits granted. Somewhat surprisingly, the total value of Japan's imports from GSP countries
($173 billion) was larger than that of the United States ($101 billion),
though smaller than that for the European Union ($280 billion). The
smaller total for the United States reflects the absence not only of China
but also of Mexico from the US program, because Mexico has duty-free
entry under its alternative NAFTA membership.

## Other Industrial Countries

The GSP schemes of other industrial countries add modestly to those of
the big three. Total GSP imports in 1997 (with the corresponding "utility
rates" to gauge against total imports) were $2.9 billion (40 percent) for
Canada, $1.5 billion (26 percent) for Switzerland, and $0.7 billion (47.6
percent) for Norway, placing the Canadian and Norwegian programs
above those of the big three in terms of generosity.

---

8. The value threshold was set at $75 million for 1996, with a scheduled increment of $5 million annually thereafter.

## Overview of the GSP Experience

Table 2.1 provides a summary of the relevant economic magnitudes for the GSP programs of the European Union, United States, and Japan in 1997 (the most recent year for which UNCTAD has compiled comparative data). The table shows the following patterns:

- Approximately $100 billion in imports entered the industrial-country markets with the benefit of GSP preferences in 1997, or 17.5 percent of total imports from GSP countries.[9]

- The countries included under the GSP account for only 24 percent of imports from all developing countries in the United States, and only 65 percent for the European Union. This reflects US coverage of Mexico under NAFTA rather than the GSP, as well as a number of exclusions of countries not deemed to need preferential treatment.[10]

- Revenue forgone under the GSP amounts to about 2 percent of the value of imports receiving GSP treatment, but only 0.4 percent of the value of total imports from GSP-eligible countries.

- The benefits of the program are concentrated in the largest suppliers, with the top five beneficiaries receiving two-thirds of benefits in the EU and US programs and three-fourths in Japan's. These shares significantly exceed the corresponding shares of total imports from the same top five countries under each program, suggesting that the largest and more sophisticated economies still eligible secure the lion's share of benefits (most notably China's 32 percent share in GSP-benefiting imports in the European Union).

- LDCs have accounted for very low shares in total imports receiving GSP benefits (about 5 percent for the United States and only 1 percent for the European Union), although the deeper cuts make their share in tariff revenue forgone somewhat higher (10 percent for the United States).

- The fraction of otherwise dutiable imports receiving GSP benefits (UNCTAD's "utility rate") is low, at 36 percent for the European Union and only 23 percent for the United States and 18 percent for Japan.

- This is partly due to product exclusion, because the products covered make up about two-thirds of the total for the European Union and

---

9. For the big three, the amount was $97 billion; including Canada, Switzerland, and Norway, it was $102 billion.

10. Major exclusions include the following. For the European Union: the Czech Republic, Hungary, Nigeria, Poland, Taiwan, and Turkey. For the United States: China, Hong Kong, Mexico, Singapore, and Taiwan.

only about 40 percent for the United States and Japan. It is also due to additional threshold screens (especially in the US program), as well in all likelihood as informational and administrative costs, which can be high relative to the size of the potential tariff preference.

- The overall effect is to cut average tariffs from about 6 to 3.4 percent in both the European Union and Japan, and somewhat less generously from 6.7 to 4.8 percent in the United States, according to UNCTAD estimates. The cuts are much steeper for LDCs for the European Union (to 0.2 percent), and moderately steeper for the United States and Japan (to 3.3 and 2.3 percent, respectively).

A study by the staffs of the IMF and World Bank (IMF and World Bank 2001, 34) notes that the often generous tariff preference margins under the GSP typically apply to products that already face low tariffs, in the range of 4 to 8 percent. It emphasizes that, in contrast, for tariff-peak products, the preferential margins tend to be lower. As a result, despite preferential treatment, GSP countries face after-preference tariffs averaging about 20 percent in the European Union, 16 percent in the United States, and 23 percent in Japan in the peak-tariff categories (table 2.1).

Overall, it is difficult to escape the conclusion that the GSP is a mechanism whose impact is close to negligible, and far smaller than might be expected given the long history of the instrument and the intense negotiating battles that have been fought on its behalf. Certainly in the aggregate, it would be hard to argue that the incentive it provides is meaningful. The best overall measure of this incentive is the amount of the tariff revenue forgone relative to the import base. When the full import base (for just the GSP countries) is considered, this incentive amounts to a mere 0.4 percent for the big three, ranging from a high of 0.57 percent for the European Union to about 0.2 percent for the United States and Japan. It is difficult to envision any investment decision being influenced by the promise that the export will benefit from a special price advantage amounting to half a percent or less of the product price. The impact of the GSP is to some extent inherently limited because the MFN tariffs are already modest at about 6 percent, and because on the most burdensome (peak) tariffs the preferences are insufficient to avoid still-high after-preference tariffs.

The key exception to this diagnosis would seem to be for the LDCs. Their deeper tariff preferences and lesser incidence of exclusions generate a much more generous outcome for the European Union, as well as a somewhat more generous result for the United States and Japan, than is the case for the other developing countries that account for the bulk of imports under the programs. This diagnosis suggests, however, that addressing the LDCs may be more effective using special regimes than under the GSP.

# Special Regimes of the European Union

Both the European Union and the United States have increasingly turned to special regimes for certain developing-country trading partners that go beyond the GSP. For most of the past three decades, these arrangements have stemmed from special cultural ties and cold war geopolitical considerations (the Lomé Convention for the European Union, and the Caribbean Basin Initiative for the United States) as well as antidrug considerations (the US Andean Trade Preference Act). More recently, both the European Union and the United States have moved toward special arrangements for the poorest countries (in the Everything But Arms initiative and African Growth and Opportunity Act, respectively). At the same time, there has been a shift from the GSP concept of temporary nonreciprocal preferences toward free trade arrangements incorporating reciprocity, albeit with a delayed phase-in of liberalization for the developing-country partner (most conspicuously in NAFTA but also in the EU's Cotonou Agreement).

## The Lomé Convention and Cotonou Agreement

The Lomé Convention comprised a series of agreements made between the European Union and 70 LDCs in Africa, the Caribbean, and the Pacific (the "ACP" states) covering trade preferences as well as development aid relationships and a commodity stabilization program.[11] All ACP industrial exports and 80 percent of agricultural exports are free from import duties and quota restrictions (UNCTAD 2001, 18). The convention was inaugurated in 1975 for 46 countries and was successively renewed and expanded every five years to encompass 70 countries by 1995.

By the late 1990s, the Lomé Convention came under increasing doubt because of the rising profile of its incompatibility with GATT rules. The European Community's single market for bananas set up in 1994 in particular precipitated confrontations with the United States and nonmember banana producers. A GATT panel found the Lomé Convention inconsistent with the GATT because being nonreciprocal, it was not a free trade arrangement, and being confined to a specific set of developing countries, it was discriminatory and thus ineligible for the Enabling Clause permitting departure from MFN treatment. Although the European Union secured a waiver through the end of Lomé IV (2000), it became necessary to rethink the arrangement (European Commission 1996). A prevailing sense that the arrangement had "not been sufficient to enhance export growth and increase diversification" (European Commission 1996, 17), and that the donor-recipient dynamics in the development assistance dimensions of

---

11. In the tradition of trade agreements, the name derives from the location of the negotiations (Lomé, Togo, and Cotonou, Benin).

the arrangement had yielded "patchy results," contributed to the decision to revamp the mechanism.

In 2000, the European Union replaced the arrangement with the ACP-EU Partnership Agreement, known as the Cotonou Agreement, with 77 countries for a period of 20 years.[12] Whereas under the Lomé Convention the European Union had granted nonreciprocal trade preferences to ACP exports, the Cotonou accord has shifted emphasis to economic integration agreements that progressively remove barriers and enhance cooperation in all areas related to trade. To this end, Regional Economic Partnership Agreements (REPAs) are to be negotiated on a regional basis by 2008, likely within the framework of existing regional organizations. Until then, the existing provisions of the Lomé Convention continue in force. The change in name is thus a signal of a new strategy rather than of any immediate change in the preferential arrangement.

## Structure

The Lomé Convention sought "stability and contractuality" through the granting of preferences for long periods, whereas GSP preferences are continually subject to modification. It provided that products originating in the ACP states were eligible to enter the European Union tariff free and exempt from quantitative restrictions. The major exceptions were for products covered under the Common Agricultural Policy, which faced tariffs and restrictions but received concessions of various sorts.

ACP countries have thus been exempted in the EU market from the textile and apparel quota regime under the Multi-Fiber Arrangement (MFA). They have benefited from "generous prices and guaranteed access for specific quantities" (European Commission 1996, 16) under commodity protocols for bananas, sugar, beef and veal, and rum.[13] Special rules of origin allow the ACP states to "cumulate origin" among themselves and count imports of intermediate goods from the European Union as having domestic origin. The agreement also includes safeguard clauses and surge protections that are less restrictive than the corresponding clauses for the EU's GSP preferences.

## Impact

Studies of the Lomé Convention have tended to conclude that it had little effect in fostering export growth. ACP countries lost rather than gained market share. Of total European Community imports, the ACP share fell

---

12. Of the 77 ACP states, 48 are in Africa (including all of SSA), 15 in the Caribbean, and 14 in the Pacific region. Out of the 49 LDCs (also covered by the EU's Everything But Arms initiative of February 2001), 40 are ACP.

13. The banana, sugar, and beef and veal protocols are discussed below. Note that in 1997 the European Union agreed with the United States to phase out the rum protocol.

from 8.5 percent in 1974 to 4 percent in 1989, whereas the share of other developing countries rose from 9.5 to 17.1 percent, with rising shares especially for the East Asian economies but also for Latin America (Grilli 1994).

Moreover, there was no apparent difference in outcomes between the original Lomé countries and those that joined later. As noted, the European Commission shares in the view that Lomé did not succeed in spurring export growth or diversification, although it cites individual success cases (Botswana, Côte d'Ivoire, Jamaica, Mauritius, and Zimbabwe; European Commission 1996). Thus, 37 of the ACP countries rely on one commodity to provide more than 50 percent of their exports to the European Union (Bjørnskov and Krivonos 2001). For Nigeria, which in 2001 accounted for 20 percent of EU imports from ACP countries, oil accounted for 81 percent of exports to the European Union (European Commission 2002b).

Grilli (1994) identifies a number of reasons for the lack of impact. First, only about 35 to 45 percent of EC imports from the ACP countries benefited from preferences, because about 5 to 10 percent were subject to Common Agricultural Policy restrictions and about 50 to 60 percent were in goods not subject to a duty (including key raw materials, e.g., oil, phosphates, and cotton, as well as copper). Second, the depth of the preferences declined over time as a consequence of multilateral trade liberalization. Third, the size of ACP preferences vis-à-vis other developing countries was small in manufactures, because of the GSP (despite Lomé's conscious attempt to maintain some preference by retaining some tariffs, unlike the zero-tariff US treatment). Fourth, an "ACP line" monitoring ceiling in practice restrained textile and apparel imports despite exemption from MFA quotas. Fifth, rules of origin were restrictive, requiring 50 to 60 percent local content, despite the allowance for cumulation.

More broadly, disincentives to exports that outweighed the potential benefit of preferences were common. These included overvalued exchange rates, export taxes, government controlled producer prices, and high domestic protection on manufactures. In addition, falling real prices for a range of commodities, and the preponderance of commodities in the exports of ACP countries, have acted as a drag on their export performance relative to other, especially Asian, exporters.[14]

Although a simple comparison of trade shares suggests little if any export stimulus from the Lomé Convention, ideally numerous other economic influences should be taken into account to detect the Lomé impact at the margin. One of the few econometric attempts to do so is that of Nilsson (2002). He applies a gravity trade model, regressing the dollar value of EU imports from countries belonging to the Organization for Economic

14. However, Grilli (1994) points out that even within commodity classes, e.g., tropical beverages, vegetable oils, and minerals, the share of African countries in world production and exports fell rapidly after the early 1970s.

Cooperation and Development (OECD) and from developing countries (deflated by the US GDP deflator) against variables meant to capture demand (EU GDP and GDP per capita) and supply (partner GNP and GNP per capita) and including distance as the "gravity" variable. Dummy variables are included for GSP and Lomé.

Nilsson's results show that in the five out of eight three-year periods from 1973 to 1992 for which both dummies are statistically significant, the GSP raised developing countries' exports by 34 to 59 percent above levels that otherwise would have been expected; and Lomé, by 45 to 69 percent. The impacts started large but fell to near zero by 1980 (for Lomé, and below zero for the GSP), before rebounding to the range of a 40 percent export impact by the period 1990–92. Nilsson attributes the earlier decline to the diminishing margin of preference as multilateral liberalization proceeded as well as the European Union's increasing use of nontariff barriers, and the rebound after the early 1980s to the reversal of the latter as well as increasing developing country export orientation.

Nilsson's results suggest that after two decades of preferential treatment under Lomé, ACP exports to the European Union stood about 50 percent above the levels they would otherwise have reached without preferences. In principle, this could be a plausible diagnosis arising from a regression technique that attributes the lagging of Lomé exports behind those from East Asia (for example) to the more rapid growth of supply in the latter (the GNP variable for exporting countries has an elasticity of about unity) rather than a negligible preference impact for the former. Even so, one wonders whether the result is not too large to be fully credible, especially considering that the corresponding GSP effect by 1990–92 is about a 30 percent increment. The latter would seem implausibly high for a preferential price impact of only 0.6 percent (measured by revenue forgone relative to total EU imports from GSP countries; see table 2.1).

More troublesome, the highest measured Lomé trade impact (an increment of 70 percent) is for the first period considered, 1973–74, yet this predates the Lomé Convention. This problem cannot be explained away by invoking the preferences already existing in the 1963 Yaoundé Convention, because that arrangement was only for the Association of African States and Madagascar (18 former French colonies), whereas the purpose of Lomé was to extend special treatment to 20 countries of the British Commonwealth following the United Kingdom's joining the European Economic Community in 1973 (Bjørnskov and Krivonos 2001). If the Lomé dummy is overestimated immediately before the arrangement, it is likely to be so for the following periods as well.

## The Cotonou Process

The shift from nonreciprocal preferences to regional free trade arrangements (FTAs) has two major implications. First, the Lomé countries will increasingly be expected to liberalize their own trade, not only with the European Union but also with regional partners. Second, the new agreements should make it possible to achieve further liberalization of the EU market for these exporters, especially in agricultural products.

The Cotonou Agreement has already revised the banana protocol after agreement by the European Union, United States, and Ecuador in 2001 (Bjørnskov and Krivonos 2001). The tariff-rate quota regime is to be converted to a tariff only by 2006. During a transition, part of the existing quota is to be shifted from ACP countries (which were only filling about three-fourths of their total quotas) to other developing-country exporters. Because of the high level of protection (EU banana imports average twice the price of those entering the United States), liberalizing the regime should provide the potential for important gains for outside suppliers and new entrants among Lomé countries, albeit at the cost of a loss in rents for the largest existing suppliers (Côte d'Ivoire and Cameroon, which account for about 5 percent each).

In sugar, where EU imports from ACP countries are at the EU-internal price—about 160 percent above world price—future trade will be governed by the REPAs to be negotiated. This seems likely to boost EU imports from such LDCs as Sudan and Zambia, probably at the expense of the current leading exporters (including especially Mauritius, with 30 percent of EU sugar imports, and Fiji and Guyana, each with about 13 percent; Bjørnskov and Krivonos 2001).

The future REPAs will also govern EU imports of beef and veal. Current imports are relatively low (only $123 million in 1999), in part because above-quota tariff rates in the tariff-rate quotas are high (22 to 56 percent). The potential for increased exports is thus high if REPA negotiations are liberalizing, although sanitary and phytosanitary standards could be an important constraint. Other agricultural goods in which REPA negotiations will be important include citrus fruit, where ACP countries face above-quota tariffs as high as about 14 percent, coffee (8 percent), fruits (7 percent), vegetables (11 percent), and tobacco (32 percent) (Bjørnskov and Krivonos 2001).

An important risk is that the REPA process will amount to a reshuffling of existing EU quotas for ACP countries, rather than a broad liberalization. At the same time, the nature of the eventual agreements will presumably be affected by the success or failure of multilateral agricultural liberalization agreed within the Doha Round, as well as more liberalized access that may arise from EU agreements with Mercosur and Mediterranean countries. The more successful the increased multilateral and other-regional access to goods from US, Latin American, and other non-ACP suppliers, the less scope will remain for dividing rents among ACP suppliers in a protected EU market.

Finally, the FTA reached between the European Union and South Africa in October 1999 (the Trade, Development and Cooperation Agreement, or

TDCA) warrants review as EU trade policymakers consider it a potential model for the REPAs.[15] South Africa did not enjoy Lomé preferential access, because the European Union had rejected its 1994 accession request on grounds of erosion of ACP preferences. The European Union instead granted qualified membership in 1998 and admission to the Cotonou Agreement in 2000, subject to negotiation of the FTA.

The TDCA provides for the elimination of tariffs on about 95 percent of South African exports (compared with 75 percent now) and 85 percent of EU exports (compared with about 55 percent now). South Africa is given 12 years to phase in the liberalization; the European Union, 10 years.[16] However, South Africa begins from considerably higher protection (10 percent average tariff, to be cut to 4.3 percent) than does the European Union (2.7 percent, to be cut to 1.5 percent). Liberalization is to be faster in industrial products on the EU side and agricultural goods on the South African side, reflecting their corresponding areas of comparative advantage. Free access will be granted to only 61 percent of South African agricultural exports by the end of the decade, and some important exports are to be excluded from liberalization (wine, citrus fruits, and apples). In contrast, EU barriers will be removed within 3 years for a range of industrial products (but more slowly for textiles, footwear, iron, and steel). The TDCA is not expected to pose major problems of trade diversion from ACP countries, because South Africa's exports are more heavily oriented toward industrial goods than is the case for most of the others.

Although the TDCA may be a model in terms of its lengthy phase-in, and perhaps as well in terms of its relatively ambitious goals for the extent of opening, it is unclear how fully it can exemplify future REPAs, for two reasons. The first is simply that South Africa is much more developed than the majority of Lomé countries. The second is that the agreement does not involve liberalization vis-à-vis third countries in the region, whereas the REPAs will do so.

## The Everything But Arms Initiative

In October 2000, the European Commission adopted an initiative, within the GSP, to admit free of duties and quotas Everything But Arms (EBA) from 48 LDCs, of which 39 were ACP.[17] This initiative, which was imple-

---

15. The description here is drawn from Bjørnskov and Krivonos (2001).

16. Note that one study, applying a computable general equilibrium (CGE) model incorporating dynamic effects, estimates that the long and back-loaded phase-in of liberalization reduces the impact of the agreement to 2 percent of South Africa's total growth during 2000–18, from a potential of 6.8 percent (Andriamananjara and Hillberry 2001).

17. The non-ACP LDCs are Afghanistan, Bangladesh, Bhutan, Cambodia, Laos, Maldives, Myanmar, Nepal, and Yemen.

mented in March 2001, removes protection on 919 agricultural line items (8-digit Harmonized System), leaving only 25 armaments tariff line items out of the total 10,500 product categories subject to restrictions. For three key products, liberalization is to be phased in gradually (2002–06 for bananas, and 2006–09 for sugar and rice; Page and Hewitt 2002).

It is less than obvious whether EBA is likely to have sizable or de minimis effects. The case for the latter includes the following:

- the LDCs account for only 1 percent of EU imports;

- 99 percent of imports from LDCs already pay no duty (Resal 1999), reflecting in part the fact that four-fifths of the LDCs already enjoy free entry for industrial and most agricultural goods as ACP countries;

- the safeguard clause in EBA allows withdrawal of LDC preferences if imports rise much above "usual levels";

- the amount of tariff revenue collected on imports from the LDCs in 1998 was a de minimis €7 million (Stevens and Kennan 2001), consistent with the de minimis 0.2 percent average after-preference tariff noted in table 2.1; and

- regulatory, sanitary, and phytosanitary standards will remain and could constrain increased trade.

The alternative case for a significant impact derives from

- the large gap between internal EU prices on key agricultural goods and the world price;

- the removal of quota limits for LDCs in these products;

- the fact that LDCs can engage in triangular trade to ship exports of their own goods to take advantage of the high EU price while filling the resulting gap in domestic demand by importing from elsewhere at the world price; and

- the availability of "cumulation" from other LDCs, EU, ASEAN, and SAARC suppliers in meeting rules-of-origin requirements (European Commission 2000).[18] LDCs need provide only 50 percent local content beyond inputs from these sources to qualify for EBA free entry.

The case for a substantial impact rests, moreover, either on sizable triangular trade or investment to develop production and export capacity beyond current levels.

---

18. The members of ASEAN, the Association of Southeast Asian Nations, are Brunei Darussalam, Cambodia, Indonesia, Laos, Malaysia, Myanmar, the Philippines, Singapore, Thailand, and Vietnam. The members of SAARC, the South Asian Association for Regional Cooperation, are Bangladesh, Bhutan, India, the Maldives, Nepal, Pakistan, and Sri Lanka.

The large gaps between domestic EU price and world price, combined with potential supply capacity, create the most plausible substantial gains in bananas (where EU prices are 83 percent above world levels), rice (100 percent), and sugar (160 percent; European Commission 2000, 4). There is, however, a trade-off for the ACP LDCs. Under their current quota access in the banana, sugar, and rice protocols, they receive a windfall rent equal to the difference between the world and EU price on the amount of the quota. If there were major export expansion, the result would be to drive down the internal EU price, reducing the unit rent, so the net effect would depend on the proportion of export expansion compared with the proportionate reduction in the rent.

The European Commission (2000) estimates that EBA could increase LDC rice exports to the European Union by 450,000 tons annually, representing €135 million at the world price and $270 million at the EU internal price. The new regime could boost LDC exports of sugar to the EU by 900,000 to 2.7 million tons, representing a corresponding range of €225 million to €540 million at the lower end and €675 million to €1.62 billion at the upper end. The EC study does not estimate the impact for bananas, given the changes already on track in that protocol and the "low competitive position" of LDCs in this category.

For other affected agricultural products (cereals, fruits, vegetables, potatoes, meat, milk, butter, and cheese), the study hypothesizes that LDC exports to the European Union could rise by 3 to 10 percent of their existing domestic production. Applying the average of the European Union and world prices reported for these products, this could add €780 million to €2.6 billion to the export impact.[19] The lower of these two estimates seems far more relevant considering that as a group the LDCs consume more than domestic production in almost all these products (European Commission 2000, 7). Applying the midpoint of the estimates for rice and sugar, EBA could thus increase LDC exports to the European Union by somewhere in the range of €1.75 billion annually. This represents about 20 percent of the base LDC exports to the European Union.[20]

An impact of this size would indeed be major from the standpoint of the LDCs, though minimal relative to total EU imports of about $430 billion from all developing countries (table 2.1). Although these magnitudes would correspondingly require investment and increases in production, the figures do suggest that the potential effect is not de minimis.

Other similar analyses tend to identify the same key product sectors, but express more doubts about the likely supply response capacity of the LDCs. A study prepared for Oxfam argues that LDCs would be unlikely

---

19. About 40 percent of this total would be in vegetables, especially tomatoes, and another 15 percent in fruits.

20. This was reported as €8.1 billion in 1997 by Resal (1999).

to boost their sugar exports to the European Union by more than about 100,000 metric tons annually, far below the EC estimate of 900,000 to 2.7 million tons noted above, considering that LDC total exports in 1997 were only 191,000 metric tons (Stevens and Kennan 2001, 14). The European Food Security Network similarly emphasizes that except for "isolated cases such as Sudan, Zambia, or Malawi," the LDCs are sugar importers rather than exporters (Resal 1999, 4).

More generally, Stevens and Kennan note that there is only a limited number of product categories in which LDCs not only currently pay import duty in the EU market but also have supply capacity. Of about 500 narrowly defined product categories in which EU imports from LDCs amount to €0.5 million or more, only 11 did not already enjoy duty- and quota-free access before EBA, concentrated in beef, cheese, maize, bananas, rice, and sugar (p. 4). They also emphasize that among LDCs, those not within the ACP will benefit more, because the ACP states already had more favorable treatment in these relevant products.

A more formal analysis of EBA is provided by Bora, Cernat, and Turrini (2002). Using a computable general equilibrium (CGE) model, they calculate that upon full implementation EBA should generate static welfare gains totaling $400 million annually for SSA (excluding southern Africa[21]) and Bangladesh, with two-thirds of the gain coming from improved terms of trade. This estimate is in the right order of magnitude for consistency with the gross export expansion effect suggested above (€1.75 billion annually). Two-thirds of the welfare gains stem from improved terms of trade, which reflects the opportunity to obtain greater access to the EU market, where key agricultural prices are far above world levels. The rest stems from increased allocative efficiency, given the opportunity for LDCs to shift further toward agricultural goods in which they have comparative advantage. For a few economies, the welfare gains are as large as 0.8 to 1.1 percent of GDP (Malawi, Tanzania, and Zambia). The global welfare effect of the EBA is calculated to be slightly positive. Welfare losses are concentrated in the European Union ($250 million). These come wholly from a terms-of-trade loss, reflecting the rising unit cost of imports from LDCs as their exports move outward along an upward-sloping supply curve.[22] Trade diversion imposes welfare losses on other areas (the United States,

21. Southern Africa includes Angola, Botswana, Lesotho, Mauritius, Namibia, South Africa, Swaziland, and Zimbabwe.

22. This somewhat counterintuitive result is in contrast to typical CGE results for multilateral liberalization, which tend to show that the elimination of relatively high agricultural protection in industrial countries provides major welfare gains (IMF and World Bank 2001, 45–46). It would appear that the differing results stem from the fact that because the LDCs are such a small fraction of global supply, the primary effect of EBA is to drive up their supply prices to the European Union rather than drive down EU consumer prices. Note also that the model indicates a shift of resources away from LDC production and exports of textiles, apparel, and other industrial goods as a consequence of the shift into agriculture.

Japan, the rest of Asia, Latin America, North Africa, southern Africa, and China, for a combined total of $123 million).

Although not quantitative, another study (Page and Hewitt 2002) raises important questions about EBA, focusing on its potential adverse effects on other developing countries. LDC-designated countries in SSA could gain at the expense of non-LDC ACP countries (Malawi and Zambia vs. neighboring Zimbabwe; Uganda and Tanzania vs. Kenya).[23] Because countries with large populations are excluded from the LDCs (excepting Bangladesh), populous poor countries (especially India, Pakistan, and Indonesia) could lose from trade diversion under EBA. Their concern about trade diversion may be exaggerated, however, because the LDCs account for such a small fraction of EU imports from developing countries (only 2.4 percent in 2000; see table 1.4 in the present study).

At the same time, the arrangement could appear to many of the Cotonou countries to undermine that agreement. The authors also make the point that in evaluating EBA it is necessary to project overall EU trade policy. The potential benefits for sugar exporters will be quite different from a baseline calculation if the European Union instead phases out the sugar protocol. Finally, the authors stress that economic impact estimates based on existing trade and production (as in European Commission 2000) can fail to capture the introduction of entirely new production. They cite the surge of apparel from 0.01 percent of Bangladesh's exports in 1977 to 51 percent in 1991 in response to its exemption as an LDC from EU textile and apparel controls (Page and Hewitt 2002, 96).

Overall, the thrust of the various estimates is that there may be scope for significant albeit not particularly large benefits to the LDCs from EBA, while all effects are likely to be extremely small in relative terms for the European Union and the rest of the world.[24] This outcome reflects the asymmetry between the very small economic and export base of the LDCs and the large EU (and rest of world) markets. The paradox of significant impact despite nearly free LDC access already stems from the opportunity to exploit further the large rents stemming from high EU protection in a few agricultural sectors. Finally, however, the caveats of Page and Hewitt (2002) suggest some possible policy costs of EBA and also serve as a reminder that if the Doha Round successfully liberalizes agricultural goods of interest to the broader range of developing countries, the LDC preference will erode over time.

---

23. The calculation of their model at more aggregated regional levels means that Bora, Cernat, and Turrini (2001) do not capture such effects.

24. Thus, in Bora, Cernat, and Turrini's (2001, 56) results, whereas the welfare effect of EBA is in the range of +0.2 to +1.1 percent of GDP for SSA (excluding South Africa), it amounts to a vanishing –0.004 percent of GDP for the European Union.

# Special Regimes of the United States

Just as in the GSP, for most of the past three decades, the United States has had much more limited special regime preferences for developing countries than the European Union. The reason is mainly that whereas the European Community had special trade ties with former colonies and associated states dating back to its formation in the Treaty of Rome in 1957, the United States had no comparably intense historical ties. In Latin America, the natural partner area for the United States, trade shares in Argentina and Brazil have actually been higher with Europe than with the United States. Mexico, with its long US border, was the one exception, and in a sense proves the rule because it is now a free trade partner with the United States in NAFTA.

Gradually, however, the US special regimes have grown to rival or surpass those of the European Union. The guerrilla warfare in El Salvador and elsewhere in Central America at the height of the cold war helped foster the Caribbean Basin Initiative (CBI) in the early 1980s; the war on drugs had a similar effect in prompting the Andean Trade Preference Act (ATPA) in the early 1990s; and the African Growth and Opportunity Act (AGOA) for SSA beginning in 2001 further extended US special regimes.

As a result, by now the special preference trade regimes of the United States (even excluding NAFTA) encompass 76 countries (24 in CBI, 4 in ATPA, and 35 AGOA-approved and 13 additional AGOA-eligible), almost the same as the EU's 77 Cotonou partners. Using 2000 trade data, the US programs aggregate to somewhat more than those of the European Union (at least using total imports as opposed to those actually using preferences), representing $50.4 billion, or 11.6 percent of US imports from developing countries, in comparison with the EU's $30.8 billion in imports from Cotonou countries, or 7.4 percent of its imports from developing countries.[25]

## The Caribbean Basin Initiative

In 1983, the Caribbean Basin Economic Recovery Act (CBERA) launched the CBI. The arrangement gives zero- or preferential-duty treatment to 24 Caribbean and Central American countries. Although inclusion is contingent on such factors as respect for worker and intellectual property rights, and benefits can be revoked by the president, only Honduras has had its CBI preferences suspended (and only briefly, in 1998, over intellectual property issues).

---

25. The US breakdown is $19.9 billion, CBI; $10.9 billion, ATPA; $15.5 billion, 35 AGOA-approved countries; and $4.1 billion, 13 other AGOA-eligible countries. Calculated from IMF (2002a).

CBERA provides more generous treatment than the US GSP. Its rules of origin are less stringent: Whereas the GSP requires 35 percent value added in the country, CBERA allows for the cumulation of inputs from other CBERA countries, and up to 20 percent from the United States, in calculating value added. Similarly, there is no phaseout after a country passes a threshold of competitive need or on a basis of per capita income. Nonetheless, important products have been excluded from, or received only limited, preferences under CBERA, including most textiles and apparel, leather goods, petroleum products, and some footwear.[26] Many agricultural products are also subject to quotas and restrictions under sanitary standards. At the same time, other preferences are also available, either under the GSP or production-sharing arrangements.[27] As a consequence, of total US imports of $22 billion in 2000 from the CBERA countries, only $6 billion were eligible for CBERA preferences, while only $2.8 billion received preferences, and of these only $1.5 billion received preferences exclusively available under CBERA (USITC 2001, 18).[28]

In part to compensate for erosion of preferences following multilateral trade negotiations and the inception of NAFTA, and in part as a response to economic damage from Hurricanes Mitch and Georges, in May 2000 preferential access was expanded under the Caribbean Basin Trade Partnership Act (CBTPA). To remain in force through 2008—when it is to be superseded by another regional agreement or by the Free Trade Area of the Americas (FTAA)—CBTPA extends NAFTA-equivalent treatment to certain sectors previously excluded from full CBERA preferences, most importantly apparel but also footwear, watches, petroleum and petroleum products, tuna, and leather goods. Although President Bill Clinton declared all 24 CBERA countries eligible, as of late 2001 only 14 had applied and qualified by meeting customs-related requirements (USTR 2001a).

The arrangements under CBTPA would appear to reflect a key strategic decision by the textile industry in particular that the best strategy for confronting the termination of MFA quotas by 2005, as negotiated in the Agreement on Textiles and Clothing in the Uruguay Round, is to enter into partnership with low-cost apparel producers in the region on a basis of exports of US fabric as inputs. This reflects a shift away from traditional outright protectionism toward emphasis on obtaining access to foreign markets for US exports of textile fabric, which tends to be amenable to

---

26. The constrained sectors are the same as those exempted from GSP, and received only a 20 percent cut from the MFN tariff, subject to a maximum 2.5-percentage-point cut.

27. Under the production-sharing arrangements of the former tariff schedule article "807" (new Harmonized Tariff Schedule 9802.00.80), tariffs on inputs assembled from US-produced components have been levied only against value added abroad.

28. About half of the $16 billion imports from the region in 2002 ineligible for CBERA preferential treatment were in just 3 oil and gas categories ($1.9 billion) and 10 apparel items ($6.1 billion; USITC 2001, 16, 19). Other key products already were duty free under MFN tariff treatment.

mechanization and can be capital intensive, in return for opening the US market to imports of apparel (including that outsourced by US firms), which tends to be labor intensive and more suited to production by developing countries. CBTPA provides that to be eligible for duty-free entry into the US market, apparel produced in CBERA countries must use fabric made and cut in the United States. If the fabric is cut in the Caribbean Basin, it must be sewn with thread produced in the United States.[29] Apparel is already the most important industry in the region, and it accounts for the largest share of US imports, displacing oil and oil products, which have fallen from about half in the early 1980s to about 10 percent now.[30]

At first glance, CBERA might not seem to have had much of an impact. The grouping's share of total US imports has actually fallen over time, from 3.1 percent in 1983–84 to 1.8 percent in 2000 (USITC 2001, 15). However, the aggregate import data disguise a more dynamic performance of nonoil goods. Whereas US imports of oil[31] actually fell from $4.2 billion in 1984 to $3.1 billion in 2000, imports of all other goods from CBERA rose from $4.5 billion to $19.0 billion. This increase by a factor of 4.2 was somewhat greater than the corresponding growth of total US merchandise imports (by a factor of 3.7; IMF 2001b). Considering that total US imports of oil rose by a factor of 2.5 during this period (US Census 2002), it would appear that the weak aggregate performance of imports from the region has much more to do with market-organization factors sharply reducing the Caribbean share in the sourcing of US oil imports than with any inefficacy of the preferential regime.[32]

At the same time, there are reasons for expecting that the impact of CBERA could have been modest. Most eligible goods were also eligible for duty-free entry either in MFN categories with zero duty or under the GSP; some important goods with a potential comparative advantage, such as textiles, were omitted; the value of the preference was limited in many covered goods where tariffs were already low; and the arrangement did not cover nontariff restrictions. The differential impact of CBERA is further difficult to evaluate in view of other influences, including unilateral trade liberalization beginning in the late 1980s by a number of the countries, and foreign exchange reforms.[33]

---

29. Similar provisions apply for NAFTA but for North American inputs

30. Other product composition changes have included a decline in tobacco and sugar, and an increase in fruits, chemicals, and plastics (USITC 2001, 16–23).

31. This is defined as mineral fuels, HTS chapter 27

32. In particular, crude oil production capacity fell by 28 percent from 1984 to 2000 in the only major producing country, Trinidad and Tobago (2002 data from US Energy Information Agency, www.eia.doe.gov).

33. Unweighted average nominal tariffs fell from 22 percent in 1987 to 7 percent in 1998 in the Central American Common Market (CACM), and from 14.5 percent to 9.5 percent for nine Caribbean economies excluding the Bahamas and Dominican Republic (USITC 2001, 108).

Nonetheless, CBERA appears to have played a role in accelerating both foreign direct investment and export growth in the region. Thus, for the six Central American economies, median inward foreign direct investment rose from 0.8 percent of GDP in 1970–83 to 1.7 percent in 1984–98; for 13 Caribbean economies, the median rose from 1.0 percent of GDP to 5.0 percent.[34] Median annual real export growth rose from 2.75 percent in the first period to 4.4 percent for the Central American economies, and from 3.25 to 7.0 percent for the Caribbean economies.[35]

The US International Trade Commission has implemented an econometric model to evaluate the impact of CBERA (USITC 2001). For a pool of six Caribbean and six Central American economies during the period 1970–98, the model estimates an equation for economic growth as a function of capital, labor, technical change, and terms of trade. It also estimates an equation for investment, as a function of the expected growth of income. The analysis includes alternative measures of CBERA in the equations (coverage and utilization of CBERA-specific preferences). The results show a small positive influence of CBERA on growth in the region, but this appears to be limited to years when the countries were undertaking unilateral trade and foreign exchange liberalization measures themselves, and decreased over time as US trade became more open. They show a strong positive impact of production-sharing agreements on both growth and investment, although this impact was significantly eroded by the advent of NAFTA. The authors emphasize that the generally strong impact of production sharing underscores the importance of the CBTPA, which extends duty-free treatment to apparel produced using US fabric.

## The Andean Trade Preference Act

In 1991, as part of the war on drugs, the United States adopted the Andean Trade Preference Act, a regime of special trade preferences for four of the five Andean Pact countries: Bolivia, Colombia, Ecuador, and Peru. These four countries are the origin of "virtually all cocaine sold in the United States" (USTR 2001b, 3). In contrast, the excluded Andean Pact member, Venezuela, has not featured prominently in coca production, and as an oil-based economy with 81 percent of its exports in petroleum (IMF 2001b) was less germane for the strategy of providing economic incentives for diversification away from coca.

---

34. Nonetheless, any acceleration of direct investment appears to have been considerably more modest than in the case of Mexico under NAFTA. Thus, in the decade 1985–95 the stock of inward direct foreign investment in the CBI economies rose 137 percent, whereas in the first decade of NAFTA the corresponding stock rose 221 percent. Calculated from United Nations (2000, 296).

35. Calculated from USITC (2001, 101).

ATPA provides duty-free treatment for imports of all goods except those on an excluded or limited-preference list. Like the CBI, it required 35 percent value added but allowed cumulation from CBERA and ATPA countries as well as 15 percent from US inputs. Also like CBERA, it exempted from duty-free treatment textile and apparel products, crude and refined petroleum, canned tuna, certain footwear, watches, sugar, and rum products. Similarly, it granted only a 20 percent reduction (or 2.5 percentage points, whichever is smaller) in duties on other sensitive items, including handbags, luggage, gloves, and leather apparel (Hornbeck 2001, 9).

The potential export incentive from ATPA is limited by the fact that (in 1999) 40 percent of US imports from the grouping are in categories that were already duty free under MFN tariffs. Zero-tariff products include several traditional exports from the region, such as coffee, bananas, shrimp, and precious metals and stones. Another 1.6 percent entered duty free under production-sharing arrangements, and 1.3 percent, under the GSP. A major share of petroleum products in the region's exports also constrains the overall potential of ATPA preferences, which exclude oil and oil products. Nonetheless, a substantial 17.8 percent of imports entered under ATPA preferences (down somewhat from 19.7 percent in 1998, as a consequence of a rebound in oil prices). Products benefiting from ATPA preferences account for about 30 percent of US imports from the region for Bolivia, 40 percent for Peru, and 12 percent for Colombia and Ecuador (USTR 2001b, 11–12).[36]

Total imports from the four ATPA countries held relatively constant at 1 percent of overall US imports from 1991 through 1999. In view of the very rapid rise in imports from some other suppliers (e.g., China and Mexico), however, this outcome is not inconsistent with some trade stimulus from the arrangement. Moreover, in the second half of the 1990s, products actually granted ATPA preferences were the leading sectors for exports to the United States, showing export growth twice that of total exports from the region. Principal ATPA-beneficiary products have included cut flowers, copper cathodes, pigments, processed tuna, and zinc plates (USTR 2001b, 11).

In terms of the objective of offering product alternatives for diversification out of coca, the evidence does show major changes in coca production, although not necessarily or even likely because of ATPA itself. From 1991 to 1999, coca production fell 55 percent in Bolivia and 68 percent in Peru. In Colombia, however, it rose 227 percent. The most suggestive in-

---

36. A study by the Congressional Research Service (Hornbeck 2001) chooses instead to emphasize that only 10 percent of US imports enter under ATPA-unique preferences. This calculation, which is premised on the fact that much of ATPA-preference trade could have entered instead under GSP, tends to understate the impact of the regional program. Unlike the frequently expiring GSP, ATPA had a secure 10-year initial horizon, providing greater certainty, and its rules-of-origin treatment was more generous.

stance of a link to ATPA was the increase in Peruvian exports of asparagus, a cash crop grown near traditional coca areas (USTR 2001b, 2, 6). In contrast, Colombian cut flowers were already established as a major export prior to ATPA and have lost share in ATPA-preference imports (though cut flowers from Colombia and Ecuador still accounted for 25 percent in 1999, down from 40 percent in 1995; p. 5).

Overall, it would appear that ATPA has had at least a mild positive effect on its member countries' exports to the United States, which has been accompanied (if not necessarily spurred) by progress in coca eradication in at least Bolivia and Peru.[37] Some positive trade impact is consistent with the findings of Hufbauer and Kotschwar (1998, 81) that in 1995 US imports from the four members in 1995 were substantially higher than predicted with a gravity trade model.[38] The arrangement also appears generally to have avoided precipitating domestic US producer calls for restrictions.[39] The combination of at least a modest contribution to the antidrug war and an absence of major domestic opposition meant that upon expiration at the end of 2001, renewal of ATPA through 2006 was approved by July 2002. The delay arose from the attachment of the Trade Promotion Authority legislation to the ATPA renewal legislation, another indication that the US administration judged the regional arrangement politically attractive.

The reauthorization of ATPA as the Andean Trade Promotion and Drug Eradication Act in August 2002, through the end of 2006, liberalizes the arrangement by granting duty-free entry to footwear, petroleum, watches, handbags, luggage, work gloves, and leather apparel, subject to presidential determination that the article is "not import sensitive." Rum remains ineligible for duty-free treatment, and sugar remains subject to the general tariff-rate quotas. Duty-free entry is granted to apparel made from US fabric. Apparel from llama, alpaca, and vicuña fabrics is also duty free, as are hand-loomed products. Apparel produced with regional fabric is duty free, subject to a cap of 2 percent (rising to 5 percent over four years) of all US apparel imports. Finally, in a provision designed to mollify competing

---

37. Note that the USTR report emphasized that even in Colombia, in 1999 there had been "record levels of coca eradication" (USTR 2001b, 3).

38. Imports were about 30 percent higher than predicted for Peru, 90 percent for Bolivia, 160 percent for Colombia, and 540 percent for Ecuador. However, the model details are not reported. Nor is it clear whether the same model would have already underpredicted US imports on the eve of ATPA, a methodological issue raised above regarding gravity-model tests for the Lomé Convention.

39. Of the leading ATPA-member exports to the United States, only cut flowers have been large enough to constitute a major share of the US market (75 percent), although at about 7 percent each, copper cathodes and gold compounds have also been significant. Nonetheless, by 1999 US producers of cut flowers had desisted from seeking antidumping and countervailing remedies, an indication that they were no longer seriously concerned by the import competition (Hornbeck 2001, 7).

Philippine producers of canned tuna (subject to a 35 percent tariff), the reauthorization permits duty-free imports of tuna in pouches ("foil or other airtight containers") but not cans.[40]

## The African Growth and Opportunity Act

The US African Growth and Opportunity Act passed Congress in May 2000. The law extended preferential market access for qualified countries in SSA within the framework of the GSP effective January 1, 2001. To be eligible for AGOA preferences, countries must be making progress toward market-based economies, strengthening the rule of law, eliminating barriers to US trade and investment, protecting intellectual property, combating corruption, protecting human rights, and eliminating certain child labor practices. As of January 2003, President George W. Bush had designated 38 of the 48 SSA countries as AGOA beneficiaries (USITC 2002; *International Trade Reporter*, January 9, 2003, 80).

AGOA adds 1,800 tariff line items to the 4,600 more generally eligible for duty-free treatment under the US GSP (out of a total of 11,800 tariff line items). The additional products include footwear, luggage, handbags, watches, and flatware. The AGOA regime of market access is assured through 2008, whereas the GSP is subject to annual review. The qualifying SSA countries are also exempt from the competitive need limitations of the GSP.

Much trade from sub-Saharan Africa is already enjoying the benefits of the regime's special treatment, although the data on utilization can be somewhat deceptive. Goods enjoying duty- and quota-free benefits specific to AGOA account for only 43 percent of US imports from countries designated as AGOA beneficiaries. However, another 29 percent enters duty free under zero MFN rates applicable to all suppliers, and a further 3 percent enters free under the GSP. Fully three-fourths of imports from AGOA beneficiaries thus enter duty free.

The full potential has not yet been met, however. In the important sector of apparel, only 38 percent of imports are duty free, and the fraction is even lower for sugar, tobacco, iron, and steel—all traditionally protected sectors in the United States. Features of eligibility approval and time horizon also unduly limit investor certainty and thus AGOA's impact on exports and job creation.

The AGOA legislation removed all existing quotas on textiles and apparel from sub-Saharan Africa (USTR 2003). In effect, for AGOA countries, this moved up by five years the date scheduled for the international elimination of textile and apparel quotas under the MFA negotiated in the

---

40. The Philippine authorities took sharp exception anyway, it turns out (*New York Times*, August 1, 2002).

Uruguay Round of multilateral trade negotiations. The apparel provisions of AGOA grant unlimited duty-free and quota-free access to SSA apparel made from US fabric, yarn, and thread. Apparel made from SSA fabric is also granted free access up to a cap set at 3 percent of overall US apparel imports, rising to 7 percent by 2008.[41]

The 2002 US Trade Promotion Act provided a modest liberalization of treatment in the sector by doubling the duty-free access for knit apparel. Countries with a per capita gross national product below $1,500 in 1998 further have duty-free access for apparel made from fabric of any origin through September 2004.[42] The use of the apparel provisions, however, is contingent on establishing effective visa systems to monitor against transshipment and counterfeiting.

In 2001, the 36 countries that qualified for AGOA benefits accounted for $17.6 billion in US imports, of which $11.0 billion (62.5 percent) was in oil (USITC 2002).[43] AGOA countries accounted for 96.4 percent of total US nonoil imports from sub-Saharan Africa, and 83.4 percent of US imports of all goods from the region (reflecting the fact that a major oil exporter, Angola, has not yet been declared eligible).

Because oil accounts for the bulk of US imports from sub-Saharan Africa, and because the MFN tariff on oil is already low at only 1.0 percent (USITC 2003), the potential impact of AGOA preferences on African growth lies primarily in the possibility of developing nonoil imports in the future.[44] Imports of apparel and textiles from AGOA countries have already shown considerable dynamism, rising from $651 million in 1999 to $789 million in 2000, $1.02 billion in 2001, and $1.18 billion in 2002 (USITC 2003). Imports of vehicles and parts have risen even more rapidly, from $121 million in 1999 to $573 million in 2002. Aggregate nonoil imports have risen from an average of $5.3 billion in 1998–99 to an average of $6.6 billion in 2000–02. For the seven quarters following passage of the AGOA legislation compared with the seven quarters before, the ratio of

---

41. This is under the limits adopted in the August 2002 revision of the law. The cap had originally been set at 1.5 percent of total US apparel imports, rising to 3.5 percent over eight years.

42. Although this Special Rule applied in 2002 to 30 of the 36 AGOA countries, it excludes South Africa as well as Gabon, Mauritius, and Seychelles. Botswana and Namibia were granted exceptional access to the Special Rule in AGOA II adopted in August 2002.

43. Oil trade is measured by Standard International Trade Classification (SITC) category 3.

44. In 2000, US imports from sub-Saharan Africa in HTS 2709.00.20 (crude oil 25° API or more) amounted to $8.6 billion, and in HTS 2710 (refined oil not elsewhere specified), $4.1 billion, comprising virtually all fuel imports. The MFN duty on the first category is 10.5 cents per barrel. The highest duty in the second category is 52.5 cents per barrel. The SSA data for this category are not broken down, so the calculation here applies the highest rate. For both categories, the rates are taken as a percent of the 1999–2001 average price per barrel for Brent oil ($23.5; IMF 2003).

## Table 2.2 US imports from AGOA countries by product and duty treatment, 2001 (thousands of dollars)

| Product category (HTS2) | | Total | Zero-duty MFN | Noneligible AGOA | Eligible AGOA | Utilized AGOA | GSP |
|---|---|---|---|---|---|---|---|
| 3 | Fish | 80,284 | 80,276 | 8 | 0 | 0 | 8 |
| 9 | Coffee, tea | 157,000 | 155,386 | 1,614 | 0 | 0 | 1,517 |
| 17 | Sugar | 38,525 | 0 | 38,525 | 0 | 0 | 29,236 |
| 18 | Cocoa | 276,109 | 264,940 | 11,168 | 0 | 0 | 21,404 |
| 24 | Tobacco | 42,135 | 2,449 | 176 | 39,509 | 8,199 | 15,769 |
| 1–23 | Other agricultural | 174,620 | 77,104 | 22,018 | 75,498 | 50,421 | 11,845 |
| 25 | Cement, etc. | 44,481 | 42,166 | 2,314 | 0 | 0 | 574 |
| 26 | Ores | 351,649 | 351,380 | 190 | 79 | 0 | 33 |
| 27 | Oil | 11,022,039 | 846,008 | 0 | 10,176,031 | 6,827,422 | 0 |
| 28 | Inorganic chemicals | 129,194 | 50,535 | 78,659 | 0 | 0 | 67,874 |
| 29 | Organic chemicals | 349,768 | 321,656 | 24,596 | 3,517 | 0 | 20,130 |
| 30–43 | Miscellaneous A | 117,798 | 41,311 | 63,701 | 12,786 | 4,564 | 52,228 |
| 44 | Wood products | 81,626 | 60,728 | 20,870 | 28 | 0 | 19,703 |
| 45–49 | Cork, straw, pulp, books | 33,155 | 30,684 | 2,006 | 464 | 66 | 1,479 |
| 50–56 | Yarns, fibers | 22,490 | 1,520 | 20,971 | 0 | 0 | 570 |
| 57–60 | Fabrics | 14,015 | 53 | 13,962 | 0 | 0 | 743 |
| 61–62 | Apparel | 938,795 | 0 | 938,795 | 0 | 355,771 | 31 |
| 63–70 | Miscellaneous B | 35,783 | 6,544 | 27,643 | 1,596 | 318 | 21,595 |
| 71 | Precious stones and metals | 2,105,331 | 2,077,584 | 27,743 | 4 | 0 | 26,822 |
| 72–73 | Iron and steel | 327,610 | 15,574 | 171,837 | 140,200 | 91,166 | 122,707 |
| 74–75 | Copper, nickel | 28,535 | 19,413 | 9,122 | 0 | 0 | 8,923 |
| 76 | Aluminum, products | 119,144 | 53,632 | 65,201 | 312 | 0 | 64,066 |
| 77–83 | Miscellaneous C | 62,557 | 28,959 | 33,415 | 183 | 2 | 13,394 |
| 84–86 | Machinery and equipment | 327,003 | 283,172 | 42,217 | 1,614 | 44 | 32,176 |
| 87 | Vehicles | 359,485 | 30,854 | 58,791 | 209,840 | 241,169 | 47,750 |
| 88–97 | Miscellaneous D | 83,833 | 58,966 | 23,365 | 1,502 | 16 | 19,611 |
| 90–99 | Special | 250,523 | 250,030 | 493 | 0 | 0 | 0 |
| | Total | 17,573,488 | 6,150,926 | 1,699,400 | 10,723,101 | 7,570,158 | 600,189 |

AGOA = US African Growth and Opportunity Act
GSP = Generalized System of Preferences
HTS2 = 2-digit Harmonized Tariff System
MFN = most-favored nation

*Source:* Calculated from USITC (2003).

US imports of nonoil goods from AGOA countries to those from other non-OECD countries rose by 3.8 percent (USITC 2003).[45] All these trends suggest a meaningful initial impact of the regime.

Table 2.2 provides the details of the duty treatment and product composition of US imports under AGOA in 2001. Clearly, there has been major

45. The ratio of course remains small, at 2.06 percent in the second period versus 1.99 percent in the first.

movement toward the objective of granting free access to the US market for AGOA countries, because three-fourths of US imports from them enter duty free. Imports granted duty-free entry by preferences specific to AGOA amount to 43 percent of US imports from the group.[46] In addition, 29 percent of imports enter duty free because they are in product categories that already had zero MFN tariff rates applicable to all suppliers. This relatively large share of MFN duty-free goods in the product mix (mainly precious stones and metals, but also large amounts in oil, chemicals, ores, machinery and equipment, and cocoa) is the major explanation for why fewer than half of total imports from AGOA use its specific duty-free provisions. If the imports entering with GSP rather than AGOA special treatment are also included ($600 million), total imports entering effectively at zero-duty treatment amounted to $13.3 billion, or 75.9 percent of the total. Three-fourths of imports from AGOA countries thus entered duty free one way or another.

The table also indicates that about $3 billion in imports was eligible for AGOA benefits but did not utilize them. This amount, however, was almost entirely in oil products. Considering the very low oil tariff, the implication seems to be that for about 30 percent of oil imports, the firms involved consider the potential tariff savings from AGOA too small to warrant the administrative procedures required to obtain them.

In contrast, the most conspicuous area in which the effective use of AGOA benefits would have had the greatest additional impact but where usage has been limited is apparel imports, where MFN tariffs are high. Only 38 percent of these imports entered with duty-free AGOA benefits in 2001, reflecting the rules of origin and ceilings discussed above. There are also significant gaps between total imports and the amounts receiving AGOA benefits (or enjoying zero MFN duties) in sugar, tobacco, inorganic chemicals, and iron and steel. It is likely no coincidence that these sectors include ones that in the past have been subject to protectionist pressures. These and other sectors included a total of $1.34 billion (7.6 percent of total imports) in goods ineligible for AGOA benefits.

## Testing for the Trade Impact of Preferential Regimes

As discussed in the previous sections, it can be difficult to detect the impact of special trade regimes for developing countries. One reason is

46. Thus, of total imports of $17.6 billion from AGOA members, the amount reported by the USITC as utilizing AGOA-specific duty-free entry benefits was $7.6 billion. Note that both the amount utilized and broader amount listed in the table as AGOA-eligible include $356 million in apparel imports, even though apparel as a whole (HTS categories 61–62) is recorded as ineligible in the summary USITC statistics, presumably because of the special rules-of-origin requirements and ceilings.

likely that these regimes tend to be established on behalf of countries whose economies and export sectors are relatively weak, so it becomes particularly important to consider the counterfactual (how exports would have performed without the arrangement) rather than merely the observed outcome. Otherwise, lackluster export growth in comparison with that of stronger developing economies may falsely be attributed to the inefficacy of the special regime.

It is useful to consider a "metatest" to determine whether there is evidence of an impact of special trade regimes on the export performance of the eligible countries. For a pool of 100 developing countries, annual real export growth in the period 1981–2001 can be related to a series of macroeconomic variables as well as to dummy variables capturing whether the country is a member of a special trade regime. Real exports are estimated as nominal dollar exports deflated by the unit value of world imports (IMF 2002a, 2002b). The first macroeconomic variable is global growth (using market rather than purchasing parity exchange rates, because it is the former that matter for effective demand) as estimated by the International Monetary Fund (IMF 1990, 2002c). Next are two variables designed to capture the country's export growth capacity. The first is the lagged average rate of growth of real GDP for the country in the previous three years. This measure separates out those countries that chronically achieve high economic performance from those that chronically fail to achieve satisfactory growth. It is to be expected that the pace of building export capacity, like that of other areas of the economy, will be greater in the former than in the latter.

The second capacity variable is purchasing power parity GDP per capita. To the extent that poor countries have a lesser capacity for export expansion than richer countries, this variable will be positively related to export growth. If instead the dominant influence is the general "convergence" trend (as found in chapter 1 for GDP per capita in 1960–2000), the sign for this variable will be negative because trade will tend to grow faster for poorer countries. The next macroeconomic variable is the real effective exchange rate. A more rapid pace of export growth can be expected from a country that has a relatively depreciated real exchange rate that provides a relative price incentive to shift resources into the production of exports and import substitutes rather than into nontradable goods. Another economic variable determining export performance is the share of exports in manufactures. In broad terms, there has tended to be a falling relative price for raw materials after the 1970s, deterring expansion of production and exports.

The impact of special trade arrangements is tested through the inclusion of a binary (1–0) dummy variable for countries (and years) in which special access was available through the Lomé or Cotonou arrangement ($D_L$), Caribbean Basin Initiative ($D_C$), or Andean Trade Preference Act

$(D_A)$.[47] Finally, in part because of the strong pattern of below-norm economic performance in SSA identified in the convergence analysis of chapter 1, a dummy variable is included for SSA countries $(D_S)$. Otherwise, given the substantial overlap between SSA and Lomé countries, the weak export performance associated with weak economies in the region could spuriously be attributed to Lomé membership.

Equation 2.1 reports the results of an ordinary-least-squares regression for pooled cross-section and time-series observations for 100 developing countries during the period 1981–2001 (t-statistics are in parentheses):

$$GX^*_{i,t} = -6.93 + 1.93GW_t + 0.41GYLAG_{i,t} + 0.079\ MFSHR_{i,t-1} + 7.76\ REER_{i,t-1}$$

$$(-1.53)\ (2.48)\qquad (1.61)\qquad\qquad (1.97)\qquad\qquad\qquad (2.36)$$

$$-0.00040\ yppp_{i,t-1} + 8.83D_L + 7.23D_C + 1.66D_A - 10.75D_S;$$

$$(-1.00)\qquad\qquad (2.36)\qquad (2.39)\qquad (0.29)\quad (-2.36)$$

Adj. $R^2 = 0.0163$; no. obs. = 1,412. $\qquad\qquad\qquad\qquad\qquad$ (2.1)

The variables are as follows: $GX^*_{i,t}$ = percentage growth rate of real exports for country $i$ in year $t$; $GW_t$ = percentage real growth rate in world GDP (at market exchange rates); $GYLAG_{i,t}$ = average real percentage growth rate of country $i$ for the three years preceding $t$; $MFSHR_{i,t-1}$ = percent of exports in manufactures for country $i$ in year prior to $t$; $REER_{i,t-1}$ = index of real effective exchange rate for country $i$ in year $t$ (1981–2002 average = 1.00); and $yppp_{i,t-1}$ = purchasing power parity GDP per capita in the year prior to $t$ (dollars).[48]

The estimated coefficients generally have the correct signs, reasonable statistical significance, and are of plausible orders of magnitude. The elasticity of developing-country real export growth with respect to growth of global GDP is about 2, and is strongly significant. The "export capacity" variable (significant at almost the 10 percent level) states that an extra percentage point in recent average growth tends to be associated with 0.4 percentage point in extra export growth, a reasonable capacity-boosting effect. As for the level of per capita income, apparently the convergence influence dominates rather than the economic capacity influence, because the coefficient is negative. Nonetheless, this variable is not statistically significant.

---

47. For four Caribbean economies—the Dominican Republic, Haiti, Jamaica, and Trinidad and Tobago—the regional preferential area is limited to the CBI rather than also attributed to the Lomé Convention in which they also participated, because their trade with the United States far exceeded that with the European Union.

48. The real effective exchange rate is calculated in terms of units of local currency per dollar, against the six major industrial countries, deflating by consumer prices and weighting by bilateral trade shares. It has a base of unity set at the 1981–2001 average for the country in question.

The manufacturing share coefficient at 0.079 (which is significant at the 5 percent level) means, for example, that a country with manufactures at 50 percent of GDP typically will have experienced 0.79 percent higher annual real export growth than a country with manufactures at 40 percent of GDP, again reasonable. The coefficient on the real exchange rate index means that, for example, if a country depreciated by 20 percent (raising the index from 1.0 to 1.25), the pace of real annual export growth would rise by 1.94 percentage point and remain at this new higher level as long as the new level of the real exchange rate remained in place.[49] The coefficient is statistically significant at the 2 percent level.

The overall degree of statistical explanation is extremely low, with an adjusted $R^2$ of only 1.6 percent. However, this is not unusual for such a large data set, especially when the dependent variable is stated in percentage change terms rather than in levels.[50]

The key variables of interest are the special regime dummies. The dummy variables for the CBI and Lomé are both large and are statistically significant at the 2 and 7 percent levels respectively. They indicate that, other things being equal, preferential regime membership has boosted real export growth by 7.2 percent annually for CBI countries and 8.8 percent for Lomé countries. The coefficient for ATPA shows a corresponding boost of 1.7 percent annually, but it is statistically insignificant (reflecting perhaps the relatively small number of observations as only four countries are in this regime). As expected, the dummy for SSA is negative; it is also large and highly significant, and it indicates that an SSA country typically had 10.7 percent lower real export growth annually than would otherwise be expected.

The CBI and Lomé dummy variables are so large that they suggest taking a second look. When the regression is run screening out the highest and lowest 1 percent of export growth observations, the result is to shrink the CBI coefficient from 7.2 to 2.2, and the Lomé coefficient, from 8.8 to 5.2. The screening also removes statistical significance.[51] The strong results from the full sample thus appear to be driven by extreme observations. On this basis, a balanced assessment would probably place the special regime effect on export growth at about 5 percent annually for Lomé and 2 percent for the CBI rather than the larger impact coefficients estimated from the full sample. The corresponding ATPA arguably could be placed at about 1.5 percent.

---

49. The more normal formulation of the exchange rate effect, a lagged percent change, was investigated (using a distributed lag of 0.25 on current year, 0.5 on previous year, and 0.25 on two years prior) but found statistically insignificant.

50. Using percentage changes avoids any question of nonstationarity.

51. The ATPA coefficient rises marginally to 1.76. The $t$-statistic for CBI falls to 1.00 (insignificant), and for Lomé, to 1.48 (significant only at the 15 percent level). In the screened test, the SSA dummy also falls, to –6.28.

This metatest, then, suggests an important favorable effect of the special regimes on export performance of their members, even after some downscaling to adjust for extreme observations. The results suggest the importance of taking into account the counterfactual of export performance given general macroeconomic variables. The more typical analyses that simply examine the export growth of preferential regime countries against nonmember countries fail to do so, and hence can attribute to regime inefficacy a weak performance that instead reflects more important macroeconomic differences between, for example, such members as Haiti, for Lomé, and nonmembers such as South Korea. Indeed, if we consider that the very reason for the existence of the special regimes is to compensate for the economic weakness of the members, the direction of bias we should expect is toward understatement (or even negative-impact estimate) in a simple (as opposed to econometric or other counterfactual) comparison between members and nonmembers.[52]

## Policy Implications

Regimes of special preferential trade access for developing countries are often considered to have provided little developmental impact and to pose distortions that make them inadvisable as a developmental strategy. The review of the GSP presented at the outset of this chapter suggests that the effects of that regime have indeed been limited, in part because of graduation provisions and product exclusions. However, closer examination of the Lomé, CBI, and ATPA arrangements suggests that these more focused programs have had greater impact, and AGOA might also do so once it has time to take effect. In the context of the relationship between trade policy and global poverty, these findings suggest that enhanced regimes of truly unencumbered market access for poor countries with a high incidence of poverty (and a high share of the poor in national income) could make an important difference to export and growth prospects. Before considering what such regimes might look like, it is important to address three related policy issues—the relationship between investment and trade, the trade diversion problem, and the relationship of deeper preferential access to multilateral and FTA liberalization.

### The Investment Connection

There is every reason to believe that the synergism between more dynamic direct foreign investment and enhanced market access opportuni-

---

52. Note also that the result here for Lomé is in the same spirit as that obtained by Nilsson (2002), cited above, but does not suffer from the inconsistency in that result whereby there was already a positive Lomé effect before the regime existed.

ties can substantially enhance the export and growth opportunities arising from special regimes for poor countries. As was noted above, direct investment in Mexico has soared under NAFTA, facilitating the expansion of production facilities to accomplish rapidly growing exports to the US market. The review of the CBI above also emphasizes the acceleration of direct investment under this regime.

The importance of the synergism between trade and investment suggests that if efforts are to be undertaken to enhance further market access as a means of reducing global poverty, these should be accompanied by measures that help spur direct investment in the countries in question. One measure especially warrants consideration: the exemption from corporate taxation of earnings on direct investment in specified poor countries or groupings (e.g., AGOA) for new investments undertaken during the next 10 to 15 years. For the United States in particular, the "residential" basis for corporate taxes means that corporate income is taxed at US rates even if it is earned in, for example, South Africa. Most other countries apply some combination of the residential principle and the "territorial" principle, whereby the tax obligation is solely to the host country. Existing US investment tax treaties do tend to provide for allowance of the host-country's taxation against US taxes otherwise due, but if the host tax is low, this still leaves the total tax obligation at the US rate. With outright exemption, the developing host country could enjoy either the tax revenue or, perhaps more relevant, the growth benefits of a stimulus to direct foreign investment through the granting of a partial or full tax holiday of a given duration (e.g., 10 years).[53]

A second instrument for spurring direct foreign investment is the use of political risk insurance (in the United States, through the Overseas Private Investment Corporation, or OPIC). For countries selected for special trade and investment treatment for purposes of alleviating global poverty, it would be possible to make particular efforts to ensure that such insurance is available, perhaps by allocating some portion of official assistance toward paying the higher risk premiums that might be required. In the specific case of OPIC, Moran (2003) argues that the agency is unduly constrained by legislative restrictions against providing insurance where there will be any loss in US jobs whatsoever, rather than taking account of US export jobs. This and other restrictions against activity in "sensitive" sectors such as textiles and apparel would need to be eliminated or suspended for investment in specified poor countries or regional groupings for perhaps 10 to 15 years to enable OPIC to play an active part in an overall trade and investment package for these countries.

---

53. CCFA (2003, 6) similarly calls for exemption from US taxation for any US company doing manufacturing or service business in any African country. Hufbauer and Wong (2002) outline possible terms for such an exemption.

## How Serious Is the Trade Diversion Problem?

A second issue that must be considered is whether preferential trade regimes are adverse in their effect because they create trade diversion. Overwhelmingly, the practical question here is simply whether the magnitudes are large enough to worry about. If special regimes for poor countries are the focus of the question, the answer is almost certainly no.

Chapter 1 observes that the three most prominent special groupings of poor countries—HIPCs, LDCs, and SSA—comprise approximately 64 countries with a combined population of 1.0 billion people, of whom 715 million are living in poverty (at the $2 per day threshold; table 1.3). Moreover, this set of countries has the highest "poverty intensity" in the imports of industrial countries, simply because the poor in these countries receive a much higher fraction of total income than they do in middle-income countries, which nevertheless also have large absolute numbers of poor people (e.g., Brazil and China).

If an enhanced special regime were to be limited to this threefold set of poor countries, on a basis of trade data for 2000 only 6.4 percent of total US imports from developing countries would be involved, only 8.5 percent for the European Union, and only 3.8 percent for Japan (calculated from IMF 2002a and from table 1.4 in this volume).[54] Moreover, as much as half or more of these imports is in oil, where protection is already extremely low. The normal concern that exports would be diverted from the other developing countries to those included in the special-access program would thus be minimized, because even a large proportionate increase in the exports of the poor countries, and even the assumption that a large fraction of this increase came out of the potential exports of other developing countries, would mean only a minor loss of export opportunities for the other, more advanced developing countries.[55]

## The Relationship to Multilateral and FTA Liberalization

Another issue that must be considered is whether preferential regimes make any sense in a world moving toward more completely free trade multilaterally and free trade in a growing number of increasingly important FTAs. These liberalizations erode the potential impact of preferen-

---

54. In absolute terms: $27.8 billion, $35.3 billion, and $5.4 billion, respectively.

55. As for the traditional static welfare effects of trade diversion, and whether there would be enough trade creation to offset them, these considerations would seem of secondary importance given the magnitudes involved, and in any event would be an inadequate basis for policy evaluation in a context in which the main objective is to address global poverty. In principle, some dollar valuation—e.g., the amount of grant development assistance that could equivalently be forgone (for the same poverty reduction impact—would be necessary to obtain more meaningful welfare estimates of trade diversion in such a regime.

tially free access. However, it will be some considerable time before global trade is truly free as a consequence of multilateral and/or FTA liberalization. The Doha Round was inaugurated in 2001. In the most recent round of multilateral negotiations, the Uruguay Round, the time lapse from the launching of the round (1986) to its full implementation (2005, for dismantling textile quotas) was 19 years. This suggests that a time horizon of some two decades remains ahead in which special market access for poor countries could retain a meaningful economic content, even if the Doha Round and the constellation of new FTAs (including a possible Free Trade Area of the Americas) were eventually to yield totally free global trade— an outcome unfortunately unlikely to be attained. Moreover, as outlined in chapter 6 below, providing a positive incentive through an immediate deepening of preferential access as part of an overall Doha Round agreement could help ensure that "at-risk" low-income countries are not tempted to block multilateral liberalization for fear of the erosion of existing preferences, a risk heightened by the new "single-undertaking" structure of WTO negotiations requiring general consensus.

## A Policy Strategy for Free Market Access for Poor Countries

Chapter 1 pointed out that the poverty intensity of industrial-country imports from HIPCs, LDCs, and SSA countries is in the range of 40 to 50 percent on a basis of the share of the poor in supplying-country income, and 60 to 70 percent on a basis of the headcount share of the poor in the populations of these countries. This chapter has broadly concluded that the preferential access regimes constructed under the EU's Lomé Convention and the United States' CBI and ATPA have had a meaningful, positive effect on the export performance of the countries in question, and there are initial signs of a positive effect even for trade under the new AGOA arrangement. Similarly, experience with the CBI (and even more so with NAFTA) suggests that the foreign direct investment effects of such regimes can be important as well.

If these strands are gathered together in pursuit of a strategy for using the trade policy instrument to combat global poverty, the following type of regime begins to suggest itself as applicable to all industrial countries and especially the United States, European Union, and Japan:

- completely duty- and quota-free entry to imports from all HIPCs, LDCs, and SSA countries (collectively, the "HLS" countries);

- exemption from corporate taxation on earnings from foreign direct investment in this set of countries for a specified period of time, such as 10 to 15 years, making it feasible for the host developing countries to adopt tax incentive regimes to spur investment to complement the new trade opportunities;

- commitment to refrain from all contingent protection, including antidumping and safeguard measures;

- sweeping simplification of rules of origin, with inputs purchased either from the importing country (e.g., textile fabric purchased from the United States) or from any poor (HLS) country counting toward local value-added measures;

- availability of trade adjustment assistance for workers deemed to have been displaced by increases in imports from HLS countries under the special-access regime;

- guaranteed continuation of the free access for a decade even if internal political conditions change.

Because the trade base of the HLS countries is small, a comprehensive free access program along these lines could make possible a large proportionate increase in their exports without breaching magnitudes of trade change that would be likely to impose significant worker displacements; even so, provision for trade adjustment assistance (e.g., along the lines of the new US Trade Promotion Act) could help provide assurance to domestic labor organizations that helping reduce global poverty would not seriously jeopardize their own prosperity.

The guarantee of continued eligibility despite possible setbacks on, for example, domestic governance, would be necessary to ensure that the regime provides investment incentives even in countries facing periodic domestic instability. The industrial-country governments could rest assured that in countries where there were sharp deteriorations in such dimensions as corruption and human rights, it would be highly unlikely that there would be robust investment and expansion of exports, so there would be little prospect that the regime could somehow "reward" governments pursuing adverse paths. Conceivably, the initial membership of eligible HLS countries could exclude the most egregious offenders under such criteria, however.

Finally, for the case of the US regime for AGOA, several major enhancements would seem desirable (Cline 2003a). Special regimes such as AGOA work only if they induce investment in productive capacity. The current structure of AGOA has three major limitations that inhibit this result. First, each country's eligibility must be reviewed annually. Second, the regime expires in 2008. Third, duty-free entry for apparel remains subject to the restrictions on source of fabric, as described.

Regarding the first of these, the desire for review is understandable, because the problem of governance has been perhaps the foremost source of disappointing growth in SSA in the past. At the same time, an annual review seems an unduly "short leash" that unnecessarily adds uncertainty to any potential investor's decisions. A useful reform would be to assure *eligibility for a period of five years* once a country has qualified. (There could be a qualification allowing the president to revoke eligibility in extreme circumstances, e.g., when a government has been deposed by force.)

Second, the *term of AGOA could be extended to 10 years* (through 2013) prior to full review of the regime (rather than through 2008, as presently provided). Moreover, the revised term could provide for indefinite continuation unless Congress passes legislation to the contrary, rather than calling for automatic expiration unless Congress acts to extend (as presently provided).

Third, the *regime for apparel could be substantially liberalized*. The general AGOA requirement for duty-free access for apparel is that it be made using fabric and yarn imported into Africa from the United States. The two exceptions to the US-fabric rule are duty-free entry up to a ceiling of 3 percent of US apparel imports, rising to 7 percent by 2008, for AGOA apparel made from fabric produced within the region itself; and, for 30 poorer SSA countries, duty-free entry for all apparel (regardless of fabric origin) but within this same volume cap and only through 2004. The presence of the volume cap and the imminent expiration date for special treatment of the 30 poorer countries act as a source of uncertainty for investors, while the actual volume of imports remains very low—only about 1.5 percent of US apparel imports in 2002 (table 2.2; USITC 2003).

An appropriate reform would be to remove altogether the volume ceiling for duty-free entry of apparel made from SSA-regional fabric. Similarly, for the poorer countries, the cap could be removed for apparel made from fabric of any source, and this provision could apply for the full 10-year horizon of an enhanced AGOA rather than expiring in 2004. This liberalization could be accompanied by provision for an automatic trigger ing of a review of whether injury has occurred warranting safeguard protection if total apparel imports from AGOA exceed, for example, 15 percent of total US apparel imports. Certainly over the longer term, it would be desirable for a major share of apparel imports to come from the poorest region in the world, in light of the underlying objective of using AGOA to reduce global poverty.

Fourth, AGOA could be amended to grant the same *exemption from safeguards protection* that applies to Canada and Mexico under NAFTA, which prohibits application of such protection unless the Canadian or Mexican share in US imports of the good is "substantial" and "contributes importantly" to the US industry's difficulties.[56] Although the existing WTO provisions already give some shelter to developing countries from safeguard

---

56. Imports from Canada or Mexico are considered "substantial" in the agreement if the country is among the top five suppliers of the product to the United States.

restrictions,[57] NAFTA-type treatment would provide a higher degree of assurance that safeguards would rarely be imposed on AGOA suppliers.

The overall effect of this policy approach would be to adopt an aggressive program of immediate free market access for goods from "at-risk" poor countries, combined with a complementary policy of tax exemption on direct investment in these countries. This track of trade policy would most directly address the concentration of about one-fourth of the global poor in countries where the share of the poor in national income is high (because the vast bulk of the population is poor). A parallel track of more generalized trade liberalization for other developing countries would be pursued to address the other three-fourths of global poverty. Chapters 3 through 5 turn to the potential poverty reduction effects of multilateral trade liberalization.

---

57. The Uruguay Round agreement provided that an industrial country could not impose safeguard protection on an import from a developing country if the amount imported did not exceed 3 percent of the industrial country's total imports of the good, and imports from developing countries collectively did not exceed 9 percent.

# 3

# Industrial-Country Protection and the Impact of Trade Liberalization on Global Poverty

The scope for reducing global poverty through improved trade policies depends importantly on the extent to which industrial-country protection remains high enough to pose a major obstacle to developing-country exports, terms of trade, and growth.[1] This chapter seeks to identify the levels of this protection and to gauge the corresponding impact that might be obtained through its liberalization. The previous chapter focused on special market access arrangements for the poor, "at-risk" countries (heavily indebted poor countries, or HIPCs; least developed countries, or LDCs; and sub-Saharan Africa, or SSA). Although these countries account for about one-fourth of the poor globally (chapter 1), they represent only about 7 percent of combined imports of the United States, European Union, and Japan from developing countries (chapter 2). Such middle-income nations as Brazil, Mexico, and South Korea, along with China in particular (a low-income but not at-risk economy) and many others, bulk far larger in total trade magnitudes. This chapter examines market access for all developing countries. Once again, however, the focus will be on industrial-country protection, rather than that maintained by the developing countries themselves.

In broad terms, protection in industrial countries is concentrated in textiles and apparel and agricultural goods. In contrast, successive rounds of multilateral trade negotiations have reduced tariffs on nontextile manu-

---

1. This chapter draws in part upon Cline (2002b).

factures to modest levels. "Contingent" protection (antidumping, countervailing duties, and safeguards) nonetheless is also a significant factor in a number of manufacturing sectors (e.g., steel).

## Tariffs on Manufactured Goods

It is generally recognized that for manufactured goods (at least outside textiles and apparel), tariffs are relatively low. Thus, Finger and Schuknecht (1999) estimate that the post–Uruguay Round average most-favored-nation (MFN) tariff of industrial countries on imports of manufactures from developing countries is only 3 percent. They note, however, that this level is about twice the corresponding average for imports from industrial-country suppliers.

The Organization for Economic Cooperation and Development (OECD 2000) provides tariff and trade data for member countries at the 6-digit Harmonized Tariff System, or HTS, level (about 4,600 categories). These data comprise import values and two alternative sets of MFN tariffs: those actually applied as of 1998, and post–Uruguay Round "bound" rates after full implementation of negotiated tariff cuts.[2] Table 3.1 reports average tariffs calculated from the OECD data for the "Quad" industrial-country importers: the United States, European Union, Japan, and Canada. The averages across the tariff-line categories are either simple (unweighted), import weighted, or "adjusted-import weighted." The latter concept, developed in appendix 3A, seeks to overcome the usual concern about import weighting: that high tariffs will suppress imports and hence be underrepresented in import-weighted averages. The approach is to weight by "adjusted" import values, based on an average between the actual and hypothetical free trade import value. As argued in the appendix, moreover, because of the arbitrariness of category width, the alternative of unweighted "simple" tariff averages may give more distorted results than weighting by import value.

All manufactured categories (HTS chapters 28–96) are included in the estimates.[3] Even though the relatively high-tariff textile and apparel sectors are included, the resulting averages are modest, especially for the bound (full-implementation Uruguay Round) levels as opposed to the 1998 applied levels. For example, on the preferred measure (adjusted-

---

2. For industrial products, Uruguay Round tariff cuts were phased in equally over five years from the beginning of 1995 to the beginning of 1999. By 2002, as a result, applied tariffs should generally have fallen fully to the new bound levels. Longer periods were given for agricultural liberalization (WTO 2002, 1).

3. The resulting aggregate imports of manufactures from developing countries in 1998 amounted to $276.6 billion for the United States (excluding from Mexico), $327.8 billion for the European Union, $83.7 billion for Japan, and $18.6 billion for Canada.

**Table 3.1    Average tariffs on manufactured goods in industrial-country markets** (percent)

| Origin of imports | United States[a] 1998 | United States[a] Bound | European Union 1998 | European Union Bound | Japan 1998 | Japan Bound | Canada[a] 1998 | Canada[a] Bound |
|---|---|---|---|---|---|---|---|---|
| **From HIOECD** | | | | | | | | |
| Simple | 5.02 | 3.44 | 5.40 | 4.01 | 3.31 | 2.49 | 7.30 | 5.71 |
| Import weighted | 3.18 | 2.20 | 5.11 | 3.91 | 1.44 | 1.16 | 5.18 | 4.05 |
| Adjusted-import weighted | 3.24 | 2.25 | 5.17 | 3.97 | 1.51 | 1.21 | 5.20 | 4.10 |
| **From developing countries** | | | | | | | | |
| Simple | 5.02 | 3.44 | 5.40 | 4.01 | 3.31 | 2.49 | 7.30 | 5.71 |
| Import weighted | 4.95 | 3.71 | 5.67 | 4.58 | 3.64 | 2.88 | 7.30 | 5.59 |
| Adjusted-import weighted | 5.09 | 3.84 | 5.75 | 4.66 | 3.78 | 2.98 | 7.56 | 5.76 |

1998 = actual applied in 1998
Bound = levels after full implementation of Uruguay Round cuts, generally by 2000
HIOECD = high-income member of the Organization for Economic Cooperation and Development
   (excluding Czech Republic, Hungary, Mexico, South Korea, Poland, and Turkey)

a. Excluding Mexico from developing countries

*Source:* OECD (2000).

import weighting), the average bound US tariff is only 2.25 percent for imports from industrial countries ("HIOECD") and 3.84 percent for developing countries (all others except Mexico, which is omitted because of free trade owing to the North American Free Trade Agreement, or NAFTA).[4]

These estimates are for MFN tariffs. The differences between tariffs facing industrial- and developing-country partners thus stem not from different tariffs at the tariff-line level, but different product weightings.[5] This is evident in the fact that the "simple" average is identical for both supplying regions (for a given importer), but the averages are no longer equal when weighting by imports or adjusted imports. The estimates in table 3.1 suggest that tariffs tend to be higher on those products that are more important to developing countries. Whereas the import-weighted tariffs are considerably lower than the simple average tariffs for HIOECD suppliers, for developing-country suppliers the import-weighted and

4. HIOECD refers to OECD countries excluding the six middle-income OECD members (see table 3.1).

5. This means that the estimates abstract from preferential entry in such arrangements as the Generalized System of Preferences, Lomé Convention, US African Growth and Opportunity Act, Caribbean Basin Initiative, and US Andean Trade Preference Act. As shown in chapter 2, however, the actual tariff revenue forgone in these arrangements has been limited by product exclusions, rules of origin, administrative costs, and other factors; and in any event, the beneficiary countries in these arrangements are mainly the high-risk low-income countries, which account for only a small portion of total developing-country supply.

adjusted-import-weighted tariff averages tend to be higher than the simple averages, especially for bound tariffs. This further suggests that the major influence of import weighting is not to understate the average tariff but to capture the actual pattern of the relevant trade. That is, if the principal effect of import weighting were to understate the incidence of high tariffs, we would observe import-weighted tariffs for imports from developing countries that are also substantially lower than the simple tariff averages, rather than higher.

On the preferred adjusted-import weighting, and using bound rates, these results confirm Finger and Schuknect's (1999) finding of higher tariffs against developing than industrial countries. The ratio between the two levels stands at 1.7 for the United States, 1.2 for the European Union, 2.5 for Japan, and 1.4 for Canada. Rather than the higher relative level of tariffs against developing countries, however, the more salient feature of the estimates is that with Quad tariffs on imports of manufactures in the range of 4 to 5 percent, this protection is now at relatively low levels by historical standards.

## Peak Tariffs: How Important Are They?

It is often suggested that low manufacturing tariffs are misleading because there are numerous tariff "peak" categories, so the protective effect is much greater than would be implied by a uniform tariff of the same average level. The typical threshold for considering a tariff peak is 15 percent or higher.

Table 3.2 considers high tariffs using a more stringent threshold of 10 percent (post–Uruguay Round bound rates). Even with a 10 percent threshold, the incidence of high tariffs is relatively limited. Thus, for the United States, 7.9 percent of tariff categories show a bound tariff of 10 percent or more, and only 2.1 percent have tariffs of 15 percent or more. Equally or more important, only 12.6 percent of manufactured imports from developing countries by value face US bound tariffs of 10 percent or more, and only 4.4 percent of import value is in categories with tariffs of 15 percent or more.[6]

The European Union and Japan show a higher incidence of categories and import values in the 10 to 14.99 percent tariff range, but lower inci-

---

6. Use of the OECD data requires the assumption that the incidence of peak tariffs using 6-digit HTS data is similar to that at the more detailed 8-digit level. Analysis of US tariff data at the 8-digit level shows that this is broadly true, depending on the thresholds considered. Manufacturing categories (HTS chapters 28–96) with applied tariffs of 10 percent and above account for 8.2 percent by category count at the 6-digit level and 8.7 percent at the 8-digit level. The proportionate divergence rises with the threshold, as follows (threshold percent, 6-digit categories, 8-digit categories): 15 percent: 2.8 percent, 4.1 percent; 20 percent: 0.6 percent, 1.6 percent; 25 percent: 0.3 percent, 1.1 percent.

**Table 3.2   Incidence of high tariffs in manufactures for industrial-country imports from developing countries** (percent)

| Measure of incidence | Tariff range | | | |
|---|---|---|---|---|
| | 10–14.99 | 15–19.99 | 20–24.99 | 25 or higher |
| **Percent of tariff categories** | | | | |
| United States | 5.8 | 1.3 | 0.5 | 0.3 |
| European Union | 6.8 | 0.4 | 0.0 | 0.1 |
| Japan | 2.9 | 0.3 | 0.2 | 0.4 |
| Canada | 8.7 | 7.3 | 0.2 | 0.1 |
| **Percent of import value** | | | | |
| United States | 8.2 | 2.5 | 0.4 | 1.5 |
| European Union | 19.1 | 1.1 | 0.0 | 0.0 |
| Japan | 8.1 | 0.2 | 0.5 | 0.9 |
| Canada | 5.8 | 14.4 | 0.1 | 0.8 |
| **Average tariff, import weighted** | | | | |
| United States | 12.4 | 17.2 | 22.1 | 27.0 |
| European Union | 11.8 | 16.7 | 20.7 | 33.9 |
| Japan | 11.0 | 17.1 | 20.6 | 33.1 |
| Canada | 13.2 | 17.6 | 20.0 | 25.0 |

Note: Rates refer to bound levels after full implementation of Uruguay Round cuts (2000).

Source: Calculated from OECD (2000).

dence for 15 percent and above. Canada has a somewhat more accentuated high-tariff structure. Fully 21.1 percent of the value of manufactured imports from developing countries is in categories with bound tariffs of 10 percent or higher, and 15.3 percent is in categories of 15 percent or higher tariffs.[7]

What is the resulting overall protective effect of tariffs on manufactures, after taking account of these high tariffs? One simple way to find out is to apply an assumed price elasticity of imports to the proportionate change in price that would be expected from complete removal of the tariff. The domestic market price includes the tariff, and is thus "1 + t" where t is the tariff (expressed as a fraction). Removal of the tariff would thus reduce the domestic price of the import by the proportion $t/(1 + t)$ at the most, and by less if the foreign supply from developing countries is less than infinitely elastic. The proportionate increase in imports from developing countries that could be expected from complete removal of manufacturing tariffs of 10 percent and higher, as a fraction of the existing level of manufactured imports, can thus be roughly approximated as $z = \beta(\Sigma\varphi_i[t_i/(1 + t_i)])$, where $\beta$ is the (absolute) value assumed for the import price elasticity of demand, $\varphi$ is the share of import value, $t$ is the tariff level, and $i$ refers to each of the tariff ranges considered.

---

7. The difference between the import and adjusted-import weighting is minimal in this range, so only the import-weighted results are shown.

Except for the import price elasticity, the elements of this calculation are straightforward. For its part, the price elasticity of import demand ($\beta$) can be inferred from the range of parameters used in leading computable general equilibrium (CGE) models of trade. Many of these models are built on a two-tier system that identifies one elasticity of substitution in demand between domestic goods and imports ($\sigma_D$) and a second elasticity for substitution among the various alternative sources of supply of imports ($\sigma_M$). The simple import price elasticity we seek is related to the first of these two substitution elasticities as follows: $\beta = \sigma_D (1 - \varphi_M)$, where $\varphi_M$ is the share of imports in total use of the product ($\varphi_M = M/[M + C_D]$, where $M$ is imports and $C_D$ is consumption of the domestically produced good).[8]

A reasonable estimate for the ratio of imports to total domestic use of manufactures is $\varphi_M = 0.25$ (imports provide one-fourth of the domestic availability of manufactures).[9] As for the elasticity of substitution between the domestic goods and imports, "based on preferred estimates from the econometric literature with some upward adjustment," Dimaranan, McDougall, and Hertel (2002, 20-2, 20-12) place this elasticity in a range of 1.8 to 5.2 for manufactures, with a simple average of 3.1. The LINKAGE model used by the World Bank for its Global Economic Prospects applies a range of 3.9 to 4.9 for manufactures, with a simple average of 4.2.[10] The CGE model of Harrison, Rutherford, and Tarr (1997a), which is used in chapter 4 below, applies a uniform value of $\sigma_D = 4.0$. The average for manufactures in these three models is thus $\sigma_D = 3.77$. Together with the estimated import share, this yields an import price elasticity of $\beta = 2.8$.

Using the simple weighted-average formula noted above, table 3.3 presents back-of-the-envelope partial equilibrium estimates of the impact of

---

8. This follows from the definition of the elasticity of substitution, which is the percentage change in the ratio of imports to domestic goods for a 1 percent decline in the corresponding price ratio. Let $x$ be the proportionate change in imports for a 1 percent fall in the import price (so $x \equiv \beta$). Let $y$ ($< 0$) be the corresponding percent change in demand for the domestic good induced by a reduction in the price of the import. Then we have two unknowns and two equations. First: $x - y = \sigma_D$. This follows from the fact that the percent change in a ratio equals the percent change in the numerator minus the percent change in the denominator. Second: $x\varphi_M + y(1 - \varphi_M) = 0$. This arises from the fact that along the indifference curve between the import and the domestic good, total use of the good remains unchanged as one is substituted for the other. This equation states that, after weighting by base-period shares, the rise in imports is just offset by the decline in the domestic good. Solving, we have: $x = \sigma_D (1 - \varphi_M)$.

9. At the world level, Dimaranan and McDougall (2002, 3–4) estimate that for manufactures, exports (which must also equal imports globally) amount to $4.16 trillion (1997 dollars) and gross output is $15.06 trillion, placing $\varphi_M$ at 0.276. The ratio will be somewhat higher for developing countries, which are less industrialized and have lower market exchange rates relative to purchasing power parity (PPP) exchange rates, and somewhat lower for industrial countries, suggesting a value of 0.25 for the latter.

10. Dominique van der Mensbrugghe, personal communication, February 10, 2004.

**Table 3.3    Illustrative impact of elimination of tariffs on manufactured imports from developing countries**
(percent)

| Measure of impact | United States | European Union | Japan | Canada |
|---|---|---|---|---|
| **Categories with tariff lower than 10 percent** | | | | |
| Average tariff | 2.02 | 2.70 | 1.73 | 2.62 |
| Import impact | 5.54 | 7.35 | 4.76 | 7.15 |
| Share in manufactured imports | 87.40 | 79.80 | 90.30 | 78.90 |
| Weighted impact | 4.85 | 5.86 | 4.30 | 5.64 |
| **Categories with tariff 10 percent and above** | | | | |
| Average tariff | 15.42 | 12.03 | 13.57 | 16.69 |
| Import impact | 37.41 | 30.06 | 33.46 | 40.05 |
| Share in manufactured imports | 12.60 | 20.20 | 9.70 | 21.10 |
| Weighted impact | 4.71 | 6.07 | 3.25 | 8.45 |
| **Total manufactures** | | | | |
| Average tariff | 3.71 | 4.58 | 2.88 | 5.59 |
| Import impact | 9.56 | 11.93 | 7.54 | 14.09 |
| Share from tariff higher than 10 percent | 49.30 | 50.90 | 43.00 | 60.00 |

Tariffs = bound rates
Import impact = percent increase assuming import demand price elasticity of −2.8 and infinite supply elasticity

*Source:* Author's calculations.

tariff removal for all manufactured imports into the main industrial countries from developing countries under extremely simplifying assumptions: a uniform import price elasticity of 2.8 (absolute value), infinite supply elasticity, an absence of quotas or other nontariff restraints, and abstraction from any indirect or general equilibrium effects. The table divides the effects into products with average tariffs below 10 percent and those 10 percent and above.

Two salient implications stand out in the table. First, the estimates suggest that the overall scope for import expansion from the removal of tariffs on manufactures is significant but nonetheless moderate, lying mainly in the vicinity of a 10 percent increase in these imports (or about $70 billion, against a base of $707 billion total manufactured imports by the Quad from developing countries in 1998).

Second, about half of this impact could be expected to arise from the removal of tariffs of 10 percent or more, even though goods in this group account for only one-eighth or less (United States and Japan) to one-fifth (European Union and Canada) of total imports of manufactures. This means that although the presence of high tariffs does not fundamentally alter the judgment that the protective effect of tariffs on manufactures is moderate, it does mean that a disproportionately large share of tariff liberalization benefits is to be found in eliminating the high tariffs.

These rough estimates might also suggest a simple but potentially powerful demand for developing countries in their Doha Round bargaining: that industrial countries reduce all tariffs on manufactured goods to no more than 10 percent. Doing so would eliminate about half of the remaining protective effect of Quad tariffs on imports of manufactured goods from developing countries even if tariffs below 10 percent were left unchanged. In exchange, leading developing countries could presumably offer to impose a ceiling on all of their own tariffs, such as 15 or 20 percent.

## Tariffs and Quotas in Textiles and Apparel

Within manufactures, the protection of industrial countries against imports from developing countries has traditionally been most severe and most important in the textile and apparel sectors. Apparel in particular tends to be unskilled-labor intensive and hence of natural comparative advantage to developing countries. Textiles and apparel account for about one-eighth of the total of all imports from developing countries into the main industrial countries.[11]

Table 3.4 reports the course of tariff protection against textiles and apparel during the past four decades for the United States, European Union, and Japan. Successive rounds of multilateral trade negotiations have reduced apparel tariffs from the range of 20–25 percent in the 1960s and early 1970s to 10–12 percent in 2002 following implementation of Uruguay Round tariff cuts. Tariffs began this period almost as high in textile fabrics, but have fallen somewhat further (to a range of 6–9 percent), reflecting the greater susceptibility of textiles to mechanized processes and hence the lesser comparative advantage for countries with abundant unskilled labor. Tariffs on the lower stage of processing—yarn and thread—have traditionally been lower. (The convergence from the relatively high rates in the United States and lower rates in Europe and Japan in 1962 toward intermediate rates by 1987 after the Tokyo Round cuts reflected the process of tariff harmonization and reduction of tariff escalation in the latter two economies.) Despite the declining trend, tariffs in the textile-apparel complex remain far higher than those for manufactures overall.

Not surprisingly, textiles and apparel are also the locus of greatest concentration for peak tariffs. As shown in table 3.5, 33 percent of textile fabric categories and 55 percent of apparel categories (62.7 percent of apparel import value from developing countries) have post–Uruguay Round bound tariffs of 10 percent or more for the United States, and 18.5

---

11. United States: 12.5 percent; European Union, 11.7 percent; Japan, 9.8 percent. Calculated from USITC (2002); WTO (2001, 114).

### Table 3.4  Tariffs in textiles and apparel[a]
(percent)

| Country or group and year | Textiles | | Apparel |
| --- | --- | --- | --- |
| | Yarn | Fabric | |
| **United States** | | | |
| 1962 | 11.5 | 24.0 | 25.0 |
| 1973 | 14.5 | 19.0 | 27.0 |
| 1987 | 9.0 | 11.5 | 22.5 |
| 1998[b] | 8.7 | 11.2 | 13.9 |
| 2002[b] | 6.7 | 7.9 | 11.5 |
| **European Union** | | | |
| 1962 | 3.0 | 17.5 | 18.5 |
| 1973 | 8.0 | 14.5 | 16.5 |
| 1987 | 7.0 | 10.5 | 13.5 |
| 1998[b] | 6.6 | 9.9 | 12.8 |
| 2002[b] | 4.3 | 8.6 | 11.7 |
| **Japan** | | | |
| 1962 | 2.5 | 19.5 | 25.0 |
| 1973 | 9.0 | 12.0 | 18.0 |
| 1987 | 7.0 | 9.5 | 14.0 |
| 1998[b] | 6.0 | 7.8 | 12.8 |
| 2002[b] | 4.7 | 6.2 | 9.8 |

a. Greater of simple and import-weighted averages.
b. Against developing countries.

*Sources:* Cline (1990, 163); OECD (2000).

percent (import-weighted) have tariffs of 15 percent or more in apparel.[12] Canada's levels are even higher, with an extraordinary 98.4 percent of apparel imports from developing countries facing tariffs of 15–20 percent (albeit with no tariffs above 20 percent). In the European Union, 22 percent of textile imports and 90–95 percent of apparel imports face tariffs of 10–15 percent, although the tariff structure has a strict ceiling and there are no tariffs in excess of 15 percent. Japan similarly has about 35–50 percent of apparel imports in categories with tariffs of 10–15 percent but no categories above 15 percent.

Table 3.5 also reports the incidence of high tariffs in manufactured goods excluding textile fabric and apparel. The striking result is a very low presence of high tariffs in manufactures outside these two sensitive sectors. In the United States, whereas 12.6 percent of imports from developing countries face post–Uruguay Round tariffs of 10 percent or higher for manufactures as a whole (table 3.2), the corresponding figure is only

---

12. Note that the estimates in table 3.5 omit textile yarn, which tends to have lower tariffs but also constitutes a much smaller import base. For example, in 1998 US imports from developing countries amounted to $6.5 billion in textile fabric and $40.9 billion in apparel, but only $0.98 billion in yarn.

**Table 3.5  Tariff peaks: Textiles, apparel, and other manufactures**
(post–Uruguay Round rates)

| Type of manufacture | United States %C | United States %V | European Union %C | European Union %V | Japan %C | Japan %V | Canada %C | Canada %V |
|---|---|---|---|---|---|---|---|---|
| **Textile fabric** | | | | | | | | |
| 10 to less than 15 percent | 28.6 | 17.9 | 10.1 | 22.3 | 5.2 | 4.8 | 74.2 | 66.8 |
| 15 to less than 20 percent | 4.4 | 5.8 | 0.0 | 0.0 | 0.0 | 0.0 | 13.7 | 19.1 |
| 20 to less than 25 percent | 0.0 | 0.0 | 0.0 | 0.0 | 0.0 | 0.0 | 0.0 | 0.0 |
| 25 percent and above | 0.0 | 0.0 | 0.0 | 0.0 | 0.0 | 0.0 | 0.0 | 0.0 |
| Total value (billions of dollars)[a] | | 6.5 | | 11.0 | | 2.2 | | 0.7 |
| **Apparel** | | | | | | | | |
| 10 to less than 15 percent | 34.9 | 44.2 | 89.9 | 95.8 | 34.0 | 50.4 | 1.7 | 1.5 |
| 15 to less than 20 percent | 12.6 | 15.1 | 0.0 | 0.0 | 0.0 | 0.0 | 95.0 | 98.4 |
| 20 to less than 25 percent | 6.7 | 2.8 | 0.0 | 0.0 | 0.0 | 0.0 | 0.0 | 0.0 |
| 25 percent and above | 0.8 | 0.6 | 0.0 | 0.0 | 0.0 | 0.0 | 0.0 | 0.0 |
| Total value (billions of dollars)[a] | | 40.9 | | 44.4 | | 11.9 | | 2.1 |
| **Manufactures excluding textiles and apparel** | | | | | | | | |
| 10 to less than 15 percent | 1.5 | 1.5 | 6.4 | 1.0 | 1.0 | 0.6 | 3.6 | 2.1 |
| 15 to less than 20 percent | 0.2 | 0.2 | 1.3 | 0.5 | 0.2 | 0.3 | 3.2 | 0.9 |
| 20 to less than 25 percent | 0.2 | 0.0 | 0.0 | 0.1 | 0.6 | 0.2 | 0.1 | 0.2 |
| 25 percent and above | 0.2 | 1.7 | 0.0 | 0.1 | 1.1 | 0.4 | 0.9 | 0.1 |
| Total value (billions of dollars)[a] | | 229.2 | | 272.3 | | 69.6 | | 15.8 |

%C = percent of categories
%V = percent of value of imports from developing countries

a. Including categories with tariff below 10 percent.

*Source:* Calculated from OECD (2000).

3.4 percent for manufactures excluding textiles and apparel (table 3.5). The same comparison shows 20.2 versus 3.5 percent for the European Union; 9.7 versus 1.5 percent for Japan; and 21.1 versus 3.3 percent for Canada (tables 3.2 and 3.5). This suggests that within manufactures, peak tariffs in industrial countries are a problem for developing countries primarily in textiles and apparel and to a far lesser extent in other goods.

In addition to high tariffs in textiles and apparel, for decades developing countries have faced quota restrictions under the Multi-Fiber Arrangement (MFA) and its precursors. A major breakthrough of the Uruguay Round of multilateral trade negotiations was to set a timetable for the elimination of these quotas by 2005. Because most industrial countries have "backloaded" the phaseouts, however, there are grounds for concern that in 2005 there will be numerous instances in which industrial countries impose safeguards or other contingent protection as a replacement for the remaining quotas.

It is significant, nonetheless, that the protective impact of quota regimes appears already to have been on a declining path during the past two

**Table 3.6   Export-tax equivalent of textile and apparel quotas under the Multi-Fiber Arrangement** (percent)

| | United States | | European Union | |
|---|---|---|---|---|
| Period | Textiles | Apparel | Textiles | Apparel |
| Mid-1980s | 12.4 | 26.5 | 17.2 | 22.8 |
| 1998–99 | 9.1 | 11.4 | 5.1 | 5.2 |

*Source:* Calculated from Gelhar et al. (1997) and François and Spinanger (2002).

decades. Studies estimating tariff-equivalents of quotas have been based in part on quota "rents" as measured by the price of quotas available for purchase, especially in Hong Kong. The Global Trade Analysis Project (GTAP) has reported estimated export tax equivalents (ETEs) for textile and apparel quotas in several successive databases. Estimates for the mid-1980s were reported in GTAP2 (Gelhar et al. 1997, 95). Updated estimates for 1998–99 are incorporated in GTAP5 (François and Spinanger 2002). Table 3.6 presents aggregated tariff equivalents from these sources for the United States and the European Union, calculated by weighting the supplier-specific GTAP estimates of ETEs by the corresponding country shares in US and EU imports of textiles and apparel.[13]

The combined effect of tariff and quota protection was extremely protective in the mid-1980s, but had fallen substantially by the late 1990s despite the back-end loading of the MFA phaseout. The total tariff-equivalent is the chained effect of the tariff and the tariff-equivalent of the quotas.[14] For the United States, in the mid-1980s with a tariff of 22.5 percent (table 3.4) and quota tariff equivalent of 26.5 percent (table 3.6), total protection amounted to 55 percent for apparel. This combined protection had fallen to 27 percent by 1998. In principle, by 2005 with the elimination of MFA quotas, protection should be down to the bound post–Uruguay Round tariff rates, or only about 11.5 percent for both the United States and the European Union (table 3.4).

The IMF and World Bank (2002) have arrived at estimates similar to those in table 3.6 using the GTAP5 database, and they further report that the ranges of the ETEs are large (e.g., 0–34 percent for US imports of apparel). The IMF–World Bank study also reports Japan's quota tariff equivalents at zero, and those of Canada at 7.8 percent for textiles and 16.8

---

13. For the United States, weights for imports from each of the GTAP countries and regions are obtained from USITC (2002) for 1989 and 2001 for the two respective periods (SITC 65 and 84). For the European Union, import weights are from partner exports as reported in World Bank (2002c), for 1985, and from WTO (2001, 146, 153) for 2000.

14. That is, $z = (1 + t)(1 + \tau) - 1$, where $z$ is the total tariff equivalent, $t$ is the tariff, and $\tau$ is the tariff equivalent (or ETE) of the quota, all expressed as fractions.

percent for apparel. The zero estimate for Japan reflects the fact that Japan traditionally did not apply MFA quotas (see, e.g., Cline 1990, 137) but instead pursued tax incentives and financial support for sectoral restructuring as it shifted from being the prime exporter of textiles and apparel in the 1950s and 1960s to facing rising import competition from developing countries by the 1970s and after.

The Agreement on Textiles and Clothing of the Uruguay Round provided for quota elimination over 10 years beginning in 1995. In the first phase (1995 through the end of 1997), 16 percent of the 1990 volume of imports was to be "integrated" into nonquota treatment consistent with other GATT (now World Trade Organization, or WTO) products. In the second phase, by the end of 2001 an additional 17 percent was to be integrated. During the third phase, another 18 percent was to be integrated, after which, at the beginning of 2005, all remaining products (a maximum of 49 percent of the 1990 base) are to be integrated. Quotas were also to rise at specified rates—which, although providing additional interim liberalization, also meant that the fraction of actual total quota volume "integrated" was increasingly less than implied by the 17 and 18 percent targets for the first two phases, because these applied to the base period volumes. As a result, by the end of 2001 the United States and the European Union had removed quotas on products amounting to only about 20 percent of textile and apparel import volume (IMF and World Bank 2002, 42).

As is shown in chapter 1, moreover, textiles and apparel are key sectors for addressing global poverty. The measure of the "poverty intensity of imports" developed in chapter 1 places textiles and apparel relatively high, with both sectors at about 47 percent on the headcount basis and 12 percent on the income-share basis (compared with 40 percent and 8.6 percent respectively for all imports from developing countries). In import value, apparel ranks second (surpassed only by oil) and textiles ranks eleventh among the top two-dozen sectors, with total US imports in 2001 of $50 billion and $8.7 billion respectively from developing-country suppliers.

On the basis of simulations using the GTAP model, IMF staff have estimated that the removal of industrial-country tariffs and MFA quotas from textiles and apparel would increase developing-country exports by $39.8 billion annually, and increase developing-country income by $23.8 billion (IMF and World Bank 2002, 44). The income gain is concentrated almost entirely ($22.2 billion) in tariff removal, implying that the modeling treats almost all quota rents as already accruing to developing-country firms and governments. In contrast, industrial countries would enjoy $14 billion annually in consumer income gains from quota removal, which would be partially offset by an income loss of $3 billion from tariff elimination (which the IMF authors attribute to terms-of-trade loss).

The simple partial equilibrium calculation of potential for increased exports from tariff elimination, set forth above for all manufactures, can also be applied to textile and apparel tariffs. Using the post–Uruguay Round tariffs reported in tables 3.4 and 3.5, the simple partial equilibrium approach using a demand elasticity of 3.0 (absolute value) yields an estimated $4.5 billion increase in Quad imports of textile fabric and $30.2 billion increase in imports of apparel from developing countries as a consequence of tariff elimination, compared with the 1998 import bases of $20.4 billion and $99.3 billion respectively (OECD 2000).[15] The increase in annual imports of textiles and apparel amounts to $13.8 billion for the United States, $16.6 billion for the European Union, $3.2 billion for Japan, and $1.2 billion for Canada. These four (the Quad) account for 89 percent of total industrial-country imports from developing countries, suggesting a corresponding total of $39.1 billion in tariff removal impact for all industrial countries for the two sectors. Textiles and apparel would thus account for about 55 percent of total developing-country gains in exports of manufactures from the removal of tariff protection in industrial countries.

This simple partial equilibrium estimate is virtually the same as the general equilibrium estimate by the IMF–World Bank team. The implication is that feedback effects (especially from a less than infinitely elastic export supply) in the general equilibrium estimates serve to damp the trade impact estimates by approximately enough to offset other factors that would yield a higher estimate (inclusion of the impact of quota removal and expansion to 2005 scale, in the IMF–World Bank calculations).

In short, textiles and apparel constitute the most important manufacturing sectors in which developing countries still stand to reap large gains from further liberalization of industrial-country protection, even after full Uruguay Round tariff cut implementation. These sectors are also important in terms of relevance to production by countries with a relatively high incidence of poverty. It follows that the actual achievement of the Uruguay Round's pledge of full elimination of MFA quotas by 2005, and avoidance of their widespread replacement by safeguards and other contingent protection, will be essential if industrial-country trade policy is to provide a major opportunity for reducing global poverty in the area of manufactured goods. It also follows that a major reduction in tariff protection for textiles and apparel will also be a key goal in the Doha Round, in addition to the effective implementation of the promised removal of MFA quotas.

## Industrial-Country Protection in Agriculture

The GTAP5 database provides estimates of post–Uruguay Round MFN bound-tariff protection against agricultural goods (Dimaranan and McDougall 2002, 4-1 to 4-6). These tariffs, which include the ad valorem

---

15. A slightly higher import price elasticity is warranted for textiles and apparel than for manufactures on average, because the two sectors tend to have above-average elasticities of substitution (domestic-import) in the CGE models that apply differing elasticities across sectors.

**Table 3.7 Agricultural tariff rates** (percent)

| Sector[a] | | Weight[b] | United States | Canada | European Union | Japan |
|---|---|---|---|---|---|---|
| 1 | pdr | 2.94 | 4.9 | 0.0 | 64.9 | 409.0 |
| 2 | wht | 2.01 | 2.6 | 62.7 | 61.4 | 249.2 |
| 3 | gro | 2.76 | 0.6 | 8.9 | 38.6 | 20.2 |
| 4 | v_f | 8.63 | 4.7 | 1.9 | 14.5 | 44.9 |
| 5 | osd | 1.85 | 17.7 | 0.0 | 0 | 76.4 |
| 6 | c_b | 0.95 | 0.7 | 0.0 | 251.4 | 0.0 |
| 7 | pfb | 0.93 | 9.7 | 0.0 | 0 | 0.0 |
| 8 | ocr | 3.14 | 21.5 | 2.4 | 3.1 | 22.1 |
| 9 | ctl | 4.03 | 1.1 | 0.2 | 36.6 | 149.1 |
| 10 | oap | 5.71 | 0.6 | 19.8 | 6.7 | 5.0 |
| 11 | rmk | 3.96 | 0.0 | 0.0 | 0 | 0.0 |
| 12 | wol | 0.45 | 0.9 | 2.3 | 0 | 54.7 |
| 13 | for | 2.53 | 0.8 | 0.7 | 0.4 | 0.2 |
| 14 | fsh | 2.80 | 0.6 | 0.4 | 9 | 4.9 |
| 19 | cmt | 4.83 | 5.3 | 16.3 | 88.9 | 36.4 |
| 20 | omt | 5.40 | 3.6 | 72.4 | 30.9 | 58.2 |
| 21 | vol | 3.17 | 4.3 | 8.6 | 11.4 | 6.6 |
| 22 | mil | 5.61 | 42.5 | 214.8 | 87.7 | 287.0 |
| 23 | pcr | 3.05 | 5.3 | 0.7 | 87.4 | 409.0 |
| 24 | sgr | 1.93 | 53.4 | 4.9 | 76.4 | 116.1 |
| 25 | ofd | 21.73 | 11.4 | 14.1 | 28.8 | 38.3 |
| 26 | b_t | 11.59 | 3.0 | 62.5 | 8.3 | 16.2 |
| **Total** | | **100.00** | **8.8** | **30.4** | **32.6** | **76.4** |

a. See table 4A.3 for sector definitions.
b. Weighted by the GTAP estimates of world output value for the corresponding products.

*Source:* GTAP5 database.

equivalents of specific tariffs, are reported in table 3.7. Where there are tariff-rate quotas, as a consequence of the Uruguay Round's conversion of quotas into tariff-rate quotas, the rates reported are the average between the in-quota and over-quota tariff rates (Gibson, Wainio, and Whitley 2002). The resulting estimated tariffs range as high as 409 percent for the protection of rice in Japan. When the protection rates are weighted by the GTAP estimates of world output value for the corresponding products (Gibson, Wainio, and Whitley 2002, 3-4, 3-5; MacLaren 1997, 214), the resulting weighted average tariff rates are 8.8 percent for the United States, 30.4 percent for Canada, 32.6 percent for the European Union, and 76.4 percent for Japan (table 3.7).[16]

In addition to tariffs, farm subsidies contribute substantially to agricultural protection. In the Uruguay Round, the amounts of these that were considered to have trade-distortive effects were summarized as the "Aggregate Measure of Support" (AMS). Under the Uruguay Round Agree-

---

16. The estimates here are lower than those in Cline (2002b) because of the availability of more detailed sectoral world output data than those used in the earlier estimates (from MacLaren 1997, 214).

ment on Agriculture (URAA), AMS levels were bound and countries committed to reducing these levels over time. These "amber box" subsidies were considered trade distorting.[17] The URAA committed industrial countries to reduce amber box subsidies by 20 percent over 6 years, and developing countries were to reduce theirs by 13 percent over 10 years (WTO 2002, 59).

As of 1998 (or closest year with AMS reported), the actual levels of the AMS were $6.2 billion for the United States, €51 billion for the European Union, ¥3.17 trillion for Japan, A$132 million for Australia, C$619 million for Canada, Kr10.9 billion for Norway, and SF3.3 billion for Switzerland (WTO 2002, 58). For the United States, a more meaningful AMS is the bound level ($20.7 billion). The reason is that new legislation in 2002 effectively set US agricultural subsidies at this level over the next decade. At 1998 exchange rates, and in light of the share of agriculture in GDP (2 percent for Canada, the United States, and Japan; and 2.3 percent for the European Union; WTO 2002, 296–97), the AMS subsidies (bound for the United States, actual for the others) amount to 2.3 percent of agricultural value added for Canada, 9.8 percent of agricultural production for the United States, 26.4 percent for the European Union, and 30.7 percent for Japan.

Some have argued that the WTO's AMS understates trade-distorting subsidies. De Gorter, Ingco, and Ignacio (2003) suggest that at least parts of the "blue box" permissible subsidies that are decoupled from production are in fact implemented in ways that stimulate output. They cite EU payments based on past acreage that are recalculated and prorated in proportion to the year's actual area planted, when the actual regional aggregate level exceeds the base level. Nevertheless, even if all blue box subsidies were added in, the AMS would not rise sharply. Thus, in 1999 the total OECD amber box subsidies were $80 billion and total blue box subsidies an additional $24 billion (de Gorter, Ingco, and Ignacio 2003, 3).[18] Considering that only some fraction of blue box subsidies would be appropriate to incorporate, the AMS measure would appear to capture the great bulk of production distorting subsidies.

The OECD provides an alternative source of subsidy estimates. Unfortunately, most reports of these estimates tend to use a total that intermixes subsidies with tariffs and tariff-rate quota effects. The OECD calculates a

---

17. The WTO treatment of agricultural subsidies has classified domestic farm support programs in categories with varying degrees of acceptability. In the main "amber box" are trade-distorting measures, e.g., production-linked subsidies and farm price support programs. The Uruguay Round adopted commitments to phase these down over time. In contrast, subsidies in a "green box," e.g., research and other support unlinked to production, are not subject to reduction commitments. Neither are certain subsidies in a "blue box" that are not gauged to current production, e.g., acreage set-asides.

18. The largest amount for the latter was the EU's $20 billion, compared with its amber box total of $50 billion.

Producer Support Estimate (PSE), which in 2002–02 averaged $234.7 billion annually (de Gorter, Ingco, and Ignacio 2003, 2). However, 63 percent of the PSE was from "border measures," for example, tariffs and tariff-rate quotas. The other 37 percent, or $87 billion, was approximately the same as the AMS used here to capture subsidies as such. For the purposes of this study, the tariff and tariff-rate quota estimates from the GTAP5 database provide a more useful basis for analyzing protection, because they make it possible to separate out the distinct influences of subsidies on the one hand and tariffs and tariff-rate quotas on the other. In this approach, it would be double counting to consider both the tariff data and additional "subsidies" calculated from the PSE rather than AMS data.

The potential confusion between production subsidies and the OECD's support estimates is even greater when the OECD measure of Total Support Estimate (TSE) is used. The TSE adds in the amount of government spending on "general services provided to agriculture," such as research and development expenditures. The TSE concept is the basis for the $350 billion figure commonly reported in the press as the magnitude of agricultural subsidies in industrial countries.[19]

The failure of much of the policy debate to distinguish between production-distorting farm subsidies on the one hand and tariffs and tariff-rate quotas on the other is potentially counterproductive in terms of its impact on the negotiating strategy of developing countries in the Doha Round. Thus far, a disproportionate amount of their attention seems to have been focused on reducing industrial-country subsidies for agriculture. To the extent that this is an accurate portrayal, the implication is that they are focusing on the wrong problem: Their efforts should go more heavily toward reducing tariffs and tariff-rate quotas and toward increasing the volume thresholds at which the latter apply. A shift in this direction—especially if linked to a new emphasis on decoupling farm subsidies from production rather than eliminating them altogether—could provide a way forward after the breakdown in the Cancún ministerial meeting of Doha Round negotiations in September 2003, which occurred largely over the entrenched EU position on subsidies (albeit with the new "Singapore issues"—investment, competition, services, and trade facilitation—as the trigger for the breakdown).

Returning to the estimates of this chapter, in order to determine total agricultural protection, it is necessary to measure the combined effects of tariffs and subsidies. Appendix 3B sets forth a methodology for obtaining the tariff equivalent of the agricultural subsidy as a function of the subsidy rate and the ratio of domestic output to imports. The key elements of this estimate are the amount of the output-distorting subsidies ($S$), the amount of domestic agricultural output valued at world prices ($Q_d$), the

---

19. The average of TSE for all OECD countries in 2000–02 was $315 billion (de Gorter, Ingco, and Ignacio 2003, 2).

## Table 3.8  Tariff equivalent of agricultural subsidies
(billions of dollars, percent and ratios)

| Category | United States | Canada | European Union | Japan |
|---|---|---|---|---|
| Gross agricultural output, 2002 ($V_d$) | 221.8 | 25.4 | 277.6 | 80.8 |
| Average tariff (percent) | 8.8 | 30.4 | 32.6 | 76.4 |
| Agricultural output at world prices ($Q_d$) | 203.9 | 19.5 | 209.4 | 45.8 |
| Output-distorting subsidies ($S$): | | | | |
|   OECD (2000–02 average) | 19.9 | 1.65 | 36.2 | 4.4 |
| Subsidy rate ($S/V_d$) (percent) | 9.0 | 6.5 | 13.0 | 5.4 |
| Imports ($M$) | 41.9 | 12.4 | 75.5 | 34.5 |
| Exports ($X$) | 57.0 | 17.4 | 70.6 | 2.4 |
| Output/imports ratio ($\lambda = Q_d/M$) | 4.87 | 1.57 | 2.8 | 1.3 |
| Import share ($\phi_m$) | 0.22 | 0.86 | 0.35 | 0.44 |
| Import price elasticity ($\beta$) | 2.80 | 0.52 | 2.33 | 2.01 |
| Tariff equivalent of subsidy ($\tau$) (percent) | 10.2 | 16.8 | 10.4 | 3.2 |

*Sources:* OECD (2003a, 2003e); WTO (2002); table 3.7.

ratio of domestic output at world prices to agricultural imports ($\lambda = Q_d/M$), and the price elasticity of demand for imports ($\beta$).

Table 3.8 reports estimates of these and other components of the calculation of the tariff equivalent of agricultural subsidies for each of the Quad countries, using the most recent data available. The table uses the closest concept for output-distorting components of the OECD's producer support subsidy estimate (average, 2000–02) as the central estimate for the amount of subsidies.[20] These OECD-based estimates turn out to be very close to the "bound" AMS figure for the United States, somewhat higher than the "actual" AMS figure for Canada, somewhat lower for the European Union, and sharply lower for Japan. Double counting tariff effects in some components of the AMS leads to a major overstatement in the WTO estimates for Japan.[21]

The price elasticity of demand for imports is needed to calculate the tariff equivalent of subsidies. As indicated in appendix 3B, when the price elasticity is high, a given subsidy rate tends to translate into a lower tariff equivalent, because the greater responsiveness of imports to price means that it takes a lower tariff to obtain the same cutback in imports.

---

20. The OECD subsidy components included are payments based on output, area planted/animal numbers, input use, overall farm income, and "countercyclical" payments (OECD 2003a, 234–78).

21. The AMS figure for Japan for 1998 is $25.8 billion, far above the OECD estimate of $4.4 billion. The AMS includes an imputed component for domestic price supports, even when the government does not make actual purchases from farmers. As a result, when tariff protection is high (as in the Japanese case) and the domestic price support program is redundant, the AMS overstates "subsidies." (I am indebted to David Orden for this point.)

The estimate of this elasticity in table 3.8 is again based on the its relationship to the elasticity of substitution between domestic goods and imports, and the share of imports in domestic use, as identified above. The average substitution elasticity for agricultural goods is 3.6 in the GTAP, World Bank Global Economic Prospects, and Harrison-Rutherford-Tarr (1996, 1997a) models. The varying import price elasticities in table 3.8 arise from the application of the varying import shares to this substitution elasticity.[22]

Using the OECD-based subsidy estimates and the method set forth in appendix 3B, and assuming that the elasticity of domestic supply is unity, the production-oriented subsidies translate into tariff equivalents of 10 percent for both the United States and the European Union, a surprisingly high 16 percent for Canada, and a low 3 percent for Japan. The low figure for Japan reflects its heavy reliance on extremely high tariff protection rather than subsidy payments to farmers as its means of agricultural protection. An equal level of the tariff equivalent for the United States and the European Union, despite the higher subsidy rate in the European Union, reflects the much higher ratio of domestic output to imports in the United States, and hence the larger impact of the boost to production relative to imports (implying a higher tariff to accomplish an equivalent import-suppressing outcome). Canada's tariff equivalent turns out to be more than twice its simple subsidy rate. This result is driven by the low price elasticity of imports, which at less than unity balloons the tariff-equivalent estimate, whereas for the other countries the price elasticity is 2 or higher and damps the tariff equivalent estimate.

The results for the tariff equivalent of subsidies are somewhat counterintuitive, for they conclude that in terms of the protective effect against imports, US agricultural subsidies are just as high as those in the European Union, and the tariff equivalents are higher for both than for Japan. This finding would not be obvious from the well-known US comparative advantage in agriculture. Nonetheless, as shown in table 3.9, when the subsidy tariff equivalents are chained to the tariff rates, for three of the four Quad countries the resulting overall protection shows the expected progression as related to comparative advantage, rising from about 20 percent in the United States to 46 percent in the European Union and a high of 82 percent in Japan. In contrast, Canada has relatively high total agricultural protection (52 percent tariff equivalent) even though its agricultural comparative advantage is much closer to that of the United States than the European Union.

---

22. Note that at the country level, imports no longer equal exports, so it is necessary to calculate domestic use as "apparent consumption": output (at world prices) plus imports minus exports, as the base for calculating the import share. The result is counterintuitive for Canada, which turns out to have a high import share even though it is a major agricultural exporter. This reflects large two-way trade, with imports about two-thirds as large as exports.

**Table 3.9  Overall protection in agriculture**
(percent tariff equivalent)

| Type of protection | United States | Canada | European Union | Japan |
|---|---|---|---|---|
| Tariffs | 8.8 | 30.4 | 32.6 | 76.4 |
| Subsidies | 10.2 | 16.8 | 10.4 | 3.2 |
| Total | 19.9 | 52.3 | 46.4 | 82.1 |

*Source:* See text.

Table 3.9 also shows that for Canada, the European Union, and Japan, the protective effect of tariffs exceeds that of domestic subsidies. Only the United States, which has relatively low agricultural tariffs, has greater protection from subsidies than from tariffs. This finding confirms the diagnosis that much of the public debate on agricultural protection has tended to overemphasize subsidies and give insufficient attention to tariffs.[23]

A common argument concerning EU agricultural protection is that preferential access sharply reduces the average tariff. Gallezot (2002, 6, 9) provides data that can serve as a basis for examining this question. For MFN agricultural tariffs, including the ad valorem equivalent of specific tariffs but excluding above-quota tariff-rate-quota tariffs, he estimates a simple average rate of 20.7 percent in 2000, down from 26.1 percent in 1997. He estimates that in 2000, the European Union had total agricultural imports of €51.6 billion. Of the total, 22.7 percent was from countries with no preferential status, and hence presumably at an average tariff of 20.7 percent. Another 44.8 percent was from Generalized System of Preferences countries at an after-preference average tariff of 17.9 percent. A further 12.6 percent was from the 70 LDCs in Africa, the Caribbean, and the Pacific at an after-preference average tariff of 5.3 percent. A final 20.3 percent was from other preferential partners, primarily in Eastern Europe, at an average after-preference tariff of only 2.7 percent. It is straightforward to calculate that the resulting weighted average tariff, after taking account of preferences, was 13.9 percent.[24] On this basis, preferences might be said to reduce otherwise-applicable EU agricultural tariffs by an average of one-third (i.e., 1 − 13.9/20.7). Even this reduction is larger than would be associated with the developing countries usually cited in regard to prefer-

23. Another study stressing tariffs is Hoekman, Ng, and Olarreaga (2002b). Using a partial equilibrium framework, they find that "the positive welfare effect of reducing [agricultural] tariffs . . . is a multiple of what can be achieved from an equivalent percentage cut in domestic support only . . . [reflecting] not only . . . the high tariff peaks in OECD countries, but the fact that developing countries use tariffs to protect domestic production" (p. 18).

24. The author himself instead places the after-preference average at only 10.5 percent. However, this estimate is based on actual tariff revenue, which is usually considered to give a downward bias in comparison with an average of applicable tariffs.

ences, such as the LDCs, and is heavily driven instead by preferential access for relatively developed trading partners in Eastern Europe.

This preference-adjusted EU tariff is an understatement, moreover, because it apparently does not include the effect of above-quota tariff-rate quotas, and it is a simple average rather than one using world production rates. One way to incorporate the preference information into a more complete estimate of tariff protection is to start from the GTAP5 tariff average of 32.6 percent (table 3.9) and adjust it downward by one-third, assuming the proportionate reduction from overall preferences inferred from Gallezot's (2002) data. This approach would yield an EU agricultural tariff average of 21.8 percent after taking account of preferences. The corresponding total agricultural protection for the European Union, including the effect of subsidies, would be a 34.5 percent tariff equivalent rather than the table 3.8 estimate of 46 percent. On this basis, it can be said that adjusting for preferential entry does not sharply reduce overall agricultural protection for the European Union, and leaves total EU agricultural protection still about 14 percentage points higher than that in the United States.

For the European Union as well as other countries, moreover, the use of simple or trade-weighted tariff averages in agriculture may substantially tend to understate the protective effect by not specifically taking account of tariff dispersion. Peak tariffs tend to be higher in agriculture than in other sectors. Martin, van der Mensbrugghe, and Manole (2003) develop an approach converting the information from detailed tariffs (hence capturing dispersion) into an overall average, in the spirit of the trade restrictiveness index proposed by Anderson and Neary (1996). Essentially, the approach takes into account the fact that the welfare triangles from tariff distortion rise with the square of the tariff rather than linearly. Martin and his colleagues calculate that the European Union, whose average agricultural tariff is usually estimated at about 35 percent, has an average tariff that is equivalent to about 46 percent when dispersion is taken into account. On this basis, it might be said that the EU agricultural tariff in table 3.9 is understated rather than overstated (although presumably the same technique would boost the averages for the other countries as well).

Returning to the main estimates of table 3.9, it is again useful to use a partial equilibrium back-of-the-envelope approach as an initial gauge of the protective effect. Using 1998 trade data, the value of agricultural imports (HTS chapters 01–24) from developing countries amounted to $2.46 billion for Canada, $52.21 billion for the European Union, $20.84 billion for Japan, and $12.77 billion for the United States (calculated from OECD 2000). Applying the import price elasticities reported in table 3.8 to these import-base values, the following rough magnitudes may be estimated for the change in imports from developing countries as a consequence of removal of all agricultural tariffs, tariff-rate quotas, and domestic farm subsidies: Canada, $0.84 billion; United States, $2.2 billion; European Union,

$16.6 billion; and Japan, $9.4 billion—for a total of $29 billion annually for the Quad.[25]

IMF staff simulations using the GTAP model arrive at estimates on the same order of magnitude (IMF and World Bank 2002, 33). OECD agricultural distortions as of 1997 (including tariffs) are calculated to cause a loss in export revenue of $22.8 billion annually for non-OECD countries.[26] Presumably the figure would be somewhat higher if the six middle-income developing countries in the OECD (Czech Republic, Hungary, South Korea, Mexico, Poland, and Turkey) were added, because except for the Czech Republic and Korea these economies tend to be net exporters of agricultural goods. Another reason the IMF simulation estimates may be smaller than the back-of-the-envelope calculation here is that they incorporate a noninfinite elasticity of supply. The corresponding income loss calculated by the IMF staff is $8.7 billion annually.[27] As reviewed below, however, alternative CGE model estimates for this concept (static annual welfare loss by developing countries from industrial-country agricultural protection and subsidies) range as high as $31 billion annually, in the World Bank's Global Economic Prospects model at 1997 prices but 2015 economic scale, corresponding to about $17 billion at 1997 prices and 1997 economic scale.[28] The CGE model applied in chapter 4 of the present study arrives at estimates closer to the upper end of this range.

In contrast, much of the public debate often crystallizes around a much larger figure based on the OECD's TSE for farm support, discussed above. Typically on the order of $350 billion annually (OECD 2002a), this figure for support is often cited in a context of calls for liberalizing agricultural trade to provide greater opportunities for developing countries.[29] As a result, the informed public could be forgiven for drawing the mistaken conclusion that agricultural protection in industrial countries somehow costs developing countries something like $350 billion annually. Instead, the

25. The estimate is again of the form $\Delta M = zM_0$, where $\Delta M$ is the increase in imports, $z = e[\Delta t/(1 + t)]$, and $e$ is the price elasticity of demand.

26. Because the six developing-country members of the OECD have agricultural exports to the OECD that are almost equal to their imports from the OECD ($15.5 billion and $16.5 billion respectively in 1998; OECD 2000), shifting them to the "non-OECD" grouping would make little difference to the IMF simulation.

27. The IMF calculations also show that both the OECD and the non-OECD experience the greatest losses from their own import restrictions rather than those imposed on their exports by the other grouping.

28. This is calculated by multiplying the absolute IMF–World Bank results by the ratio of the World Bank percentage of GDP results to those from the IMF–World Bank study (table 3.12 below).

29. Thus, in his speech to the 2002 Annual Meeting, World Bank president James D. Wolfensohn remarked, "We know that agricultural subsidies in rich countries, at $1 billion per day, squander resources and profoundly damage opportunities for poor countries to invest in their own development" (Wolfensohn 2002).

great bulk of the cost is imposed on the industrial-country consumers and taxpayers themselves.[30] As indicated in chapter 4, the annual static welfare costs to developing countries resulting from agricultural protection (including their own) as estimated in the CGE model of the present study are about $45 billion, or only about one-eighth as large as the frequently cited $350 billion figure. Even so, these agricultural protection costs are high, and they are much higher if dynamic effects are taken into account.

Finally, an important dimension of the impact of agricultural protection is the question of whether developing countries suffer mainly from industrial-country protection of agriculture or, instead, mainly from their own protection. Some estimates (including those summarized in table 3.14) suggest that developing countries experience far greater welfare losses from their own agricultural protection and that of other developing countries than they do from industrial-country protection of agriculture. In a negotiating context, this point has been used to criticize the position of those developing countries that insist on reductions in industrial-country agricultural subsidies and protection but seek to avoid a reduction of their own agricultural protection on the grounds of "special and differential treatment." This issue will be examined in greater detail in chapter 4, where runs of the CGE model are implemented to shed additional light on this question. For the purposes of this chapter, however, it can simply be said that the estimates of total agricultural protection by industrial countries shown in table 3.9 suggest that this protection is extremely high, and that the potential benefits for developing countries from its reduction should be neither downplayed (e.g., by shifting attention to developing-country protection) nor exaggerated (e.g., by loose use of the $350 billion TSE figure as implicitly a direct cost to developing countries).

## Aggregate Protection Against Developing Countries

The sectoral estimates of protection for textiles and apparel, other manufactures, and agriculture discussed above, and corresponding weighted average tariffs for oil and other nonagricultural raw materials, are combined in table 3.10 to obtain an Aggregate Measure of Protection (AMP) against developing countries for each of the four large industrial-country importers (i.e., the Quad). The adjusted-import-weighting method set forth in appendix 3A is applied for this purpose. All tariff rates are post–Uruguay Round bound levels; import shares are for 1998 (calculated from OECD 2000). The textile and apparel rates exclude the protective ef-

---

30. For 2001, the OECD places the estimate of TSE at $311 billion. This derives from $164 billion in transfers from consumers and $170 billion transfers from taxpayers, with a modest offset of $23 billion in budget revenue (OECD 2002a, 40).

# Table 3.10 Aggregate Measure of Protection against developing countries (tariff equivalent, percent)

| Sector | United States | European Union | Japan | Canada |
|---|---|---|---|---|
| **I. Import-weighted average tariff** | | | | |
| Manufactures, excluding textiles and apparel | 2.10 | 3.20 | 1.49 | 3.48 |
| Textiles and apparel | 10.87 | 11.62 | 9.20 | 16.45 |
| Agriculture | 19.92 | 46.37 | 82.05 | 52.26 |
| Oil, other | 0.92 | 0.58 | 0.29 | 0.93 |
| **II. Import shares** | | | | |
| Manufactures, excluding textiles and apparel | 0.699 | 0.618 | 0.480 | 0.680 |
| Textiles and apparel | 0.145 | 0.119 | 0.097 | 0.120 |
| Agriculture | 0.039 | 0.117 | 0.144 | 0.106 |
| Oil, other | 0.117 | 0.145 | 0.279 | 0.094 |
| **III. Adjusted-import share weights** | | | | |
| Manufactures, excluding textiles and apparel | 0.694 | 0.607 | 0.465 | 0.666 |
| Textiles and apparel | 0.149 | 0.121 | 0.097 | 0.124 |
| Agriculture | 0.041 | 0.131 | 0.169 | 0.119 |
| Oil, other | 0.116 | 0.141 | 0.269 | 0.091 |
| **IV. Aggregate Measure of Protection** | | | | |
| Import weighted | 3.93 | 8.00 | 13.48 | 9.96 |
| Adjusted-import weighted | 4.01 | 9.53 | 15.55 | 10.68 |
| *Memorandum:* excluding oil, other: | | | | |
| Import-weighted | 4.33 | 10.31 | 18.59 | 10.89 |
| Adjusted-import-weighted | 4.42 | 10.99 | 21.16 | 11.65 |

*Source:* Author's calculations.

fect of MFA quotas, because the estimates are for complete post–Uruguay Round protection and hence assume the full removal of quotas by 2005. Agricultural estimates include the tariff equivalent of subsidies, as discussed above.

The AMP estimates show substantial differences in the level of overall protection against developing countries, among the four big industrial-country areas. This is in contrast to the relatively homogenous industrial-country protection levels against developing countries in manufactures, including textiles and apparel. The differences are driven by the large differences in the summary protection measure for agriculture. Thus, because the EU agricultural protection measure is at a relatively high 46 percent tariff equivalent, whereas the US level is considerably lower at 20 percent, the overall AMP for the European Union stands at 10 percent, more than twice as high as the US 4 percent, even though the two areas' manufacturing protection levels are comparable at about 11 percent for textiles and apparel and 2 to 3 percent for other manufactures. The even higher Japanese protection in agriculture (82 percent) similarly places its overall AMP at an even more restrictive 16 percent.[31]

Even though the AMP measures show substantial overall protection, for some purposes they are underestimated by including oil. All industrial countries impose minimal tariffs (below 1 percent) on oil, and this low protection of oil has little to do with a forthcoming approach to openness of markets to goods from industrial countries more generally. Japan in particular is more heavily dependent on oil imports, so inclusion of oil tends to reduce the AMP disproportionately for Japan. As shown in table 3.10, if the sector of oil and other nonagricultural raw materials is excluded, the AMPs rise by about 1 percentage point each for the European Union and Canada but by about 5 percentage points for Japan.

## The Impact of Industrial-Country Agricultural Trade Liberalization on Global Poverty

The high level of protection in agriculture is only one reason the sector deserves special attention. The other reason is that agriculture is unique in two important dimensions for analyzing the impact of its liberalization on poverty. First, because a large share of the global poor are in the rural sector, their incomes are likely to be closely related to world agricultural prices, which are artificially held down by the existing structure of international protection and subsidies. Second, food comprises a large share of the consumption budget of the poor, and induced real income losses from higher food prices must be carefully considered in drawing a balance on the overall impact of liberalization on global poverty.

Appendix 3C below sets forth a simple quasi-accounting model of this impact. It turns out, under simplifying assumptions, that a good approximation of the condition for industrial-country agricultural liberalization to reduce rather than increase global poverty incidence is that the share of food in the consumption basket of the poor be smaller than the fraction of the poor located in the agricultural sector. This result is for static welfare effects. If dynamic gains are added, there can be net gains for the poor even if somewhat more of them than this fraction live in the urban sector, and under optimistic assumptions about dynamic effects there can even be net gains for the urban poor.

The driving force behind poverty reduction in the rural sector and increase in the urban sector is the rise in world food prices when industrial

31. The AMP estimates here are different from those in Cline (2002b) because: (1) this version uses a more standardized database (OECD 2000); (2) the estimates here exclude the tariff equivalent of quotas on textiles and apparel because these are to be eliminated after full implementation of Uruguay Round commitments; and (3) new sectoral weights place the weighted average agricultural tariff levels lower than before for, especially, the European Union and Japan (table 3.7).

countries eliminate agricultural subsidies and agricultural protection. Because this liberalization will result in lower agricultural production in industrial countries, and this reduction will be offset only partially by an induced rise in agricultural production in developing countries, world agricultural prices will rise. This increase will in turn cause upward pressure on food prices within the developing countries themselves. The rural poor will tend to gain, because the rise in agricultural prices will affect nearly the entirety of their income but boost their living costs only by the proportion associated with food costs in the consumption basket. The rise in food prices will cause a real income loss for the urban poor from the impact on food consumption cost. This static effect may or may not be offset by eventual gains from induced economywide dynamic effects.

Appendix table 3C.1 reports the central case results of applying the model. For the 72 countries with relevant data available, accounting for 2.53 billion persons in poverty ($2 per day, purchasing power parity definition), a rise of world agricultural prices by 10 percent as the consequence of agricultural trade liberalization would reduce the incidence of poverty by 201.5 million persons, or by about 8 percent. The 10 percent rise in world prices is based on existing trade model estimates (see appendix 3C). This net effect comprises a large net reduction in poverty in most countries (i.e., 56 countries, with a net reduction of 204.3 million persons), which would be slightly offset by a net rise in poverty in a smaller number of countries (16, with an aggregate net increase in poverty of 2.8 million).

The principal influence leading to this result is that the poor predominantly live in the rural areas.[32] For the 72 countries, the aggregate portion of poor living in rural areas amounts to 74.7 percent.[33] Latin America is an important exception, because in several key countries more poor people live in urban than rural areas. With only about 14 percent of the poor in the rural areas of Argentina and 18 percent in Chile's, poverty rises by about 5 percent in each case. In contrast, there is virtually no change in poverty for Brazil, where the 39 percent portion of the poor living in rural areas is almost identical to the share assumed for food costs in the consumption basket.

---

32. Note, however, that poverty incidence also falls in urban areas in a handful of countries (9 of 72) where one of two conditions occurs. Where the poor population is almost entirely in the rural area (e.g., Vietnam), the static gains base on which the dynamic gains are extrapolated is sufficiently large relative to the number of urban poor that the dynamic gains for the urban poor outweigh the direct losses from higher food costs. Alternatively, where the fraction of agricultural production exported is especially high (e.g., Costa Rica), the static gains base applicable for the dynamic gains extrapolation is also large, leading to the same result (see appendix 3C).

33. The unweighted average portion of the poor living in rural areas is 59 percent. For the key large-population economies, however, this share is considerably higher, ranging from about 70–72 percent for India, Indonesia, Nigeria, and Pakistan to 89 percent for China and 94 percent for Bangladesh (see appendix 3C).

These results do show considerable sensitivity to the parameter assumptions. Under the set of unfavorable assumptions, global agricultural liberalization actually increases world poverty slightly, by 0.5 percent (14 million people). In contrast, under the set of favorable assumptions, poverty reduction reaches an impressive 18.5 percent, accounting for a massive 471 million reduction in the number of poor persons.

Although these calculations provide reassurance that global agricultural liberalization would not be injurious to the world's poor even though foodstuffs are crucial to their consumption budgets, the impacts on the urban poor do give one pause. Thus, even though the aggregate impact is a global reduction in poverty of about 200 million persons, within each country the urban poor tend to lose. The aggregate increase of urban poverty amounts to 54 million, whereas the aggregate reduction in rural poverty reaches 255 million. The winners among the poor thus outnumber the losers from global agricultural liberalization by a factor of almost five to one. Even so, the prospect for increased urban poverty suggests that in at least some countries, such mechanisms as food stamps might be important in helping to cushion the effect on the urban poor.

Concern about adverse effects on the urban poor is even more relevant if one considers the recent outbreaks of famine in sub-Saharan Africa. From a global standpoint, there is something inconsistent in pursuing policies that raise agricultural prices as a way to help the global poor, on the one hand, and ignoring adverse effects on those already facing famine, on the other. This suggests the possible desirability of a "famine relief box" of permissible agricultural subsidies if they are linked in some appropriate way to donations of agricultural goods for famine relief. For example, each year the Food and Agriculture Organization could designate (and update quarterly) a list of low-income countries experiencing famine conditions. Subsidies for food exports to these countries could then be exempt from general commitments reducing or eliminating agricultural export subsidies.

A recognition of the broad divergence of the impacts on rural as compared with urban sectors also illuminates a crucial aspect of the poverty impact of agricultural liberalization: internal income redistribution. Because most of the effects in question come from "transfer rectangles" rather than "welfare triangles," a major part of the reduction in poverty arises from what amounts to a transfer from the urban population (including, or especially, the urban nonpoor) to the rural population domestically, rather than from industrial-country farmers to poor-country farmers. Thus, in the model developed in appendix 3C, even a country that has no agricultural exports or imports at all experiences a reduction in rural poverty as a consequence of the transfer of income from the urban sector associated with higher food prices, so long as there is a sympathetic rise in domestic agricultural prices when world agricultural prices rise.

Finally, it should be noted that the analysis here abstracts from changes in developing countries' own protection of agriculture. As discussed in chapter 4, however, protection tends to be relatively high in agriculture in developing as well as industrial countries. The average level of agricultural tariffs in industrial countries is high at 36 percent, but in developing countries the average is not far behind at 30 percent (table 4.4). Nonetheless, as discussed in the next section of this chapter, the bulk of the world's poor live in countries that are net agricultural exporters, or at least have a comparative advantage in agriculture. This suggests that the high levels of protection tend to be redundant, or that the tariffs contain "water." That is, the local cost of agricultural production is low enough to compete on world markets, and the tariff is not the binding influence determining the level of imports because domestic supply is available at world prices.[34]

Even so, the presence of significant agricultural protection in developing countries does suggest that the central estimate of 200 million poverty reduction from agricultural liberalization may tend to be an overstatement for a scenario of global agricultural liberalization in which both developing and industrial countries remove protection. That is, if developing countries' protection is not redundant, its removal would tend to reduce prices to farmers, offsetting the rise in world prices and potentially even turning the net income effect for farmers negative.

These considerations suggest that in multilateral trade negotiations, developing countries should be prompt to offer to remove any agricultural protection that in practice is redundant, in order to increase the willingness of industrial countries to remove their protection in a somewhat reciprocal manner, rather than relying on unilateral industrial-country liberalization. However, where developing countries (especially net agricultural importers) do have significant binding (as opposed to redundant) agricultural protection, then considerations of poverty impact would point toward partial rather than complete liberalization and implementation on a lengthier timetable than otherwise.

## Food Trade Balance and Poverty

A reasonable concern about global agricultural trade liberalization is that by pushing up prices of food, it could bring losses to poor countries that are net importers of foodstuffs. For this reason, it is of special interest to consider more closely whether poor countries tend on balance to be food importers.

---

34. One indication of redundancy is that applied agricultural tariffs in developing countries tend to be significantly lower than bound tariffs, whereas the two are much closer in industrial countries (WTO 2002, 51–52). In principle, the tariffs in the GTAP5 database (see table 4.4 in this study) are applied rather than bound tariffs, but in practice the bound levels are used in a number of cases for developing countries, especially in Africa (Rozanski, Kuwahara, and Amajadi 2002).

The GTAP database used in chapter 4 below for modeling the impact of multilateral trade liberalization provides a convenient summary of data that can be brought to bear on this question. This database, which in its most recent version (GTAP5) reports trade data for 1997, aggregates trade into 57 product groups and 66 countries or regions. The regions and products are enumerated in appendix 4A (tables 4A.1 and 4A.3).

Table 3.11 reports the exports, imports, and trade balance of food products in this database for the 41 countries or regions that are relevant for global poverty. The products include rice (paddy and processed); wheat; other cereal grains; vegetables, fruits, and nuts; oil seeds; other crops; meat and dairy products; and other food products.[35] They exclude raw and processed sugar, which although a foodstuff is mainly a tropical export that could give a misleading impression of degree of dependence on food imports.

The strong pattern in table 3.11 is that developing countries are net exporters of food. China (CHN in the table) and India (IND) are both net exporters by a small margin. So is Indonesia (IDN). The only country toward the top of the list of number in poverty with a negative food trade balance is Pakistan (XSA), which on balance imports only a net $8 per capita in food. In Africa, Botswana (BWA) is a substantial net food importer (at $73 per capita), but otherwise the region tends to be a net exporter. South Africa (XSC), Malawi (MWI), Mozambique (MOZ), Tanzania (TZA), Zambia (ZMB), Zimbabwe (ZWE), and Uganda (UGA) are all net food exporters. The important aggregate case of the "rest of sub-Saharan Africa" (XSS), numbering 477 million people, is also a net exporter of food, although only slightly so. This does mean that some individual countries may be substantial net importers, but the dominant pattern is of broad food trade balance in this key grouping.

The developing countries that are clear net food importers tend to be upper middle income. These include especially South Korea (KOR), with net food imports of $119 per capita annually; Russia and other former Soviet Union countries (XSU); and the rest of Eastern Europe (XSE, and POL, Poland), with the strong exception of Hungary (HUN). The Middle East and North Africa (XME and XNF) are also relatively large net food importers. In Latin America, only Mexico (MEX) and Venezuela (VEN) are net food importers, and in amounts that are relatively small in Mexico ($8 per capita) and moderate in Venezuela ($40).

In sum, the data in table 3.11 should provide considerable reassurance that the problem of the adverse impact of agricultural liberalization on global poverty because of the poor's reliance on food imports is at most a selective and limited one. It is obvious from the table that any poverty-weighted net food trade balance would show that, on balance, the poor

---

35. These correspond to the product groups 1–5, 8–11, 19–23, and 25 in table 4A.3 in this volume.

# Table 3.11   Food trade balance in developing countries, 1997

| Economy or region | Exports (millions of dollars) | Imports (millions of dollars) | Balance (millions of dollars) | Population (millions) | Food balance (per capita dollars) |
|---|---|---|---|---|---|
| 3 CHN | 11,891.8 | 10,433.5 | 1,458.3 | 1,253.6 | 1.2 |
| 6 KOR | 2,188.2 | 7,761.7 | −5,573.5 | 46.9 | −118.8 |
| 8 IDN | 5,487.6 | 3,485.0 | 2,002.6 | 207.0 | 9.7 |
| 9 MYS | 5,805.7 | 3,823.4 | 1,982.3 | 22.7 | 87.3 |
| 10 PHL | 1,835.0 | 2,865.3 | −1,030.3 | 74.3 | −13.9 |
| 12 THA | 7,340.4 | 2,843 | 4,497.4 | 60.3 | 74.6 |
| 13 VNM | 1,969.7 | 431.2 | 1,538.5 | 77.5 | 19.8 |
| 14 BGD | 382.9 | 987.4 | −604.5 | 127.7 | −4.7 |
| 15 IND | 6,532.0 | 2,114.8 | 4,417.2 | 997.5 | 4.4 |
| 16 LKA | 521.4 | 521.1 | 0.3 | 19.0 | 0.0 |
| 17 XSA | 806.7 | 2,109.4 | −1,302.7 | 159.3 | −8.2 |
| 20 MEX | 5,368.1 | 6,504.3 | −1,136.2 | 96.6 | −11.8 |
| 21 XCM | 7,074.6 | 5,368.0 | 1,706.6 | 55.0 | 31.0 |
| 22 COL | 3,927.3 | 1,519.1 | 2,408.2 | 41.5 | 58.0 |
| 23 PER | 2,006.4 | 1,045.9 | 960.5 | 25.2 | 38.1 |
| 24 VEN | 518.2 | 1,465.5 | −947.3 | 23.7 | −40.0 |
| 25 XAP | 3,116.9 | 735.5 | 2,381.4 | 20.6 | 115.9 |
| 26 ARG | 11,885.7 | 1,577.8 | 10,307.9 | 36.6 | 281.8 |
| 27 BRA | 12,538.1 | 5,127.2 | 7,410.9 | 168.0 | 44.1 |
| 28 CHL | 3,668.2 | 1,104.8 | 2,563.4 | 15.0 | 170.7 |
| 29 URY | 1,220.9 | 317.5 | 903.4 | 3.3 | 272.9 |
| 30 XSM | 1,011.9 | 388.0 | 623.9 | 5.4 | 116.4 |
| 48 HUN | 2,255.2 | 969.0 | 1,286.2 | 10.1 | 127.7 |
| 49 POL | 2,531.4 | 3,274.3 | −742.9 | 38.7 | −19.2 |
| 50 XCE | 2,306.2 | 3,854.2 | −1,459 | 48.3 | −30.2 |
| 51 XSU | 6,502.1 | 17,679.0 | −11,176.9 | 257.3 | −43.4 |
| 52 TUR | 4,008.2 | 3,176.4 | 831.8 | 64.4 | 12.9 |
| 53 XME | 3,002.4 | 13,500.1 | 10,505.7 | 120.7 | −87.1 |
| 54 MAR | 1,347.7 | 986.0 | 361.7 | 28.2 | 12.8 |
| 55 XNF | 1,168.4 | 7,555.3 | −6,386.9 | 102.1 | −62.6 |
| 56 BWA | 78.1 | 194.6 | −116.5 | 1.6 | −73.3 |
| 57 XSC | 2,258.0 | 1,645.8 | 612.2 | 42.1 | 14.5 |
| 58 MWI | 432.6 | 10.9 | 421.7 | 10.8 | 39.1 |
| 59 MOZ | 136.3 | 82.3 | 54.0 | 17.3 | 3.1 |
| 60 TZA | 441.2 | 188.7 | 252.5 | 32.9 | 7.7 |
| 61 ZMB | 44.9 | 21.9 | 23.0 | 9.9 | 2.3 |
| 62 ZWE | 956.0 | 171.5 | 784.5 | 12.0 | 65.4 |
| 63 XSF | 178.9 | 572 | −393.1 | 13.5 | −29.1 |
| 64 UGA | 486.2 | 39.9 | 446.3 | 21.5 | 20.8 |
| 65 XSS | 6,920.0 | 3,364.9 | 3,555.1 | 477.4 | 7.4 |
| 66 XRW | 3,102.2 | 5,078.0 | −1,975.8 | 58.7 | −33.7 |

Note: The codes given above for economies and regions are spelled out in the GTAP5 column.

Source: GTAP5.

globally live in net food-exporting rather than food-importing countries (a result ensured by the estimates for China and India).

Two further dimensions of this issue warrant exploring. The first is whether this judgment is valid for the LDCs as well as for developing countries overall. The second is a more subtle but crucial economic point: Just because a country has a food (or agricultural) trade deficit, it does not follow that it will be adversely affected by a rise in relative food (or agricultural) prices following global trade liberalization. What matters is whether the country has a comparative advantage in food (or agriculture).

Appendix 3D reports estimates on both of these further questions. Consider first the simple question of whether LDCs have trade deficits in food and agriculture. As indicated in the table, the answer is a clear yes. Of the 45 LDCs for which data are available, on average 35 (including Bangladesh) had food trade deficits in the period 1999–2001. Thirty (including Bangladesh) also had agricultural trade deficits. If the analysis stopped there, as it usually does, the implication would be that higher world food and agricultural prices resulting from trade liberalization will be disadvantageous to LDCs.

The analysis needs to recognize, however, that these countries typically are not just trade deficit countries in food (and/or agriculture). They are trade deficit countries in everything, reflecting large inflows of foreign assistance that pays for a substantial portion of imports. If a country's trade deficit is relatively more extreme in nonfood products, however, then it can actually benefit from global trade liberalization, even though the relative world price of food rises and it is a net food importer. The reason is that it gains more in the *reduction* of the relative price of manufactured and other nonfood imports than it loses in the rise in the relative price of food, because it is more intensively a net importer of nonfood than it is of food.

Consider the following logic. First, global trade liberalization raises the relative price of food (as discussed above). Second, global trade liberalization should not raise average prices, because if it did, it would be welfare reducing rather than welfare increasing. Third, it follows that global trade liberalization reduces the price of nonfood products. This means that even a food deficit country can obtain a welfare gain from improved terms of trade, as long as it has a comparative advantage in food.

A measure of revealed comparative advantage is the ratio of exports to imports. So the key test for the net impact of liberalization on food importers is whether the ratio of food exports to food imports (which will be less than unity by definition) is greater than or less than the ratio of nonfood exports to nonfood imports. As shown in appendix 3D, it turns out that *fewer than half of LDCs have a comparative disadvantage in food.* More than half have a higher ratio of food exports to food imports than their ratio of nonfood exports to nonfood imports. Moreover, *excluding Bangladesh, countries with a comparative disadvantage in food account for only 29 per-*

*cent of the total number of poor people in LDCs.* The corresponding conclusion is that 71 *percent of the poor in LDCs (excluding Bangladesh) live in countries that should benefit from improved terms of trade as world food prices rise from global trade liberalization.*

This finding should counter the view that it is not in LDCs' general interest to have liberalization in global agriculture because food prices will rise. Basically, that view ignores the fact that these countries tend to have a comparative advantage in food despite their trade deficits in agriculture. Thus, the general equilibrium effect will be that the direct adverse effect of higher prices for their net agricultural (or food) imports will be more than offset by relative declines in nonfood goods, which are even more important in these countries' imports and less important in their exports. As shown in appendix 3D, this same set of conclusions applies if the focus is shifted from food to all agricultural products.

Finally, the crucial exception of Bangladesh warrants special attention. Bangladesh accounts for about one-fifth of the total poverty population of LDCs. As a major exporter of textiles and apparel in particular, this country has a comparative disadvantage in both food and agriculture. Its ratio of exports to imports for food and also for agricultural goods is less than one-tenth of its ratio of exports to imports for all other goods. This indicates that Bangladesh would lose from global trade liberalization from the standpoint of higher relative agricultural prices. However, as will be found in the CGE estimates of chapter 4, Bangladesh turns out to have positive overall welfare effects from global trade liberalization, so increased export opportunities in textiles and apparel and other manufactures more than offset higher relative prices for its food and agricultural imports.

## Contingent Protection

In addition to tariffs (including quota-rate tariffs in agriculture after conversion of quotas in the Uruguay Round) and the remaining MFA quotas in textiles and apparel, developing-country exporters face "contingent" or "process" protection in industrial-country markets. These have primarily included antidumping duties, countervailing duties to offset export subsidies, and "safeguard" (GATT Article XIX) restrictions. In practice, and since the Uruguay Round banned the so-called voluntary export restraint, antidumping duties have become the instrument of choice for contingent protection, not only in industrial countries but increasingly also in developing countries. This is because antidumping can be levied against individual exporting countries instead of on an MFN basis; it is unilateral and requires no WTO compensation; its injury test is typically softer than that for safeguards; its unfair trade rhetoric facilitates imposition politically; and the legal and administrative costs are borne by the exporter (Finger, Ng, and Wangchuk 2001).

**Table 3.12  Intensity of antidumping initiations per dollar of imports, 1995–99**

| Against | By | | | |
|---|---|---|---|---|
| | United States | European Union | Japan | Canada |
| Industrial economies | 61 | 22 | 0 | 64 |
| China | 186 | 681 | 0 | 262 |
| Transition economies | 672 | 517 | 0 | 2,897 |
| Other developing countries | 133 | 150 | 0 | 209 |
| All: Index | 100 | 100 | 0 | 100 |
| All: Number | 136 | 160 | 0 | 50 |

*Source:* Finger, Ng, and Wangchuk (2001).

Moreover, instead of being strictly limited to the traditional test of selling at a lower price in the export market than at home, antidumping in recent years has increasingly been based on a constructed cost methodology based on questionable measures of cost (including exaggerated imputed profit rates). This has meant, correspondingly, that pricing treated as unfair under antidumping would rarely have been questioned under domestic competition law (Lawrence 1998; Lindsey 1999).

Developing countries have tended to face a disproportionate incidence of antidumping investigations in industrial-country markets. This is especially true for transition economies, perhaps in part because of the appeal of imputing constructed costs on grounds that (earlier) nonmarket economies did not have meaningful cost data. As indicated in table 3.12, compared with an index of 100 for the average ratio of number of antidumping initiations relative to total import value, the intensity of antidumping has been well below 100 for imports from industrial economies, and well above 100 for imports from developing countries. The intensity index is in the range of 130–200 in the US, EU, and Canadian markets for goods from most developing countries; in a range of about 200–700 for imports from China; and reaches 500–700 for imports from transition economies (and nearly 3,000 in the case of the Canadian market).

It should be stressed that antidumping has also been employed by the developing countries themselves. Indeed, whereas traditionally the instrument was used primarily by industrial countries, after the Uruguay Round there were actually more antidumping initiations by developing countries than by industrial countries (566 vs. 463 during the period 1995–99; Finger, Ng, and Wangchuk 2001, 12). It may also be noted that Japan has been the prime exception, and has not used antidumping measures.

Unfortunately, there appear to be no major estimates of the economic impact of antidumping measures. Most estimates are confined to counts of initiations (or number of tariff lines involved), so it is difficult to tell whether the protective effect is large or small, and where it ranks in comparison with tariff and other nontariff protection. The simple number of

**Table 3.13　Core nontariff barriers, 1996[a]** (percent of tariff lines)

| Type of manufacture | United States | European Union | Japan | Canada |
|---|---|---|---|---|
| Food, beverages, tobacco | 2.8 | 17.2 | 5.9 | 0.4 |
| Textiles and apparel | 67.5 | 75.2 | 31.9 | 42.9 |
| Wood, wood products | 0.6 | 0 | 0 | 3.2 |
| Paper, paper products | 1.1 | 0.7 | 0 | 0.4 |
| Chemicals, petroleum products | 3.3 | 2.9 | 0.9 | 0.6 |
| Nonmetallic mineral products | 3.6 | 0 | 0 | 0 |
| Basic metal industries | 30.4 | 0.6 | 5.1 | 1.7 |
| Fabricated metal industries | 5.9 | 0 | 0 | 2.2 |
| Other manufacturing | 1.7 | 0 | 0 | 0.9 |
| All manufacturing | 17.9 | 13.4 | 10.3 | 7.8 |

a. Antidumping and countervailing actions, export restraints, and other quantitative restrictions, export price restraints, variable charges, and nonautomatic licensing.

*Source:* WTO (2002).

antidumping initiations is modest (e.g., 136 cases for the United States in a five year period; table 3.12) Moreover, it would appear that the cases are concentrated in certain sectors (especially steel, for the United States).

The OECD has compiled data on the incidence of "core nontariff barriers" (NTBs) that include not only antidumping measures but also countervailing duties, quotas (notably under the MFA), export price restraints, variable charges, and nonautomatic licensing. As shown in table 3.13, for 1996 these core NTBs were extremely high in textiles and apparel (in which about 70 percent of tariff lines were affected, in the United States and the European Union). They were also quite high for "basic metal industries" (which include steel) in the case of the United States (30 percent). Otherwise, the principal instance of relatively high core-NTB coverage is for food, beverages, and tobacco in the European Union (17 percent). Considering that MFA quotas are to be eliminated by 2005, and keeping in mind that most agricultural restraints in 1996 were quotas (i.e., the EU core NTBs just cited) but that quotas have been converted to tariff-rate quotas by the Uruguay Round, the implication is that after full implementation of the Uruguay Round, contingent protection will be relatively limited and concentrated in basic metal industries.

The most conspicuous recent instance of contingent protection is the safeguard protection imposed on US steel in 2002. Steel has long been one of the main US industrial sectors periodically receiving major protection. Antidumping and countervailing have been the principal instruments in recent years. As of early 2001, approximately 80 percent of steel imports were subject to antidumping orders (Hufbauer and Goodrich 2002, 4). In June 2001, President George W. Bush requested an investigation by the International Trade Commission under the safeguards law (Section 201) providing for temporary protection for sectors experiencing injury from imports.

In the eventual presidential decision issued in March 2002, tariffs of 30 percent were imposed on flat rolled steel, tin mill products, and hot-rolled bar and cold-finished bar steel; 15 percent on rebar (used in construction), pipes, and stainless rod and bar steel; and 8 percent on stainless wire (*Wall Street Journal*, March 6, 2002). The timetable called for the 30 percent tariffs to fall to 24 percent in the second year, 18 percent in the third year, and then expire (with a corresponding degression to 12 percent in the second year and 9 percent in the third year for the 15 percent tariffs). The executive decision was oriented toward imposing the heaviest protection on steel from China, the European Union, Japan, South Korea, and Taiwan. In contrast, partial special exemptions were granted for key political allies (Turkey) and some politically important developing countries (Argentina, Brazil, Russia). NAFTA partners were also exempt but were warned not to create a surge in exports. The decision provided that "consistent with WTO rules," developing countries that exported only "small amounts" of steel to the United States would also be exempted. As a result, the only developing countries subject to the safeguard duties, and only for selected products, were Brazil, India, Moldova, Romania, Thailand, Turkey, and Venezuela (USTR 2002).

The basis for US steel safeguards was technically in doubt because any surge in imports had occurred in the late 1990s rather than in the period immediately preceding the investigation. It can be argued that the move (along with the mid-2000 escalation in planned US agricultural subsidies) was a necessary tactical movement to ensure congressional passage of the Bush administration's Trade Promotion Act granting fast-track negotiating authority for the Doha Round and a number of prospective free trade arrangements (most notably, the Free Trade Area of the Americas, or FTAA) (Bergsten 2002). Nonetheless, the European Union threatened retaliation carefully targeted toward politically sensitive US products and regions. Subsequent US exemptions of products of special interest to the European Union facilitated the postponement of any EU retaliation before the completion of the lengthy WTO review process.[36]

In late 2003, the WTO declared the US steel safeguard tariffs illegal. The Bush administration then removed the tariffs, bringing this episode to a close. This decision was facilitated by the changing politics of protection for the sector, as opposition to the tariffs by steel-using sectors in several industrial states increasingly offset any political gains in steel-producing states. From the standpoint of impact on developing countries, however, the main point would seem to be that the latest round of contingent protection in US steel was unusually benign, because it largely exempted

---

36. For an analysis of developments through late 2002, see Hufbauer and Goodrich (2003).

developing-country suppliers, and it may even have created some temporary export opportunities through trade diversion from the main industrial-country suppliers.

In short, if the recent US steel episode is any indication, the impact of contingent protection against developing countries in manufactured goods may be diminishing, especially considering that this sector has been the most prominent (outside agriculture and textiles and apparel) for this type of protection (table 3.13).

## General Equilibrium Model Estimates of Trade Liberalization Effects

In an important sense, the most meaningful measure of the extent of remaining industrial-country protection against developing countries is a calculation of the prospective gains in exports and economic welfare that could be obtained by developing countries as a result of the removal of industrial-country barriers. Numerous CGE model estimates have been prepared in recent years providing estimates of the impact of trade liberalization.[37]

At the simplest level, the traditional "partial equilibrium model" for trade liberalization comprises a series of product-specific "elasticities" of supply and demand, confronted with changes in price when the tariff or quota is eliminated to obtain an estimate of the change in trade volume and net consumer and producer welfare (e.g., see the illustrations in appendices 3A and 3B). In such models, highly detailed tariff-line calculations can be made, although the availability of reliable empirical estimates of elasticities is typically problematic.

In contrast, the CGE models tend to be far more aggregative, comprising, for example, one- or two-dozen product sectors and "countries" or regions. There tends to be far richer variety in the styles of one model or another. For example, perfect competition will tend to generate the solution that a country either exports or imports a given product but does not have two-way trade in a single product sector. To approximate reality, often the "Armington assumption" is made that a product imported from one region is "differentiated" from the same product imported from a different region. Alternatively, the "new trade theory" emphasizing two-way trade resulting from imperfect competition, economies of scale, and heterogene-

---

37. For example, for a description of one of the most widely used CGE models, the GTAP model, see Hertel and Tsigas (1997). The model comprises accounting equations (e.g., product value equals the sum of factor and input costs; import price equals foreign f.o.b. export price plus transportation cost and import tax), behavioral equations (firms' choice of factor combinations, households' constant-share budget expenditure systems), and "closure" rules (e.g., fixing the current account balance). Reducing a tariff causes changes in consumption and production that must work through this system until all of the market-clearing conditions (e.g., uniform price for a given factor of production) obtain.

## Table 3.14 Impact of complete trade liberalization on developing-country income (billions of dollars; percent in parentheses)

| Liberalizing group, type of impact, and source | Agriculture | Textiles and apparel | Other | Total | Notes |
|---|---|---|---|---|---|
| **I. Industrial countries** | | | | | |
| **Static** | | | | | |
| AFHHM | 11.6 | 9.0 | 22.4 | 43.1 | a |
| DFS (OECD) | n.a. | n.a. | n.a. | 43 | b |
| IMFWB | 8.7 (0.14) | 23.8 (0.39) | n.a. | n.a. | c |
| WBGEP | 31 (0.27) | 19 (0.17) | 26 (0.23) | 75 (0.65) | d |
| **Total, including dynamic** | | | | | |
| WBGEP | 99 (0.86) | 20 (0.17) | 7 (0.06) | 124 (1.08) | d |
| DFS (OECD) | n.a. | n.a. | n.a. | 292 (3.1) | |
| **II. All countries** | | | | | |
| **Static** | | | | | |
| AFHHM | 43.0 | 12.6 | 52.6 | 108.1 | a |
| DFS (OECD) | n.a. | n.a. | n.a. | 18 (0.2) | b |
| BDS | n.a. | n.a. | n.a. | 370 (5.8) | e |
| IMFWB | 30.4 (0.51) | 51.8 (0.87) | n.a. | n.a. | c |
| WBGEP | 142 (1.23) | 24 (0.21) | 20 (0.17) | 184 (1.6) | d |
| **Total, including dynamic** | | | | | |
| DFAT | n.a. | n.a. | n.a. | — (3.5) | f |
| DFS (OECD) | n.a. | n.a. | n.a. | 455 (4.9) | b |
| WBGEP | 390 (3.4) | 123 (1.1) | 27 (0.23) | 539 (4.7) | d |

n.a. = not available

a. 2005 scale, 1995 dollars.
b. 2010 scale, 1995 dollars. Case I includes a 50 percent tariff cut for developing countries.
c. 1997 scale and dollars. Welfare measure.
d. 2015 scale, 1997 dollars.
e. 2005 scale, 1995 dollars. Includes economies of scale, monopolistic competition, and product heterogeneity effects.
f. Includes liberalization of services.

*Sources:* AFHHM: Anderson et al. (2000); DFS: Dessus, Fukasaku, and Safadi (1999); IMFWB: IMF and World Bank (2002); WBGEP: World Bank (2002a); BDS: Brown, Deardorff, and Stern (2001); DFAT (1999).

ity is adopted in some models, requiring correspondingly greater information. Another crucial dimension of the differences among CGE models is whether or not dynamic effects are added to static effects. Within the dynamic effect models, some may be based upon induced capital formation, whereas others are premised on induced productivity growth changes.

Table 3.14 reports recent estimates of leading CGE models for the impact of post–Uruguay Round trade liberalization. A number of important generalizations can be inferred from these estimates:

- The gains to be obtained from removal of post–Uruguay Round protection remain substantial, even after the tariff cuts and reductions in

NTBs in that round. Static gains for developing countries from the liberalization of industrial-country markets tend to be in the vicinity of $60 billion annually at mid-1990s prices but scaled to a future, larger economic base as of 2005 to as late as 2015. This magnitude is on the order of two-thirds of 1 percent of GDP for developing countries. It is also about the same as the current annual flow of concessional development assistance, although in the case of trade liberalization the benefits would be much more heavily oriented toward the large middle-income economies rather than the low-income countries that receive most of concessional aid.

- The gains are highly concentrated in agriculture and in textiles and apparel, with all other sectoral gains (almost wholly manufactures, given already typically free entry in such key raw materials imports as oil) about comparable in magnitude to either agriculture or textiles-apparel singly.

- In the studies summarized in table 3.14, developing countries' estimated gains tend to be even larger from the liberalization of their own markets and those of their developing-country peers than from the liberalization of industrial-country markets.[38] However, as examined in chapter 4, the CGE analysis of the present study finds just the opposite, as does recent CGE modeling by the OECD (2003c).

- Dynamic gains tend to be larger than static gains. The most conspicuous example is World Bank's Global Economic Prospects model (WBGEP)—in which total gains, including dynamic ones, are two to three times static gains, depending on whether liberalization is just by industrial countries or developing countries remove their barriers as well. The inclusion of dynamic gains tends to boost total estimated gains to the range of 3 to 5 percent of developing-country GDP for global liberalization, and 1 to 3 percent of developing-country GDP for liberalization only by industrial countries.

- Model coverage can matter as much as the inclusion or exclusion of dynamic gains. Thus, primarily because of the inclusion of liberalization of barriers in services trade, the model of Brown, Deardorff, and Stern (2001) estimates higher gains (5.8 percent of developing-country GDP) than any of the other models considered, even though it captures only "static" effects.[39]

---

38. A sharp exception is the model of Dessus, Fukasaku, and Safadi (1999), which places heavy emphasis on the loss of tariff revenue to developing countries when they are included in the imports liberalized.

39. The overall percent of GDP estimate for the model of Brown and her colleagues is inferred from their country- and region-specific welfare estimates (Brown, Deardorff, and Stern 2001, 40). Liberalization of services accounts for 64 percent of total gains in this model.

The incorporation of "new trade theory" effects in model structure, as in the Brown-Deardorff-Stern model, also tends to boost estimated welfare effects. In the traditional static model, the upward-sloping supply curve means that marginal cost is rising. Under economies of scale, marginal cost is falling. It follows that when production for exports expands, the traditional model will show much less welfare gain than a model incorporating economies of scale.[40] The inclusion of imperfect competition arises as a natural concomitant of economies of scale, and it boosts potential welfare effects because the erosion of monopoly power through increased import competition makes it possible for production to move closer to the socially efficient level. The inclusion of product differentiation allows for two-way trade in a given product sector instead of complete specialization.[41]

Similarly, the intuition behind the "dynamic productivity effects," such as those included in the WBGEP model, is straightforward, if somewhat ad hoc in terms of traditional trade theory. The broad notion is that exposure to international trade acts as a stimulus to technical change and hence productivity growth. The World Bank (2002a, 180) calibrates this effect by positing the relationship $\gamma^e = \chi^0(E/X)^\eta$ for a given sector, where $\gamma^e$ is the additional productivity growth attributable to openness, $E/X$ is the ratio of exports to output, $\eta$ is the elasticity of productivity growth with respect to this openness ratio, and $\chi^0$ is a constant set so that $\gamma^e$ contributes an average of 40 percent of productivity growth. The model appeals to economies of scale through increased exports as one motivation for this treatment, as an alternative to incorporating scale economies directly in the model.

The central question on the induced-productivity dynamics is simply how to obtain robust estimates of these parameters. The parameters assumed in the WBGEP model seem plausible.[42] Chapter 5 examines the

---

40. There will be partially offsetting losses of economies of scale in import-competing industries, but because these are less efficient, the losses will be smaller than the gains in the export sectors.

41. As reviewed in chapter 4, however, Harrison, Rutherford, and Tarr (1996) find that in the increasing-returns-to-scale version of their CGE model, the increase in static welfare effects above those estimated in the constant-returns-to-scale version is considerably smaller than is often asserted in other studies.

42. Thus, consider a sector with exports equal to 20 percent of output and productivity growth of 3 percent. The trade influence accounts for 40 percent of productivity growth, or 1.2 percent. Suppose trade liberalization boosts the trade ratio by 10 percent. With an elasticity of unity ($\eta$ is set at unity in WBGEP), the result is to raise this trade component to 1.32 percent. Over a decade, the extra 0.12 percent annual productivity growth boosts output by about 1.2 percent. This order of magnitude is consistent with the difference between the static and total effect in the WBGEP results for case I in table 3.14, where only industrial countries liberalize. The larger difference for case II (liberalization by developing countries as well) is heavily concentrated in the agricultural sector, suggesting that the model shows high increases in agricultural trade ratios when the developing countries liberalize their own barriers.

literature on this question and arrives at its own summary parameters, which are broadly consistent with the WBGEP measurement of this effect.

In summary, the leading CGE models tend to place the gains to developing countries from post–Uruguay Round elimination of protection at about two-thirds of 1 percent of GDP (static) to 2 percent of GDP (total including dynamic) from the removal of industrial-country protection, and at about 2 percent (static) to 5 percent (total including dynamic) if developing countries also remove their own protection. Although the total effects are more relevant in principle, the conceptual basis for and empirical estimates of the dynamic effects are far less widely agreed on than is true for the traditional static effects.

## The Poverty Impact of Trade Liberalization

The World Bank (2002a) has considered the implications of its trade liberalization estimates for global poverty. The WBGEP model estimates include calculations on changes in factor incomes. These indicate that complete trade liberalization would raise unskilled wages in developing countries by 5.7 percent from the baseline reference path without trade liberalization by 2015 for the static model, and by 7.4 percent for the model including dynamic productivity gains (World Bank 2002a, 173). Applying a poverty elasticity of –2, the World Bank thus estimates that trade liberalization would reduce global poverty by 15 percent (2 × 7.4), or by 320 million people in 2015 (p. 174). Of particular importance, the World Bank estimates imply that even in the baseline without trade liberalization, global poverty at the $2 per day threshold should have declined from 2.9 billion today (chapter 1) to 2.13 billion (= 320/0.15). This means in effect that complete trade liberalization would boost the rate of reduction of the absolute number of the global poor from 2 to nearly 3 percent annually.[43]

A subsequent World Bank study uses the same GEP model to estimate the trade and poverty impact of a more realistic liberalization scenario (World Bank 2003, 48–51). Industrial countries are assumed to cut agricultural tariffs to no more than 10 percent and a target average of 5 percent, and to reduce tariffs on manufactured goods to no more than 5 percent and a target average of 1 percent. Developing countries are assumed to implement corresponding ceilings and averages of 15 and 10 percent for agriculture and 10 and 5 percent for manufacturing, respectively. There

---

43. The World Bank baseline suggests a greater optimism about growth and poverty reduction during the next 15 years than the in the past decade. The institution estimates that from 1990 to 2000 the absolute number in poverty remained unchanged, because population growth offset a reduction in poverty rates (see chapter 1). In contrast, the projection through 2015 implies an annual reduction of about 2 percent in the absolute number of poor people (baseline without trade liberalization).

would be complete elimination of export subsidies, specific tariffs and tariff-rate quotas, and antidumping penalties. This scenario would achieve an estimated three-fourths of potential gains from complete free trade. In this outcome, the number of poor people in developing countries at the $2 per day threshold would decline by 144 million from the baseline level.[44] In contrast to the results of chapters 4 and 5 below, the largest absolute reductions would be in sub-Saharan Africa (67 million) and Asia (45 million; World Bank 2003, 52). As discussed in chapter 5, this study finds a greater concentration of poverty reduction in Asia, in part because the poverty elasticity tends to be higher there than in Latin America and sub-Saharan Africa.

This earlier World Bank estimate is consistent in order of magnitude with that identified above in this chapter as the static poverty reduction impact of liberalization in agriculture alone (an 8 percent reduction in global poverty). Conceptually, the two effects are different, because the World Bank estimate is largely driven by a real income effect, whereas the agricultural estimate in the present chapter implicitly also involves an internal redistribution from the nonpoor urban to poor rural population. There is considerable congruence as well, however, because presumably much of the rise in real unskilled wages in the World Bank estimates reflects higher rural wages from agricultural liberalization (especially in view of the outsized share of agriculture in the total liberalization gains, including dynamic, in the WBGEP model; see table 3.14).

Chapters 4 and 5 below present new CGE-based estimates of the potential reduction in global poverty resulting from trade liberalization. Chapter 4 estimates the static welfare and poverty impacts. Chapter 5 incorporates dynamic effects from productivity gains and induced capital investment, and it arrives at an overall central estimate of about 540 million people as the number who could be lifted out of poverty by global free trade during a 15-year period. *The estimates of this study for the poverty-reducing impact of global free trade are thus about two-thirds larger than the corresponding estimates by the World Bank*, and nearly four times the World Bank's more recent "realistic scenario" calculation. The reasons for the differences are set forth in chapter 5.

It is important to reiterate that in the World Bank (and some other) estimates, much of the potential for welfare gains and poverty reduction in developing countries is sacrificed if the developing countries do not liberalize their own markets. The WBGEP welfare estimates (including dynamic effects) are only 23 percent as high for developing countries if the only markets liberalized are those of industrial countries. The implication is that about three-fourths of the potential poverty reduction would be sacrificed if developing countries do not liberalize, cutting the reduction in absolute

---

44. It is not reported why the poverty impact is less than half the free trade total, whereas the welfare gains are three-fourths as large.

number of poor people (from the baseline) from 320 million to only 80 million. In agriculture, the more recent (i.e., realistic scenario) World Bank estimates attribute fully 80 percent of developing country welfare gains to the reduction of barriers in the developing-countries themselves, and for manufactures the share is 57 percent (World Bank 2003, 51), a politically salient point that tends to undermine developing-country complaints that the industrial countries are the main source of the problem.[45]

This finding is surprising considering that industrial-country protection of agriculture tends to be higher than that in developing countries, and it is explored further in chapter 4, where a greater relative impact of industrial-country liberalization is found. Specifically, it is found there that industrial-country liberalization provides from about half to two-thirds of the total potential welfare gains to developing countries from trade liberalization, whereas developing countries' liberalization conversely provides only about a third to a half. The reasons for these divergent results are set forth in chapter 4.

An important recent direction in CGE research on this issue, finally, is to combine a cross-country general equilibrium trade model with detailed household survey data for individual countries, to obtain a richer analysis of the impact of trade liberalization on poverty incidence. Hertel, Preckel, Cranfield, and Ivanic (2002; hereafter, "HPCI") use the GTAP model in combination with national household survey data for seven developing countries for this purpose. They concentrate on the impact of liberalization on factor income. They divide households into those primarily dependent on (1) self-employed agriculture, (2) nonagricultural enterprises, (3) wages, (4) transfers (public and private), and (5) all other. For each group, they map the income distribution by 5-percentage-point steps. They then trace the impact of multilateral trade liberalization on the income of the representative "marginal" household in the group located at the poverty line ($1 per day).[46] The effects derive from both the influence of product price changes on the consumption basket and from factor price changes on income.

The HPCI study finds that the complete removal of protection existing as of 1997 reduces poverty in Indonesia, the Philippines, Thailand, Uganda, and Zambia but increases it in Brazil and Chile. Even so, within Brazil and Chile, there are large reductions in poverty (more than 30 percent) for agriculture-specialized households.[47] This group also experiences 7 to 9 percent poverty reductions in the Philippines and Thailand, as do wage

---

45. See, e.g., The Economist, September 6, 2003, 60.

46. This choice somewhat attenuates the inherent interest of the findings, because it confines the initial poverty group to only 2 percent of households in Thailand, 4 percent in Chile, and 5 percent in Brazil, although the share rises to 73 percent in Zambia.

47. The poverty measure chosen is Foster, Greer, and Thorbecke's (1984) concept of the transfer required to lift all households in poverty up to the poverty threshold.

labor households in Indonesia and the Philippines. There are increases of poverty by 5 to 11 percent, however, for self-employed nonagricultural households in Indonesia and labor-specialized households in Brazil and Chile.

The HPCI findings tend to confirm the importance of global agricultural liberalization for reducing global poverty, as well as the nuance that this liberalization has at least the potential to raise poverty in countries where the bulk of the poor are urban rather than rural. Thus far, this line of research has not generated sufficient results for global aggregation like that in the WBGEP analysis at the country level, because the individual country data requirements are demanding. It does, however, shed light on key influences, such as the finding that differences in the household source of factor income are more important than differences in consumption patterns in tracing the impact of trade liberalization on poverty incidence. The estimates of chapter 4 below pursue a parallel approach that seeks to take into account factor shares at the poverty level and the impact of trade liberalization on factor prices.

## Protection in Services

Economists and trade negotiators have increasingly recognized that the liberalization of trade in services might generate gains that are as large as, or larger than, those attainable through further liberalization in merchandise trade. The Uruguay Round created a framework for negotiations in the General Agreement on Trade in Services. The WTO has identified four "modes" of services trade. Mode 1 is "cross-border" services, illustrated by the electronic transmission of back-office and software service activities.[48] This is a relatively new area and has not acquired a backlog of protection, but it has become increasingly salient as fears mount about the outsourcing of white-collar jobs to low-income countries. The main challenge now is to ensure that new protection does not arise that would choke off cross-border service opportunities for developing countries. Mode 2 is "consumption abroad," including most prominently tourism but also education and medical services. Here also, protection would not seem rampant, particularly in tourism, although it can be argued that liberalization measures should be adopted to extend (for example) eligibility for medical insurance reimbursement to procedures undertaken abroad.

Most analysis of services trade liberalization seems to concern mode 3. This is "commercial presence," and it refers primarily to the right of establishment for foreign affiliates of multinational firms (i.e., foreign direct investment). The implications of liberalization are much more profound,

---

48. India in particular has advanced rapidly in these areas, with software exports rising from $225 million in 1992–93 to $1.75 billion in 1997–98 (World Bank 2002a, 73).

however, for mode 4, the "movement of individuals," which is difficult to distinguish from immigration, the sole distinction being the temporary nature of mode 4 services. Yet from an economic standpoint, the relative abundance of different factors is what matters, and it makes little difference whether there is a large increase in the availability of, say, unskilled labor through a permanent increase in the stock of immigrants by X, or an annual inflow of X additional temporary unskilled workers who next year are replaced by another X temporary workers.

Immigration is perhaps the most socially and politically charged dimension of international economic relations, because it raises ethical and cultural issues absent from trade policy. The questionable political feasibility of large-scale temporary labor programs may account for the relative dearth of analyses of mode 4 liberalization, but this seems likely to be an area of increasing analysis. In particular, the early 2004 proposal of the Bush administration in the United States for a temporary work program to absorb previously illegal immigrants could place this area more centrally on the policy agenda.

This study does not include trade in services, either in the estimates of protection or in the calculations of the potential trade and poverty effects of liberalization. From this standpoint, the main estimates in this study for the potential poverty reduction resulting from trade liberalization will tend to be understated rather than overstated. There are two broad reasons why services are omitted. First, at the policy level free trade in services remains much further removed from the realm of political feasibility than free trade in goods. The best example, as just suggested, is in mode 4. The absolutely free entry of temporary workers, like absolutely unconstrained immigration, would surely mean the arrival of tens, or even hundreds, of millions of workers from low-income countries into industrial countries. Even though the welfare effects of such flows could be calculated, they would be largely an exercise in fantasy. Even the main pragmatic area of services trade liberalization—mode 3—faces considerably greater resistance in developing countries than most areas of merchandise trade liberalization.

The second broad reason for the absence of services in the calculations of this study is that the data on protection and the analytical techniques for quantifying liberalization effects are far less reliable than those for merchandise trade. The main estimates available to date have tended to rely on considerably more heroic assumptions than are needed to analyze merchandise trade. In particular, in the absence of direct measures of protection, several studies have relied on the "gross operating margins" in services sectors as a guide to protection.[49] Implicitly, they are examining mode 3 trade, and by implication they are assuming that opening services to di-

---

49. This is the ratio of revenue minus cost to cost.

rect investment by foreign competitors would eliminate excess profits. But this approach raises serious doubts about the meaning of protection.

Studies that use this approach tend to adopt the lowest-gross-margin country as the benchmark and then to assume that countries with higher gross operating margins have "protection" (Hoekman 2000; Brown, Deardorf, and Stern 2001; Robinson, Wang, and Martin 2002). Unfortunately, this approach yields what would appear to be implausible levels of protection. For example, Robinson, Wang, and Martin (2002) rely on other analysts' estimates of gross operating margins to estimate that "protection" amounts to about 100 percent in construction, trade and transport, private services, and public services in the European Union, and it stands at 70 percent for trade and transport and private services in the United States.

But what is this protection? In what manner do "private services" in the United States impose a 70 percent penalty for participation by foreign producers? What assurance is there that after the entry of foreigners, monopolistic practices will not persist, leaving the supposed "protection" embodied in excess profits unchanged? And for that matter, why would these margins be the highest in the European Union, where the influence of services-sector competition from within the single market should by now be among the most advanced?

Not only are the protection levels likely overestimated by this approach, but the welfare gains from liberalization then tend to be ballooned by the simple fact that the services sectors are a large share of the economy, so assumed liberalization takes place on a larger base than that for merchandise trade. For these reasons, great caution would seem warranted in considering the estimates of large liberalization gains that such studies tend to generate. Thus, Robinson, Wang, and Martin (2002), who acknowledge that "our goal is to find large numbers" (p. 1), succeed in doing so as they estimate that "a 100 percent elimination of protection in all manufacturing sectors generates less gain in GDP than a 50 percent cut in the protection level in one service sector for most economies in the model" (p. 12). For its part, the World Bank (2002a, 172) draws on this school of work to estimate that the adoption of free trade in four services sectors (trade and transportation, communications, financial services, and "other private services") by the developing countries alone would provide static welfare gains for these countries amounting to 7.7 percent of GDP, far larger than the World Bank's estimate of 1.7 percent of GDP static welfare gains from free trade in goods.[50]

If one placed great faith in such estimates, the implication would be that the potential for global poverty reduction through liberalization even of just mode 3 services would be several times that for merchandise trade

---

50. The main source of the gains in the World Bank's calculation is the assumption that free trade in services would provide a "10 percent increase in efficiency" in the four services sectors.

liberalization. Unfortunately, the existing services estimates would appear to remain too speculative at present to warrant such a conclusion. Nonetheless, even if exaggerated, these estimates provide an ample cushion to help ensure that the estimates of poverty reduction in the present study, which exclude services liberalization, are unlikely to be overstated.

## Conclusion

The broad conclusion of this chapter is that even though the Uruguay Round made important progress in reducing global protection, industrial-country protection against developing countries remains substantial, and its removal could make an important contribution to reduction of global poverty. More specifically:

- Outside textiles and apparel, protection in manufactures has fallen to low levels, about 2 to 3 percent for US and EU protection against developing countries.

- Post–Uruguay Round protection in textiles and apparel will remain high, however, at about an 11 percent average tariff for the United States and European Union, and much higher if the industrial countries fail to deliver on their pledge to eliminate quotas by 2005. Even so, the level of total tariff and quota protection has already fallen steeply, from about 55 percent for the tariff equivalent in apparel in the mid-1980s to about 27 percent in the late 1990s. A back-of-the-envelope partial equilibrium calculation suggests that removal of the remaining post–Uruguay Round industrial-country tariffs in textiles and apparel would boost developing-country exports by about $39 billion annually (at 1998 scale and prices), or about 55 percent of the total increase that could be expected from the elimination of industrial-country protection on all manufactures.

- Despite special concerns about tariff peaks, it turns out that the tariff peak problem is almost wholly concentrated in textiles and apparel and agriculture. Excluding textiles and apparel, for other manufactures only 0.6 percent of tariff categories (representing only 1.9 percent of the value of imports of manufactures from developing countries) have bound tariffs of 15 percent or more in the United States; the corresponding incidence is 1.3 percent (categories) and 0.7 percent (value) for the European Union.

- The highest remaining protection is found in agriculture, where the combined effects of tariffs, tariff-rate quotas after conversion from physical quotas in the Uruguay Round, and domestic subsidies amount to an overall tariff equivalent of about 20 percent in the United States,

46 percent in the European Union, 52 percent in Canada, and 82 percent in Japan. A simple partial equilibrium calculation suggests that the removal of this protection would raise developing-country exports by about $30 billion annually (at 1998 scale and prices), or by about three-fourths of the increase in exports from liberalization in all manufactures including textiles and apparel.

■ The aggregation of protection in textiles and apparel, other manufactures, agriculture, and oil and other nonagricultural raw materials yields an Aggregate Measure of Protection against developing countries of about 4 percent for the United States, 10 percent for the European Union, 11 percent for Canada, and 16 percent for Japan (tariff-equivalent). Overall industrial-country protection against developing countries thus remains substantial, although not particularly high by postwar standards.

■ A simple model developed in appendix 3C calculates that industrial-country removal of agricultural subsidies and protection could reduce global poverty by about 8 percent, or about 200 million people for 72 countries included in the calculation. The driving force is a rise of about 10 percent in global agricultural prices, resulting from the induced cutback in industrial-country agricultural output. So long as the rural share in the poor population exceeds the share of food in the low-income consumer budget, rising world agricultural prices tend to reduce global poverty. For the 72 developing countries, in aggregate about 75 percent of the poor are in the rural sector, whereas the likely share of food in their household budgets is only about 40 percent. Exceptions include some Latin American countries (e.g., Argentina and Chile), where the bulk of the poor are in the urban sector. The same pattern of differing results depending on the concentration of rural or urban poverty is found in recent work combining CGE models with detailed household surveys.

■ Much of the poverty reduction effect of industrial-country agricultural liberalization would stem from a redistribution from the urban sector (especially the urban nonpoor) to the rural sector within developing countries, rather than a redistribution from industrial to developing countries. Despite losses by the urban poor, the rural gainers among the poor would outnumber the urban losers by about five to one. Urban losses are smaller under more optimistic assumptions about dynamic gains from liberalization.

■ Despite the prominence of agricultural liberalization in potential poverty reduction, a careful reading of the various model estimates shows much smaller welfare gains for developing countries from the removal of industrial-country agricultural protection (about $9 billion to $17 billion annually at 1997 scale for static gains, and about three times as much including dynamic ones) than the $350 billion annual figure frequently cited in public debate, including by leading international officials, as the amount of industrial-country "subsidies" to agriculture. The latter figure actually refers to industrial-country "support" for agriculture, and the great bulk of this support comes from the price-raising effect of tariffs and tariff-rate quotas, not from fiscal grants to farmers that might arguably be reallocated to international development assistance. Similarly, the corresponding transfers are primarily from consumers and taxpayers to farmers in rich countries, rather than from farmers in poor countries to farmers in rich countries. The new estimates in chapter 4 below suggest, however, that the existing models may understate the proportion of gains to developing countries stemming from agricultural liberalization in industrial countries.

■ A review of the data on net agricultural and food trade balances suggests that, for the most part, the diagnosis of a favorable effect on global poverty from rising relative prices of food and agricultural products after global liberalization is not reversed by the food-importing status of some developing countries. The poor predominantly live in net food-exporting rather than food-importing countries. A further analysis of the least developed countries shows that although a majority of them are net food importers, they predominantly have a comparative advantage in food and agriculture. Overall, even the LDCs should thus gain rather than lose from the terms-of-trade effects of global liberalization, after taking account of the reduction in relative prices of their nonagricultural imports (which bulk even larger than their food imports).

■ A brief review of contingent protection (i.e., antidumping, countervailing duties, and safeguards) suggests that although this type of protection has been disproportionately applied to imports from developing countries, the removal of quotas in textiles and apparel and in agriculture should leave the principal incidence of contingent protection in the steel sector. In this sector, the US safeguard measures adopted in 2002 went a considerable way toward exempting developing countries and were to be phased out after three years, even before they were cut short by an adverse WTO ruling. Much will depend, however, on whether there is a surge in safeguard protection in textiles and apparel to replace quotas after their removal by 2005.

This chapter concludes with a brief survey of leading recent CGE models of the impact of removing the remaining post–Uruguay Round protection. These models tend to find the following:

■ The remaining benefits of further liberalization are still large. If only the industrial countries remove their protection, the developing countries experience welfare gains in the vicinity of two-thirds of 1 percent of GDP for static effects and 2 percent of GDP if dynamic effects are included. If the developing countries themselves also remove their trade barriers, these developing-country gains rise to about 2 percent of GDP for static effects and 5 percent of GDP including dynamic effects.

- The World Bank has applied a CGE model to estimate the corresponding impact on global poverty. It finds that if all countries remove all barriers, in its model including dynamic gains from stimulus to productivity growth, welfare gains in developing countries amount to about 5 percent of GDP, and unskilled wages in these countries would rise by 7.4 percent. Applying a "poverty elasticity" of 2, the World Bank study concludes that global trade liberalization would reduce global poverty ($2 per day definition) by 15 percent, or by 320 million people in the year 2015.

- Chapter 5 will show that, on the basis of new CGE estimates and taking account of long-term productivity and induced-investment effects, the potential poverty reduction from global free trade could be even larger.

The salient overall finding of this chapter, even without including the additional new estimates of chapters 4 and 5, is that the reform of trade policy contains substantial potential for reducing global poverty. Ensuring the successful removal of textile and apparel quotas by 2005, as already agreed on in the Uruguay Round, and further reducing tariffs in this sector will be crucial to realizing this potential. Even more critical will be major progress in removing agricultural protection, and it is inescapable that if the Doha Round is truly to be a development round, deep reductions in agricultural barriers will have to be on the negotiating table.

The estimates also contain important caveats. At the most fundamental level, even in their most sweeping form, the various estimates tend to show that trade policy is a useful but by no means sufficient instrument for addressing global poverty. Thus, in the extreme case of completely free trade, and even using the larger estimates developed in chapter 5 below, trade reform might reduce global poverty by about a fourth from its baseline level by 2015. This means that other domestic economic policies will have to be employed to attack the other three-fourths.

# Appendix 3A
# Weighting Protection

This study proposes "adjusted-import weighting" as the best approach to obtaining an aggregated weighted measure of tariffs or tariff equivalents of protection.[51] The adjustment obtains an average between the observed import level and a measure of the import value that would occur if the protection were removed. For simplicity and transparency, this approach assumes a unitary price elasticity of demand for imports and a global supply elasticity of infinity. The free trade import volume equals the original volume plus a percent equal to the percent change in price resulting from removal of the tariff-equivalent protection. Thus,

$$M_1 = M_0 + M_0\left(-\alpha\left[\frac{-\tau}{1+\tau}\right]\right) \tag{A.1}$$

where $\alpha$ is the absolute value of the price elasticity of demand for imports, $\tau$ is the tariff equivalent, and $(1 + \tau)$—often called the "force of the tariff"—is the ratio of the domestic price including protection to the world price. We seek as the basis for weighting an adjusted-import base $M^*$ that is equal to the average of the actual import base $(M_0)$ and the hypothetical free trade import base $(M_1)$. Assuming $\alpha = 1$, then we have

$$M^* = \frac{M_0 + M_1}{2} = \frac{M_0}{2}\left(\frac{2+3\tau}{1+\tau}\right) = M_0\left(\frac{1+1.5\tau}{1+\tau}\right) \tag{A.2}$$

Adjusted-import weights along these lines should be preferable to actual import weights because of the problem of endogeneity of the latter (higher tariffs cause lower imports). An even simpler approach that avoids this problem is the use of simple unweighted tariffs, but these in turn are susceptible to distortions caused by arbitrary differences in the coverage of individual tariff-line categories. In support of the proposition that more error is introduced by using unweighted tariff category tariff averages than by weighting by adjusted (or even unadjusted) import values, consider figure 3A.1. For 115 categories drawn at random from the Harmonized Tariff System of the United States (about 1 percent of the total US nomenclature), the figure shows on the vertical axis the natural logarithm of the value of imports (in millions of dollars), and on the horizontal axis

---

51. This appendix is from Cline (2002b).

**Figure 3A.1   Log value and log tariff: 8-digit Harmonized Tariff System of the United States**

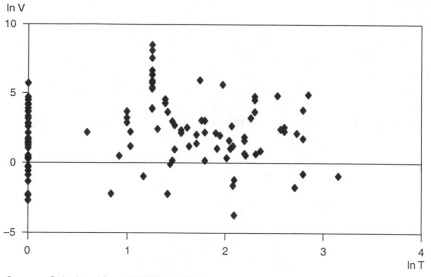

*Source:* Calculated from USITC (2002).

the natural logarithm of the percentage rate ad valorem tariff.[52] If the value scope of each tariff-line item were about the same, and the main influence were that higher tariffs compress imports to lower levels, we would observe a downward-sloping line with minimal dispersion around the line. If instead there is very wide variation between some categories with huge import values and some with small import values, and if there is little if any relationship between the difference in import value magnitudes and the tariff rate, we should instead observe a relatively random dispersion. It is evident from the figure that the latter is the case.

To illustrate the arbitrariness of the categories, in this sample the largest import value occurs in item 8708.29.50, amounting to $4.8 billion; the smallest, in 2915.40.20, comprising only $24,000.[53] The value multiple is a factor of 200,000. So if a minimally important category has an unrepresentative tariff, the potential distortion to the average can be significant.

---

52. Note that unity (i.e., 1 percent) is added to each tariff before taking the logarithm, because the numerous cases of zero tariff would yield undefined logarithms. Note also that the negative figures on the vertical axis occur because in these categories imports are less than $1 million.

53. These two items are, respectively: "other" under "other parts and accessories of bodies . . . of motor vehicles"; and "aromatic" under "saturated acyclic monocarboxylic acids, other."

# Appendix 3B
# The Tariff Equivalent of Agricultural Subsidies

In figure 3B.1, the domestic supply curve would be $S$ without the subsidy, but shifts rightward to $S'$ with the subsidy, which reduces production cost by the vertical distance between the two curves. This increases domestic output volume from $OA$ to $OB$. Domestic demand is given by curve $DD$. World supply is available at price $p_w$, but because of the tariff $t$ the price to the consumer is $p_w(1 + t)$. In the absence of the subsidy, imports would be the amount $AC$. In the presence of the subsidy, they are only $BC$. The question is thus: What is the tariff equivalent that would have the same effect as the subsidy, that is, in suppressing imports from $AC$ to $BC$?

Let $V_d$ be the value of domestic agricultural output at domestic prices. Then defining $Q_d$ as the value of domestic output at international prices, we have $Q_d = V_d/(1 + t)$. Suppose the domestic subsidy is the fraction $s$ of domestic market value of agricultural output (where the market value excludes the amount of the subsidy because the consumer does not pay it). Suppose the elasticity of domestic supply is $\varepsilon$. Then we can obtain the counterfactual level of domestic output (at world prices) in the absence of subsidy, or $Q_d^*$, as

$$Q_d^* = Q_d / (1 + s\varepsilon) \tag{B.1}$$

That is, an increase in the producer price of the good in the proportion $s$ will raise supply by the proportion $s\varepsilon$, and in the absence of the subsidy output would have been observed output divided by unity plus this proportion.

Now consider what would have been the level of imports in the absence of the subsidy:

$$M^* = M + (Q_d - Q_d^*) = M + (s\varepsilon) \cdot \frac{Q_d}{(1 + s\varepsilon)} \tag{B.2}$$

The proportionate reduction in imports attributable to the subsidy is thus

$$\frac{\Delta M}{M^*} = \frac{-[(s\varepsilon) / (1 + s\varepsilon)]Q_d}{M + [(s\varepsilon) / (1 + s\varepsilon)]Q_d} = \frac{-[(s\varepsilon) / (1 + s\varepsilon)]}{[1 / \lambda] + [(s\varepsilon) / (1 + s\varepsilon)]} \tag{B.3}$$

where $\lambda$ is the ratio of domestic output at world prices ($Q_d$) to imports ($M$).

If protection is implemented through a tariff rather than through domestic subsidies, the proportionate impact of an ad valorem tariff of $\tau$ on imports will be

## Figure 3B.1 Impact of farm subsidies on imports

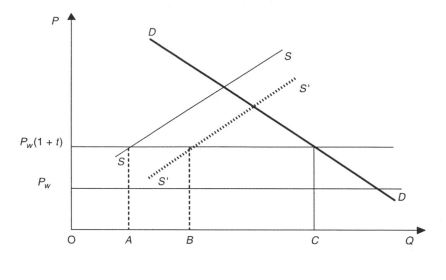

$$\frac{\Delta M}{M^*} = -\tau\beta \qquad (B.4)$$

where $\beta$ is the absolute value of the price elasticity of import demand. To obtain the tariff equivalent $\tau$ of a given ad valorem subsidy rate $s$, equations B.3 and B.4 can be equated. After rearranging, this yields

$$\tau = s\frac{\lambda}{\beta}\frac{\varepsilon}{1 + s\varepsilon + \lambda s\varepsilon} \qquad (B.5)$$

A potentially counterintuitive result of this estimation is that the tariff equivalent of the domestic subsidy rises with the ratio of domestic output to imports ($\lambda$). The economic meaning is that a country that has a small volume of imports and large amount of domestic output will be causing a proportionately large further reduction in imports with only a modest subsidy. The tariff equivalent also varies positively with the size of the elasticity of supply ($\varepsilon$), reflecting the fact that a higher supply elasticity causes a greater expansion of domestic output and contraction of imports in response to a given subsidy rate. In contrast, the size of the tariff equivalent of the subsidy varies inversely with the (absolute) size of the price elasticity of demand for imports ($\beta$), because a larger elasticity means that a smaller tariff accomplishes the same reduction in imports.

# Appendix 3C
# The Impact of Industrial-Country Agricultural Import Liberalization on Poverty Incidence in Developing Countries

The removal of protection on and subsidies to agriculture in industrial countries will tend to reduce global agricultural supply and raise world agricultural prices. This will benefit developing countries by increasing their export opportunities, but it will tend to raise their consumers' food prices. As a consequence, whereas its effects will tend to be favorable for poor farmers in developing countries, they will tend to be unfavorable in the first instance for the urban poor. Even so, losses by the urban poor from higher food prices may be mitigated or conceivably offset by spill-over dynamic gains to the economy from the increased agricultural export opportunities.

## Static Effects

Let $z$ be the proportionate change in real income per person, and $w$ the proportionate increase in world food prices from industrial-country agricultural liberalization. Let $\theta$ be the share of food in the consumption basket of the poor. Let $\gamma$ be the elasticity of the local food price with respect to the world food price. Let $\beta$ be the elasticity of rural income with respect to the farm-gate agricultural price, and let $\alpha$ be the elasticity of the farm-gate price with respect to the world price. Let subscripts $R$ refer to rural and $U$ to urban.

The direct price effect on the real income of the rural poor, expressed as a proportionate change, is then

$$z_R^1 = \alpha\beta w - \theta_R \gamma_R w = w(\alpha\beta - \theta_R \gamma_R) \tag{C.1}$$

There is an additional component of static gain for agriculture associated with the increase in exports. Figure 3C.1 shows the demand and supply for agricultural output. The horizontal axis shows output volume; the vertical axis, price. Industrial-country liberalization raises the world price from $P_0$ to $P_1$. The domestic demand curve is shown for simplicity as completely inelastic (vertical line $D_d$). Output $d$ is consumed domestically; exports are total initial production minus domestic consumption, or $Q_0 - d$. When prices rise, agricultural income on the original output volume rises by areas $A + B$. Area $A$ is merely a transfer from domestic consumers to farmers. Area $B$ is a net welfare gain from improved terms of trade on exports. In addition, area $C$ is a net welfare gain on the increase in output

## Figure 3C.1 Impact of liberalization of agricultural export markets

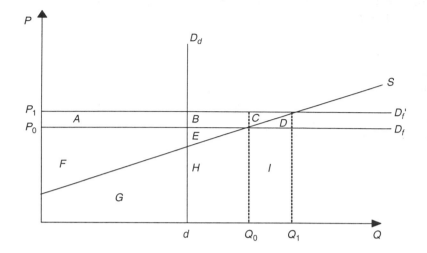

undertaken to meet increased exports, which are equal to $Q_1 - d$ after output rises to $Q_1$. (Area $D + I$ is the opportunity cost of the additional output.)

The first part of the direct price gain in equation C.1, or $\alpha\beta w$, corresponds to the area $A + B$, expressed as a ratio to the total original value added, or ratio $(A + B)/(F + E + H + G)$. In the figure, total agricultural output value is initially $P_0 Q_0$. The farm-gate price rises by the proportion $\alpha w$, so $P_1 = P_0(1 + \alpha w)$. Area $A + B$ is thus $(P_0 Q_0)\alpha w$. Area $C$ is $0.5 \Delta P \Delta Q$. If the price elasticity of domestic supply is $\Omega$, then $\Delta Q = \alpha w \Omega Q_0$, and area $C$ is $(0.5\alpha w P_0)(\alpha w \Omega Q_0)$. The total static gain to farmers, expressed as a proportion of initial farm income, is thus $\{(P_0 Q_0)\alpha w + (0.5\alpha w P_0)(\alpha w \Omega Q_0)\}/P_0 Q_0$, or $\alpha w(1 + 0.5\alpha w \Omega)$. This proportionate change must be dampened by elasticity $\beta$ to translate agricultural gain into a rural income gain. Finally, it is assumed that the rural poor share proportionately in the change in rural income. The resulting direct price effect on rural household income, augmented to incorporate the static welfare gain on increased export volume, and expressed as a proportion of total income of the rural poor, is

$$z_R^s = \beta\alpha w(1 + 0.5\Omega\alpha w) - \theta_R \gamma_R w = w(\beta\alpha[1 + 0.5\Omega\alpha w] - \theta_R \gamma_R) \quad (C.2)$$

In the urban sector, the static real income effect of the rise in food prices is

$$z_U^s = -\theta_U \gamma_U w \quad (C.3)$$

That is, real income falls by the proportionate rise in urban food prices times the weight of food in the consumption basket of the urban poor. The rise in urban food prices equals the proportionate rise in world food prices times the urban elasticity of food prices with respect to the world price.

Define $\varepsilon$ as the absolute value of the elasticity of the incidence of headcount poverty with respect to household income. Define $\pi$ as the poverty rate, and use the circumflex to denote proportionate change. Then the proportionate changes in the rural and urban poverty rates resulting from static effects of (industrial-country) agricultural trade liberalization will be

$$\hat{\pi}_R^s = -\varepsilon z_R^s \, ; \, \hat{\pi}_U^s = -\varepsilon z_U^s \tag{C.4}$$

If the share $\varphi_R$ of the country's poor are in rural areas, and the share $\varphi_U$ are in urban areas ($\varphi_R + \varphi_U = 1$), then for the country as a whole the proportionate change in the incidence of poverty will be a weighted average of the rural and urban changes, or, with subscript $T$ denoting the total:

$$\pi_T^s = \phi_R \hat{\pi}_R^s + \phi_U \hat{\pi}_U^s \tag{C.5}$$

Substituting, we have

$$\hat{\pi}_T^s = \varepsilon w \{ \phi_R [\theta_R \gamma_R - \beta\alpha(1 + 0.5\Omega\alpha w)] + \phi_U \theta_U \gamma_U \} \tag{C.6}$$

From the standpoint of static effects, then, the condition for industrial-country agricultural liberalization to reduce rather than increase poverty in developing countries ($\hat{\pi}_T^s < 0$) is

$$\phi_R \theta_R \gamma_R + \phi_U \theta_U \gamma_U < \phi_R \beta\alpha(1 + 0.5\Omega\alpha w) \tag{C.7}$$

Inequality C.7 states that the increase in poverty incidence stemming from the reduction in real income associated with the rise in food prices in both the rural and urban areas (left-hand side) must be smaller than the reduction in poverty incidence arising from the boost in real farm income attributable to higher prices for farm exports (right-hand side). The central core of this condition can best be illuminated by making the not unreasonable assumption that several of these parameters, $\alpha$, $\beta$, $\gamma$, and $\Omega$, are all unity; and that there is no difference between their values in the rural and urban sectors, nor is there any difference between the two sectors for the share of food in the consumption basket. Under these assumptions, the condition for poverty reduction rather than poverty increase becomes

$$\theta < \phi_R(1 + 0.5w) \tag{C.8}$$

Essentially, inequality C.8 states that the share of food in the consumption basket of the poor ($\theta$) must be smaller than the share of the country's poor found in agriculture ($\theta_R$) for industrial-country agricultural liberalization to reduce rather than increase poverty in developing countries. The condition is a bit more lenient, because the test more precisely is against the share of the poor in agriculture augmented by half the percentage rise in world agricultural prices. For example, if the share of food in the consumption budget is 0.5, and if the rise in world food prices is 10 percent, then for poverty reduction rather than poverty increase, the share of the country's total poor population to be found in the agricultural sector must be at least $0.5/1.05 = 0.48$.

From inequality C.8, it becomes immediately clear that where the great bulk of the poor are in the rural sector, global liberalization of agricultural trade is likely to reduce poverty, but where most of the poor are in urban areas the reverse will be true, at least for the static effects.

On balance, a consideration of the differences in the list of parameters from unity seems likely to make the poverty reduction condition less stringent. In particular, the elasticity of domestic food prices with respect to the international price may well be less than unity, especially in the rural sector ($\gamma_R$), where foodstuffs grown for home consumption may differ from products grown for export. Similarly, in the rural area, the share of food in the consumption basket of the poor could be less than in the urban area, given the availability of low-opportunity-cost subsistence crops. Partly offsetting this may be a less than unitary elasticity of the farm-gate price to the world price ($\alpha$). Unity is a reasonable value for the elasticity of rural income with respect to farm-gate price ($\beta$), however. The presence of intermediate input costs suggests this elasticity could be higher than unity (a given percent rise in product price yields a greater percent increase in income net of input costs), but the presence of nonagricultural rural activity (e.g., services sector) would make the elasticity less than unity, with the two effects tending to offset each other. Finally, for the agricultural supply elasticity, an assumption of unity would seem reasonable.

Plausible central values for these parameters thus might be as follows: $\theta_R = 0.4$; $\theta_U = 0.5$; $\gamma_R = 0.8$; $\gamma_U = 0.9$; $\alpha = 0.9$; $\beta = 1.0$; and $\Omega = 1.0$. If the rise in the world price is 10 percent ($w = 0.1$), then inequality C.7 becomes $\phi_R$ (0.4)(0.8) + $\phi_U$ (0.5)(0.9) < $\phi_R$ (0.9)(1.0)(1.05). Under these assumptions, agricultural liberalization by industrial countries reduces poverty for those developing countries where $\phi_U < 1.65\ \phi_R$, which means $\phi_U < 0.58$. This will usually be the case, because for most countries the share of the total poor population to be found in the rural area will be well above half rather than below half.

At the same time, the simple fact that these conditions must be met for the impact of industrial-country agricultural liberalization to reduce rather than increase poverty in developing countries suggests that the poverty reduction gains from this reform might be smaller than many of the strong calls for this reform might imply. However, if there are dynamic as well as static gains from liberalization, the poverty reduction gains will be larger than those identified so far.

## Dynamic Effects

It has long been recognized that there can be dynamic as well as static gains from trade liberalization. The "welfare triangles" theory of static gains is well worked out, but this is not the case for dynamic gains. The latter (broadly defined) include gains from economies of scale, gains associated with imperfect competition, stimulus to technical change (X-efficiency), and perhaps macroeconomic gains from an increased availability of foreign exchange. Although some models have specified particular forms for these gains (e.g., Rutherford and Tarr 1998), for the purposes here it is sufficient to recognize their presence and consider their likely magnitude relative to the static gains. In addition to incorporating a component of gains for dynamic effects, it is necessary to consider their allocation between the urban and rural sectors, and within each sector, between the poor and nonpoor, in order to obtain a more complete analysis of the impact on poverty incidence.

Suppose that total gains including dynamic ones (e g., as measured, say, by the annual rate in the fifth year) amount to the multiple $\psi$ of static gains. Dynamic gains alone are thus ($\psi - 1$) times static gains. We seek first the total static and dynamic gains for the economy, and then the amounts accruing to the poor.

Returning to figure 3C.1, the static welfare gains on which we seek to build an estimate of dynamic gains must be the net welfare gains ($B + C$), not the gross gains to farmers including transfers from consumers ($A + B + C$). If we define the ratio of home-consumed agricultural output to the total as $h$, then from the figure $h = A/(A + B)$. So the net static welfare gain base corresponding to the gross base $w(\beta\alpha[1 + 0.5\Omega\alpha w])$ in equation C.2 will be $w(\beta\alpha[1 + 0.5\Omega\alpha w - h])$.

Per rural poor person, these net static gains amount to $y_{PR}w(\beta\alpha [1 + 0.5\Omega\alpha w - h])$, defining original income per rural poor person as $y_{PR}$. If the total number of poor people in the rural sector is $N_R$, if the share of the poor in total rural income is $S_R^P$, and if we assume that the share of the rural poor in the static liberalization gains is equal to their share in sectoral income generally, then we may estimate the implied aggregate static gains as

$$G_s = \frac{N_R}{S_R^P} y_{PR}[w\beta\alpha(1 + 0.5\Omega\alpha w - h)] \tag{C.9}$$

That is, per poor worker, the static gains amount to original income $y_{PR}$ multiplied by the proportionate increase in income in the bracketed expression. The first right-hand-side component (the fraction) then balloons the per-poor-person gains into aggregate sectoral gains by first multiplying by the number of the rural poor and then expanding by the inverse of the share of the poor in rural income.

Total dynamic gains, by construction, are merely

$$G_d = (\Psi - 1)G_s \qquad (C.10)$$

It is useful to recall, at this point, that the approach here is to use a benchmark relationship between dynamic and static gains from trade liberalization as the basis for incorporating dynamic gains. Because the liberalization in this case is rather special—unilateral liberalization by the industrial-country trading partners of the developing countries—it is worth making explicit the fact that the core static gains are from terms-of-trade improvement for exports, and the welfare triangle on export expansion. The more usual gains from import liberalization (net welfare triangle from lower consumer prices) are absent here. This means, correspondingly, that the dynamic gain estimates are substantially reduced if there is no export base.[54]

Intuitively, the dominant role of exports in measuring the dynamic gains is attractive. It coincides with the broad notion that the developing countries that are most likely to benefit from industrial-country agricultural liberalization are the agricultural exporters, whereas those that import agricultural goods could be adversely affected. It is also consistent with the strong implied role of exports in the various arguments invoked about dynamic gains, especially economies of scale and specialization in product varieties under imperfect competition.[55] Note further that the entire analysis could be recalculated to incorporate reciprocal import liberalization by developing countries. That, however, is not the focus here, which instead is on the effects on developing countries caused by agricultural protection in the industrial countries.

With a gauge of total dynamic gains in hand (equation C.10), the next step is to allocate them between the rural and urban sectors, and then add them to the static effects on the rural and urban poor. Suppose the fraction $\rho$ of these total dynamic gains accrues to the rural sector itself, and the fraction $1 - \rho$ provides economywide gains. Suppose the share of agriculture in GDP is given as the variable $a$. The total dynamic gains accruing to the rural poor will thus be

---

54. If $h = 1$, there are no base-period exports. The construction here nonetheless attributes dynamic gains to the new exports obtained from the expansion of domestic production, so the welfare triangle $C$ in figure 3C.1 persists even if the domestic demand curve $D_d$ is located further to the right and domestic consumption $d$ coincides with output $Q_0$.

55. The argument of stimulus to technical change, however, applies equally well to import liberalization.

$$G_{dPR} = S_R^P(\rho + [1-\rho]a)G_d \qquad (C.11)$$

Expressed as a proportionate change in income of the rural poor, these dynamic gains are

$$z_R^d = \frac{G_{dPR} / N_R}{y_{PR}} \qquad (C.12)$$

Substituting and simplifying,

$$z_R^d = (\rho + [1-\rho]a)(\Psi - 1)(w\beta\alpha[1 + 0.5\Omega\alpha w - h) \qquad (C.13)$$

The total dynamic gains accruing to the urban poor correspondingly amount to

$$G_{dPU} = S_U^P(1-\rho)(1-a)G_d \qquad (C.14)$$

The corresponding proportionate increase in real income per urban poor person amounts to

$$z_U^d = \frac{G_{dPU} / N_U}{y_{PU}} \qquad (C.15)$$

Once again substituting, simplifying, and in addition making the assumption that the household income of the urban poor is equal to that of the rural poor ($y_{PU} = y_{PR}$), and recognizing that $N_R/N_U = \phi_R/\phi_U$, we obtain

$$z_U^d = \frac{S_U^P\phi_R}{S_R^P\phi_U}(1-\rho)(1-a)(\Psi - 1)w\beta\alpha(1 + 0.5\Omega\alpha w - h), \qquad (C.16)$$

where $S_U^P$ is the share of the urban poor in urban income. The initial right-hand-side term is essentially a scaling factor. The intuition is straightforward with respect to the term $S_U^P$, because there will be a larger impact for the poor where they have a larger share of urban income. Division by the fraction of poor in the urban sector $\phi_U$ is also intuitive, because there will be more income per urban poor person if there are fewer of them. Less intuitively, the rest of the initial scaling fraction gives a larger impact where there are more rural poor people, because this means the aggregate of the per-person amounts is larger, and when the share of the rural poor in rural income is smaller, because this means there is larger ballooning to the aggregate dynamic gains from the amount received by the rural poor.

Reasonable central values for the parameters required to estimate these dynamic effects are as follows. The total welfare gains might reasonably amount to twice the static gains, or $\psi = 2$. The share of dynamic gains specific to the agricultural sector itself might plausibly be set at two-thirds in the central case, or $\rho = 0.67$.

## Combined Effects

The total static and dynamic gains to the poor in developing countries from industrial-country liberalization of agricultural trade, expressed as a proportionate change in real income, thus amount to $z_R = z_R^s + z_R^d$, in the rural sector, and $z_U = z_U^s + z_U^d$ in the urban sector. The corresponding proportionate change in total poverty incidence for the developing country is

$$\hat{\pi}_T^T = -\varepsilon[\phi_R z_R + \phi_U z_U] \tag{C.17}$$

Substituting, and for convenience setting $\Gamma = \beta\alpha(1 + 0.5\Omega\alpha w - h)$, $c = \rho + a - \rho a$, and $\mu = (S_U^P/S_R^P)(\phi_R/\phi_U)$, we have

$$\hat{\pi}_T^T = -\varepsilon w[\phi_R\{\Gamma(1+c[\Psi-1])-\theta_R\gamma_R\}+\phi_U\{\Gamma\mu(1-c)(\Psi-1)-\theta_U\gamma_U\}] \tag{C.18}$$

## Data and Results

The most important data for the calculations are the proportions of the poor located in the rural and urban areas, $\phi_R$ and $\phi_U$. These are derived from World Bank estimates of the incidence of rural, urban, and national poverty (World Bank 2002d).[56] The term $h$, referring to the fraction of domestic agricultural production that is consumed domestically rather than exported, is estimated as $h = \min\{1.0; 1 - [X - M]/Q\}$, where $X$ is agricultural exports, $M$ is agricultural imports, and $Q$ is agricultural value added. Export and import data are for International Standard Industrial Classification categories 1, 2, and 5 (revision 3) from the World Bank's World Integrated Trade Solution database. Agricultural value added is from World Bank (2002d), in current dollars. The trade and agricultural production data are for 2000. The share of agriculture in GDP, the variable

---

56. The World Bank reports the fraction of households in poverty at the national level ($\eta$), and for the rural and urban areas ($\eta_R$ and $\eta_U$, respectively). Because the national rate must equal a weighted average of the rural and urban rates, we can infer that $\eta = m_R\eta_R + m_U\eta_U$, where $m$ is the fraction of total population in each respective sector. These population shares can thus be estimated as $m_R = (\eta - \eta_U)/(\eta_R - \eta_U)$; $m_U = 1 - m_R$. With some manipulation, it can then be shown that the desired estimate of the share of total poor residing in rural areas can be obtained as $\varphi_R = (\eta_R/\eta)m_R$. Then, $\varphi_U = 1 - \varphi_R$. Note also that whereas the urban and rural poverty rates are reported using the national definition of poverty, for calculating the cross-country aggregates the international ($2 PPP per day) definition is used, along with the assumption that the allocation of poor people between the two sectors is the same under that definition as well.

*a*, is from World Bank (2002d). A single standard elasticity of poverty with respect to income, $\varepsilon$, is set at $-2$, the central value identified in most past empirical work (see chapter 1).

Table 3C.1 reports the results of the model estimates for the 72 countries for which data are available. These central estimates assume that global agricultural liberalization raises world agricultural prices by 10 percent ($w = 0.1$).[57] Key features of the central estimates include the following:

- Global agricultural liberalization substantially reduces global poverty. The number of poor people in the 72 countries falls by 201.5 million, or by 7.9 percent.

- The net impact comprises a large net reduction in poverty for 56 countries (by 204.3 million) and a small net increase in poverty for 16 countries (by 2.8 million).

- The results are heavily driven by the fraction of the total poor population found in rural areas. The minority of cases where poverty rises tend to have uncharacteristically high fractions of the poor living in urban areas. Notable cases include Argentina, Chile, and Mexico.

- As is true for the underlying poverty numbers, the impacts are concentrated in a limited number of large countries (especially China, a reduction by 72 million; India, 59 million; Bangladesh, 12 million; and Pakistan, 10 million).

- Most countries experience a reduction in rural poverty but an increase in urban poverty. The aggregate effect for the 72 countries in the rural sector is a reduction of 255 million in poverty; the corresponding urban aggregate is an increase of 54 million in poverty.

- Poverty reduction is greater where the export base is larger (i.e., *h* is smaller) and/or where the rural share of the total poor population is extremely large (e.g., 90 percent or more). Both factors tend to boost the dynamic gains experienced by the urban poor.

- In the central results, by far the dominant effects are the static impacts. Static rural income gains are 6.2 percent, and static urban income losses are 4.5 percent. Simple average dynamic rural income gains are 0.97 percent, and dynamic urban income gains are 0.57 percent. This result derives mainly from the typically relatively low ratio of net agricultural exports to agricultural production (i.e., a relatively close value of *h* to unity) for most countries.

---

57. IMF staff estimates using a CGE model find that freeing world trade in agriculture would raise world prices by 4 percent for cotton; 2–8 percent for rice, sugar, and wheat; 7 percent for beef; and 23 percent for milk (IMF 2002d, 89).

# Table 3C.1   Impact of global agricultural liberalization on poverty

| Country | Percent of poor in rural areas | Domestic consumption (*h*) | Share of agriculture in GDP | Change in poverty Percent | Change in poverty Millions |
|---|---|---|---|---|---|
| Albania | 74.8 | 1.00 | 0.51 | −7.6 | −0.1 |
| Algeria | 69.6 | 1.00 | 0.09 | −6.4 | −0.3 |
| Argentina | 13.5 | 0.69 | 0.05 | 5.4 | 0.3 |
| Azerbaijan | 52.7 | 1.00 | 0.19 | −2.7 | −0.1 |
| Bangladesh | 94.0 | 1.00 | 0.25 | −11.8 | −12.0 |
| Belarus | 36.8 | 1.00 | 0.15 | 0.9 | 0.0 |
| Benin | 71.1 | 0.82 | 0.38 | −8.9 | −0.4 |
| Bolivia | 42.9 | 1.00 | 0.22 | −0.5 | 0.0 |
| Botswana | 61.3 | 1.00 | 0.04 | −4.6 | 0.0 |
| Brazil | 38.8 | 0.92 | 0.07 | 0.0 | 0.0 |
| Bulgaria | 36.8 | 0.94 | 0.15 | 0.5 | 0.0 |
| Burundi | 95.0 | 0.90 | 0.51 | −13.6 | −0.8 |
| Chile | 18.4 | 0.82 | 0.11 | 4.4 | 0.1 |
| China | 88.9 | 1.00 | 0.16 | −10.6 | −72.1 |
| Colombia | 74.9 | 0.86 | 0.14 | −9.0 | −1.1 |
| Costa Rica | 50.6 | 0.22 | 0.09 | −8.7 | −0.1 |
| Côte d'Ivoire | 66.2 | 0.49 | 0.29 | −11.2 | −0.9 |
| Czech Republic | 30.7 | 1.00 | 0.04 | 2.2 | 0.0 |
| Ecuador | 61.0 | 0.28 | 0.10 | −11.3 | −0.7 |
| Egypt, Arab Republic | 55.4 | 0.90 | 0.17 | −4.3 | −1.5 |
| El Salvador | 44.9 | 0.92 | 0.10 | −1.5 | −0.1 |
| Estonia | 41.7 | 0.93 | 0.06 | −0.6 | 0.0 |
| Gambia | 82.1 | 0.99 | 0.38 | −9.3 | −0.1 |
| Georgia | 45.5 | 1.00 | 0.32 | −1.1 | 0.0 |
| Ghana | 62.7 | 0.85 | 0.35 | −6.6 | −0.7 |
| Guatemala | 73.6 | 0.78 | 0.23 | −9.9 | −0.7 |
| Guinea | 82.1 | 1.00 | 0.24 | −9.2 | −0.4 |
| Honduras | 64.2 | 0.60 | 0.18 | −10.0 | −0.4 |
| India | 70.5 | 0.99 | 0.25 | −6.8 | −59.2 |
| Indonesia | 72.3 | 0.99 | 0.17 | −7.1 | −9.9 |
| Jamaica | 53.9 | 1.00 | 0.06 | −2.9 | 0.0 |
| Jordan | 31.9 | 1.00 | 0.02 | 2.0 | 0.0 |
| Kazakhstan | 61.9 | 0.66 | 0.09 | −8.2 | −0.2 |
| Kenya | 83.8 | 0.61 | 0.20 | −14.8 | −2.8 |
| Latvia | 38.0 | 0.95 | 0.04 | 0.3 | 0.0 |
| Lithuania | 39.2 | 1.00 | 0.08 | 0.3 | 0.0 |
| Malawi | 95.0 | 0.80 | 0.42 | −15.2 | −1.3 |
| Mauritius | 72.3 | 1.00 | 0.06 | −7.0 | 0.0 |
| Mexico | 31.9 | 1.00 | 0.04 | 2.0 | 0.8 |
| Moldova | 66.2 | 0.77 | 0.28 | −8.3 | −0.1 |
| Mongolia | 45.8 | 0.99 | 0.33 | −1.3 | 0.0 |
| Morocco | 66.3 | 1.00 | 0.14 | −5.7 | −0.1 |
| Nepal | 94.8 | 1.00 | 0.40 | −12.0 | −2.3 |
| Nicaragua | 62.2 | 0.75 | 0.32 | −7.2 | −0.2 |
| Nigeria | 70.6 | 1.00 | 0.30 | −6.7 | −7.7 |
| Pakistan | 72.5 | 0.85 | 0.26 | −8.9 | −10.4 |
| Panama | 77.3 | 0.74 | 0.07 | −10.8 | −0.1 |
| Paraguay | 29.3 | 0.78 | 0.21 | 1.5 | 0.0 |
| Peru | 47.8 | 1.00 | 0.08 | −1.6 | −0.2 |
| Philippines | 71.3 | 1.00 | 0.16 | −6.8 | −2.0 |
| Poland | 41.7 | 1.00 | 0.04 | −0.2 | 0.0 |
| Portugal | 44.1 | 1.00 | 0.04 | −0.8 | 0.0 |

*(table continues next page)*

**Table 3C.1** *(continued)*

| Country | Percent of poor in rural areas | Domestic consumption (h) | Share of agriculture in GDP | Change in poverty Percent | Change in poverty Millions |
|---|---|---|---|---|---|
| Romania | 31.8 | 1.00 | 0.13 | 2.0 | 0.1 |
| Russia | 33.1 | 1.00 | 0.07 | 1.7 | 0.6 |
| Senegal | 65.0 | 1.00 | 0.18 | −5.5 | −0.4 |
| Sierra Leone | 77.2 | 0.90 | 0.47 | −9.4 | −0.4 |
| Slovak Republic | 52.7 | 1.00 | 0.04 | −2.7 | 0.0 |
| Slovenia | 61.3 | 1.00 | 0.03 | −4.6 | 0.0 |
| South Africa | 55.2 | 0.86 | 0.03 | −4.4 | −0.7 |
| South Korea | 22.1 | 1.00 | 0.05 | 4.1 | 0.0 |
| Tanzania | 88.3 | 0.90 | 0.45 | −12.0 | −2.4 |
| Thailand | 61.5 | 0.92 | 0.10 | −5.4 | −0.9 |
| Trinidad and Tobago | 71.4 | 1.00 | 0.02 | −6.9 | 0.0 |
| Tunisia | 60.4 | 1.00 | 0.12 | −4.3 | 0.0 |
| Turkey | 30.7 | 1.00 | 0.16 | 2.2 | 0.3 |
| Turkmenistan | 67.4 | 0.82 | 0.27 | −7.9 | −0.2 |
| Uganda | 95.0 | 0.93 | 0.42 | −13.1 | −2.2 |
| Uruguay | 11.0 | 1.00 | 0.06 | 6.6 | 0.0 |
| Venezuela | 15.9 | 1.00 | 0.05 | 5.5 | 0.5 |
| Vietnam | 90.1 | 0.70 | 0.24 | −15.1 | −6.3 |
| Zambia | 67.8 | 0.98 | 0.27 | −6.2 | −0.6 |
| Zimbabwe | 90.8 | 0.80 | 0.18 | −13.7 | −1.1 |
| Total | | | | | −201.5 |

*Source:* See text.

## Sensitivity Analysis

The results of this analysis are relatively sensitive to the parameters assumed. Table 3C.2 shows pessimistic, central, and optimistic parameter assumptions and the corresponding principal results. The elasticity of agricultural supply ($\Omega$) could be high at 2.0 or low at 0.5. The elasticity of the farm-gate price with respect to the world price ($\alpha$) could be optimistically as high as unity but pessimistically as low as 0.6; the elasticity of rural income with respect to the farm-gate price ($\beta$) could be optimistically as high as 1.1 but pessimistically as low as 0.7; and the elasticities of food costs in the consumption basket with respect to the farm-gate price ($\gamma_R$, $\gamma_U$) could be as low as 0.6 on the optimistic side.[58] The ratio of total welfare effects including dynamic gains to static gains ($\psi$) could plausibly be as high as 4 but as low as 1.5. The agriculture-specific portion of dynamic gains ($\rho$) could be as high as 0.9, on the pessimistic side, or as low as 0.5 (permitting greater economywide gains), on the optimistic side.

---

58. On the pessimistic side, considering that the farm price is set at a relatively low elasticity with respect to the world price in the pessimistic case, the elasticity of consumption food price with respect to the world price may appropriately be left unchanged from the central case, because the alternative of raising it would tend to create an implausible divergence between domestic agricultural production and consumption prices.

# Table 3C.2   Sensitivity analysis for poverty impact of global agricultural liberalization

| Parameter or results | Less favorable impact | Central | More favorable impact |
|---|---|---|---|
| **Parameter** | | | |
| $\Omega$ supply elasticity | 0.5 | 1.0 | 2.0 |
| $\alpha$ farm price elasticity | 0.6 | 0.9 | 1.0 |
| $\beta$ rural income elasticity | 0.7 | 1.0 | 1.1 |
| $\gamma_R$ food cost elasticity | 0.8 | 0.8 | 0.6 |
| $\gamma_U$ food cost elasticity | 0.8 | 0.9 | 0.6 |
| $\Psi$ ratio, total/static gains | 1.5 | 2.0 | 4.0 |
| $\rho$ agriculture-specific portion of dynamic gains | 0.9 | 0.67 | 0.5 |
| | | | |
| Results (72 countries) | | | |
| Poverty | | | |
|     Percent | 0.5 | −7.9 | −18.5 |
|     Millions | 13.9 | −201.5 | −470.7 |
| Rural poverty | | | |
|     Percent | −2.3 | −13.5 | −24.8 |
|     Millions | −43.8 | −255.1 | −469.5 |
| Urban poverty | | | |
|     Percent | 9.0 | 8.3 | −0.2 |
|     Millions | 57.7 | 53.7 | −1.2 |
| Income change (percent) | | | |
|     Rural static | 1.06 | 6.21 | 9.7 |
|     Rural dynamic | 0.23 | 0.97 | 4.0 |
|     Urban static | −4.50 | −4.50 | 3.0 |
|     Urban dynamic | 0.03 | 0.90 | 4.3 |

*Source:* Author's calculations.

As indicated in table 3C.2, under the optimistic assumptions, world agricultural liberalization could reduce global poverty by an impressive 18.5 percent, or by 471 million people for the 72 principal developing countries examined. Under the pessimistic assumptions, however, the result could be a slight increase in global poverty, by 0.5 percent or 14 million people for the countries listed in table 3C.1.

# Appendix 3D
# Trade Balance and Comparative Advantage in Food and Agriculture for Least Developed Countries, 1999–2001

| Country | (FX – FM)/T | (AX – AM)/T | ZF | ZA | Poor (millions) | Number of countries |
|---|---|---|---|---|---|---|
| Afghanistan[a] | -0.11 | -0.15 | 3.98 | 5.09 | 19.3 | |
| Angola | -0.03 | -0.04 | 0.00 | 0.00 | 8.5 | |
| Bangladesh | -0.06 | -0.11 | 0.07 | 0.09 | 99.3 | |
| Benin | -0.07 | 0.04 | 1.36 | 177.96 | 4.5 | |
| Burkina Faso | -0.15 | -0.09 | 0.68 | 3.99 | 9.4 | |
| Burundi | 0.11 | 0.10 | 20.57 | 18.11 | 5.5 | |
| Cambodia | -0.02 | -0.11 | 0.03 | 0.08 | 7.5 | |
| Cape Verde | -0.22 | -0.29 | 0.03 | 0.05 | 0.1 | |
| Central African Republic | -0.04 | -0.02 | 0.23 | 0.42 | 3.0 | |
| Chad | 0.07 | 0.18 | 8.43 | 69.50 | 5.7 | |
| Comoros | -0.11 | -0.14 | 1.87 | 1.53 | 0.3 | |
| Congo, Democratic Republic of | -0.06 | -0.08 | 0.09 | 0.10 | 38.2 | |
| Djibouti | -0.06 | -0.15 | 0.20 | 0.09 | 0.5 | |
| Equatorial Guinea | 0.00 | 0.00 | 0.33 | 0.22 | 0.1 | |
| Ethiopia | 0.02 | 0.05 | 10.28 | 34.64 | 48.0 | |
| Gambia, The | -0.21 | -0.22 | 0.55 | -1.38 | 0.8 | |
| Guinea | -0.07 | -0.09 | 0.04 | 0.05 | 4.0 | |
| Guinea-Bissau | 0.19 | 0.16 | 8.51 | 7.74 | 1.0 | |
| Haiti | -0.18 | -0.23 | 0.25 | 0.20 | 5.2 | |
| Kiribati | -0.12 | -0.13 | 0.00 | 0.59 | 0.1 | |
| Laos | -0.01 | -0.03 | 1.35 | 0.69 | 2.9 | |
| Liberia | -0.01 | 0.00 | 0.59 | 9.22 | 2.3 | |
| Madagascar | 0.02 | 0.01 | 1.86 | 1.65 | 13.4 | |
| Malawi | 0.05 | 0.36 | 5.18 | 49.12 | 9.2 | |
| Maldives | 0.09 | -0.11 | 0.00 | 0.00 | 0.1 | |
| Mali | -0.01 | 0.07 | 9.41 | 358.18 | 9.6 | |
| Mauritania | -0.09 | -0.13 | 0.29 | 0.20 | 0.6 | |
| Mozambique | -0.08 | -0.10 | 0.63 | 0.70 | 13.6 | |
| Myanmar | 0.04 | 0.00 | 3.30 | 1.48 | 32.8 | |
| Nepal | -0.03 | -0.08 | 1.06 | 0.59 | 19.3 | |
| Niger | -0.04 | -0.10 | 1.39 | 0.93 | 9.0 | |
| Rwanda | -0.04 | -0.08 | 3.30 | 2.36 | 7.0 | |
| Samoa | -0.04 | -0.04 | 0.66 | 1.18 | 0.0 | |
| Sao Tomé and Príncipe | 0.03 | -0.09 | 3.21 | 1.74 | 0.1 | |
| Senegal | -0.14 | -0.13 | 0.21 | 0.60 | 6.3 | |
| Sierra Leone | -0.36 | -0.41 | 2.04 | -0.52 | 3.7 | |
| Solomon Islands | -0.07 | 0.06 | 0.30 | 0.14 | 0.2 | |
| Somalia | -0.02 | -0.04 | 4.16 | 3.61 | 7.1 | |
| Sudan | -0.02 | 0.01 | 1.59 | 2.03 | 21.1 | |
| Tanzania | 0.04 | 0.07 | 6.50 | 93.59 | 19.7 | |
| Togo | 0.00 | 0.02 | 2.81 | 6.28 | 2.9 | |
| Uganda | 0.10 | 0.11 | 30.96 | 5.28 | 16.6 | |
| Vanuatu | -0.03 | 0.00 | 1.28 | 2.68 | 0.1 | |
| Yemen | -0.11 | -0.13 | 0.03 | 0.04 | 6.1 | |
| Zambia | 0.00 | 0.02 | 1.70 | 2.36 | 9.1 | |
| **Total** | | | | | 470.4 | 45 |
| Excluding Bangladesh | | | | | 374.1 | 44 |
| Of which: food trade deficit | | | | | 213.4 | 34 |
| agriculture trade deficit | | | | | 175.1 | 29 |
| food comparative disadvantage | | | | | 110.2 | 21 |
| agriculture comparative disadvantage | | | | | 129.3 | 20 |

F = food; A = agriculture; X = exports; M = imports; T = total trade turnover; ZF = ratio of food exports to food imports, divided by ratio of nonfood exports to nonfood imports; ZA = same ratio for agricultural goods.

a. 1999.

*Source:* FAO (2003); IMF (2003).

# 4

# Modeling the Impact of Trade Liberalization on Global Poverty

This chapter applies one of the leading computable general equilibrium (CGE) models of international trade and a prominent international database on trade and protection to estimate the impact of alternative trade liberalization scenarios on trade, welfare, and global poverty. The purpose is to extend and complement the estimates developed and surveyed in chapter 3, and to obtain a better understanding of the forces and interactions that determine the poverty impact of trade liberalization.

For these estimates, the analysis applies the CGE model developed by Harrison, Rutherford, and Tarr (1996, 1997a; hereafter, the HRT model). When combined with the Global Trade Analysis Project (GTAP) database developed by a network of researchers centered at Purdue University (Dimaranan and McDougall 2002), the HRT model is capable of estimating the change in trade flows, economic welfare, and product and factor prices that can be expected to result from changes in protection and subsidies. Varying aggregations by sector and country can be applied, depending on the focus in question and subject to computational feasibility.

The strategy of this chapter is to examine the effects of alternative scenarios for international trade liberalization, and particularly their impact on factor prices, as the basis for then calculating the corresponding impact on global poverty. For this purpose, the principal production factor of interest is unskilled labor, which accounts for the bulk of income of households at the poverty level. It is possible to combine the factor price estimates from simulations using the HRT model with the poverty elasticity estimates of chapter 1 to arrive at estimates of changes in global poverty that might be expected from alternative trade liberalization scenarios. The country and regional detail is chosen taking into account the most important country concentrations of poverty. The combined model of this chapter, centered on the HRT CGE model as tailored to the poverty-oriented regions and extended to derive poverty-impact estimates, may be called the Poverty Effects–HRT, or PEHRT, model.

## The Harrison-Rutherford-Tarr CGE Model

The HRT model is in the family of "Walrasian" CGE models. More broadly, CGE models are descendants of early multisectoral planning or policy models and, like the earlier multisectoral models, are built around a core input-output structure required for interindustry consistency. The more Walrasian of these models are based on optimizing the behavior of representative agents (e.g., the representative firm, for production, and the representative household, for consumption) in a framework of welfare economics. They can be distinguished from "macrostructuralist" CGE models, which also involve the simultaneous determination of sectoral quantities and prices in response to exogenous or policy shocks, but which may depart from optimizing behavior in favor of ad hoc components designed to increase empirical relevance (Thissen 1998; Robinson 1989).

The underlying analytical structure of the HRT model closely follows that developed by de Melo and Tarr (1992).[1] Producers maximize profits, subject either to constant returns to scale or increasing returns to scale. The representative firm in each industry purchases factors of production (e.g., unskilled and skilled labor) and intermediate input goods from domestic or foreign suppliers, in combinations that minimize cost for any given level of production. Sectoral output equals the amount demanded domestically by consumers and intermediate users, plus the amount sold in exports. There is a "constant elasticity of transformation" (CET) between production allocated to the domestic market and that placed on the export market, and producers make this allocation in the light of domestic and export prices so as to maximize profits.[2]

---

1. De Melo and Tarr (1992) display a full set of model equations. The various published versions of the HRT model do not do so. Instead, for the core economic equations, the HRT model relies on a computer-code version incorporated into the General Algebraic Modeling System (GAMS) software system (Rutherford 1998).

2. The CET has the same functional form as the more widely known constant elasticity of substitution (CES) function. This form is $z = a[\delta_x x^{-\rho} + (1 - \delta_x) y^{-\rho}]^{[-1/\rho]}$, where $z$ is production (or total output to be sold), $x$ is one factor of production (or output allocated to one market, domestic) and $y$ is the other factor (or output allocated to the other market, foreign). The parameter $\rho$ is equal to $\rho = [1/\sigma - 1]$, where $\sigma$ is the absolute value of the elasticity of substitution.

The "representative" consumer purchases domestic goods and imports so as to maximize utility. Demand is "nested" at successive stages. At the top level, demand is Cobb-Douglas among the various sectoral products, which means that the share of total spending on each sector will be constant with a higher (or lower) price offsetting a lower (higher) volume.[3] For each composite good, at the next level down there is a constant elasticity of substitution (CES) aggregation between the aggregate import and the domestic good, with a base-case elasticity of substitution of 4.[4] Within the aggregate import, the composition of the goods from the various country suppliers is obtained with an ("Armington") CES aggregate applying a base-case elasticity of substitution of 8. Thus, there is closer substitutability among imports from varying sources than between overall imports of the good and the domestic variety.[5]

Consumer income is determined by the model outcome for factor prices and hence payments to households for factors, plus transfers. Consumer income equals expenditures on commodities, with the composition but not the total affected by relative prices. The equality of expenditure on commodities available (supply) with consumer income (demand) is the feature of the model that enforces "Walras's law." The government collects trade taxes (tariffs and export taxes) and redistributes them to consumers in a manner that does not affect consumer behavior ("lump-sum" payments). The government operates under a balanced budget. The real exchange rate is assumed to adjust to maintain the base period current account balance unchanged.

The model is first "benchmarked" or calibrated so that the initial equilibrium solution replicates actual sectoral production, consumption, and factor use in the base year. Trade policy experiments can then be conducted by shocking the model, reducing specified import tariffs or export taxes. The model solution is driven by the required equality of the unit cost of production for each sector with the market-clearing price of consumption in each sector. To reach a new equilibrium after the shock, the nonlinear programming algorithm varies the sectoral assignment of factors and trade patterns so as to meet all the simultaneous equations once again. If these equations are met, welfare is maximized.[6] Thus, elimina-

---

3. Harrison, Rutherford, and Tarr (1997a, 1408). The Cobb-Douglas consumption is of this form: $C = a(X^\beta Y^{(1-\beta)})$, where $\beta$ is the share of the consumer budget spent on good $X$.

4. That is, a rise of 1 percent in the ratio of the price of imports to domestic supply will cause a 4 percent decline in the ratio of the volume of the import to the domestic good.

5. There is similar CES nesting of domestic varieties on the production side, in the increasing-returns-to-scale version of the model, which specifies a number of firms rather than just a single representative firm, as in the constant-returns-to-scale (CRTS) version.

6. Welfare is measured by Hicks's Equivalent Variation (EV) and Compensating Variation (CV). The first uses initial prices and asks how much income would have to be given to consumers to make them as well-off as they would become after liberalization. The second uses

tion of a high tariff will tend to reduce the relative price of the good in question, increase its consumption and the volume of imports, and reduce domestic production as the lower price makes the good less profitable for the domestic representative firm. The model treats voluntary export quotas (most important, in the textile and apparel sector) as export taxes imposed by the supplying country. It treats export subsidies (important in agriculture) as negative export taxes, which make the good more attractive to foreign purchasers.

The change in composition of domestic production resulting from the array of changes in import tariffs and export taxes will change the relative demand for the various factors of production (land, capital, skilled labor, and unskilled labor), inducing a change in their relative prices. More generally, product prices will change in each sector, and factor prices will change for each factor, such that each of the product sector and factor markets will "clear" (no "excess demand" or "excess supply").

Production for a given sector is CES at the level of intermediates between domestic and imported intermediates. It is also CES among the various factors in the production of sectoral value added. Given the production functions, factor prices are obtained using Shephard's lemma, which states that the quantity of a factor demanded is the partial derivative of the cost function with respect to the price of the factor in question. Production is "Leontief" (fixed-coefficient) between the aggregate intermediate input and the aggregate value added, to arrive at final sectoral output. For each sectoral good, there is similarly a CES composite aggregating the domestic and imported product. The sectoral import, for its part, is a CES Armington composite of imports from all the various supplying countries and regions.

The HRT model used in the analysis below is the version that is publicly available.[7] The model is solved using the General Algebraic Modeling System, or GAMS (Meeraus 1983; Brooke et al. 2003).

There are three variants of the HRT model: constant returns to scale (CRTS), increasing returns to scale (IRTS), and the "Steady State." In their calculations of the impact of the Uruguay Round, the three authors find that in their methodologically preferred IRTS version, the results are "striking" in their similarity to the CRTS estimates (Harrison, Rutherford,

---

the new prices and asks how much income would have to be taken away from consumers after liberalization to make them no better off than they were before. In an indifference curve diagram showing alternative combinations of two goods generating the same utility, both measures can be thought of as the distance between the before-shock (lower utility) and after-shock (higher utility) indifference curves. In the CRTS model, profits are zero, so the welfare gains are fully appropriated by consumers in the form of increased consumer surplus.

7. The model can be downloaded from http://dmsweb.badm.sc.edu/Glenn/ur_pub.htm. Rutherford has prepared software for use of the HRT model with the GTAP databases. This GTAPinGAMS software is available at http://nash.colorado.edu/tomruth/gtapingams/html/gtapgams.html.

and Tarr 1996, 236). Against benchmark 1992 levels of world GDP and trade, full implementation of the Uruguay Round liberalization is estimated to bring annual welfare gains of $96 billion (0.418 percent of global GDP) in the IRTS version, compared with welfare gains of $93 billion (0.405 percent) in the CRTS version.

Harrison, Rutherford, and Tarr emphasize that this difference is far smaller than usually believed. They suggest two reasons. First, on the basis of their review of the empirical literature on returns to scale, they use more modest implied gains from scale economies than are often assumed. They define the cost disadvantage ratio (CDR) as the ratio of average cost to marginal cost. For the 13 of their 22 product sectors in which they apply increasing returns, the maximum CDR shows the average cost at 13 percent above the marginal cost; the minimum, 3 percent; and the median, only 5 percent (Harrison, Rutherford, and Tarr 1996, 234).

Second, they judge that numerous CGE models that have quantified the effect of shifting from constant to increasing returns have changed other parameters (e.g., elasticities) at the same time, biasing the estimated impact of considering increasing returns. In part because the IRTS results appear to be close to the CRTS results, the estimates below rely on the CRTS version, despite the analytical elegance of the IRTS variant.[8]

The third version, the Steady State, does yield major differences in the estimated effects. In this version, instead of assuming that all factors remain at their initial economywide endowments, it is assumed that the stock of capital is allowed to increase to the point where the marginal return on investment after liberalization falls once again to its preliberalization level. Although this variant must be interpreted with care, as discussed below, it does provide insight into the important distinction between static and much larger dynamic welfare gains from trade liberalization.

## The GTAP5 Trade and Protection Database

The empirical data set used for the calculations in this chapter is that compiled in the Global Trade Analysis Project (GTAP) system. Whereas the Harrison, Rutherford, and Tarr (1996, 1997a) results for the Uruguay Round applied the 1992 benchmark GTAP data (GTAP2), the estimates here apply the successor GTAP5 database, which has trade and protection data primarily for 1997 but in agriculture for 1998. The data include estimates of sectoral production, taxes, interindustry input flows, and factor payments.

The GTAP data for bilateral merchandise trade are primarily from the United Nations' COMTRADE database. The data are screened for consis-

---

8. An additional reason is that implementation of the IRTS model requires additional software expense.

tency between exports reported by a country and the corresponding imports reported by its relevant trading partner. The tariff data for manufactures are from the UN Conference on Trade and Development's Trade Analysis and Information System (TRAINS) database, and apply the World Bank's World Integrated Trade Solution (WITS) software to combine the trade and protection data for purposes of aggregation. The tariffs on food and agricultural goods are from the Agricultural Trade Policy Database of the Economic Research Service of the US Department of Agriculture. These data in turn are largely from the Agricultural Market Access Database (AMAD) compiled jointly by the Department of Agriculture and certain international counterparts and official agencies. Agricultural export subsidies are from country submissions to the World Trade Organization (WTO). Domestic support in agriculture is divided into output subsidies, intermediate input subsidies, land-based payments, and capital-based payments, which are drawn from the Organization for Economic Cooperation and Development's (OECD's) producer subsidy equivalent (PSE) statistics.

All protection data are most-favored nation (MFN) rates, so a given country's protection for a given aggregate product varies across partners only because of varying subcategory product composition. Protection rates are not adjusted for preferential access, such as that under the Generalized System of Preferences (GSP). Bilateral trade among partners in the principal free trade arrangements, or FTAs (European Union; North American Free Trade Agreement, or NAFTA; Australia–New Zealand, and South African Customs Union), is treated as having zero protection, however.[9] Other details are given in Dimaranan and McDougall (2002).

The absence of specific treatment of preferential market access under the GSP and other special regimes considered in chapter 2 (the Everything But Arms, or EBA, program of the European Union; and the African Growth and Opportunity Act, or AGOA, Caribbean Basin Initiative, or CBI, and Andean Trade Preference Act, or ATPA, programs of the United States) raises the question of whether and by how much the welfare gains and poverty reduction from global trade liberalization will be overestimated. The broad answer is that the overstatement is unlikely to be large in the aggregate but may be significant for individual countries enjoying special-regime preferences. Nonetheless, several considerations should tend to limit overstatement.

First, the special-regime countries represent only a small fraction of developing-country trade. As noted in chapter 2, the heavily indebted poor countries (HIPCs), the least developed countries (LDCs), and sub-Saharan Africa (SSA) account for only 6.4 percent of US imports from developing countries, 8.5 percent for the European Union, and 3.8 percent for Japan.

---

9. However, zero-duty partner trade is not captured for Mercosur and other more recent FTAs.

Second, as reviewed in chapter 2, the special regimes have tended to have numerous restrictions (especially in agriculture and textiles-apparel, and especially under the GSP as opposed to the narrower regimes) that have meant the market access provided is far from full free entry. Third, that portion of welfare gains arising from own-country liberalization (the traditional welfare triangles) rather than terms-of-trade gains associated with foreign market liberalization should be accurately captured by the protection database. Fourth, estimates of export terms-of-trade gains from foreign market liberalization will not be overstated for that portion of exports going to other developing countries and to industrial countries not providing special-regime access (including Japan except for the GSP).

The database provides information at the level of 57 product sectors and 66 countries or regions. Some aggregation is necessary because the full detailed set of countries and products is beyond the computational capacity for the CGE model. The analysis of this chapter aggregates the data into the same 22 product groups as used in Harrison, Rutherford, and Tarr (1996). This disaggregation gives considerable attention to agricultural and food products (8 of the 22 sectors) and textiles and apparel (2 sectors), so it is already appropriate for estimations of special interest to developing countries.

The choice of countries and regions for the PEHRT model application of this chapter is tailored even more toward developing countries and especially those with major concentrations of poverty. One variant (B25) is for 25 "big" countries that are important in international trade; the other variant (P26) emphasizes the 26 economies relatively more important in the totals for global poverty.

The economy disaggregation for the B25 version is close to that in the 24-region HRT model (Harrison, Rutherford, and Tarr 1996).[10] The B25 version provides somewhat more detail on regions important for poverty, however (Central America, India, South Africa, Turkey), while aggregating other economies without poverty at the $2 per day level (Australia is combined with New Zealand; and Singapore, Hong Kong, and Taiwan are treated as a single region).

The P26 version provides still greater detail for poverty-relevant countries (separating out Bangladesh, Mozambique, Pakistan, Tanzania, Uganda) while aggregating other economies into broader regions (South Korea is combined with Hong Kong, Singapore, and Taiwan; Malaysia with Other Asia; Argentina with Other Latin America; and Turkey with the Middle East and North Africa). Because the B25 version provides greater detail on countries that bulk large in international trade, it is used for the main simulations oriented toward reviewing alternative trade liberalization policies, whereas a combination of the B25 and P26 versions is

---

10. The computational constraints for a GAMS solution appear to begin to be relevant as the model reaches the size of about 25 sectors and 25 regions.

used for the estimates of poverty impacts. Appendix 4A shows the GTAP5 regions and product sectors, along with the aggregations applied in the analysis here.[11]

Finally, it should be noted that using the GTAP5 database to calculate the effect of the Doha Round of trade liberalization likely involves a modest overstatement of the prospective gains from unfinished business in trade liberalization. Doha Round cuts apply to protection levels that already incorporate complete implementation of the Uruguay Round cuts. Yet the 1997 data for manufactures and 1998 data for agriculture will generally reflect incomplete Uruguay Round reductions, although by this period the bulk of reductions should have occurred. The Uruguay Round cuts were to begin in 1995 and be completed in 1999 (WTO 2002, 1), so some exaggeration of the post–Uruguay Round protection level is likely involved in using 1997–98 data as the protection base. For agriculture, this is probably a lesser problem than in manufactures, because the Uruguay Round in effect largely converted existing agricultural protection from quotas to tariff-rate quotas rather than lowering its level.

One specific area in which truly post–Uruguay Round protection would be lower than in the 1997 GTAP5 data would be for textile and apparel quotas. These are supposed to be phased out entirely by 2005 under the Uruguay Round agreements. Nonetheless, the model estimates below do incorporate effects from the removal of these quotas insofar as they were still present in 1997. As noted below, however, the level of their protection in the GTAP5 database was already far below that in the earlier 1992 GTAP2 database (albeit likely more for reasons of different methodology than because of major elimination of quotas during the intervening period).

## Trade Liberalization Simulation Results

The first step in evaluating the impact of global trade liberalization on world poverty is to calculate the change in economic welfare and factor prices that would result from liberalization. The size of the welfare gains for developing countries will depend on the particular scenario considered (e.g., global free trade, different depth of liberalization for industrial vs. developing countries, and different degrees of liberalization for different major sectors). The estimates will also depend on whether the calculations are only for static effects or also seek to incorporate dynamic effects using the Steady State model. For policy purposes, a key issue in the

---

11. The aggregation from GTAP5 data to the regions and sectors used here is done using the GTAPinGAMS software referred to above.

various calculations is the share of total potential gains for developing countries that arises from the liberalization of industrial-country markets as opposed to the liberalization of developing countries' own markets.

## Static CRTS: Free Trade

Trade liberalization is simulated in the HRT model by reducing or eliminating the benchmark rates of tariffs, export subsidies (e.g., on agricultural goods), export taxes (in particular, those representing voluntary export restraints under the Multi-Fiber Arrangement, or MFA), and input subsidies (e.g., those in agriculture included in the PSE estimates). Table 4.1 reports the welfare impact estimates of completely eliminating protection, using the CRTS version of the model. For the B25 groupings, free trade increases global welfare by $227.8 billion annually against the 1997 trade and production base, or by 0.93 percent of world GDP. Separate detail is shown as a memorandum item for the five additional countries treated individually in the P26 variant of the model.[12]

For comparison to the earlier results for the Uruguay Round, the model was also applied using the "full" Uruguay Round cuts in protection used in Harrison, Rutherford, and Tarr (1996) but as implemented with the GTAP5 data and PEHRT regions. This calculation yielded global welfare gains of $85.5 billion annually, or 0.35 percent of world GDP. This is about the same nominal level as found for the actual Uruguay Round in the original HRT results ($92.86 billion; Harrison, Rutherford, and Tarr 1996, 221), but smaller as a proportion of world GDP (the original result was 0.405 percent). A lower expected level of further welfare gains from applying a second round of the same proportionate cuts in protection is thus nearly offset by the rise in the nominal base of trade and GDP values (with world GDP expanding from $22.9 trillion in the GTAP2 database for 1992 to $24.6 trillion in the GTAP5 database for 1997).

Table 4.1 shows the sectoral composition of the potential gains from free trade. There are three broad sectors: agriculture and food; textiles and wearing apparel; and other manufactures and nonagricultural goods, abbreviated in the table as "manufactures." The contribution of each sector to total gains is obtained by running the model with free trade for all sectors except the one in question, and then subtracting the result from the result for total free trade. There is thus a residual that implicitly arises from the interaction of joint liberalization of all sectors, which is also displayed in the table.

---

12. The P26 model gives a nearly identical aggregate estimate of $224.7 billion. The sectoral decomposition is carried out only for the B25 and thus is not included in the memorandum for additional P26 country detail.

## Table 4.1 Welfare effects of free trade: CRTS model
(billions of dollars or percent of GDP)

| Region or economy | Agriculture | Textiles and apparel | Other manufactures | Interaction effect | Total | Total percent of GDP |
|---|---|---|---|---|---|---|
| **B25** | | | | | | |
| ANZ | 8.42 | 0.07 | 0.04 | 0.64 | 9.17 | 2.41 |
| CAN | 3.98 | 1.31 | −0.44 | −0.46 | 4.39 | 0.90 |
| USA | 22.31 | 8.04 | 2.00 | 6.85 | 39.20 | 0.57 |
| JPN | 21.67 | 1.25 | 14.03 | −5.25 | 31.70 | 0.85 |
| KOR | 5.92 | 1.19 | 4.48 | −2.14 | 9.44 | 2.41 |
| E_U | 21.62 | 6.25 | 14.94 | −3.85 | 38.96 | 0.61 |
| IDN | 0.20 | −0.02 | 1.15 | 0.10 | 1.43 | 0.74 |
| MYS | −0.71 | 0.05 | 0.86 | −0.22 | −0.02 | −0.02 |
| PHL | 1.39 | −0.21 | −0.16 | 0.17 | 1.20 | 1.50 |
| THA | 0.64 | −0.01 | 2.01 | 0.44 | 3.08 | 2.21 |
| CHN | 1.64 | 1.64 | 0.97 | 0.21 | 4.47 | 0.62 |
| AG3 | 2.05 | 1.85 | 3.32 | 0.08 | 7.30 | 1.55 |
| ARG | 3.62 | −0.03 | 1.15 | 0.52 | 5.27 | 1.65 |
| BRA | 5.83 | 0.23 | 3.95 | 0.20 | 10.20 | 1.54 |
| MEX | −1.42 | −0.46 | −0.04 | −0.14 | −2.06 | −0.60 |
| OLA | 2.64 | 0.13 | 1.26 | 0.09 | 4.12 | 1.23 |
| SSA | 1.32 | 0.07 | 1.22 | 0.04 | 2.66 | 1.41 |
| MNA | 9.56 | 1.14 | 10.77 | −4.42 | 17.05 | 3.00 |
| EIT | 3.71 | 0.67 | 2.18 | −0.37 | 6.20 | 0.82 |
| XAS | 3.44 | 0.03 | 1.63 | 0.34 | 5.45 | 1.33 |
| EFTA | 6.83 | 1.01 | 12.54 | −2.52 | 17.86 | 5.73 |
| IND | 0.82 | 0.57 | 0.43 | 0.40 | 2.22 | 0.63 |
| TUR | 2.24 | 0.17 | 0.53 | 0.14 | 3.08 | 1.72 |
| XCM | 2.32 | 0.08 | 1.51 | 0.18 | 4.09 | 4.03 |
| XSC | 0.46 | 0.10 | 0.89 | −0.09 | 1.37 | 1.28 |
| GDC | 45.68 | 7.20 | 38.09 | −4.46 | 86.51 | 1.35 |
| DEV | 84.83 | 17.94 | 43.11 | −4.59 | 141.29 | 0.78 |
| WLD | 130.51 | 25.14 | 81.20 | −9.05 | 227.80 | 0.93 |
| *Memorandum:* From P26 results | | | | | | |
| BGD | n.a. | n.a. | n.a. | n.a. | 0.39 | 0.90 |
| XSA | n.a. | n.a. | n.a. | n.a. | 0.98 | 1.51 |
| MOZ | n.a. | n.a. | n.a. | n.a. | 0.12 | 3.24 |
| UGA | n.a. | n.a. | n.a. | n.a. | 0.09 | 1.33 |
| TZA | n.a. | n.a. | n.a. | n.a. | 0.29 | 4.11 |

CRTS = constant returns to scale
n.a. = not available

Note: For definitions of the B25 and P26 economies, see the text above. For the meanings of the codes used for regions and economies, see table 4A.2 below.

*Source:* Author's calculations.

For services, the GTAP5 database includes tariff protection data for only one sector (electricity), and this tariff level is zero for most countries (Dimaranan and McDougall 2002, 4–6 to 4–11). This protection database thus clearly does not attempt to capture the large protection estimated in some other studies for the services sector (e.g., using departures from benchmark gross operating margins as proxies for services protection; see chapter 3). The trade liberalization estimates here should thus be interpreted as essentially referring to merchandise trade only.[13] Moreover, the protection database does not include estimates of the protective effect of antidumping measures, product standards, or other "process" protection instruments.

The estimates in table 4.1 tend to confirm several important stylized facts of trade liberalization. The first is that agriculture accounts for a major part of the remaining gains from opening trade. Of the total gains (prorating the "interaction effect"), agriculture accounts for 55 percent globally, 58 percent for industrial countries (DEV), and 50 percent for developing countries (DGC).[14] The high gains for industrial countries reflect removal of high protection, in the cases of the European Union, the European Free Trade Area (EFTA), and Japan, and benefits from major export opportunities opened up, in the cases of the United States, Australia–New Zealand, and Canada.[15]

Similarly, the results confirm that high protection in textiles and apparel means that they are second only to agriculture in providing potential gains from liberalization that are large relative to the trade base. Thus, moving to free trade in textiles and apparel would generate 31 percent as much in global welfare gains as would adopting free trade in all other manufactured and nonagricultural goods. This ratio is much higher than the respective shares in world trade (worldwide imports of textiles and apparel are only 7.3 percent of global imports of other manufactures and nonagricultural goods in the GTAP5 database).[16]

The results also confirm the view that developing countries have much to gain from global trade liberalization. Their combined gains from global free trade amount to about 1.4 percent of their GDP, about three-fourths

---

13. Thus, the difference in world welfare gain from complete liberalization and liberalization excluding the services sector is only $0.090 billion.

14. DGC refers to all developing countries, the same group as referred to as LDC in Harrison, Rutherford, and Tarr (1996).

15. This is a distinct difference from the Harrison, Rutherford, and Tarr (1996) estimates for Uruguay Round cuts. In those results, the gains for agriculture are large for Japan and the European Union ($43.7 billion together), but relatively small for the United States, Canada, Australia, and New Zealand (a combined total of $2.9 billion). Although it is clear that free trade should generate much larger total gains in agriculture than the Uruguay Round (which was modeled in HRT as reducing agricultural tariffs by 36 percent in industrial countries and by 24 percent in developing countries), it is not clear why the composition of gains would have shifted so much toward the exporters in the free trade variant.

16. Total global imports (and exports) in the GTAP5 database for 1997 are $6.72 trillion. Agricultural and food products account for $321.2 billion; textiles and apparel, $385.5 billion; services, $758.8 billion; and other manufactures and nonagricultural goods, $5.25 trillion.

larger than the 0.78 percent of GDP gains for industrial countries.[17] The gains relative to GDP tend to be even higher for some of the countries identified separately in the poverty-oriented P26 grouping (with welfare gains reaching 3.2 percent of GDP in Mozambique and 4.1 percent in Tanzania). However, as recognized above, the absence of special treatment of non-MFN access already available to the LDCs and sub-Saharan African countries under various special regimes means that the estimates of welfare gains for some of these countries will tend to be exaggerated.

The positive results identified for developing countries differ in important ways from the earlier HRT finding using the same model that sub-Saharan Africa, the Middle East and North Africa, Eastern Europe, and Hong Kong would suffer welfare losses from liberalization in the Uruguay Round (Harrison, Rutherford, and Tarr 1996, 221).[18] They attributed these losses to adverse terms-of-trade effects for food importers in the face of reduced European Union and other subsidies for agricultural production, and to losses of quota rents for textile and apparel exporters as the MFA is dismantled. Neither of these broad diagnoses seems to be confirmed in the results here. Even though the earlier results were for Uruguay Round cuts only and could thus be expected to differ from estimates for free trade, the differing qualitative results suggest that extrapolating the earlier findings to full free trade could be misleading.

Thus, table 4.1 shows gains for all the developing-country regions that were identified as losing in the earlier HRT results. The findings here receive some additional support by virtue of their greater country detail, with separate estimates for several countries or regions not treated individually in the HRT Uruguay Round results (Bangladesh, BGD in the table; Central America, XCM; India, IND; Mozambique, MOZ; Pakistan, XSA; Tanzania, TZA; Turkey, TUR; and Uganda, UGA). The only developing countries to experience losses in the results here are Mexico (MEX, –0.6 percent of GDP welfare effect) and Malaysia (MYS, –0.02 percent). Mexico's loss is understandable as a reversal of the present strong preferential entry into the large US market under NAFTA, once free trade gives other suppliers equal status. Malaysia's loss is less transparent but in any case minimal.

---

17. The largest gains for industrial countries are for EFTA (comprising mainly Switzerland and Norway), where high protection of manufactures and especially agriculture means that free trade would raise welfare by 5.7 percent of GDP. Thus, the unweighted average import tariff in agricultural goods stands at 114 percent in Switzerland and 185 percent in other EFTA member countries (mainly Norway), compared with 51 percent for the European Union and 8.1 percent for the United States (Dimaranan and McDougall 2002, 4-10, and GTAP5 database).

18. Note that this study's implementation of the HRT model (using the software MRTMDL and MRTCAL) was first applied to their "full" Uruguay Round formula using their original regions and GTAP2 data, and successfully replicated the results reported in Harrison, Rutherford, and Tarr (1996). Comparisons of the results therefore should not be biased by nonreplication problems.

The loss in terms of trade for agricultural importers as diagnosed by the earlier HRT estimates does not seem to dominate welfare effects in the results here. The overall terms of trade do fall under the free trade scenario here for the three regions identified by HRT: by 0.4 percent for "other" sub-Saharan Africa (SSA),[19] 3.1 percent for the Middle East and North Africa (MNA), and 0.8 percent for Eastern Europe (EIT). Nonetheless, as noted, these three areas show net welfare gains from free trade. Table 4.1 shows, moreover, that the addition of agriculture to the sectors liberalized generates net welfare gains even for these three areas. The implication is that the welfare gains from increased efficiency of factor use are more important than the welfare losses from terms-of-trade movements. Once again in agriculture, only Malaysia and Mexico have negative welfare effects from agricultural liberalization in the estimates here.

Neither do the results here confirm the earlier HRT diagnosis of adverse effects for developing economies from textile and apparel liberalization. In the results here, as a group the developing economies gain $7.2 billion from this liberalization, concentrated in China ($1.64 billion), South Korea (KOR, $1.19 billion), Hong Kong–Singapore–Taiwan (AG3, $1.85 billion), and India ($0.57 billion). Although it is true that some developing countries lose (Indonesia, IDN; the Philippines, PHL; Thailand, THA; Argentina, ARG, and Mexico), their combined losses of $0.73 billion are far smaller than the gains of the developing countries that show positive welfare effects in the sector. These results are consistent with intuition, considering that the group of gainers is broadly the set of countries facing textile and apparel quota constraints, whereas the losers include Mexico, which already has open access to the US market, and other countries likely to be pressed by more competition as markets are opened to the East Asian suppliers.

Harrison, Rutherford, and Tarr (1996, 221) find instead that developing economies combined would experience a welfare loss of $2.3 billion in textiles and apparel from Uruguay Round liberalization, with the combined losses of South Korea, Hong Kong, Taiwan, and Singapore placed at $2.8 billion. Instead, in the results of table 4.1 here, these four economies experience combined gains of $3.0 billion in textiles and apparel. HRT emphasized that it was the loss of export tax revenue from the elimination of quotas that caused the sectoral losses for these East Asian suppliers.

An important difference between the GTAP5 database and the GTAP2 database used by HRT, however, is that the more recent database sharply reduces estimates of export tax equivalents of these quotas. For the supply from Asia and Latin America, the GTAP2 database used export tax equivalents of MFA quotas that averaged 14.7 percent and 20.3 percent

---

19. In this chapter, because "SSA," as specified here, refers to a code for a subset of only some sub-Saharan African countries, the abbreviation "SSA" is not used to refer to the region, as it is elsewhere in the book.

for textiles in the North American and EU markets, respectively, and 34 percent and 31.7 percent for apparel in the North American and EU markets, respectively (Yang, Martin, and Yanagishima 1997, 260). In contrast, in the GTAP5 database the corresponding export tax equivalents average only 2.7 percent for textiles and 5.7 percent for apparel (Dimaranan and McDougall 2002, 4-12 to 4-15).[20] The GTAP5 estimates rely in part on new surveys of quota-rent values in Hong Kong and China, and they expressly take into account the fraction of imports not covered by the quotas (François and Spinanger 2002).[21]

The downward revision of textile and apparel export tax equivalents is one important reason for the earlier estimated losses from liberalization to diminish or disappear. Another reason for the change is that the Uruguay Round tariff (as opposed to export tax) cuts simulated by HRT were quite modest for apparel imports into the United States (only a 9 percent cut in the tariff) and the European Union (a 13 percent cut). This is a sharp contrast to the free trade scenario of table 4.1 (a 100 percent cut). The overall effect is that the textile and apparel data and scenario in Harrison, Rutherford, and Tarr (1996) tended to overstate the negative effects for developing countries (by exaggerating the levels of export tax equivalents and hence export tax losses from liberalization) and understate the potential positive effects (by specifying small cuts in the tariffs in the key markets), or at least to overstate and understate in these areas relative to conditions in the late 1990s and relative to a free trade scenario.

## Alternative Liberalization Scenarios

In order to approximate more realistic scenarios than complete free trade, and in addition to highlight some key issues such as whether developing countries should liberalize their imports, it is useful to consider alternative trade policy shocks using the PEHRT model. Once again, the B25 groupings are used as the most relevant basis for comparison, given their greater detail on several major trading nations than in the poverty-oriented P26 grouping.

---

20. In both cases, the averages here are unweighted. The GTAP5 data are for Asian and Latin American exports to all markets, but North America and the European Union (E_U) should dominate. Note that the export subsidies (rather than taxes) of Uruguay and "other South America" are excluded from the GTAP5 averages, as are the zero rates of Mexico in view of NAFTA.

21. The GTAP2 export tax equivalents had been based on East Asian market conditions in the mid-1980s and assuming 100 percent product coverage. To update, the GTAP2 authors cut the rates by 30 percent for three economies (South Korea, Hong Kong, and Taiwan) but left them unchanged for exporters on grounds that rising protection offset any overstatement from assumed 100 percent coverage. Rates were extrapolated to other regions based on assumed ratios to the rates for China (the most restricted East Asian economy) at, e.g., the full China rate for South Asia and one-half the China rate for Latin America (Gelhar et al. 1997, 94–95).

# Table 4.2 Welfare effects of alternative trade liberalization scenarios (billions of dollars or percent of free trade potential)

| Region or economy | 2-tier liberalization | | Asymmetric free trade | | Differential liberalization | | US Swiss formula with 50 percent agriculture cut | |
|---|---|---|---|---|---|---|---|---|
| | Dollars | Percent | Dollars | Percent | Dollars | Percent | Dollars | Percent |
| ANZ | 2.72 | 29.7 | 7.20 | 78.5 | 2.56 | 27.9 | 1.27 | 13.8 |
| CAN | 1.93 | 43.9 | 2.43 | 55.4 | 2.78 | 63.2 | 1.00 | 22.8 |
| USA | 21.44 | 54.7 | 17.51 | 44.7 | 13.63 | 34.8 | 21.80 | 55.6 |
| JPN | 20.97 | 66.2 | 18.70 | 59.0 | 10.18 | 32.1 | 10.47 | 33.0 |
| KOR | 6.37 | 67.5 | 1.47 | 15.6 | 12.11 | 128.3 | 3.17 | 33.6 |
| E_U | 39.60 | 101.6 | 7.66 | 19.7 | 24.80 | 63.6 | 18.26 | 46.9 |
| IDN | 1.25 | 87.2 | 1.70 | 118.7 | 2.02 | 140.9 | 0.62 | 43.2 |
| MYS | 0.89 | — | −0.15 | — | 2.15 | — | 0.49 | — |
| PHL | 0.19 | 16.1 | 1.53 | 127.7 | 0.51 | 42.6 | 0.11 | 9.2 |
| THA | 2.82 | 91.6 | 3.44 | 111.7 | 3.64 | 118.1 | 1.33 | 43.2 |
| CHN | 4.42 | 98.8 | 6.99 | 156.3 | 9.48 | 212.0 | 3.83 | 85.6 |
| AG3 | 4.64 | 63.6 | 4.48 | 61.4 | 9.35 | 128.1 | 2.22 | 30.4 |
| AHG | 2.89 | 54.9 | 3.66 | 69.5 | 4.95 | 94.0 | 1.49 | 28.3 |
| BRA | 6.04 | 59.2 | 4.35 | 42.6 | 10.94 | 107.2 | 2.88 | 28.2 |
| MEX | −0.59 | 28.6 | −2.63 | 127.8 | −0.15 | 7.3 | −0.33 | 16.0 |
| OLA | 2.30 | 55.9 | 3.73 | 90.7 | 3.70 | 89.8 | 1.10 | 26.7 |
| SSA | 1.86 | 70.1 | 3.00 | 113.0 | 2.14 | 80.5 | 0.88 | 33.1 |
| MNA | 13.63 | 80.0 | 3.27 | 19.2 | 14.48 | 84.9 | 6.12 | 35.9 |
| EIT | 3.57 | 57.7 | 8.03 | 129.6 | 0.00 | 111.1 | 2.03 | 32.8 |
| XAS | 3.06 | 56.3 | 4.78 | 87.7 | 3.53 | 64.9 | 1.70 | 31.2 |
| EFTA | 17.44 | 97.6 | 15.52 | 86.9 | 16.19 | 90.6 | 7.55 | 42.3 |
| IND | 1.80 | 81.1 | 1.31 | 59.1 | 2.66 | 119.8 | 1.14 | 51.4 |
| TUR | 1.52 | 49.4 | 2.20 | 71.7 | 2.35 | 76.5 | 0.87 | 28.3 |
| XCM | 2.49 | 61.0 | 4.41 | 107.9 | 2.74 | 67.0 | 1.04 | 25.4 |
| XSC | 1.19 | 86.7 | 0.98 | 71.5 | 1.59 | 116.2 | 0.61 | 44.7 |
| LDC | 60.35 | 69.8 | 56.55 | 65.4 | 95.05 | 109.9 | 31.30 | 36.2 |
| DEV | 104.09 | 73.7 | 69.02 | 48.9 | 70.12 | 49.0 | 60.36 | 42.7 |
| WLD | 164.44 | 72.2 | 125.57 | 55.1 | 165.17 | 72.5 | 91.67 | 40.2 |

— = not meaningful because of near-zero free trade estimate

Note: For the meanings of the codes used for regions and economies, see table 4A.2 below.

Source: Author's calculations.

The first alternative scenario, two-tier liberalization, applies free trade to manufactures (and other goods, as well as the GTAP services sectors), but only a 50 percent cut in tariffs, export taxes and subsidies, and input subsidies for agriculture and for textiles and apparel. This scenario is designed to address the reality that these are the two broad areas of persistent hard-core protection. As shown in table 4.2, this scenario would achieve about two-thirds of the free trade potential for developing countries and almost three-fourths for the industrial countries. This gain ($164 billion globally) turns out to be somewhat more than would be calculated simply taking the full gains from manufactures and half of the gains from agriculture and textiles and apparel in table 4.1 ($159 billion). The PEHRT model thus exhibits mild nonlinearity of welfare effects in the direction that would be expected (greater proportionate welfare gains from cuts in higher tariffs), in contrast to the linear welfare effects in at least one recent CGE model (Brown, Deardorff, and Stern 2001).[22] The greatest shortfalls from the free trade potential in this scenario are in the main agricultural exporters (Australia–New Zealand achieve only 30 percent of potential, Canada 44 percent, and the United States and Argentina 55 percent).

There is an important departure from the general pattern of welfare effects in this scenario that is most evident in the case of the European Union. Its welfare gains are slightly *larger* with two-tier liberalization than in the case of free trade. Further examination with a run of the model applying a 60 percent cut in agricultural, textile, and apparel protection (rather than 50 percent) elicits a cluster of four other countries that also do better under two-tier than full liberalization. In the 60 percent case, the ratios of welfare gains to free trade welfare gains are as follows: China, 146 percent; European Union, 104 percent; and EFTA, India, and Indonesia, 102 percent. In sharp contrast, the corresponding ratio for all other countries is only 67 percent.

The explanation for the paradox for these five countries seems to be that their initial agricultural protection is so high that it is far above an optimum-tariff protection level; that as the protection is cut down to about 40 percent of its initial level, the increase in welfare to consumers increasingly exceeds any loss of terms of trade; but that as the protection is cut further, additional losses in terms of trade begin to dominate. This interpretation is consistent with the high level of protection identified for the European Union in chapter 3, at overall tariff-equivalent protection of 46 percent in agriculture. The significance of implicit optimum-tariff effects in the underlying HRT model is discussed below in connection with the differential liberalization scenario.

Some might interpret the findings for the two-tier scenario as evidence that it is not in the interest of the European Union to cut agricultural (and textile) protection by more than about 50 or 60 percent, because of optimum-tariff losses beyond that point. A more appropriate interpretation is that though there is little difference between such cuts and 100 percent cuts for the European Union, there is a large difference for other countries that would experience a considerable sacrifice of potential welfare gain in the two-tier as opposed to free trade outcome. The results nonetheless suggest the caveat that in trade negotiations, EU negotiators might be expected to seek increasing reciprocal opening in other products and dimensions as they are asked to make reductions in agricultural protection (in particular) that go well beyond the 50 to 60 percent range.

---

22. In static welfare estimates, the welfare cost of a tariff rises with the square of the tariff (see, e.g., Cline 1995).

The next alternative scenario is "asymmetric liberalization." In this case, industrial countries grant free trade in all sectors and eliminate agricultural input and export subsidies.[23] In contrast, developing countries do not change protection at all. Global welfare gains fall further, to only 55 percent of their free trade potential. Developing countries achieve only 65 percent of the welfare gains possible if they also liberalize their markets.

However, there is a somewhat surprising pattern in which a number of developing countries and regions actually increase their welfare gains above the levels under total free trade, including Indonesia, the Philippines, Thailand, China, SSA (but not South Africa, XSC), Eastern Europe, and Central America. These extra gains are more than outweighed by losses (relative to free trade) in other developing countries, especially South Korea, the East Asian Group of 3, Latin America, and the Middle East and North Africa.[24] The difference between the gainers and losers depends in part on their degree of dependence on developing-country markets in their exports. Thus, the seven developing countries showing gains relative to free trade have an average of 32.5 percent of their exports going to developing countries, whereas the eight showing relative losses have a corresponding average of 42.5 percent.[25] Similarly, the loss in welfare gains compared with free trade is greater for the European Union, for which 44.1 percent of (non-intra-EU) exports go to developing countries, than for the United States, for which 35.3 percent of exports go to developing countries, excluding its free trade partner Mexico.

The results of asymmetric liberalization contrast sharply with those in some other CGE studies in one crucial dimension: the share of potential gains achieved by developing countries even if they do not liberalize their own trade This share is approximately the opposite of what is estimated in the World Bank Global Economic Prospects (WBGEP) model and the IMF-World Bank CGE runs. As shown in table 3.12 above, for static welfare effects the WBGEP model calculates that 59 percent of developing countries' potential gains stem from removal of their own protection, and only 41 percent from the elimination of protection by industrial countries.[26] In contrast, in table 4.2 it is found with the PEHRT model that only 35 percent of developing countries' potential free trade gains can be at-

23. Developing countries also eliminate export taxes on textiles and apparel, as industrial-country protection in these sectors including quotas is removed.

24 Note that the changes in the table for especially Malaysia but also Mexico are not meaningful, because both countries experience small welfare losses in the free trade base case, and a large "increase" in the welfare effect is thus an even larger loss (which can be manyfold because of the near-zero base).

25. This excludes the disparate rest of Asia grouping, XAS.

26. Total static welfare gains for developing countries are $184 billion annually at 1997 prices and 2015 economic scale. Of this amount, only $75 billion is attributable to liberalization by industrial countries.

tributed to their own liberalization, while 65 percent stems from liberalization by industrial countries.

This contrast carries important policy implications. Some commentators have criticized the developing-country Group of 21 (G-21) for having blocked the progress of the Doha Round negotiations at the Cancún ministerial meeting in September 2003 and have argued that this was self-defeating, citing (for example) the World Bank's estimates that 80 percent of developing-country potential gains in agriculture come from liberalizing their own agricultural protection rather than that of industrial countries (*The Economist*, October 6, 2003, 60). If the PEHRT results are correct, however, this argument tends to lose force, and the alternative argument gains strength: that the developing countries appropriately chose a confrontational strategy in an attempt to break open the industrial-country market for agricultural goods, in recognition that liberalizing export markets there was at least as important as achieving gains from liberalizing their own markets and their markets for each other.

The analysis below returns to this question. It is useful to note, however, that the "optimum-tariff" influence discussed below in explaining the results of other scenarios is also likely to play a part in the seeming mirror image of the PEHRT results from the World Bank results for the asymmetric liberalization scenario. The parameters applied tend to give the underlying HRT model somewhat stronger terms-of-trade and "optimum-tariff" effects than does the CGE model used by the World Bank. As discussed below, an even more important influence generating relatively higher importance for opening export markets in industrial countries than for opening own-import markets in developing countries is that the PEHRT model is comparative-static against today's world economy, whereas the World Bank model applies to a projected future world for 2015 in which industrial-country agricultural markets are relatively less important and developing-country markets for manufactures are relatively more important.

A third alternative scenario, "differential free trade," applies free trade in industrial countries except for limiting reductions in protection and subsidies to half their initial levels in agriculture and in textiles and apparel. For developing countries, protection is cut by only half in all goods, except that free trade is granted to imports from other developing countries. Global welfare gains in this variant are almost the same in the variant of two-tier liberalization, at about 72 percent of the total free trade potential. This time, however, nine developing countries and regions gain more than under full free trade, and because they tend to be larger economies than the eight that gain less than in free trade, overall the developing countries achieve about 10 percent larger welfare gains than in the full free trade scenario. In contrast, for the industrial countries, this scenario is as unfavorable as the asymmetric free trade case, with both generating slightly less than half the welfare gains possible under global free trade.

Finally, table 4.2 reports estimates for an approximation of the US proposal in the Doha Round of trade negotiations. That proposal calls for nonagricultural tariffs to be cut according to a particular "Swiss formula," namely: $t_1 = [t_0 \times 8]/[t_0 + 8]$.[27] For agriculture, the US proposal applies a more lenient formula (with the 8 replaced by 25), and moreover the formula does not apply to the tariff-quota rates (although the threshold volumes for these would be expanded at a target rate).[28] Because the extreme protection is in tariff-rate quotas, the overall effect of the agricultural proposal is moderate, so the scenario here simply models it as a cut of agricultural protection (including input and export subsidies) by half.

Global welfare gains in the US formula are the lowest of the scenarios considered, at only 40 percent of the free trade gains. This reflects the fact that the depth of liberalization is less in the US formula than in any of the other scenarios here, which all call for free trade in nonagricultural and non-textile-apparel goods on the part of at least the industrial countries. The gains are especially low for the developing countries under the US formula, at only 36 percent of the free trade potential.

The welfare-effect findings are provocative in that they indicate that developing countries might do better with less liberalization of their own markets than that offered by industrial countries. Although this might seem sensible to the layperson, it is somewhat counterintuitive to the economist. Usually even unilateral free trade will be better for a country than retaining protection, in the static welfare model, which emphasizes gains in consumer surplus from lower prices on imported goods. The main exception arises with the "optimum-tariff" argument, in which a country that unilaterally liberalizes its imports could experience a terms-of-trade loss, because by increasing its demand for the imported good, it would tend to drive up the price of the import; and by exporting more to pay for the increased imports, it would tend to drive down the price of its export. The optimum tariff argument, however, is usually reserved for the case of a large country capable of influencing the world price.

Similarly, the relatively unfavorable results for developing countries in the US formula case appear largely to be the opposite side of the coin from the differential liberalization scenario. As a harmonization formula, the US formula cuts higher tariffs proportionately more than lower tariffs. Because they tend to have higher tariffs in manufactures than industrial countries, developing countries will be cutting their protection by a larger rather than smaller proportion than industrial countries in this scenario. So the optimum-tariff influences in the HRT model will act to their disfavor rather than to their favor, as in the differential liberalization scenario.

---

27. For example, a 10 percent tariff would be cut to 4.44 percent (= $[10 \times 8]/[10 + 8]$).

28. With this formula, a 10 percent tariff is cut to 7.1 percent, and a 50 percent tariff is cut to 16.7 percent.

Again, however, the question arises as to why optimum-tariff effects should apply to small countries.

The explanation of the paradox of optimum-tariff results for developing countries in the PEHRT model lies in its use of Armington imperfect substitution among goods. This assumption is required if there is to be two-way trade in a given good. But the imperfect-substitution assumption also in effect makes every country, no matter how small, capable of affecting the price of its export good. In this framework, it is possible for free riders to do better than full liberalizers, because they obtain the gains of lower prices on international supply without pushing down the prices of their own exports.

More specifically, Harrison, Rutherford, and Tarr (1997b) have shown that in trade models using the two-tiered Armington elasticity structure (e.g., the HRT model used here), with one tier for substitution between the domestic good and all imports of the good ($\sigma_D$) and a second tier for substitution among alternative country supplies of the import in question ($\sigma_M$), the optimal tariff is inversely related to the second-tier elasticity. The argument starts from the price elasticity of demand for the country's exports. For sectors in which the country has a small share in world supply, and with other countries having a uniform second-tier elasticity of demand among alternative suppliers equal to $\sigma_M$, this will also be the price elasticity of demand for the country's export ($\varepsilon$). The optimal export tax is $1/(\varepsilon - 1)$, which collapses to zero when foreign demand is infinitely elastic. The authors then appeal to the Lerner symmetry theorem (stating that an import tariff is equivalent to an export tax) to conclude that the optimal tariff equals $1/(\sigma_M - 1)$. Applying the uniform value of $\sigma_M = 8$ in the main runs of the HRT model here, the implied optimum tariff is $1/7 = 14$ percent. Because developing countries tend to have tariffs above this level, deep liberalization scenarios cut the tariffs below the optimal level, tending to erode the welfare gains from multilateral liberalization.

A test was conducted for the optimum-tariff causation of the better outcome for developing countries in the differential liberalization (DL) scenario by examining the terms-of-trade impact in comparison with free trade (FT). It was found that in all 19 developing-country areas in the B25 model, there was an increase in the terms of trade in the DL scenario relative to the free trade scenario, by a median 1.2 percentage point. Confirming this interpretation, for the industrial-country areas in the model, the changes in terms of trade were systematically less favorable under DL than under FT. Thus, US terms of trade rise 1.3 percent under FT but remain unchanged under DL; Australia–New Zealand's terms of trade rise 8.4 percent under FT but only 2.1 percent under DL; and Japan's terms of trade fall 0.6 percent under FT and fall 1 percent under DL.

A further test of the same issue (i.e., an optimum-tariff explanation for the puzzle of higher developing-country gains under DL than under FT) was carried out by magnifying the key second-tier substitution elasticity by 50 percent (raising $\sigma_M$ from 8 to 12). With a higher elasticity, the optimum tariff should be lower. In this test, the ratio of developing-country welfare gains under DL to those under FT fell to 1.044, from a ratio of 1.10 in the base runs of tables 4.1 and 4.2. This shrinkage of the relative extra gains from differential liberalization as the import–import substitution elasticity increases further confirms the optimum-tariff interpretation of the more advantageous (for developing countries) results of the differential liberalization scenario.[29]

The results showing greater benefits for developing countries in the differential liberalization scenario should perhaps be taken with a grain of salt. Broadly, the experience of developing countries in the past several decades has tended to be one of unfortunate inefficiencies associated with domestic protection. The relationship of trade openness to growth performance is revisited in chapter 5. For the purposes of the present chapter, however, the specific alternative-scenario results warrant consideration from the standpoint of forcing one to think further about the usual free trade recommendation, but they probably do not warrant a strong inference that partial (free-rider) liberalization would be better than full liberalization for the developing countries. In any event, for the developing countries as a whole, differential liberalization gives gains that are just 10 percent higher than gains under free trade. Moreover, it is crucial to keep in mind that in the differential liberalization scenario developing countries do grant free trade access to imports from each other.

## Developing-Country Versus Industrial-Country Liberalization Impact

As highlighted in the discussion above of the results of asymmetric liberalization, a key issue for global trade policy is whether the potential gains for developing countries stem primarily from the opening of their own import markets, primarily from the opening of industrial country markets for their exports, or a relatively balanced combination of the two. Differing perceptions generate different views of what type of reform is "fair." Some of those who believe that the great bulk of potential developing country gains can be achieved by their own unilateral liberalization will naturally be led to question why the developing countries should risk the collapse of the Doha Round by insisting on the deep liberalization of

29. In the high import–import elasticity runs, developing countries achieve welfare gains of $110.2 billion under free trade and $115 billion under differential liberalization. Industrial countries achieve gains of $159 billion under free trade but only $85 billion under differential liberalization. Thus, whereas the ratio of developing-country to industrial-country welfare gains goes from 0.61 under FT to 1.36 under DL in the base runs (tables 4.1 and 4.2), this ratio goes from 0.69 under FT to 1.12 under DL in the higher import–import elasticity runs. This narrowing of the relative free-rider benefits for developing countries goes in the expected direction from the curbing of terms-of-trade (or optimum-tariff) effects by the use of a higher elasticity.

industrial-country agricultural markets, a risk that arose in the collapse of the Cancún ministerial meeting of the WTO in September 2003 over this issue as well as the new "Singapore issues" (investment, competition, government procurement, and trade facilitation).

In a partial equilibrium model in which world supply is assumed to be perfectly elastic (horizontal world supply curve for imports) and the products are homogeneous, welfare gains from global trade liberalization arise solely on the import side. In a general equilibrium model in which the export good is differentiated, a reduction of foreign protection increases the demand for and price of the export good. In this case, simple consumer welfare gains from lower protection (consumer welfare triangles) must be compared with terms-of-trade effects that arise from an induced rise in exports needed to cover the additional import bill after liberalization. In this context, whether the foreign trading partner liberalizes will have an important effect in avoiding a terms-of-trade loss (or achieving a terms-of-trade gain).

The HRT model appears to have strong welfare gains on the export side, reflecting terms-of-trade gains from increased demand in newly opened export markets. The cleanest test of this proposition is the case of the HRT results for Singapore, which has zero protection in 37 of the 42 GTAP5 merchandise trade categories and average protection of less than 9 percent in the other 5 (which are agricultural sectors). With near-zero protection overall, Singapore should gain nothing from global trade liberalization in a partial equilibrium world with homogeneous goods, because it has no tariffs to reduce and hence no unexploited consumer welfare triangles to harvest. Yet in the HRT model results for the Uruguay Round effects, Singapore turns out to have one of the largest welfare gains of any country, at 2.1 percent of GDP (Harrison, Rutherford, and Tarr 1996, 221).

As noted above, the WBGEP model finds that about 60 percent of developing countries' potential welfare gains from global free trade arise from the liberalization of their own markets. In contrast, the results of the PEHRT model for asymmetric liberalization (table 4.2) suggest that 65 percent of developing countries' potential gains come instead from increased export opportunities associated with the liberalization of industrial-country markets. The sources of this divergence are analyzed below. First, however, it is important to recognize that the attribution question of whose liberalization confers the benefits on developing countries suggests that even the question itself is inherently ambiguous. The answer will depend on whether the scenario tested involves liberalization by developing countries only, liberalization by industrial countries only, or some combination.

The World Bank (2002a, 171) presents free trade attribution results that are noncontingent and strictly additive, in the following sense. With $W_{ijk}$ as the welfare effect of free trade in sector $i$ (e.g., agriculture) conferred by the liberalization of market $j$ (e.g., industrial countries as a group) and received by group $k$ (e.g., developing countries), global welfare is simply $W = \Sigma_{ijk}W_{ijk}$. To report such results requires the implicit assumption that the welfare impact of developing countries' own liberalization is independent of whether industrial countries liberalize, that the welfare gains from agricultural liberalization are independent of whether manufactures are liberalized, and so forth.

A further analysis suggests instead that decomposing the welfare gains by source generates a range of estimates contingent on how the question is posed. We seek to estimate what fraction of developing-country total gains can be attributed to their own liberalization. One way to pose this question is as is done in table 4.2: Compute asymmetric liberalization in which developing countries do not liberalize, and subtract the results from the estimates for total free trade in order to estimate the additional contribution attributable to developing countries' own liberalization. This formulation of the question attributes only 35 percent of total potential developing-country gains to the liberalization of their own markets (i.e., table 4.2 shows 65 percent of potential free trade gains occurring even with developing countries leaving their own protection intact).

Now suppose instead that the scenario is reversed and that only developing countries liberalize while industrial countries are the free riders. In this reverse asymmetry scenario, global static welfare gains are $100.45 billion, of which $41.11 billion is for developing countries and $59.34 billion is for industrial countries. When this is the viewpoint, developing countries' own liberalization generates 48 percent of the total free trade potential. There are two main points. First, these estimates from the PEHRT model are in a range of 35 to 48 percent, well below the 60 percent point estimate in the WBGEP model as the share of potential total gains attributable to developing countries' own liberalization. Second, a single point estimate for such source-of-gain attribution does not seem to be well defined. One can estimate own-liberalization effects on each side with zero liberalization on the other and obtain two alternative estimates of the fraction of global free trade gains attributable to the group's own liberalization. The two different answers arise because in one case the developing countries are the ones that gain from the optimum-tariff (terms-of-trade) effects of being the free riders, whereas in the other case it is the industrial countries that obtain these gains. The source-attribution question would thus seem inherently to require a range answer rather than a point estimate answer.

Table 4.3 shows the range of source estimates corresponding to this diagnosis, using the PEHRT (B25) model. Row A shows welfare gains when only developing countries (DGC) liberalize (reverse asymmetry). Row B shows gains when only industrial countries (DEV) liberalize (the asymmetric liberalization scenario above). Row C shows the simple sum of the first two. Row D shows the results for joint global free trade, in which both

**Table 4.3  Decomposition of static welfare gains between developing and industrial countries**

| Liberalizing area | DGC (billions of dollars) | Percent of DGC total | DEV (billions of dollars) | Percent of DEV total | Total (billions of dollars) | Percent of global free trade |
|---|---|---|---|---|---|---|
| | | | **Beneficiary** | | | |
| A. DGC only | 41.11 | 47.5 | 59.34 | 42.0 | 100.45 | 44.1 |
| B. DEV only | 56.55 | 65.4 | 69.02 | 48.8 | 125.57 | 55.1 |
| C. Simple sum | 97.66 | 112.9 | 128.36 | 90.8 | 226.02 | 99.2 |
| D. Global free trade | 86.51 | 100.0 | 141.29 | 100.0 | 227.80 | 100.0 |
| E. Interaction effect | −11.15 | −12.9 | 12.93 | 9.2 | 1.78 | 0.8 |

DGC = developing countries
DEV = industrial countries

*Source:* Author's calculations.

sides liberalize. And row E shows the divergence of global free trade results from the simple sum of the two asymmetric scenarios.

As the table shows, row A attributes 47.5 percent of potential free trade gains for developing countries to their own liberalization. In contrast, row B arrives at 34.6 percent for the same source-attribution estimate. (That is, in row B, 65.4 percent of total potential developing-country gains are obtained when only the industrial countries liberalize, implying that only 34.6 percent of potential gains for developing countries arise from their own liberalization.) The simple sum of the two asymmetric scenarios *exceeds* the global free trade potential, for developing countries, because interaction effects tend to erode their gains. There is a mirror image pattern for gains in industrial countries, where global free trade generates a larger welfare outcome than the simple sum of the two unilateral (or asymmetric) cases. At the world level, the interaction term disappears, and global gains for total free trade are virtually the same as the sum of the two asymmetric cases.

In sum, the results here suggest that about half to two-thirds of developing countries' potential gains from multilateral free trade arise from increased opportunities in industrial-country markets rather than from the efficiency effects of liberalizing their own markets and the terms-of-trade effects of obtaining full access to each others' markets. Three further runs of the PEHRT (B25) model for agriculture alone do show a greater relative weight of developing countries' own-market impact on their gains, but once again to a lesser degree than in the World Bank estimates. Thus, free trade in agriculture alone generates global gains of $120.0 billion, developing-country gains of $40.3 billion, and industrial-country gains of $79.7 billion.[30] When only developing countries liberalize agri-

---

30. These "direct" agricultural estimates are close to the "indirect" agricultural estimates in table 4.1. The difference is that in table 4.1, the sector's contribution is obtained by subtracting from global free trade results the results with the sector in question excluded from liberalization.

culture, the respective gains are $31.5 billion, $22.8 billion, and $8.7 billion. When only industrial countries liberalize agriculture, the respective gains are $85.4 billion, $17.4 billion, and $68.0 billion. For this sector, both of the asymmetric estimates generate virtually the same result for the developing-country gains attributable to the liberalization of their own agricultural markets ($22.8 billion for the reverse-asymmetric case, and $40.3 − $17.4 = $22.9 billion for the asymmetric case). These own-liberalization gains amount to 57 percent of the total in agriculture for developing countries. Even though in agriculture the developing countries thus obtain more than half of their potential gains just by freeing their own markets, this share remains well below the 80 percent estimated for the agricultural sector by the World Bank (2003, 51).

A similar but even more extreme finding is obtained in a recent study by the OECD (2003c). Using the standard GTAP CGE model (Hertel 1997), the OECD authors obtain a benchmark estimate of $97 billion as annual global static welfare gains from removing all tariffs.[31] In this model, the developing countries obtain the greater part of global gains ($68 billion, or 70 percent). More dramatically, the sourcing of developing-country gains comes heavily from the removal of protection in industrial-country markets ($59 billion, or 79 percent of developing-country total gains).[32] Perhaps most dramatic, industrial countries obtain more than the entirety of their gains from increased export opportunities in developing-country markets ($31.6 billion), because their terms-of-trade losses mean that the liberalization of their own markets generates net negative effects (of $2.8 billion).

The differences between the OECD, WBGEP, and PEHRT model attributions for the source of developing-country gains appear to stem in considerable part from the different values used for the (Armington) elasticity of substitution between alternative sources of import supply. As discussed above, this elasticity turns out to drive the optimum tariff. In this study's PEHRT model, this elasticity is set at a uniform value of 8. In contrast, the simple average of the sectoral values for this elasticity in the OECD study is 5.6, almost identical to that in the standard GTAP model.[33] This means that that the implicit optimum tariff in the OECD model is 1/(5.6 − 1) = 21.7 percent, higher by about half than in the PEHRT model. This difference would appear easily large enough to explain why the OECD model has much stronger terms-of-trade effects than the PEHRT model, and correspondingly why the OECD results attribute the great bulk of developing-country gains from multilateral liberalization to the opening of industrial-country markets.

---

31. The study estimates that this gain is additional to an initial $18 billion from completion of tariff-cut implementation of Uruguay Round cuts beyond those already adopted as of 1998, the GTAP database year.

32. Like the World Bank, the OECD is silent on the question of source-attribution ambiguity.

33. Douglas Lippoldt, OECD, personal communication, November 28, 2003.

On the other side, the average for the import-import substitution elasticity in the WBGEP model is 8.8 (van der Mensbrugghe 2004). The implication is that whereas the OECD model has a much higher optimum tariff than the PEHRT model, the PEHRT model has only a modestly higher optimum tariff than the WBGEP model.[34] Although there is no close agreement among CGE modelers about the appropriate value for this elasticity, the fact that the PEHRT elasticity is intermediate between the OECD and WBGEP values provides some comfort that the estimates are not substantially biased in one direction or the other. Moreover, recent econometric estimates by a key author of the GTAP model used by the OECD suggest that the proper average value for the elasticity of substitution between alternative sources of imports is approximately 7, rather than the lower value of 5.3 in the basic GTAP parameter set (Hertel, Hummels, et al. 2003).

Nonetheless, for the PEHRT versus WBGEP results, the divergent values for the import–import substitution elasticity are insufficient to explain fully the difference in attribution of developing-country welfare gains between industrial- and developing-country liberalization. Instead, there are two other more dominant sources of this divergence.[35] First, the WBGEP model (LINKAGE) essentially deals with the world as it is projected to be in 2015, not 1997. A major difference by 2015 is that China and other major developing countries will represent a far larger share of world output than they do today. Moreover, because developing countries tend to have high protection in manufacturing, and because their economies will evolve toward larger shares of manufacturing, the result is that their share in protection-weighted global production will rise even more, above the share of developing countries in protection-weighted production today.

This ballooning of developing countries' measured share in the amount of global protection is accentuated further by a second model difference. The HRT model has "Cobb-Douglas" consumption, which holds each sector's share constant as income rises, reflecting an income elasticity of unity for each sector in consumption. The WBGEP model instead uses a consumption structure with an extremely low income elasticity for agricultural goods, for industrial countries.[36] The result is that agricultural demand falls sharply as a share of industrial-country consumption in the baseline projection to 2015. Yet agriculture is the high-protection sector for industrial countries. So the effect is to shrink the share of highly protected goods in the projected market of industrial countries.

---

34. The optimum tariff stands at 21.7 percent, 14.3 percent, and 12.8 percent for the three models respectively, based on values for $\sigma_M$ of 5.6, 8.0, and 8.8, respectively.

35. I am indebted to Dominique van der Mensbrugghe (2004) for special runs of the WBGEP model to elucidate the differences and similarities of the two models.

36. WBGEP-LINKAGE uses an Extended Linear Expenditure System and places the income elasticity for agricultural goods at only about 0.04 for the industrial countries.

With the future-year basing of the WBGEP model involving the relative expansion of high-protection developing-country market shares and the relative contraction of high-protection industrial-country market shares, it is not difficult to understand why the World Bank projects that the liberalization of developing-country markets becomes the main potential source of welfare gains from trade liberalization. The question then becomes whether this approach or the comparative-static approach in PEHRT based on today's global economic profile is more relevant for policy purposes. Implicitly, the PEHRT model is more ambitious in reflecting the consequences of immediate liberalization, whereas the WBGEP model is much more gradualist in achieving free trade only by 2015. The World Bank approach may be closer to political reality, but it would seem further removed from the proper basis on which to make statements about whose protection—that of the developing countries or that of the industrial countries—is more important *today* in thwarting welfare gains that otherwise could be obtained by developing countries. The answer to that question, which is the question that is relevant for the current trade debate, would seem more accurately to be provided by the PEHRT results than by the WBGEP results. Even so, as emphasized by van der Mensbrugghe (2004), in most regards (of particular importance, including the magnitudes of the overall welfare effects and their division as between developing and industrial countries), when scaled to the same base year, the PEHRT and WBGEP results are quite similar.[37]

## Relative Level of Protection

There is, of course, one case in which developing countries would be unambiguously responsible for failing to harvest the gains of free trade: if their protection were extremely high already and industrial-country protection were extremely low. In this case, even a model sensitive to export demand and terms of trade would not pick up much gain beyond the unilateral liberalization of developing-country imports. This is not the reality, however. In general, industrial countries tend to have higher protection than developing countries in agriculture, whereas the reverse is true for manufactures other than textiles and apparel.

Table 4.4 reports average tariff levels in industrial and developing countries for all merchandise trade divided into four groups: agriculture and food, textiles and apparel, all other manufactures, and energy (mainly oil) and nonagricultural raw materials. These tariff levels are from the GTAP5 database (Dimaranan and McDougall 2002, 4-6 to 4-11), and they include

---

37. Thus, the WBGEP model, which as a dynamic recursive model incorporates new investment over time, has an aggregate welfare effect of global trade liberalization that, after scaling back to 1997 economic level, is intermediate between the static and the steady state versions of the PEHRT model (i.e., the results in tables 4.1 and 4.5).

# Table 4.4 Most-favored nation tariff protection, 1997–98 (percent)

| Economy group | Agriculture, food | Textiles, apparel | Other manufactures | Energy, nonagricultural raw materials |
|---|---|---|---|---|
| **Industrial countries**[a] | 35.6 | 11.6 | 3.1 | 0.1 |
| Australia | 3.7 | 22.1 | 4.4 | 0.0 |
| Canada | 30.4 | 18.0 | 4.1 | 0.1 |
| European Union | 32.6 | 10.6 | 4.3 | 0.0 |
| Japan | 76.4 | 10.2 | 1.2 | 0.0 |
| New Zealand | 5.6 | 15.4 | 5.7 | 0.0 |
| Norway | 153.5 | 15.3 | 3.8 | 0.2 |
| Switzerland | 118.9 | 1.9 | 0.2 | 1.0 |
| United States | 8.8 | 12.1 | 2.8 | 0.1 |
| **Developing economies**[a] | 30.3 | 18.2 | 11.5 | 0.7 |
| Bangladesh | 19.8 | 29.0 | 17.7 | 0.9 |
| China | 29.9 | 27.9 | 15.3 | 0.5 |
| Hong Kong | 0.0 | 0.0 | 0.0 | 0.0 |
| India | 31.5 | 31.6 | 24.6 | 1.1 |
| Indonesia | 19.6 | 19.2 | 11.5 | 0.6 |
| Korea | 50.7 | 7.9 | 6.9 | 0.4 |
| Malaysia | 17.8 | 16.9 | 10.2 | 0.4 |
| Philippines | 19.2 | 17.0 | 8.7 | 0.7 |
| Singapore | 4.2 | 0.0 | 0.0 | 0.0 |
| Sri Lanka | 36.7 | 30.8 | 18.1 | 5.7 |
| Taiwan | 17.2 | 8.9 | 6.5 | 0.4 |
| Thailand | 33.3 | 31.7 | 16.7 | 0.8 |
| Vietnam | 22.5 | 38.2 | 14.2 | 1.2 |
| Argentina | 12.5 | 18.6 | 14.0 | 0.2 |
| Brazil | 22.9 | 17.6 | 15.4 | 0.4 |
| Chile | 13.5 | 11.1 | 10.9 | 2.0 |
| Colombia | 14.7 | 18.0 | 11.9 | 0.8 |
| Mexico | 22.1 | 22.8 | 10.8 | 1.0 |
| Peru | 15.0 | 17.2 | 12.1 | 2.1 |
| Venezuela | 14.6 | 18.0 | 12.6 | 1.0 |
| Hungary | 33.3 | 10.8 | 7.9 | 0.2 |
| Poland | 59.0 | 18.9 | 12.3 | 0.5 |
| Turkey | 43.6 | 8.3 | 6.4 | 0.1 |
| Morocco | 57.3 | 31.5 | 14.6 | 0.2 |
| Botswana | 7.0 | 7.6 | 5.7 | 2.6 |
| Malawi | 20.9 | 36.3 | 21.4 | 0.1 |
| Mozambique | 17.6 | 31.0 | 13.1 | 0.6 |
| South Africa | 37.8 | 19.3 | 7.8 | 0.2 |
| Tanzania | 22.8 | 17.3 | 20.3 | 2.2 |
| Uganda | 20.2 | 19.2 | 14.6 | 2.3 |
| Zambia | 14.0 | 21.8 | 13.5 | 2.4 |
| Zimbabwe | 25.3 | 50.9 | 20.7 | 2.8 |

a. Weighting by average of shares in group GDP and trade turnover.

*Source:* GTAP5, using world output weights (Dimaranan and McDougall 2002).

the effect of tariff-rate quotas in agriculture. However, they exclude the effect of agricultural subsidies and MFA quotas in textiles and apparel. Within each broad product group, product subsectors are weighted by their respective shares in global production (Dimaranan and McDougall 2002, 3-1 to 3-5). For the aggregate estimates for industrial and developing countries, respectively, the individual country or region tariff averages in all product categories are weighted by an average of the country's share in world output and its share in trade turnover (exports plus imports) in the world total (Dimaranan and McDougall 2002, 2-4 to 2-5, and GTAP5 database).[38]

There are two principal patterns of protection in table 4.4. First, the sectoral ranking of protection is remarkably similar across both industrial and developing countries. Protection is highest in agriculture, relatively high in textiles and apparel, somewhat lower in all other manufactures, and close to zero for oil and other nonagricultural raw materials. Actual protection is even higher in the first two categories because of the exclusion of subsidies and MFA quotas. The second broad pattern is that protection tends to be higher in agriculture in industrial countries and higher in manufactures in developing countries.

These data confirm the estimates in chapter 3 in suggesting that there is sizable protection in especially agriculture but also textiles and apparel in industrial countries. Correspondingly, one should expect that a sizable fraction of welfare gains to developing countries from global liberalization should arise from the opening of industrial-country markets in these sectors, especially considering that they are precisely the sectors in which developing countries tend to have a comparative advantage. A parallel implication is that one should be cautious about model results that show a very limited role for industrial-country liberalization in potential gains for developing countries from global free trade.

Table 4.4 also shows, however, that protection remains relatively high in developing countries (though by no means as high as in the heyday of import-substituting industrialization in the 1970s). It is therefore reasonable to expect that industrial-country negotiators will insist on some degree of reciprocal liberalization by at least middle-income countries (including China and low-income India) in the process of the Doha Round negotiations.[39]

## Dynamic Effects

In addition to the CRTS and IRTS static variants of the HRT model (of which only the CRTS is used in PEHRT), there is a Steady State (SS) vari-

---

38. This excludes intra-EU trade for the trade turnover weights.

39. Whether China's liberalization already undertaken as the price of WTO entry will suffice for this purpose is unclear.

ant designed to capture one important dimension of dynamic effects. In this version, instead of holding total factor endowments for each economy constant, the model stipulates that there is an expansion of the capital factor sufficient to bring the postliberalization rate of return on investment back down to the preliberalization rate. The idea is that over an undefined medium-term horizon, firms can be expected to respond to the new opportunities offered by trade liberalization by making new investments, thereby raising the capital stock. The welfare gains in this approach to measuring dynamic effects must be interpreted with care, because they are not a windfall gain but require additional resources. Nonetheless, they help establish a range that shows how large total effects, including dynamic responses, might be. Although Harrison, Rutherford, and Tarr (1996) do not do so, it is possible to interpret the SS results further in terms of net welfare gains by imputing an opportunity cost of capital to the extra capital resources estimated and by deducting this cost from the total SS welfare gains.

The return on investment in the HRT model depends on two influences. The first is the real factor price of capital (i.e., "rental price" or "real return"). The second is the "price of a new unit of investment." The SS version of the model expands the capital stock until the ratio of the rental price of capital to the price of a new unit of investment falls back to its preliberalization level. The source of this effect can be a rise in the rental price of capital, a decline in the unit price of investment, or both. For developing countries, removing protection against imported capital goods can be a major source of an increased attractiveness of investment, because it reduces the denominator of this ratio.[40] It is somewhat more counterintuitive that the rental price of capital (the numerator) can also rise, considering that the Stolper-Samuelson theorem in its extreme form would imply an absolute reduction in the rental price of capital for developing countries where capital is relatively scarce (Stolper and Samuelson 1941).

In the HRT model, however, the rental price of capital can rise from liberalization even for developing countries, although typically it will rise by less than the price of unskilled labor, yielding a change in the relative factor prices in the Stolper-Samuelson direction.[41] Important influences in the HRT model that are not present in the extreme version of the Stolper-Samuelson model include four production factors instead of just two: terms-of-trade effects as foreign markets are opened and imperfect substitutability between the domestic good and the imported variety. These and perhaps other influences make it possible for the absolute level

---

40. This is a common finding of CGE models of global trade liberalization. Thomas Hertel, personal communication, October 23, 2003.

41. Thomas Rutherford, personal communication, November 5, 2003.

of the rental price of capital to rise in the HRT model even for developing countries.[42]

Table 4.5 shows the results of applying the HRT SS model to the PEHRT regions using the GTAP5 trade and protection data. The gross welfare gains are far larger than the static CRTS gains, amounting to $613.8 billion globally, or 2.5 percent of 1997 world GDP. The gains are especially large for developing countries, reaching 5.5 percent of GDP on average and as high as an estimated 12.6 percent for Central America and 31.2 percent for Thailand. Although the latter case appears to be an aberration, the overall pattern is one of relatively large gains.[43]

It is evident in table 4.5, however, that these large gross welfare gains come at the expense of a considerable increase in capital stock. The percentage increases in capital stock are shown in the third column. Weighting by GDP, for developing countries capital stock would rise by 15.8 percent, and for industrial countries by 2.15 percent. In order to estimate net welfare gains after taking account of the opportunity cost of the additional capital, it is possible to apply capital-output ratios to the various economies and regions (taken from Cline 1997, 183). These ratios are typically in the range of 3. The fourth column in table 4.5 shows the rise in capital stock expressed as a percentage of GDP, obtained by multiplying the percent rise in capital stock by the economy's capital-output ratio.

The final two columns report net welfare gains after deducting the annual opportunity cost of the extra capital, which is imputed using a real interest rate of 7 percent.[44] The net welfare gains are still relatively high at $343 billion globally, compared with a $604 billion gross welfare gain. The net welfare gains in the SS version are 50 percent larger than the global welfare gains in the static version of the model ($228 billion, table 4.1). The increment is higher for developing countries, however. For these countries, the net welfare gains in the SS version reach $162 billion, or 2.5 percent of GDP. This is about 90 percent more than the $87 billion (1.35 percent of GDP) in the static version.

---

42. Brown, Deardorff, and Stern (2001) report similarly that "we routinely find in our CGE modeling that both labor and capital gain from liberalization" (p. 9) They emphasize the "additional sources of gain from trade due to increasing returns to scale, competition, and product variety . . . [which] are shared across factors."

43. As before, the table includes the SS estimates for five additional country-detail cases from the P26 run of the SS model, which as before generates a result very close to that for the B25 groupings (global welfare gain of $608 billion annually, compared with $614 billion in the B25 version). For the case of Thailand, the outsized estimate likely reflects the fact that in the GTAP5 database the share of capital (including resources) in total factor payments is an inordinately large 80 percent.

44. The estimation of a net welfare effect deducting cost of capital is not part of the underlying HRT model.

## Table 4.5 Steady state welfare gains from free trade (billions of dollars, percent of GDP, and percent change in capital stock)

| Region or economy | Billions of dollars | Percent of GDP | Percent change in capital | dK as percent of GDP | Net change in welfare[a] Billions of dollars | GDP |
|---|---|---|---|---|---|---|
| **B25** | | | | | | |
| ANZ | 21.90 | 5.76 | 11.32 | 37.58 | 11.89 | 3.13 |
| CAN | 6.53 | 1.34 | 1.80 | 4.88 | 4.86 | 1.00 |
| USA | 80.23 | 1.17 | 1.92 | 5.22 | 55.06 | 0.80 |
| JPN | 44.25 | 1.18 | 1.78 | 5.85 | 28.92 | 0.77 |
| KOR | 16.44 | 4.20 | 17.88 | 48.44 | 3.17 | 0.81 |
| E_U | 89.34 | 1.41 | 1.90 | 5.69 | 64.02 | 1.01 |
| IDN | 7.06 | 3.64 | 13.98 | 33.28 | 2.55 | 1.31 |
| MYS | 3.21 | 3.73 | 22.91 | 54.53 | −0.07 | −0.09 |
| PHL | 3.91 | 4.91 | 14.81 | 35.25 | 1.95 | 2.44 |
| THA | 43.39 | 31.16 | 67.03 | 159.53 | 27.84 | 19.99 |
| CHN | 6.46 | 0.90 | 14.14 | 33.51 | −10.45 | −1.45 |
| AG3 | 16.06 | 3.42 | 9.69 | 26.27 | 7.42 | 1.58 |
| ARG | 15.66 | 4.89 | 11.53 | 34.93 | 7.83 | 2.44 |
| BRA | 40.13 | 6.04 | 12.85 | 38.94 | 22.02 | 3.32 |
| MEX | 3.47 | 1.02 | 3.41 | 10.04 | 1.07 | 0.31 |
| OLA | 27.32 | 8.16 | 17.92 | 54.31 | 14.60 | 4.36 |
| SSA | 13.90 | 7.36 | 19.80 | 51.48 | 7.09 | 3.75 |
| MNA | 50.60 | 8.91 | 18.40 | 47.83 | 31.58 | 5.56 |
| EIT | 24.55 | 3.26 | 10.82 | 36.24 | 5.44 | 0.72 |
| XAS | 26.90 | 6.58 | 18.20 | 43.31 | 14.51 | 3.55 |
| EFTA | 20.98 | 6.73 | 6.37 | 21.14 | 16.37 | 5.25 |
| IND | 23.86 | 6.74 | 21.99 | 51.46 | 11.10 | 3.14 |
| TUR | 9.76 | 5.45 | 9.72 | 25.28 | 6.59 | 3.68 |
| XCM | 12.72 | 12.55 | 37.42 | 113.37 | 4.67 | 4.61 |
| XSC | 5.22 | 4.88 | 13.10 | 34.06 | 2.67 | 2.49 |
| DGC | 350.62 | 5.48 | 15.75 | 42.18 | 161.59 | 2.52 |
| DEV | 263.22 | 1.45 | 2.15 | 6.46 | 181.13 | 1.00 |
| WLD | 613.84 | 2.50 | 5.70 | 15.77 | 342.71 | 1.40 |
| *Memorandum:* From P26 results | | | | | | |
| BGD | 1.72 | 3.94 | 13.66 | 32.52 | 0.73 | 1.67 |
| XSA | 14.11 | 21.72 | 69.07 | 164.39 | 6.64 | 10.21 |
| MOZ | 0.38 | 9.84 | 25.99 | 67.84 | 0.20 | 5.09 |
| UGA | 0.32 | 4.90 | 13.37 | 34.89 | 0.16 | 2.45 |
| TZA | 0.91 | 12.89 | 33.10 | 86.40 | 0.48 | 6.84 |

dK = change in capital stock

a. At a capital cost of 7 percent.

Note: For definitions of the B25 and P26 economies, see the text above. For the meanings of the codes used for regions and economies, see table 4A.2 below.

*Source:* Author's calculations.

It could be argued that any excess of the SS welfare gains over the static gains should not be considered because capital markets already optimize the intertemporal choice between consumption and investment. Under this argument, any induced-investment effect from free trade bears an extra cost that fully offsets the additional welfare gains.[45] However, this argument would seem to miss the point that trade liberalization is a positive shock that alters the optimal intertemporal saving equilibrium by boosting the rate of return to investment. Even if the intertemporal equilibrium is optimal ex ante, it will no longer be so ex post as free trade opens up new opportunities.

Consider the analogy of a technological breakthrough, such as the invention of the steam locomotive. It would make no sense to discard welfare gains from such an invention on the grounds of the intertemporal equilibrium argument, that the extra investment required by definition has a cost that fully offsets the potential gains from applying the innovation. Neither should this argument be invoked to discard welfare effects from induced investment in the case of trade liberalization, as long as a reasonable opportunity cost has already been applied to the capital required. In the estimates here, the 7 percent real rate for capital opportunity cost is relatively high, so ample allowance has already been made for the capital costs of the induced investment.[46]

It should be noted, finally, that Rutherford currently considers that the calibration of the HRT model in Harrison, Rutherford, and Tarr (1996; the model used here) may have generated excessive SS welfare estimates.[47] In a balanced SS growth path, the gross rental value of capital would be the stock of capital multiplied by the SS interest rate plus the depreciation rate. The level of gross investment would be the stock of capital multiplied by the SS growth rate plus depreciation. With reasonable values for growth (e.g., 2 percent), real interest rate (5 percent), and depreciation (7 percent), the ratio of gross capital rental value to gross investment would be about 1.3. The benchmark calibration of this ratio instead placed it considerably higher (at about 1.8).

At the same time, the more fundamental question is whether the SS model overstates the dynamic effects of trade liberalization. Rutherford and Tarr (2002) develop a dynamic version of the HRT model that incorporates productivity gains, driven by an increased number of "varieties" of inputs in a Dixit and Stiglitz (1977) framework. In that model, welfare gains from trade liberalization are far higher than in the traditional static welfare estimates.[48] So whereas the Harrison, Rutherford, and Tarr (1996)

---

45. This view is held by Dani Rodrik; comment on a draft of this study; personal communication, October 20, 2003.

46. For example, during the 1990s the 10-year US Treasury bond had an average nominal interest rate of 6.4 percent. Average inflation was 2.8 percent, so the average real interest rate was 3.5 percent, only half the rate used here.

47. Personal communication, November 5, 2003.

48. Their central estimate in the dynamic productivity model is that a 10 percent tariff cut leads to a 10.6 percent increase in welfare, far higher than in the traditional static welfare triangles method.

SS model may in retrospect overstate potential dynamic gains from the standpoint of induced investment, the authors would now consider that it substantially understates total dynamic gains by not incorporating the productivity gains associated with increased varieties of inputs.

In short, in the context of the overall set of models developed by these authors, the estimates of net welfare effects in the SS version in table 4.5 are likely to understate rather than overstate the overall dynamic effects. For the purposes of the present study, in chapter 5 a specific attempt is made to estimate the dynamic productivity gains separately. Only half of the estimated SS net welfare and poverty effects are used in the consolidated estimates of that chapter, making some allowance for possible overstatement in the model calibration along the lines just reviewed, as well as for possible limits to the feasibility of mobilizing the additional capital for the potentially induced investment.

## Factor Price Effects

The PEHRT model's estimates of changes in factor prices form the basis for the estimates of the impact of trade liberalization on global poverty. Table 4.6 reports the estimated percentage changes in real factor prices resulting from free trade in the CRTS static model.

Because the HRT model generates only relative price changes against a "numeraire," it is necessary to subtract the change in the numeraire price from all factor price changes calculated. In the model, the US representative agent consumer is the numeraire entity. The unit price of consumption in the United States falls by 0.7 percent in the free trade results, so 0.7 percent is added to the price changes reported in the HRT results to obtain the real factor price changes presented in table 4.6.

The factor price changes generally go in the expected direction.[49] The expected (Stolper-Samuelson) change in relative factor prices, with an increase of the relative price of the country's relatively abundant factor—inherent in the Heckscher-Ohlin model of international trade based on relative factor abundance—is evident in the estimates in that the change in the price of the country's most abundant factor tends to rise the most. This effect is dramatic in the case of land, where the changes are large. There are increases of well over 100 percent in the real price of land for Australia–New Zealand (ANZ) and Canada (CAN), a rise of more than 50 percent for South Africa (XSC), and increases on the order of 25 to 35 percent in the five Latin American countries or subregions and Tanzania. The

---

49. For the purposes of discussing relative factor price changes, the direct estimates in table 4.6 are cited for convenience. As discussed below, however, these are subsequently adjusted to ensure consistency with the overall welfare estimate, for the purposes of estimating the poverty impact.

# Table 4.6 Impact of free trade on real factor prices and welfare: CRTS static model (percent change)

| Region | Land | Unskilled labor | Skilled labor | Capital and resources | Weighted sum | Welfare | Lambda |
|--------|------|-----------------|---------------|-----------------------|--------------|---------|--------|
| **B25** | | | | | | | |
| ANZ | 124.9 | 4.5 | 1.9 | 1.8 | 3.62 | 3.3 | 0.91 |
| CAN | 140.5 | 2.1 | 1.8 | 2.3 | 2.80 | 1.2 | 0.43 |
| USA | 4.8 | 1.0 | 1.0 | 1.0 | 1.02 | 0.7 | 0.69 |
| JPN | −70.9 | 3.5 | 4.0 | 3.7 | 3.50 | 1.3 | 0.37 |
| KOR | −31.2 | 9.4 | 9.6 | 9.6 | 8.54 | 4.0 | 0.47 |
| E_U | −51.3 | 1.2 | 1.7 | 1.4 | 0.96 | 0.8 | 0.83 |
| IDN | 8.6 | 2.4 | 1.4 | 2.0 | 2.63 | 1.1 | 0.42 |
| MYS | −0.6 | 8.6 | 8.3 | 8.5 | 8.07 | 1.0 | 0.12 |
| PHL | 12.4 | 5.2 | 3.4 | 3.2 | 4.46 | 2.0 | 0.45 |
| THA | 51.3 | 10.6 | 5.8 | 5.2 | 7.44 | 3.6 | 0.48 |
| CHN | 0.7 | 8.3 | 8.5 | 8.2 | 7.89 | 1.1 | 0.14 |
| AG3 | 6.4 | 3.7 | 3.1 | 3.3 | 3.41 | 2.3 | 0.68 |
| ARG | 36.5 | 2.5 | 1.2 | 1.5 | 2.94 | 2.1 | 0.71 |
| BRA | 23.4 | 1.6 | 1.7 | 2.3 | 2.27 | 2.0 | 0.88 |
| MEX | −2.3 | 1.0 | 1.1 | 1.1 | 0.97 | −0.8 | −0.83 |
| OLA | 32.5 | 4.3 | 2.6 | 2.6 | 3.89 | 1.6 | 0.41 |
| SSA | 18.9 | 6.0 | 4.0 | 3.9 | 5.12 | 1.7 | 0.33 |
| MNA | −22.4 | 9.6 | 11.4 | 12.2 | 10.91 | 4.2 | 0.38 |
| EIT | 10.8 | 1.4 | 4.0 | 4.0 | 4.25 | 1.1 | 0.26 |
| XAS | 7.2 | 5.0 | 4.6 | 4.4 | 4.83 | 1.7 | 0.35 |
| EFTA | −65.3 | 12.9 | 12.9 | 12.0 | 11.97 | 7.9 | 0.66 |
| IND | 3.4 | 2.8 | 2.5 | 2.5 | 2.71 | 0.9 | 0.33 |
| TUR | 14.3 | 4.3 | 3.3 | 3.5 | 3.85 | 2.4 | 0.62 |
| XCM | 26.5 | 9.7 | 8.1 | 9.2 | 9.91 | 5.2 | 0.52 |
| XSC | 56.0 | 4.3 | 4.1 | 5.0 | 4.81 | 1.7 | 0.35 |
| *Memorandum: P26* | | | | | | | |
| BGD | 4.7 | 6.4 | 5.5 | 5.4 | 5.8 | 1.1 | 0.19 |
| XSA | 7.2 | 9.7 | 10.0 | 9.0 | 9.1 | 1.9 | 0.21 |
| MOZ | 8.3 | 6.5 | 6.2 | 6.0 | 6.3 | 3.9 | 0.62 |
| UGA | 3.3 | 2.8 | 2.3 | 2.3 | 2.6 | 1.6 | 0.61 |
| TZA | 32.4 | 8.8 | 2.1 | 3.4 | 7.3 | 4.9 | 0.67 |

CRTS − constant returns to scale

Note: For definitions of the B25 and P26 economies, see the text above. For the meanings of the codes used for regions and economies, see table 4A.2 below

*Source:* Author's calculations.

opposite side of this coin is a sharp decline in land prices in the countries and groups with relatively less land and relatively high protection of agriculture: Japan (−71 percent), the European Union (−51 percent), the EFTA (−65 percent), and South Korea (−31 percent).

The relative prices of skilled versus unskilled labor also tend to move in the expected direction, although far less sharply. For major industrial countries where skilled labor is abundant relative to unskilled labor, there tends to be a rise in the price of the former relative to that of the latter. Thus, for the European Union, the real price of skilled labor rises 1.7 percent, while that of unskilled labor rises 1.2 percent; for Japan, the corresponding comparison is 4.0 percent with 3.5 percent. The effect is not particularly strong, however, and for both the United States and the EFTA the rise in the price of skilled and unskilled labor is identical. For their part, Australia–New Zealand and Canada contravene the expected pattern, because the price of unskilled labor rises more than that of skilled labor. The explanation here may be the strong influence of the agricultural sector (in view of the extreme increases in land price), coupled with a relatively greater intensity of unskilled labor in agriculture than manufactures.

For the developing countries, the expected factor price effect is generally confirmed, although again often this effect is only mild. For South Korea, by now the economy is relatively skill-abundant, so the finding of a slightly greater increase in the price of skilled than unskilled labor is consistent with the theory. For the 18 other developing countries shown in the table, the expected increase in the price of unskilled labor relative to the price of skilled labor is confirmed. Usually the differences are moderate, however. In the two cases where the unskilled labor price rises sharply more than that of skilled labor, Tanzania and Thailand, the explanation likely again lies in the connection with agriculture (given the large land price outcomes in these two cases) rather than the relative skill intensity in the mix of manufacturing products. The same agricultural explanation likely explains why the unskilled-labor price rises less than that of skilled labor in the Middle East and North Africa, considering that this region has a sizable decline in land price.

An important surprise for the relative price of unskilled versus skilled labor is for China, where the former rises slightly less than the latter. The other exceptions to the developing-country rule (Brazil and Pakistan, XSA) show only very small differences between the increases for unskilled and skilled labor.[50]

Again confirming the Heckscher-Ohlin expectation, in 20 of the 25 developing countries or regions in table 4.6, the price of unskilled labor rises more than that of the capital.[51] The overall finding that the factor price for unskilled labor tends to rise relative to that of skilled labor and capital for the developing countries is extremely important for the globalization debate, because it confirms standard international trade theory and contradicts the fears of antiglobalists that trade liberalization will increase the inequality of income in developing countries.

The final column of table 4.6 shows the ratio of the estimated percentage increase in welfare to the weighted sum of the real factor price increases, weighting by ex ante factor shares in each country (see appendix

---

50. The results for Mexico are ambiguous, because in some sense it already has free trade because of NAFTA and the strong dominance of the US market in its trade.

51. Note that in the PEHRT model the GTAP5 "capital" factor is aggregated with its "resources" factor. In the underlying data, capital is by far the more important in the aggregate.

table 4A.4). In principle, these should be equal, apart from the question of whether ex ante or ex post weights are used. In practice, the ratio is systematically less than unity, having a median of 0.42 in these CRTS static effects of free trade. The discrepancy arises primarily from the HRT model's treatment of the fiscal constraint. When import tariffs and export taxes are removed, their original revenue must be replaced by other taxes to keep the fiscal balance unchanged. The model applies "lump-sum" factor taxes to offset the loss of trade tax revenue. The factor price increases reported are gross of taxes, so the net factor price increases are smaller than the reported increases. A test confirms that the revenue treatment is the main source of divergence between the weighted sum of factor price increases and the percent rise in welfare.[52]

To adjust for the trade revenue effect as well as any other sources of divergence between welfare and factor price change, the poverty estimates below shrink the factor price increase estimates if their weighted sum exceeds the welfare estimates. Thus, the analysis uses the *minimum* of two estimates. The first is the direct estimate, that is, the weighted sum of real factor price changes, weighting by factor shares *at the poverty household level*:

$$\hat{z} = \sum_f \hat{y}_f \varphi_f^p,$$

where $\hat{z}$ is the proportionate change in real income for poverty-level households, $\hat{y}$ is the proportionate change in the real factor price, $\varphi$ is the factor share, $f$ refers to the factor in question, and $p$ refers to households at the poverty threshold. The second is the same measure but multiplied by the economywide aggregate ratio of the proportionate change in welfare divided by the weighted sum of proportionate increases in real factor prices (this time weighting by the economywide factor shares), or by

$$\lambda = \hat{w} / [\sum_f \hat{y}_f \varphi_f].{}^{53}$$

The estimated proportionate increase in real income at the poverty level is thus $\hat{z}$ if $\lambda \geq 1$, and $\lambda \hat{z}$ if $\lambda < 1$.

Finally, it should be noted further that the percentage welfare increase in table 4.6 is systematically somewhat higher than the change in welfare

---

52. For the regions of the B25 model (excluding Malaysia), the simple average ratio of import and export tax revenue to the base magnitude of welfare is 3.83 percent. The simple average excess of the factor-share-weighted sum of factor price increases over percent increase in welfare is 2.57 percent, in the same order of magnitude. A regression across the 24 countries of the latter on the former yields $d = 0.19 + 0.62r$, where $d$ is the excess of weighted factor price percent increases over percent increase in welfare and $r$ is trade tax revenue as a percentage of base welfare, with an adjusted $R^2$ of 0.73 and a $t$-statistic of 7.9 on $r$.

53. Factor shares in the GTAP5 database for the PEHRT regions are shown in table 4A.4.

as a percentage of GDP shown in table 4.1, because the welfare base refers to private consumption plus investment (net of depreciation) rather than full GDP.[54]

## Poverty Effects: Static

With the real factor price effects of trade liberalization in hand, the next step is to calculate the corresponding impact on global poverty. This involves two components: estimating the percent increase in the factor prices relevant to households at the poverty level; and multiplying this percent change by the "poverty elasticity" examined in chapter 1 to obtain the corresponding percentage reduction in countrywide poverty.

In the first instance, a good approximation of the relevant factor price change at the poverty level should be the rise in the real price of unskilled labor, because this will be the principal source of income at this level. Ideally, additional detail would be included to take account of any income stemming from poverty households' endowments of land, skilled labor, and capital as well. Obtaining data on factor shares at the poverty level is difficult, however. Household surveys typically do not carefully divide income into that attributable to each of the principal factors of production.

One set of empirical estimates is available for Brazil in Harrison, Rutherford, Tarr, and Gurgel (2002). This study finds the following sources of household income at the poverty level in the rural areas of Brazil: land, 0; unskilled labor, 80.2 percent; skilled labor, 8.3 percent; capital, 0.2 percent; and transfers, 11.3 percent. For urban households at the poverty level, the corresponding shares are 0.3 percent, 67.2 percent, 18.1 percent, 0.6 percent, and 13.9 percent.[55] The shares of the total number of poor people located in the rural (38.8 percent) and urban (61.2 percent) areas (table 3C.1 above) can then be applied to obtain the economywide factor shares for households in poverty in Brazil.

These data raise the question of how to treat transfers. The approach taken here is simply to apply the economywide proportionate gain in welfare to estimate the proportionate rise in transfers, on the grounds that nonpoor relatives and the government are at least as likely to use the

---

54. The simple average ratio of the welfare base to GDP for the B25 countries is 0.725. The exclusion of capital depreciation (the difference between GDP and net national product) in limiting the welfare base is straightforward. The exclusion of "government provision" from the welfare base is somewhat more ambiguous, however. Nonetheless, as the welfare percent increase is already being used to shrink the direct estimates of real factor price increases, and because use of welfare change as a percentage of GDP would contain a clear understatement bias as the denominator includes capital depreciation, the direct estimate of the welfare percent change is the more reasonable to use for estimating $\lambda$.

55. These are the shares for the second of the 10 household groupings arrayed by ascending income, in both the rural and urban areas (Harrison et al. 2002, 42).

gains from liberalization to increase their transfers to poor households as they are to use them for other purposes.

Unfortunately, comparable factor shares at the poverty-household level are not available for other countries.[56] On the basis of the Brazil estimates, the calculations below assume for all other countries that transfers account for 10 percent of poverty-household income. Otherwise, the principal calculation assumes that the remaining 90 percent of poverty-level income comes from unskilled labor, which is surely the dominant factor endowment of the poor. A sensitivity test is conducted in which it is assumed instead that transfers account for 10 percent, unskilled labor for 70 percent, and land for 20 percent. The reason for an alternate incorporating significant weight to land is that where smallholder agriculture is present, the land factor could be important in household income. As indicated in table 4.6, because of the importance of agricultural liberalization, the most dramatic factor price changes tend to be for land, so this sensitivity test should provide a good indication of the possible range of effects.

The poverty-impact calculations here do not take special account of any differential effect of trade liberalization on the consumption basket of the poor as opposed to at the aggregate national level. There might be grounds for concern that the prices of consumption items of greater importance to the poor might be less favorably affected than those on average (or even adversely affected, given the expectation of an increase in global agricultural prices; see chapter 3 and appendix 3C). The existing research suggests, however, that such effects on the consumption-composition side are minor relative to the effects on the factor payments side (Hertel et al, 2002).

Table 4.7 reports the results of the poverty-impact calculations for free trade using the CRTS model, static effects. The estimates are made for 25 developing countries or regions in the B25 and P26 model results discussed above. The table first repeats the World Bank estimate of the number of poor people at the $2 per day threshold (see chapter 1). The next column reports the poverty elasticity using the lognormal distribution as applied to the Gini coefficient and the ratio of average to poverty-level income in the country in question, applying equation B.9 from appendix 1B. As discussed in chapter 1, this elasticity estimate can be extremely high in countries where the ratio of mean to poverty-level income is high and the Gini coefficient is moderate or low. As a result, a ceiling of 3.5 is imposed on the absolute size of the poverty elasticity (the next column of table 4.7),

---

56. The data compiled in Hertel, Preckel, Cranfield, and Ivanić (2002) for seven developing countries come close, but do not provide overall factor shares for households at the poverty level. Instead, their data are organized by household type (i.e., agricultural enterprises, nonagricultural enterprises, households dependent on wage and salary labor, households dependent on transfers, and "diversified" households). It is unclear what share of income in each household type is derived from each of the factors of production, as well as what fraction of the total poverty population is in each of the household types.

# Table 4.7 Impact of free trade on global poverty: CRTS static model

| Region and economy | | Poor (millions) | Poverty elasticity | | Percent change in real poverty-level income | | Change in number of poor (millions) | |
|---|---|---|---|---|---|---|---|---|
| | | | Estimated | Constrained | Base case | Alternative | Base case | Alternative |
| **Asia** | | | | | | | | |
| Bangladesh | BGD | 99.3 | 5.8 | 3.5 | 1.2 | 1.1 | −4.2 | −4.0 |
| China | CHN | 673.2 | 5.1 | 3.5 | 1.2 | 0.9 | −27.2 | −22.2 |
| India | IND | 859.9 | 5.0 | 3.5 | 0.9 | 1.0 | −27.7 | −28.9 |
| Indonesia | IDN | 136.8 | 6.6 | 3.5 | 1.0 | 1.5 | −4.9 | −7.4 |
| Malaysia | MYS | 5.6 | 3.2 | 3.2 | 1.0 | 0.8 | −0.2 | −0.1 |
| Pakistan | XSA | 114.2 | 9.4 | 3.5 | 2.0 | 1.9 | −8.1 | −7.7 |
| Philippines | PHL | 29.2 | 3.0 | 3.0 | 2.3 | 3.0 | −2.0 | −2.6 |
| South Korea | KOR | 0.9 | inf | 3.5 | 0.2 | −2.7 | 0.0 | 0.1 |
| Thailand | THA | 17.0 | 5.9 | 3.5 | 4.9 | 8.8 | −2.9 | −5.3 |
| Hong Kong, Taiwan, and Singapore | AG3 | 0.0 | n.a. | 2.0 | 2.5 | 2.9 | 0.0 | 0.0 |
| Other | OAS | 84.8 | n.a. | 2.0 | 1.3 | 1.1 | −2.3 | −1.9 |
| *Subtotal* | | 2,020.9 | | | | | −79.5 | −79.9 |
| **Latin America** | | | | | | | | |
| Argentina | ARG | 5.4 | 3.1 | 3.1 | 1.8 | 6.6 | −0.3 | −1.1 |
| Brazil | BRA | 29.2 | 1.0 | 1.0 | 1.5 | 5.3 | −0.4 | −1.5 |
| Central America and Caribbean | XCM | 26.6 | n.a. | 2.0 | 5.1 | 6.8 | −2.7 | −3.6 |
| Mexico | MEX | 41.1 | 2.0 | 2.0 | 0.8 | 0.2 | −0.7 | −0.1 |
| Other | OLA | 45.9 | n.a. | 2.0 | 1.7 | 4.1 | −1.6 | −3.7 |
| *Subtotal* | | 148.2 | | | | | −5.7 | −10.1 |
| **Central and Eastern Europe** | EIT | 92.2 | n.a. | 2.0 | 1.1 | 1.5 | −2.1 | −2.7 |
| **Middle East and North Africa** | | | | | | | | |
| Turkey | TUR | 11.6 | 6.1 | 3.5 | 2.6 | 3.9 | −1.1 | −1.6 |
| Other | MNA | 76.4 | n.a. | 2.0 | 3.7 | 1.3 | −5.7 | −1.9 |
| *Subtotal* | | 88.0 | | | | | −6.7 | −3.5 |
| **Sub-Saharan Africa** | | | | | | | | |
| Mozambique | MOZ | 13.6 | 1.4 | 1.4 | 4.0 | 4.2 | −0.8 | −0.8 |
| South Africa | XSC | 15.1 | 1.2 | 1.2 | 1.5 | 5.1 | −0.3 | −0.9 |
| Tanzania | TZA | 19.7 | 0.6 | 1.0 | 5.8 | 9.0 | −1.1 | −1.8 |
| Uganda | UGA | 16.6 | 2.3 | 2.3 | 1.7 | 1.8 | −0.7 | −0.7 |
| Other | SSA | 328.4 | n.a. | 2.0 | 2.0 | 2.8 | −12.8 | −18.4 |
| *Subtotal* | | 393.2 | | | | | −15.6 | −22.6 |
| **Total** | | 2,742.5 | | | | | −109.7 | −118.8 |

CRTS = constant returns to scale
inf = infinite
n.a. = not available

*Source:* Author's calculations.

based on international patterns as reviewed by the World Bank (2001, 54). The ceiling tends to apply to the Asian countries, except for the Philippines, where the Gini coefficient is somewhat higher. The direct estimate of the poverty elasticity applies to the three individually identified Latin American countries, reflecting their higher Gini coefficients. For countries in sub-Saharan Africa, the direct estimates are also low enough to be the relevant poverty elasticities, reflecting the fact that in these economies the ratio of mean income to the poverty-level income tends to be much lower because such a large fraction of the population is poor. For regions where individual Gini coefficients and mean/poverty income estimates are not available, a standard poverty elasticity of 2 is applied (the general value used in World Bank 2001).

The next two columns of table 4.7 show the percent change in the weighted average real factor price (and transfers) for poverty-level households in the country in question, using the factor shares just discussed and the constrained factor price effects discussed above (i.e., direct estimates or these multiplied by $\lambda$, table 4.6). The base case applies the direct estimates for poverty-level factor shares for Brazil and the standard set of assumed shares (90 percent unskilled labor, 10 percent transfers) for all other countries; the alternative estimates apply 20 percent land, 70 percent unskilled labor, and 10 percent transfers.

The final two columns of table 4.7 apply the percent change in poverty obtained by multiplying the poverty elasticity by the percent change in real income for poverty-level households, to the number of poor in each country. The results show that free trade systematically reduces poverty in the developing countries. The largest absolute reductions are in India and China, reflecting their large poor populations. For Asia as a whole, the two alternative estimates place the reduction in poverty at about 80 million, or about 4 percent of the poor in the region. The reduction in Latin America is 6 to 10 million, or about 5 percent of the region's poor. In sub-Saharan Africa, in the base case the number of poor falls by about 16 million, or by 4 percent; but in the alternative case, postulating a 20 percent factor share of land, the reduction is by about 23 million, or 5.7 percent. In the Middle East and North Africa and in Eastern Europe, the poverty reduction estimates range from 2.3 to 7.6 percent of the current population in poverty.

The aggregate reduction of 110 to 120 million in the number of poor globally is smaller than the suggested estimate of 200 million in chapter 3 for the impact of complete agricultural liberalization, using the simple model of hypothesized price effects and rural-urban elasticities relating real income to agricultural prices. A number of influences could contribute to this divergence.

First, the back-of-the-envelope model developed in appendix 3C postulates a 10 percent rise in global agricultural prices as the consequence of free trade, based on a few aggregative product price increases reported in

CGE estimates elsewhere (IMF 2002d). In the central version of that simple model, this translates into a 9 percent rise in the real domestic agricultural price at the farm gate. The corresponding price increase in PEHRT could be smaller. Second, the rural-urban dichotomy in the earlier model is not present in the PEHRT model. Although the latter does treat each production sector as occupied by a "representative firm," it treats all households identically as the "representative consumer." Third, and related, the underlying HRT model treats factors as mobile across sectors within the country. Implicitly, the simple model of appendix 3C treats rural and urban households as fixed within their existing production sectors.[57]

For these reasons, it is not overly surprising that the PEHRT results differ from those of the simple rural-urban poverty model. Nor is it surprising that the difference is in the direction found, considering that the rural-urban detail in the PEHRT model is essentially missing and in view of the fact that the driving force in the earlier model is the much greater share of poor households located in the rural than the urban sectors.

As for the first possible source of the difference noted above, it turns out that in the PEHRT free trade scenario, the rise in the real domestic price to agricultural producers is 8.5 percent if weighted by the agricultural exports of seven major exporting countries (ANZ, CAN, USA, ARG, BRA, OLA, and XCM). This is almost identical to what is assumed in the model of chapter 3. However, for the countries more directly relevant for poverty effects, the rise is substantially less. Weighting by country shares in global poverty, the rise in the domestic agricultural production price turns out to be only 2.7 percent in the PEHRT free trade static results. This average is dragged down by heavily weighted India (an increase of 2.9 percent) and especially China (an increase of only 0.55 percent). It is important to keep in mind, however, that especially for the relatively homogeneous agricultural goods, the HRT Armington substitution assumptions may tend to permit a greater gap between the domestic agricultural price increase and the global export price increase than would in fact occur.

The principal implications of a comparison of the results in table 4.7 with those of appendix 3C, then, are that the simple model of chapter 3 may tend to overstate somewhat the poverty reduction from agricultural liberalization; but also that the poverty estimates from the static version of the PEHRT model may tend to understate rather than overstate the scope for global poverty reduction through trade liberalization.

---

57. It might be asked whether a fourth source of the divergence is that implicitly the earlier model imputes land income as well as unskilled-labor income to rural households, whereas the land factor has a zero share in poverty-level factor payments in the PEHRT model's base case. However, all that is required for the model of appendix 3C to be consistent with a zero land share for the poor is for the unskilled wage in the rural sector to rise at least proportionately with total farm income, not that land factor income accrues to the poor.

# Poverty Effects: Steady State

The results for poverty impact can be calculated for the steady state (SS) effects of free trade as well, corresponding to the welfare effects shown in table 4.5. Table 4.8 reports the SS model estimates of real factor price changes.[58] Once again, it is necessary to check the factor price changes against the welfare changes, in this case using the net welfare estimates after deducting the imputed cost of induced capital investment. Once again, most countries (24 of 30) show the weighted sum of factor price changes as higher than the increase in net welfare as a percentage of the welfare base, so again in most cases the relevant factor price increase is multiplied by the term $\lambda$ to obtain the adjusted factor price increase.

As would be expected, the real factor price increases are typically much larger in the SS results than in the static results. The exception is for capital, because by design this version of the model allows the quantity of capital to rise until the rate of the return on investment is brought back down to the preliberalization level. In about half of the countries, this involves an absolute reduction in the factor price for capital, whereas there was an increase in all capital factor prices in the static case (table 4.6). The implication is that for about half of the countries, the price of investment goods falls sufficiently that in order for the ratio of the rental price of capital to the unit cost of investment to be brought back down to its original level, capital must be increased by enough so that its rental price falls below the level before liberalization.

Table 4.9 reports the results of applying the real factor price changes of table 4.8 to obtain the poverty-level real income changes and resulting changes in the number of poor in each country or region. The sequence of steps in the calculation is the same as that set forth for the static poverty-impact effects discussed above.

The poverty-impact estimates are far larger for the SS case than for the static case. Thus, the average of the base and alternative estimates amounts to 587 million globally lifted out of poverty, or 20 percent of the global poor population. This impact is 5.1 times as great as that in the static case, whereas the corresponding aggregate net welfare gains for developing countries are only 1.9 times as high (tables 4.5 and 4.1). A key difference is that in the SS, India, "other" sub-Saharan Africa (SSA), and Pakistan experience much larger increases in poverty-level real incomes (on the order of 8, 10, and 25 percent respectively) than in the static case (only about 1, 2, and 2 percent respectively). The greater poverty reduction relative to aggregate welfare increase in the steady state case than in the static

---

58. As before, these are the direct PEHRT calculations minus the percent change in the price for the consumer representative agent in the numeraire country (United States), which in this case adds 1.5 percent to the B25 factor price changes and 1.4 percent to the P26 changes.

# Table 4.8 Impact of free trade on real factor prices and welfare: Steady State CRTS model (percent change)

| Region or economy | Land | Unskilled labor | Skilled labor | Capital and resources | Weighted sum | Net welfare | Lambda |
|---|---|---|---|---|---|---|---|
| **B25** | | | | | | | |
| ANZ | 142.7 | 7.9 | 4.5 | −0.1 | 4.52 | 4.28 | 0.95 |
| CAN | 156.6 | 3.3 | 2.9 | 2.4 | 3.61 | 1.33 | 0.37 |
| USA | 10.2 | 2.2 | 2.1 | 1.4 | 1.92 | 0.98 | 0.51 |
| JPN | −69.4 | 4.8 | 5.4 | 4.2 | 4.51 | 1.19 | 0.26 |
| KOR | −27.5 | 14.2 | 14.0 | 5.6 | 9.44 | 1.35 | 0.14 |
| E_U | −48.9 | 2.7 | 3.0 | 1.9 | 1.98 | 1.31 | 0.66 |
| IDN | 15.9 | 6.9 | 4.7 | −2.0 | 2.93 | 1.96 | 0.67 |
| MYS | 11.8 | 16.2 | 14.0 | 2.8 | 7.86 | 3.69 | 0.47 |
| PHL | 20.7 | 9.5 | 6.2 | −0.4 | 4.90 | 3.24 | 0.66 |
| THA | 74.4 | 38.3 | 21.6 | −1.8 | 6.60 | 32.54 | 4.93 |
| CHN | 5.0 | 12.7 | 12.0 | 3.2 | 8.45 | −2.57 | −0.30 |
| AG3 | 12.6 | 7.0 | 5.9 | 1.6 | 4.38 | 2.34 | 0.53 |
| ARG | 45.7 | 6.5 | 4.4 | −1.0 | 3.93 | 3.12 | 0.79 |
| BRA | 37.6 | 5.7 | 4.6 | −0.1 | 3.17 | 4.32 | 1.36 |
| MEX | 2.1 | 3.2 | 2.9 | 1.0 | 1.70 | 0.42 | 0.25 |
| OLA | 46.7 | 10.6 | 6.4 | −0.9 | 4.53 | 5.67 | 1.25 |
| SSA | 31.4 | 12.6 | 7.2 | −2.4 | 5.49 | 4.53 | 0.83 |
| MNA | −11.9 | 15.5 | 15.2 | 6.9 | 10.84 | 7.78 | 0.72 |
| EIT | 18.4 | 7.7 | 6.5 | 1.2 | 4.91 | 0.97 | 0.20 |
| XAS | 18.4 | 10.2 | 7.7 | −0.6 | 5.38 | 4.53 | 0.84 |
| EFTA | −62.6 | 14.9 | 14.9 | 10.4 | 12.68 | 7.24 | 0.57 |
| IND | 16.0 | 8.6 | 5.0 | −4.2 | 3.03 | 4.50 | 1.48 |
| TUR | 24.6 | 9.2 | 7.1 | 2.0 | 4.87 | 5.13 | 1.05 |
| XCM | 48.2 | 19.9 | 13.1 | −0.6 | 9.46 | 5.94 | 0.63 |
| XSC | 72.7 | 8.2 | 7.0 | 1.51 | 5.68 | 3.31 | 0.58 |
| *Memorandum:* P26 | | | | | | | |
| BGD | 14.5 | 10.3 | 7.4 | 0.7 | 6.11 | 2.05 | 0.33 |
| XSA | 42.5 | 26.4 | 14.4 | −11.3 | 9.43 | 12.86 | 1.36 |
| MOZ | 23.8 | 14.3 | 10.1 | −2.9 | 6.64 | 6.38 | 0.96 |
| UGA | 9.1 | 6.8 | 4.2 | −2.3 | 3.23 | 2.84 | 0.88 |
| TZA | 55.5 | 21.0 | −9.6 | 4.1 | 13.61 | 8.13 | 0.60 |

CRTS = constant returns to scale

Note: For definitions of the B25 and P26 economies, see the text above. For the meanings of the codes used for regions and economies, see table 4A.2 below.

*Source:* Author's calculations.

case reflects the greater increase in the factor price for unskilled labor relative to the percent increase in net welfare. This in turn reflects the rise in the capital/labor ratio from induced investment in the steady state case.

China is the one case in which the SS net welfare effects turn negative (table 4.8), indicating that the increased gross welfare effects are smaller than the increased capital cost when imputed at the standard 7 percent real interest rate. It makes no sense, however, to attribute a corresponding estimate of negative poverty reduction (i.e., a poverty increase), because under these circumstances the additional investment would not take place

**Table 4.9  Impact of free trade on global poverty: Steady State CRTS model**

| Region and economy | | Percent change in real poverty-level income | | Change in number of poor (millions) | |
|---|---|---|---|---|---|
| | | Base | Alternative | Base | Alternative |
| **Asia** | | | | | |
| Bangladesh | BGD | 3.3 | 3.5 | −11.3 | −12.3 |
| China | CHN | 0.0 | 0.0 | 0.0 | 0.0 |
| India | IND | 8.2 | 9.7 | −246.5 | −291.0 |
| Indonesia | IDN | 4.4 | 5.6 | −20.9 | −26.6 |
| Korea | KOR | 1.9 | 0.8 | −0.1 | 0.0 |
| Malaysia | MYS | 7.2 | 6.8 | −1.3 | −1.2 |
| Pakistan | XSA | 25.0 | 28.3 | −100.1 | −113.0 |
| Philippines | PHL | 6.0 | 7.4 | −5.2 | −6.5 |
| Thailand | THA | 37.7 | 44.9 | −22.4 | −26.7 |
| Hong Kong, Taiwan, and Singapore | AG3 | 3.6 | 4.2 | 0.0 | 0.0 |
| Other | OAS | 8.2 | 9.5 | −13.8 | −16.2 |
| *Subtotal* | | | | −421.6 | −493.6 |
| **Latin America** | | | | | |
| Argentina | ARG | 4.9 | 11.1 | −0.8 | −1.9 |
| Brazil | BRA | 5.4 | 11.9 | −1.6 | −3.5 |
| Central America and Caribbean | XCM | 11.9 | 15.4 | −6.3 | −8.2 |
| Mexico | MEX | 0.8 | 0.7 | −0.6 | −0.6 |
| Other | OLA | 10.1 | 17.3 | −9.3 | −15.0 |
| *Subtotal* | | | | −18.6 | −30.1 |
| **Central and Eastern Europe** | EIT | 1.5 | 1.9 | −2.7 | −3.5 |
| **Middle East, North Africa** | | | | | |
| Turkey | TUR | 8.8 | 11.9 | −3.6 | −4.8 |
| Other | MNA | 10.8 | 8.9 | −16.5 | −10.5 |
| *Subtotal* | | | | −20.1 | −15.3 |
| **Sub-Saharan Africa** | | | | | |
| Mozambique | MOZ | 13.0 | 14.8 | −2.4 | −2.8 |
| South Africa | XSC | 4.6 | 12.1 | −0.8 | −2.2 |
| Tanzania | TZA | 12.2 | 16.3 | −2.4 | −3.2 |
| Uganda | UGA | 5.7 | 6.1 | −2.2 | −2.3 |
| Other | SSA | 9.9 | 13.0 | −64.8 | −85.3 |
| *Subtotal* | | | | 72.6 | −95.8 |
| **Total** | | | | −535.7 | −638.2 |

*Source:* Author's calculations.

and thus the negative welfare effect would not occur. For the SS estimates of poverty impact (table 4.9), the entries for China are thus set at zero. This is a conservative approach, because it could be argued that instead the poverty reduction could be at least as great as in the static case (27 million, table 4.7). The conservative use of zero is consistent with a probabilistic interpretation of the estimates, in which one should expect overstatement for some countries and understatement for others. Setting the SS poverty impact at zero for China helps lean against any possible overstatement of the results for other countries, in particular for India, where the estimates are large at somewhat more than half of the global total.

The SS results do raise the question of feasibility. The extra capital required would amount to 42 percent of developing-country GDP (table 4.5), or $2.7 trillion (at 1997 GDP scale and prices). This amount is not as impossibly large as it might seem at first glance. Suppose the developing countries themselves achieved extra saving amounting to, say, 3 percent of GDP annually (raising the saving rate by about one-tenth in Asia and one-seventh in Latin America). Suppose net capital flows to developing countries rose to 4 percent of developing-country GDP annually, or $256 billion. This figure is actually smaller than the 1996 peak of $330 billion in net capital flows to emerging-market economies, although it is far above the 2000–02 average of $145 billion in the aftermath of the East Asian, Russian, and Argentine financial crises (IIF 2003). The result would be potentially an extra 7 percent of developing-country GDP in annual capital formation, so after 6 years the additional capital to support the SS scenario would be in hand. (There would be some leakage of foreign capital to extra consumption and capital depreciation, but an offset from a growing GDP base and hence larger absolute scale corresponding to the extra 7 percent of GDP capital formation.)

The main implication of these considerations is that there is a central role for mobilizing capital, both domestically and from abroad, as a necessary counterpart to trade liberalization to permit the potential gains of free trade to be fully realized. For poor countries, this probably means "trade and aid," not one or the other; and for middle-income countries, it highlights the importance of strengthening global capital markets after their severe difficulties from financial crises and occasional conspicuous defaults in recent years.

There is another relevant question about the SS results: Even if somehow the extra capital could be mobilized, would this be an efficient way to attack global poverty? The extra $2.7 trillion in capital to reduce poverty by an extra 393 million (the difference between the results in tables 4.7 and 4.9) works out to about $6,900 per person removed from poverty, or an annual cost of about $480, applying a real opportunity cost of capital of 7 percent. Once again the dimensionality is not as disproportionate as the large numbers might at first suggest, considering that the extra annual income even just for those near the poverty line would be about $50 (using an illustrative 7 percent increase on the basis of the median identified in table 4.9), and more fundamentally, that the gains of the 393 million lifted out of poverty would be only a small portion of the economic gains from liberalization with capital accumulation, because the bulk would accrue to the general economy and not just to that set of the poor near the poverty line.

It should be stressed that even the SS model does not necessarily capture the full dynamic effects of trade liberalization. As noted in chapter 3 and examined further in chapter 5, there is a strong tradition in the literature holding that the increased competitive pressure from trade liberalization will stimulate technological change and the pace of total factor productivity growth. Increased productivity growth would be additive to effects from a more rapid accumulation of capital. Chapter 5 takes productivity gains into account, and it obtains consolidated dynamic effects by adding the estimated productivity gains to a conservative estimate (i.e., half) of the incremental SS gains.

## Preference Erosion

The estimates of this chapter are based on the removal or reduction of protection as reported in the GTAP5 database. Except for NAFTA (for Mexico) and trade within the South African Customs Union, for developing countries these data refer to MFN protection. They do not make explicit allowance for existing preferential entry under the GSP, the EU's Cotonou and EBA arrangements, and the US arrangements under CBI, APTA, and AGOA (see chapter 2). The question thus arises as to whether the estimates significantly overstate global poverty reduction from the move to free trade by failing to take account of the erosion of preferences as MFN protection declines.

The broad answer to this question is that aggregate global poverty reduction is unlikely to be overstated by much as a consequence of absence of specific attention to existing preferential entry. As noted in chapter 2, the three "at-risk" country groupings—LDCs, HIPCs, and sub-Saharan Africa—account together for only about 4 percent of imports from developing countries into Japan, 6 percent for the United States, and 8 percent for the European Union. Yet these are the groups of countries eligible for the more meaningful existing regimes of preferences. The broader GSP, which in principle applies to middle-income countries as well, in practice has had so many restrictions that it does not provide meaningful free entry.

Whereas the CGE model estimates of this chapter should therefore give a broadly accurate calculation of aggregate global poverty reduction from free trade, they may significantly overstate poverty reduction for some of the poorer regions and countries. It is possible to examine this question further using a tailored run of the PEHRT model for the P26 groupings, which provide the greatest detail on the poor countries eligible for these arrangements. The US AGOA regime and the European Union's EBA arrangement represent perhaps the most open special regimes for poor countries, although even these programs contain considerable restrictions (see chapter 2). A relatively strong test of the "preference erosion effect" can thus be obtained by leaving unchanged the measured protection by the United States

**Table 4.10   Test for overstatement of gains from exclusion of preference erosion**

(welfare effects, billions of dollars)

| Region or economy | Free trade (P26) | Free trade except unchanged US and EU protection against P7 |
|---|---|---|
| SSA | 2.36 | −0.02 |
| MOZ | 0.13 | 0.09 |
| UGA | 0.09 | 0.07 |
| XSC | 1.33 | 0.28 |
| TZA | 0.29 | 0.24 |
| XCM | 4.02 | 1.78 |
| BGD | 0.39 | −0.20 |
| Subtotal (P7) | 8.61 | 2.24 |
| | | |
| DGC | 82.78 | 77.43 |
| DEV | 141.92 | 142.25 |
| WLD | 224.69 | 219.68 |

Note: For definitions of the P7 and P26 economies and for the meanings of the codes used, see the text.

Source: Author's calculations.

and the European Union against the relevant P26 countries in a scenario that otherwise applies global free trade.[59] The test should overstate rather than understate preference erosion effects because existing entry for the relevant poor countries is not fully free, even in the US and EU markets.[60]

Table 4.10 reports the results of this test. US and EU protection is frozen against Mozambique (MOZ), Uganda (UGA), South Africa (XSC), Tanzania (TZA), "other" sub-Saharan Africa (SSA), Central America (XCM), and Bangladesh (BGD), while global free trade is implemented otherwise. The result is to reduce static welfare gains for these seven regions ("P7") from $8.6 billion (table 4.1) to $2.2 billion annually. However, the striking finding is that these countries nonetheless enjoy positive benefits, except for very small losses in other sub-Saharan Africa and Bangladesh. Moreover,

59. That is, if in reality the applicable tariff against country X is zero but the database says it is the MFN tariff of 10 percent, then the tariff erosion effect of eliminating US tariffs against all other countries can be approximated by applying the model with the US tariff against country X left unchanged at the base value of 10 percent while eliminating US tariffs against all other countries. The proportionate change in the price of supply from country X relative to that from other countries will be the same, and hence so will the calculated shift of supply away from X to the other countries, as if the database had accurately reported the base tariff against country X as zero and had then eliminated protection against all countries.

60. This fact should more than offset any understatement from limiting the protection freeze to the United States and the European Union, because the preference programs of most other industrial countries tend to be more restrictive and the import bases smaller. Thus, whereas the United States and the European Union together accounted for a total of $18 billion in imports from the LDCs in 2000, Japan and Canada together accounted for only $1.2 billion (table 1.4).

this strong test of preference erosion only reduces aggregate developing-country welfare gains from free trade by 6.5 percent.

A key message of table 4.10 is that the countries already enjoying the most complete preferential access to the US and EU markets can nonetheless expect to reap further gains, instead of suffer losses, from global free trade.[61] The reason is that their losses from the erosion of existing preferential entry are more than offset by their gains from removing their own protection and from increased market opportunities in other countries (including developing countries) not currently providing free entry. The policy implication is that negotiators for LDCs and other at-risk countries should not fear global free trade liberalization, because the new opportunities it gives their countries should outweigh the preference erosion that results. This conclusion would of course be even stronger if the Doha Round outcome included a "parallel track" of immediate deepening of free entry (and tax incentives for direct investment) for the at-risk countries, as proposed in this study (chapters 2 and 6).

The test for preference erosion effects can be extended to decompose the welfare gains for the P7 countries between own-liberalization and effects of liberalization of non-US and non-EU markets. This distinction is of relevance because some might judge that own liberalization is not a benefit of multilateral negotiations, because countries can carry out the removal of their own protection without the help of WTO negotiations. (This concern is questionable, because both the authorities and business groups in even the poorer countries are likely to seek to maximize their export opportunities by linking the liberalization of their own markets to requests made in multilateral negotiations, probably in support of a bloc of countries making requests on the same set of products.)

When the P26 model is run, freezing not only US and EU protection against the P7 countries but also the protection of the P7 countries themselves, welfare gains for the P7 fall by very little: from $2.24 billion (table 4.10) to $2.06 billion.[62] The strong implication is that there are considerable gains from liberalization of non-US and non-EU markets facing the at-risk countries, so that gains from global free trade outweigh preference erosion even after setting aside the gains arising solely from the removal of these countries' own protection.

---

61. The single important exception appears to be that of Bangladesh, where the costs from preference erosion would amount to an estimated $200 million per year, or 0.4 percent of GDP. This suggests the appropriateness of a special development assistance initiative for Bangladesh to accompany a Doha Round agreement achieving deep multilateral liberalization.

62. For the residual sub-Saharan Africa grouping (SSA), welfare effects actually rise in this run, from −$0.02 billion to $0.29 billion. In contrast, the main instance of lower welfare gains when own-protection is frozen is the case of South Africa (XSC), where the gains fall from $0.28 billion (table 4.10) to −$0.01 billion. The implication is that relatively high trade between SSA and XSC leads to significant terms-of-trade differences between the case in which these countries liberalize their own protection and the case in which they do not.

## Poverty Effects in Alternative Scenarios

Although the calculations for tables 4.7 and 4.9 could be repeated for each of the other trade liberalization scenarios considered above, the effects of these alternatives can more readily be approximated by comparing their corresponding relative welfare effects. For this purpose, each country's welfare effect needs to be weighted by its share in global poverty.

The poverty-weighted welfare effects show the following gains in welfare as a percentage of GDP for developing countries as related to poverty effects (B25 results). Static free trade (CRTS) shows 0.95 percent of GDP gains; SS free trade, 5.26 percent; two-tier liberalization, 0.71 percent; asymmetric liberalization, 0.90 percent; differential liberalization, 1.07 percent; and the US formula, 0.43 percent.[63] Thus, with the poverty-weighted impact of static free trade at an index of 100, the other scenarios generate poverty impacts with index values of 554 (steady state), 74.7 (two-tier), 94.7 (asymmetric), 112.6 (differential), and 45.3 (US formula).

The broad implication is that the more restrictive liberalization scenarios fall short of the poverty reduction potential of (static) free trade, especially the variant cutting agriculture and textile-apparel by only half. The sole exception is the differential liberalization case in which developing countries grant each other free trade but cut protection against industrial countries by only half, while industrial countries extend free trade to all. As discussed above, however, it is a moot point whether the differential scenario would be better for developing countries (and their poor populations) than outright free trade. The special characteristics of the CGE model say so, but there is a strong presumption in the bulk of the mainstream economic literature to the contrary, as terms-of-trade and optimum-tariff effects are more typically considered to be less affected by a "small" country's own liberalization than is implied in the CGE structure.[64]

## Implications

This chapter has implemented one of the leading CGE models, coupled with the leading trade and protection database available for trade modeling, to estimate the factor price changes and hence changes in poverty that could be expected to result from international trade liberalization. The results show that trade has a large potential to reduce global poverty. In the static free trade version of the model, free trade would reduce the

---

63. These are percentage increases in welfare, not in welfare as a percentage of GDP, as discussed above.

64. Specifically, the use of a less than infinite "Armington" elasticity of substitution among trading partners' alternative sources of imports yields a price elasticity of export demand low enough for even small countries to influence their terms of trade.

number of the poor globally by an estimated 110 million, or by 4 percent. In the Steady State version of the model, which captures an important dimension of dynamic effects by allowing capital investment to respond to new trade opportunities, the medium-term reduction in poverty could amount to about 500 million, or by 17 percent.

The static estimate is likely a lower-bound estimate for free trade effects. A simple model for the response of rural and urban poverty to free trade in agriculture alone, developed in chapter 3 above, places the central estimate at a reduction of 200 million in poverty from removing protection and subsidies in agriculture. The dynamic SS estimate, conversely, is likely an overstatement for practical purposes, because it would imply large increases in capital that in turn would require boosts in investment by about 7 percent of GDP annually for 6 years. Even so, the SS estimate does not include effects on productivity growth and technical change, which could be a partial replacement for the large capital increases otherwise needed. Chapter 5 draws together the static and SS poverty estimates in combination with dynamic productivity-impact estimates developed in that chapter.

There are eight important additional features in the model estimates. First, agriculture is the most important sector to liberalize globally. It provides about half of total welfare gains from free trade.

Second, textiles and apparel constitute the next most important sector. They contribute about 11 percent of total welfare gains under free trade.

Third, developing countries gain the most from free trade, which generates welfare gains equal to 1.35 percent of GDP for developing countries and 0.78 percent for industrial countries, in the static model, and 2.5 percent of GDP for developing countries versus 1.0 percent for industrial countries in the dynamic SS version.

Fourth, concerns about adverse effects for numerous developing countries identified in earlier results should be allayed by the present results. The HRT model's authors estimated in 1996 that the Uruguay Round cuts in protection would cause welfare losses for sub-Saharan Africa, the Middle East, and Eastern Europe. They attributed the losses to higher agricultural prices facing food importers and to losses of quota rents in textiles and apparel. The new results here—applying the same model to more recent trade and protection data with greater disaggregation for developing countries—show instead that all these areas gain from global free trade. The difference from the earlier results stems in part from lower estimates of textile-apparel quota rents in the more recent data, and from the application of free trade rather than the limited reductions in protection for agriculture and textiles and apparel in the earlier estimates. The only developing country estimated to experience loss is Mexico, where global free trade means a loss of preferred status in the US market.

Fifth, the model results for alternative liberalization scenarios suggest that a differential formula in which industrial countries grant free trade while developing countries cut protection only in half could generate welfare gains for developing countries that are about the same or even modestly larger than those from full free trade, but only if the developing countries grant free trade access to each other as part of such a package. This result depends in part on the special features of the model, suggesting that it is at least as likely that full free trade would generate better results for developing countries and their poor populations.

Sixth, results from "asymmetric" liberalization tests suggest that between 52 and 65 percent of total potential welfare gains for developing countries stem from the liberalization of industrial-country markets rather than developing-country liberalization. This finding contradicts the view that developing-country losses from global protection are primarily of their own making. The driving force in this finding is that the HRT model provides significant terms-of-trade impact estimates, although not as large as those in the findings of the OECD (GTAP) model, which attributes an even higher fraction of developing-country gains to industrial-country liberalization than estimated here. In contrast, the more widely cited results of the WBGEP (LINKAGE) model attributing the bulk of developing-country gains to their own rather than industrial-country liberalization would seem potentially misleading. They refer to a world in 2015 when relatively highly protected developing-country manufactures are projected to be a much higher share of the world economy, and highly protected industrial-country agriculture is projected to be a much lower share of the world economy, than is true today.

Seventh, the SS results underscore how important it will be that global capital markets achieve renewed strength to provide capital flows to developing countries. A return to capital market flows to emerging markets on the order of $250 billion annually, as reached before the financial market crises of the late 1990s, would potentially provide somewhat more than half of the extra capital required to raise the capital stock and achieve the large potential dynamic welfare gains (about $350 billion annually for developing countries).

Eighth, special tests with the PEHRT model suggest that concerns about injury to poor countries from the erosion of trade preferences as a consequence of global free trade are largely misplaced. These countries generally have more to gain from the liberalization of markets in which they do not enjoy free entry, and from removing their own protection, than they stand to lose from preference erosion.

Overall, these results confirm that trade liberalization could contribute in a major way to the reduction of global poverty. Moreover, the estimates are understated rather than overstated from the standpoint that they exclude the effects of liberalizing services-sector trade. They nonetheless also serve as a reminder that even in the most optimistic formulation (the medium-term SS version), freeing up trade would provide only a partial solution to the problem of global poverty.

# Appendix 4A
# PEHRT Model Definitions

## Table 4A.1   Mapping of GTAP5 to PEHRT regions

| GTAP5 | | | PEHRT B25 | PEHRT P26 | GTAP5 | | | PEHRT B25 | PEHRT P26 |
|---|---|---|---|---|---|---|---|---|---|
| 1 | AUS | Australia | 1 | 1 | 36 | DEU | Germany | 6 | 5 |
| 2 | NZL | New Zealand | 1 | 1 | 37 | GBR | United Kingdom | 6 | 5 |
| 3 | CHN | China | 11 | 10 | 38 | GRC | Greece | 6 | 5 |
| 4 | HKG | Hong Kong | 12 | 8 | 39 | IRL | Ireland | 6 | 5 |
| 5 | JPN | Japan | 4 | 4 | 40 | ITA | Italy | 6 | 5 |
| 6 | KOR | Korea | 5 | 8 | 41 | LUX | Luxembourg | 6 | 5 |
| 7 | TWN | Taiwan | 12 | 8 | 42 | NLD | Netherlands | 6 | 5 |
| 8 | IDN | Indonesia | 7 | 6 | 43 | PRT | Portugal | 6 | 5 |
| 9 | MYS | Malaysia | 8 | 17 | 44 | ESP | Spain | 6 | 5 |
| 10 | PHL | Philippines | 9 | 7 | 45 | SWE | Sweden | 6 | 5 |
| 11 | SGP | Singapore | 12 | 8 | 46 | CHE | Switzerland | 21 | 18 |
| 12 | THA | Thailand | 10 | 9 | 47 | XEF | Rest of EFTA | 21 | 18 |
| 13 | VNM | Vietnam | 20 | 17 | 48 | HUN | Hungary | 19 | 16 |
| 14 | BGD | Bangladesh | 20 | 26 | 49 | POL | Poland | 19 | 16 |
| 15 | IND | India | 22 | 19 | 50 | XCE | Rest of Central | | |
| 16 | LKA | Sri Lanka | 20 | 17 | | | European | | |
| 17 | XSA | Rest of South Asia | 20 | 20 | | | Association | 19 | 16 |
| 18 | CAN | Canada | 2 | 2 | 51 | XSU | Former Soviet Union | 19 | 16 |
| 19 | USA | United States | 3 | 3 | 52 | TUR | Turkey | 23 | 15 |
| 20 | MEX | Mexico | 15 | 12 | 53 | XME | Rest of Middle East | 18 | 15 |
| 21 | XCM | Central America | | | 54 | MAR | Morocco | 18 | 15 |
| | | and Caribbean | 24 | 25 | 55 | XNF | Rest of North Africa | 18 | 15 |
| 22 | COL | Colombia | 16 | 13 | 56 | BWA | Botswana | 17 | 14 |
| 23 | PER | Peru | 16 | 13 | 57 | XSC | Rest of South African | | |
| 24 | VEN | Venezuela | 16 | 13 | | | Customs Union | 25 | 23 |
| 25 | XAP | Rest of Andean Pact | 16 | 13 | 58 | MWI | Malawi | 17 | 14 |
| 26 | ARG | Argentina | 13 | 13 | 59 | MOZ | Mozambique | 17 | 21 |
| 27 | BRA | Brazil | 14 | 11 | 60 | TZA | Tanzania | 17 | 24 |
| 28 | CHL | Chile | 16 | 13 | 61 | ZMB | Zambia | 17 | 14 |
| 29 | URY | Uruguay | 16 | 13 | 62 | ZWE | Zimbabwe | 17 | 14 |
| 30 | XSM | Rest of South America | 16 | 13 | 63 | XSF | Other South Africa | 17 | 14 |
| 31 | AUT | Austria | 6 | 5 | 64 | UGA | Uganda | 17 | 22 |
| 32 | BEL | Belgium | 6 | 5 | 65 | XSS | Rest of sub-Saharan | | |
| 33 | DNK | Denmark | 6 | 5 | | | Africa | 17 | 14 |
| 34 | FIN | Finland | 6 | 5 | 66 | XRW | Rest of world | 20 | 17 |
| 35 | FRA | France | 6 | 5 | | | | | |

Note: See table 4A.2 for the PEHRT regions.

## Table 4A.2    PEHRT regions

| Big 25 (B25) | | | Poverty 26 (P26) | | |
|---|---|---|---|---|---|
| 1 | ANZ | Australia and New Zealand | 1 | ANZ | Australia and New Zealand |
| 2 | CAN | Canada | 2 | CAN | Canada |
| 3 | USA | United States | 3 | USA | United States |
| 4 | JPN | Japan | 4 | JPN | Japan |
| 5 | KOR | Korea | 5 | E_U | European Union |
| 6 | E_U | European Union | 6 | IDN | Indonesia |
| 7 | IDN | Indonesia | 7 | PHL | Philippines |
| 8 | MYS | Malaysia | 8 | AG4 | South Korea, Hong Kong, |
| 9 | PHL | Philippines | | | Singapore, and Taiwan |
| 10 | THA | Thailand | 9 | THA | Thailand |
| 11 | CHN | China | 10 | CHN | China |
| 12 | AG3 | Hong Kong, Singapore, | 11 | BRA | Brazil |
| | | and Taiwan | 12 | MEX | Mexico |
| 13 | ARG | Argentina | 13 | OLA | Other Latin America |
| 14 | BRA | Brazil | 14 | SSA | Other sub-Saharan Africa |
| 15 | MEX | Mexico | 15 | MNA | Middle East, North Africa, |
| 16 | OLA | Other Latin America | | | and Turkey |
| 17 | SSA | Other sub-Saharan Africa | 16 | EIT | Eastern Europe |
| 18 | MNA | Middle East and North Africa | 17 | OAS | Other Asia |
| 19 | EIT | Eastern Europe | 18 | EFTA | European Free Trade Association |
| 20 | XAS | Rest of Asia | 19 | IND | India |
| 21 | EFTA | European Free Trade Area | 20 | XSA | Pakistan and other South Asia |
| 22 | IND | India | 21 | MOZ | Mozambique |
| 23 | TUR | Turkey | 22 | UGA | Uganda |
| 24 | XCM | Central America and Caribbean | 23 | XSC | South African Customs Union |
| 25 | XSC | Southern African Customs | 24 | TZA | Tanzania |
| | | Union | 25 | XCM | Central America and Caribbean |
| | | | 26 | BGD | Bangladesh |

# Table 4A.3　Mapping of GTAP5 to PEHRT product sectors

| GTAP5 sectors | | | Allocated to PEHRT | PEHRT sectors | | |
|---|---|---|---|---|---|---|
| 1 | pdr | Paddy rice | 1 | 1 | pdr | Paddy rice |
| 2 | wht | Wheat | 2 | 2 | wht | Wheat |
| 3 | gro | Cereal grains n.e.c. | 3 | 3 | gro | Grains excluding wheat, rice |
| 4 | v_f | Vegetables, fruits, nuts | 4 | 4 | ngc | Nongrain crops |
| 5 | osd | Oil seeds | 4 | 5 | for | Forestry, fishing, lumber, |
| 6 | c_b | Sugar cane, sugar beet | 4 | | | wood, paper, and wool |
| 7 | pfb | Plant-based fibers | 4 | 6 | pcr | Processed rice |
| 8 | ocr | Crops n.e.c. | 4 | 7 | mlk | Milk products |
| 9 | ctl | Cattle, sheep, goats, horses | 17 | 8 | tex | Textiles |
| 10 | oap | Animal products n.e.c. | 7 | 9 | wap | Wearing apparel |
| 11 | rmk | Raw milk | 7 | 10 | crp | Chemicals, rubber, plastics |
| 12 | wol | Wool, silk-worm cocoons | 5 | 11 | i_s | Primary iron and steel |
| 13 | for | Forestry | 5 | 12 | nfm | Nonferrous metals |
| 14 | fsh | Fishing | 5 | 13 | fmp | Fabricated metal |
| 15 | col | Coal | 18 | 14 | trn | Transport industry |
| 16 | oil | Oil | 18 | 15 | t_t | Trade and transport |
| 17 | gas | Gas | 18 | 16 | cgd | Investment goods |
| 18 | omn | Minerals n.e.c. | 19 | 17 | mea | Meat products, livestock |
| 19 | cmt | Bovine meat products | 17 | 18 | enr | Energy and products |
| 20 | omt | Meat products n.e.c. | 17 | 19 | min | Minerals and products |
| 21 | vol | Vegetable oils and fats | 20 | 20 | foo | Food, beverages, and tobacco |
| 22 | mil | Dairy products | 7 | 21 | mac | Machinery, equipment, |
| 23 | pcr | Processed rice | 6 | | | and other manufacturing |
| 24 | sgr | Sugar | 20 | 22 | ser | Services and utilities |
| 25 | ofd | Food products n.e.c. | 20 | | | |
| 26 | b_t | Beverages and tobacco products | 20 | | | |
| 27 | tex | Textiles | 8 | | | |
| 28 | wap | Wearing apparel | 9 | | | |
| 29 | lea | Leather products | 9 | | | |
| 30 | lum | Wood products | 5 | | | |
| 31 | ppp | Paper products, publishing | 5 | | | |
| 32 | p_c | Petroleum, coal products | 18 | | | |
| 33 | crp | Chemical, rubber, plastic products | 10 | | | |
| 34 | nmm | Mineral products n.e.c. | 19 | | | |
| 35 | i_s | Ferrous metals | 11 | | | |
| 36 | nfm | Metals n.e.c. | 12 | | | |
| 37 | fmp | Metal products | 13 | | | |
| 38 | mvh | Motor vehicles and parts | 21 | | | |
| 39 | otn | Transport equipment n.e.c. | 21 | | | |
| 40 | ele | Electronic equipment | 21 | | | |
| 41 | ome | Machinery and equipment n.e.c. | 21 | | | |
| 42 | omf | Manufactures n.e.c. | 21 | | | |
| 43 | ely | Electricity | 22 | | | |
| 44 | gdt | Gas manufacture, distribution | 22 | | | |
| 45 | wtr | Water | 22 | | | |
| 46 | cns | Construction | 22 | | | |
| 47 | trd | Trade | 15 | | | |
| 48 | otp | Transport n.e.c. | 14 | | | |
| 49 | wtp | Water transport | 14 | | | |
| 50 | atp | Air transport | 14 | | | |
| 51 | cmn | Communication | 22 | | | |
| 52 | ofi | Financial services n.e.c. | 22 | | | |
| 53 | isr | Insurance | 22 | | | |
| 54 | obs | Business services n.e.c. | 22 | | | |
| 55 | ros | Recreational, other services | 22 | | | |
| 56 | osg | Public administration, defense, education, health | 22 | | | |
| 57 | dwe | Dwellings | 22 | | | |

n.e.c. = not elsewhere classified

## Table 4A.4   Economywide factor shares (percent)

| Region or economy | Land | Unskilled labor | Skilled labor | Capital and resources |
|---|---|---|---|---|
| **B25** | | | | |
| ANZ | 0.8 | 31.4 | 21.8 | 46.1 |
| CAN | 0.5 | 42.1 | 16.7 | 40.7 |
| USA | 0.6 | 36.1 | 25.6 | 37.7 |
| JPN | 0.3 | 37.2 | 22.8 | 39.8 |
| KOR | 2.4 | 38.4 | 16.0 | 43.2 |
| E_U | 0.8 | 32.9 | 21.9 | 44.4 |
| IDN | 8.0 | 34.3 | 6.6 | 51.1 |
| MYS | 4.8 | 27.0 | 8.9 | 59.2 |
| PHL | 6.5 | 32.2 | 11.3 | 50.0 |
| THA | 3.4 | 12.1 | 4.2 | 80.4 |
| CHN | 5.2 | 44.6 | 10.4 | 39.8 |
| AG3 | 0.7 | 32.3 | 22.4 | 44.6 |
| ARG | 3.2 | 36.6 | 12.8 | 47.4 |
| BRA | 1.4 | 33.8 | 16.4 | 48.4 |
| MEX | 3.2 | 22.7 | 8.6 | 65.6 |
| OLA | 2.7 | 28.5 | 11.9 | 56.9 |
| SSA | 2.4 | 40.5 | 10.5 | 46.6 |
| MNA | 0.9 | 33.7 | 14.4 | 51.0 |
| EIT | 1.4 | 39.8 | 16.8 | 42.0 |
| XAS | 7.0 | 34.7 | 10.8 | 47.5 |
| EFTA | 0.8 | 37.1 | 26.3 | 35.9 |
| IND | 12.2 | 32.4 | 6.8 | 48.6 |
| TUR | 1.4 | 27.9 | 10.7 | 60.0 |
| XCM | 4.0 | 31.7 | 11.8 | 52.5 |
| XSC | 0.5 | 40.7 | 19.6 | 39.2 |
| | | | | |
| **P26** | | | | |
| BGD | 6.3 | 39.4 | 43.0 | 11.3 |
| PAK | 12.8 | 32.1 | 48.3 | 6.9 |
| MOZ | 4.5 | 42.4 | 45.0 | 8.1 |
| UGA | 6.2 | 48.4 | 38.9 | 6.5 |
| TZA | 5.6 | 43.5 | 45.5 | 5.4 |
| OAS | 5.6 | 29.1 | 56.1 | 9.2 |

*Source:* GTAP5 database.

# 5

# The Impact of Trade on Poverty Through Growth Effects

Chapter 4 provided estimates of the impact of multilateral trade liberalization on global poverty, based on one-time efficiency gains. This chapter focuses on the additional poverty alleviation that could be expected from the ongoing dynamic growth effects of higher levels of trade. This second tranche of dynamic gains is conceptually different from the "steady state" gains estimated in chapter 4 under the hypothesis of additional capital investment in response to new trade opportunities. These dynamic gains refer to increases in total factor productivity, rather than increases in output per worker from increased capital per worker.

There is an extensive literature on the interaction between trade and growth.[1] This chapter first surveys this literature to identify key parameters that can serve as a basis for estimating dynamic gains from increased trade. It then uses these parameters in combination with the estimates developed in previous chapters to arrive at a comprehensive calculation of the potential for global trade policy reform to reduce global poverty over time. Before doing so, however, it surveys the recent empirical debate on the link between trade policy and growth. The main controversy is about whether the liberalization of the developing countries' own trade regimes will spur, curb, or leave unaffected their own growth. In contrast, even trade policy skeptics will tend to agree that developing countries would be better off if industrial countries liberalized market access.

---

1. Recent surveys include Berg and Krueger (2003) and Baldwin (2003). Edwards (1993, 1998) and Sachs and Warner (1995) are prominent protrade empirical studies, while Rodriguez and Rodrik (2000) lead in the skeptical backlash.

Two components of the trade-growth relationship can be separated. The first is the influence of trade on growth. The second is the influence of trade policy on growth, presumably through its influence on trade. The discussion treats each in turn before synthesizing the parameters needed to estimate the growth and poverty effects of trade liberalization.

## The Impact of Trade on Growth

The tradition that international trade enhances domestic growth goes back at least to Adam Smith. Trade permits increased specialization. Specialization permits increased attainment of economies of scale, especially for countries with relatively small domestic markets. It also permits fuller utilization of the country's abundant factor of production. Increased imports, for their part, provide increased competitive pressure that helps prompt domestic firms to improve their technologies. Increased economic integration with the outside world also stimulates technical change through the diffusion of new technologies, especially from more advanced countries at the technological frontier to developing countries. Increased imports also curb domestic monopoly power that holds production below and prices above socially optimal levels.

Cross-country regression analyses to determine the sources of growth have proliferated in recent years. A relatively early study that sounded a strong cautionary note was that by Levine and Renelt (1992). They tested for robustness in the by then already extensive literature. They first identify four core variables influencing growth: the share of investment in GDP, the initial secondary school enrollment rate, GDP per capita in 1960, and the rate of population growth. Using data for 119 countries for the period 1960–89, they find the predicted signs for all four variables and significance at the 5 percent level except for population growth. The results confirm conditional convergence (negative coefficient on initial income per capita), and a strong positive influence of capital accumulation and human capital. Their objective, however, is to explore the robustness of additional variables (especially policy variables) when they are added to the core set. The method is essentially to see whether a particular variable remains significant and of the right sign when an alternative set of up to three control variables is added.

For all the resulting sets of regressions including the variable of interest, Levine and Renelt identify the highest and lowest value of the coefficient that cannot be rejected at the 5 percent level (Leamer's "extreme bounds"; Leamer 1983). If the highest and lowest values estimated for the coefficient remain significant and of the same sign, the variable's results are considered robust. By this test, "almost all results are fragile." A broad array of fiscal, monetary, and political variables are found not robustly correlated with growth or the investment share.

Levine and Renelt's results for trade are of special interest to this chapter. They find that while a trade variable is not robust when entered in addition to the four core variables, there is "a positive and robust correlation between the share of investment in GDP and the average share of trade in GDP." They thus conclude that there is a "two-step" positive influence of trade on growth, working through the influence of trade on investment. They note that this is somewhat surprising, considering that usually the trade influence is thought to work more through technical change than through induced capital accumulation. Their results also show a significant influence of trade if the investment rate is left out of the core variable set. Moreover, they find that it does not matter whether trade is measured by the ratio of exports, imports, or their sum, to GDP. This is important, because whereas exports as a positive component of GDP would be expected to generate spurious correlation through a simultaneous-equation accounting relationship, imports as a negative component would be expected to generate a spurious negative relationship from this standpoint.

Although it will be suggested below that the Levine-Renelt extreme bounds tests may be too stringent, it is important to note that the influence of trade does seem to pass even this strong test for their results through the two-step interaction with investment. In particular, they estimate a coefficient of 17.5 on the investment variable, indicating that each percentage point of GDP in additional investment will boost the per capita growth rate by 0.175 percentage point. They also estimate a (robust) coefficient of 0.14 on exports as a fraction of GDP in an equation explaining investment share.[2] This implies that an extra 10 percentage points of GDP in the export ratio will boost per capita annual growth by 0.245 percent, raising the level of per capita income above the baseline by 2.5 percent over a decade and 5 percent over two decades.[3] The average share of exports in GDP in their sample is 0.32 for countries with per capita growth above the mean of 1.92 percent, and 0.23 for countries below mean growth.[4] Thus, the mean export ratio is about 0.28. In turn, a 0.1 rise in the export ratio is equivalent to a 36 percent increase against its mean. This in turn implies an elasticity of the level of output per capita with respect to the export ratio of 0.14 over two decades.[5]

---

2. Their text says as a percent of GDP, but their specific example in a footnote makes it clear that a fraction is being used (p. 954).

3. That is, a 10-percent-of-GDP rise in the export variable generates a 0.1 rise in X (e.g., from 0.2 to 0.3, or from 20 to 30 percent of GDP). This rise in turn generates $0.1 \times 0.14 = 0.014$ increase in the investment share. The combined impact on the per capita growth rate is $0.014 \times 17.5 = 0.245$ percent per year.

4. The difference is statistically significant, with $t = 2.3$.

5. That is, there is a 5 percent increase in level over two decades, against a 36 percent increase in the export ratio. The translation of various studies' results into this long-term elasticity is discussed further below.

One of the most convincing tests of the influence of trade on growth in the more recent literature is the instrumental variable approach used by Frankel and Romer (1999) and Frankel and Rose (2000). This approach seeks to deal with the problem of reverse causality (i.e., from growth to trade rather than the other way around) by using a "gravity model" of trade to estimate an instrumental variable for the trade variable (exports plus imports relative to GDP) and then applying two-stage least squares (2SLS) to estimate the relationship between growth per capita and the trade ratio.

Concern about endogeneity in the trade-growth relationship is well placed. As shown in chapter 1 (figure 1.3), there is a clear positive relationship between export growth and GDP growth in international experience. But exports, after all, are part of GDP, so contemporaneous data will inherently have a "simultaneous equations" bias relating the two. More fundamentally, it has long been considered a standard pattern of consumption that imports tend to be "income elastic" goods, so as per capita incomes rise the share of imports (and hence, to pay for them, exports) in GDP would be expected to rise as a consequence rather than cause of growth.

Frankel and Romer (1999) cut through this identification problem by using the by now well-known empirical strength of a gravity trade model. The gravity model states that the exports of one nation to another are greater if the two countries are geographically closer to each other (especially if they share a border), and if they are larger and hence offer larger markets to each other. Their core gravity equation is simply that the logarithm of the ratio of exports plus imports to GDP (which will be called the "trade ratio" in this chapter) is a function of the logarithm of distance between the two (negative coefficient) and of the logarithms of the "size" of the two (positive coefficients). The equation is enhanced with dummy variables for landlocked countries and countries with a common border. Both population and land area variables are included to capture size.

With predicted trade ratios from the gravity model in hand as the "instrument" for the actual trade ratio, Frankel and Romer then regress the logarithm of per capita income on the trade ratio, log population, and log area. The trade ratio is statistically significant, and indeed it is larger with 2SLS than with ordinary least squares (OLS).[6] The authors then decompose the source of the trade influence, using 1960 as a base and estimating the influence of the trade share on the change in capital, education, and total factor productivity from 1960 to 1985. They find that trade influences growth both by increasing physical and human capital deepening and, even more, by boosting total factor productivity growth. Their overall estimate is that a rise in the trade ratio by 1 percentage point of GDP (e.g., from 0.7 to 0.71) raises per capita income by at least 1 percent.

---

6. If endogeneity were a major problem, the reverse would be true.

Frankel and Rose (2000) apply the same method to examine the influence of currency unions on growth, working through their influence on trade. Using panel data for 180 countries from 1970 through 1995, they refine the underlying estimate of the trade-growth relationship to estimate that "every one percent increase in trade (relative to GDP) raises income per capita by roughly ⅓ of a percent over twenty years."[7] Moreover, in an appendix they show that their result is robust to the inclusion of distance from the equator.[8] A related paper by Irwin and Tervio (2000) extends the Frankel-Romer analysis to eight benchmark years from 1913 to 1990 and generally confirms the results, but it finds that prior to the 1985 period examined by Frankel and Romer the inclusion of a latitude variable removes the significance of the trade ratio. The implication is that although climate may have dominated trade as an influence on economic performance through much of the 20th century, by its final two decades that was no longer the case.

Frankel and his coauthors are careful not to equate trade with trade policy. Indeed, a key feature of the instrumental variable approach is that it suggests an independent benefit from the good fortune of being located in the right spot for high trade. The further implication is that if some other influence, such as trade policy, can act as a substitute to attain comparable high trade, there will be economic benefits from that policy.

A second and even stronger finding that trade enhances growth is set forth in Alcalá and Ciccone (2001). Three features distinguish their study. First, they use Generalized Method of Moments (GMM) estimation rather than OLS or 2SLS.[9] The GMM approach is an alternative to 2SLS as a vehicle for addressing simultaneity. Second, and centrally, they place the purchasing power parity (PPP) valuation of GDP in the denominator of the trade ratio, rather than GDP at the national exchange rate. The reason for this approach is basically the Balassa-Samuelson effect. In this effect, as countries achieve catch-up growth, their productivity tends to grow more rapidly in tradables than in nontradables, so the very process of growth will tend to shrink the observed rise in the trade ratio by ballooning the relative price and therefore national valuation of nontradables in the denominator. There will be a downward bias in the measured influ-

7. Note that this time the percent change in the trade ratio is stated proportionately rather than as a percentage point of GDP.

8. This further test answers queries by Hall and Jones (1999) and Rodriguez and Rodrik (2000).

9. See Wooldridge (2001) for a brief description of the Generalized Method of Moments. In essence, this method takes advantage of known or postulated relationships between the moments (e.g., mean and variance) of a distribution to obtain parameter estimates as a weighted average of alternatively based relationships in an overdetermined set (more equations than unknowns). The method is especially helpful for increasing the efficiency of estimates in nonlinear and time-series models. It also addresses heteroskedasticity (i.e., the size of the disturbance term not independent of the underlying variables), although for correction of this in OLS alternative methods are approximately as effective.

ence of the trade ratio on growth unless this is corrected for by using PPP GDP in the denominator of the trade ratio measure. Third, the authors include institutional quality in their explanatory variables, addressing the growing concern in this literature that institutions determine everything.

The equation estimated in Alcalá and Ciccone is as follows: The logarithm of per-worker PPP GDP is a function of the logarithm of real openness, an economic scale variable (logarithm of the total workforce), the logarithm of land area (for comparability with Frankel-Romer), an index of institutional quality, and geography controls (distance from equator and continent dummies). Once again, the gravity model is used to obtain the instrument for the trade variable. The data are cross-sectional for 1985 and 1990. Their central result is that the elasticity of average labor productivity with respect to real openness is 1.44. For example, a country moving from median real openness (31 percent) to the 60th percentile (39 percent, or a proportionate rise by 8/31 = 0.26) increases productivity by 37 percent (= 26 × 1.44). On a comparable basis, this is about twice as large as the Frankel-Romer estimate, even in the higher (2SLS) variant in that study.

Alcalá and Ciccone further explore the relationship of openness to trade policy. They use GMM estimation of the logarithm of observed real openness against the gravity model's predicted real openness instrument, "years open" between 1960 and 1985 (based on the measure used by Sachs and Warner 1995) as instrumented by English language incidence and population size, the fraction of GDP in mining and quarrying, and geography controls.[10] They find that these variables have a strong positive effect on real openness. To address Rodriguez and Rodrik's (2000) critique that various components of Sachs and Warner's variable measure something other than trade policy, they repeat the test replacing "years open" by an alternative measure of trade policy, the nontariff and tariff component of the Sachs and Warner variable. They find that doing so raises rather than reduces the influence of the trade policy variable on real openness. Pursuing this line further, they obtain similarly strong results using import duties as a percent of the value of imports to explain real openness. The basic finding is that not only does higher openness drive higher productivity but lower protection also drives higher openness.

A prominent study relating growth to trade is that by Dollar and Kraay (2001b). They use decade-average panel data for the 1980s and 1990s for about 100 countries to estimate growth in real per capita income (from the first decade to the second) as a function of the corresponding growth in the previous decade (1970s to 1980s), the change in a set of control variables from the 1980s to 1990s, and a decadal-shift "period effect" common to all countries. Among the control variables is the key "trade volume"

---

10. The incidence of the English language is used, somewhat heroically, to capture a favorable attitude toward free market policies, and population size is used to capture the scope for scale benefits, even without open trade.

variable, the ratio of imports plus exports to GDP. They argue that use of change in trade rather than trade level itself circumvents the problem that the level of the trade variable is highly influenced by such factors as geography, because the change over time is not.

Similarly, they argue that the decadal-difference approach avoids the problem of omitted variables, such as the rule of law or colonial history, because these change little over a decade. They maintain that their approach also deals naturally with the problem of reverse causation. In particular, they include the level of "trade volume" in the 1970s (which cannot be caused by economic shocks in the subsequent decades) as an instrument for trade openness, as well as the level of income in the 1970s as an instrument for lagged growth.

In their OLS regression, Dollar and Kraay estimate a relatively high coefficient of change in growth on change in trade. The coefficient indicates that a 100 percent increase in the ratio of trade to GDP has the effect of raising GDP per capita by 25 percent over a decade. When instrumental variables are included for initial income and trade ratios, the coefficient nearly doubles, from 0.25 to 0.48. The much larger coefficient in the 2SLS result is reminiscent of the same contrast found by Frankel and Romer (1999), in that it once again indicates that taking endogeneity into account tends to strengthen rather than reduce the trade-growth relationship. Robustness experiments with a number of additional variables tend to show them as insignificant and to leave the trade influence significant and intact. The authors interpret this pattern as confirming their expectation that the use of decadal differences will largely remove the influence of slow-moving omitted variable influences such as institutional quality.

In short, the Dollar-Kraay study appears to provide additional evidence that trade matters as an influence on growth. It is considerably less clear that it also shows that trade policy matters, because, as discussed below, many factors could have altered the trade ratios between the two decades other than trade policy.

Easterly (2003) provides additional information on the influence of trade on growth. In a dynamic panel regression of growth on inflation, the government budget balance, M2 relative to GDP, the logarithm of the black market premium, the logarithm of overvaluation, government consumption relative to GDP, private credit as a fraction of total credit, and a trade variable—exports plus imports divided by GDP—he estimates a surprisingly large and significant coefficient on trade. The coefficient averages 0.066 over four variants. A unit increase in the trade ratio would thus boost the long-term annual per capita growth rate by 6.6 percent. The mean trade ratio in the sample is 0.7, so a 10 percent rise in the trade ratio would amount to 0.07, which when applied to the coefficient would raise annual per capita growth by 0.46 percentage point, so that over the course of a decade per capita income would rise 4.7 percent, and over 2 decades, 9.6 percent.

This result is much larger than in corresponding OLS regressions (where the coefficient is only 0.01). It is notable that Easterly's GMM result is high, just as the Alcalá-Ciccone GMM result is high. At the same time, it should be noted that despite his seemingly strong results, Easterly is skeptical that trade or any of his other policy indicators affect growth.[11] The results, however, can also be interpreted as capable of speaking for themselves. It should also be noted that whereas he interprets the trade ratio as a policy indicator, for the discussion here it is considered as an economic characteristic but not necessarily a proxy for trade policy.

Choudhri and Hakura (2000) provide a methodologically attractive analysis of the influence of trade on total factor productivity growth. Their approach draws on Krugman's technology gap model, and thereby focuses on a central and concrete dimension of the openness argument: that it promotes technological transfer. Using panel data for 33 developing and 11 industrial countries for the period 1970–93, they conduct tests relating total factor productivity growth to sectoral shares and sectoral changes in trade ratios. They find a relatively strong impact of the import ratio in medium-technology industries (International Standard Industrial Classification categories 33, wood and wood products; 36, nonmetallic mineral products except fuel; and 37, basic metal industries). For these sectors, a rise by 0.1 in the ratio of imports to value added increases total factor productivity growth by 0.6 percent annually. If we place the median ratio of imports to value added at, say, 0.3 for these sectors, the implication is that a 33 percent rise in the openness indicator elicits a 6 percent rise in output in this part of the economy over a decade. For other sectors, however, there is no statistically significant relationship. Moreover, these medium-growth (and medium-technology) sectors account for only about 3 percent of GDP for developing countries.

The World Bank (2002a) has developed a computable general-equilibrium (CGE) model that incorporates the influence of trade on productivity growth. As set forth in chapter 3, when this dynamic effect is included, the World Bank's Global Economic Prospects (WBGEP; World Bank 2002a) model boosts the estimate of the impact of free trade by 2015 from $355 billion static gains annually (in 1997 prices) to $832 billion annually, or from 0.9 percent of global product to 2.1 percent (World Bank 2002a, 168–69). The study cites the following arguments for why these dynamic productivity effects should occur (p. 181): (1) Higher incomes from the static trade liberalization gains lead to higher saving and investment. (2) Tariffs are often imposed on investment goods, so liberalization will tend to boost investment. (3) Incorporating economies of scale and imperfect competition increases welfare gain estimates above the static estimates.

---

11. Easterly seems to reject the GMM approach summarily because he considers that it requires "the rather dubious assumption that the lagged right-hand side variables do not themselves enter the growth equation" (2003, 41).

(4) Opening trade increases the extent to which domestic firms can take advantage of new technologies and foreign research and development, and move toward international standards (which they call an "endogenous growth" or "productivity" effect). (5) International capital flows can enhance growth through capital deepening and improved technologies associated with foreign investment; by implication, some increase in capital flows is considered likely to arise from increased export opportunities.

To provide a basis for comparison of the welfare gain effect, ideally the WBGEP model's estimate of increased trade from the elimination of barriers would be used. Because this is not reported, the free trade impact estimates of chapter 4 in the present study can serve as a benchmark. The main free trade scenario generates import increases that, when weighted by base levels of imports, yield an aggregate increase in import volume of 1.53 percent globally. This implies that a 1.5 percent rise in the ratio of trade to GDP leads in the WBGEP model to a long-term productivity increase of 1.2 percent (the difference between the static gains as a percentage of GDP and the dynamic gains).

Finally, in a recent study on the sources of growth in 21 of its member countries, the Organization for Economic Cooperation and Development (OECD 2003f, 88) has estimated that a rise in the trade exposure ratio by 10 percent of GDP increases long-term per capita GDP by 4 percent. Trade exposure is close to, but not the same as, the sum of exports plus imports relative to GDP.[12] In an appealing refinement, the OECD researchers use an adjusted trade measure—the deviation of the trade exposure ratio from a cross-country regression line relating exposure to country population size—rather than the raw trade exposure measure itself, as the gauge of the influence of trade. This simple but powerful approach makes the trade variable in their regressions much closer to a policy variable than a state-of-nature parameter. In other words, if a country has considerably more trade than would be predicted by its size, the chances are that it has pursued policies that tend toward integration externally rather than toward closure or neutrality.

In regressions obtaining "pooled mean group estimators" for the 21 countries during the period 1971–98, the OECD authors obtain highly significant coefficients of per capita growth on prior year growth (negative coefficient indicating convergence), the investment rate, human capital, inflation (negative), the standard deviation of inflation (negative), government capital formation, taxes (negative), and adjusted trade exposure (p. 82). The coefficient of the logarithm of per capita income on the logarithm of adjusted trade exposure is persistently about 0.20 across six

---

12. The actual underlying measure is $[x + (1 - x)(M/\{Y - X + M\})]$, where $x$ is the ratio of exports to GDP, $X$ is exports, $M$ is imports, and $Y$ is GDP. Basically, an import penetration ratio against apparent consumption is used rather than imports relative to GDP for the import part of the trade measure.

model variants and also consistently significant (at the 1 percent level in four of the six variants). Given the log-log specification, this implies that the elasticity of per capita GDP with respect to trade exposure is 0.2. This is consistent with the OECD's summary interpretation that an increment of trade exposure by 10 percent of GDP yields a welfare gain of 4 percent of GDP if the average trade exposure ratio is 50 percent.[13]

Because the OECD study includes Hungary, Mexico, Poland, South Korea, and the Slovak Republic, as well as the main industrial countries, its results are of relevance to effects in developing countries more generally. At the same time, because at least one key component of the stimulus to growth from trade—the transfer of technological know-how—should be smaller for countries already at the technology frontier, one should expect that the OECD growth elasticity with respect to trade should be lower than that applicable to most developing countries. For the purposes of this study, then, the OECD estimate likely represents a lower-bound calculation of this elasticity.

It is possible to synthesize these various estimates more generally into a comparable "long-term elasticity of productivity with respect to trade intensity." The discussion of the estimates of Levine and Revelt (1992) above infers this elasticity for 20 years. Frankel and Rose (2000) explicitly give a 20-year horizon for their estimate; Alcalá and Ciccone (2001) and Easterly (2003) use cross-section data and do not specify a time horizon. Choudhri and Hakura (2000) provide an annual productivity growth estimate that can be cumulated for a decade. Dollar and Kraay's (2001b) results are for the difference between two decades and hence imply a decade as the time horizon. The WBGEP estimate is for the effects of free trade over the course of a decade. The OECD authors interpret their model to refer to "long-run" or "steady state" output per capita (p. 87). A horizon on the order of 20 years thus seems implied by their results.

Table 5.1 compiles the direct or implied long-term elasticity of productivity with respect to the trade/GDP ratio in these various studies. This is simply the ratio of the percent rise in productivity over the long term (typically one to two decades) divided by the percent rise in the ratio of trade to GDP, for each of the studies in question.

There is a striking feature of table 5.1: None of these estimates is negative.[14] Despite all the debate about whether openness contributes to

---

13. That is, a 10-percent-of-GDP rise would amount to a 20 percent rise in the trade exposure measure, which when applied to an elasticity of 0.2 would generate a 4 percent rise in per capita GDP.

14. Even the recent study by Yanikkaya (2003), which as discussed below purports to find that "trade barriers are positively . . . associated with growth" (p. 57), finds that there is a "strong and positive relationship between trade intensity ratios and growth" (i.e., the ratio of trade to GDP shown here in table 5.1), and thus that "it is probably safe to conclude that trade barriers may have negative repercussions on growth through reducing the size of the external sector of a country" (p. 69).

## Table 5.1 Various studies' estimates of the long-term elasticity of output per capita with respect to trade relative to GDP (10–20 year horizon)

| Study | Estimate |
|---|---|
| Levine and Revelt (1992) | 0.14 |
| Frankel and Rose (2000) | 0.33 |
| Alcalá and Ciccone (2001) | 1.44 |
| Dollar and Kraay (2001b) | 0.25–0.48 |
| Easterly (2003) | 0.14–0.96 |
| Choudhri and Hakura (2000)[a] | 0.18 |
| World Bank Global Economic Prospects (World Bank 2002) | 0.80 |
| OECD (2003f) | 0.20 |

a. Medium-technology manufacturing.

growth, if the issue were truly one warranting nothing but agnosticism, we should expect at least some of these estimates to be negative (and statistically significantly negative). The uniformly positive estimates suggest that the relevant terms of the debate by now should be about the size of the positive influence of openness on growth, and probably also about how trade policy is related to observed openness, rather than about whether increased levels of trade relative to GDP have a positive effect on productivity and growth. The preponderance of theoretical considerations on this side of the argument reinforces this judgment, because theory should presumably weigh substantially in interpreting the econometric results (as indeed "Bayesian" econometrics formally recognizes).

The simple average of the central values of these estimates is a long-term elasticity of output on trade of 0.5. This represents a powerful influence of trade on growth and a major potential source of increased growth, especially for those economies with currently low trade ratios. It is unclear, however, how much of this relationship represents windfall gain from technical change (for example), as opposed to extra output purchased at the price of increased capital investment.

Several of the studies do seek to distinguish between these two sources, however, and they tend to find the greater part of the effect resides in the pure productivity (e.g., technological) shift effect. The Frankel and Rose (2000) study is one of the more explicit on this issue. Its "uncontrolled" productivity elasticity is 0.79 (OLS) to 1.22 (2SLS), but its central estimate of the elasticity (0.33) is from equations that control for the investment ratio (as well as original income and human capital variables). Alcalá and Ciccone (2001) conduct further analysis suggesting that the trade-growth relationship is driven by a pure labor productivity effect, whereas physical and human capital accumulation are driven by institutional quality.

Overall, a fair summary would seem to be that in the econometric estimates relating productivity change to the trade ratio, the bulk of the effect is from an efficiency shift rather than induced capital and/or human capital deepening. On this basis, an appropriate central estimate for the pure productivity gain elasticity might be on the order of 0.4 (i.e., the bulk of the 0.5 simple average).

Finally, an important recent study by Wacziarg and Welch (2003) suggests that the impact of trade on growth could be even higher than the range in table 5.1. This study focuses on the impact of trade liberalization on trade, growth, and investment. The authors find that, after controlling for time trend, for 133 countries over the full period 1950–98 annual growth in per capita income was 1.4 percentage point higher in postliberalization than in preliberalization periods. On average, liberalization raised the ratio of imports plus exports to GDP by 5 percentage points. Their formulation does not clarify how long the additional growth rate persists. Under an extreme endogenous growth model, it might persist indefinitely; under a more traditional neoclassical growth model, the boost to growth would only be transitional, as the economy moved from the original output baseline to a higher one thanks to increased efficiency. If we assume that the Wacziarg and Welch increment to growth persists for only 15 years, this amounts to an eventual rise in output by 23 percent from the baseline. For 118 countries with available data, the average ratio of exports plus imports to GDP in 1990 was 56 percent, and the median ratio was 48 percent (World Bank 2002d). So the 5-percentage-point increase identified by Wacziarg and Welch amounts to about a 10 percent rise in the trade/GDP ratio. This implies an output elasticity with respect to the trade ratio of 2.3 (23 percent divided by 10 percent), which is higher than any of the entries in table 5.1. Although the Wacziarg and Welch study implies a higher dynamic growth effect of openness than will be used here, it finds that about the same proportion of this effect is attributable to induced investment as is assumed here (one-fifth).

## The Impact of Trade Policy on Growth

Although empirical studies often seem to leap from the observed trade ratio to an inference about trade policy, the two are separate. A larger economy will tend to have a lower ratio of trade to GDP even under free trade than a smaller economy, because of the greater potential for economies of scale in the domestic market. An economy with an impoverished natural resource base will tend to have a higher trade ratio than an economy with abundant agricultural land, minerals, and energy reserves, because it will need to specialize more in exporting manufactures to obtain food and fuel through imports.

Similarly, movements in the ratio of trade to GDP will not necessarily be driven by changes in trade policy. Commodity-dependent countries may exhibit a prolonged decline in the ratio of their trade to GDP even though they have no tariff or nontariff barrier (NTB) protection (or have not increased this protection), because of adverse trends in global commodity prices.

The challenge of moving from observed trade to inferred trade policy is illustrated by Dollar and Kraay's (2001b) analysis discussed above. The authors interpret an increase in the ratio of trade to GDP as an indication of an opening in trade policy. They divide their sample into three groups, by change in trade ratio. Their top one-third of developing countries by this measure increased their ratio of imports plus exports to GDP from 16 to 33 percent from 1980 to 2000. In contrast, the remaining two-thirds of developing countries experienced a *decline* in the trade/GDP ratio. Their "globalizers" had an increase in growth rates from 2.9 percent in the 1970s to 3.5 percent in the 1980s and 5 percent in the 1990s; the rest experienced a decline, from 3.3 percent in the 1970s to 0.8 percent in the 1980s and 1.4 percent in the 1990s.

After taking note of the Rodriguez-Rodrik critique of attempts to relate trade policy variables to growth, and after noting the difficulty of obtaining "clean measures" of trade policy, Dollar and Kraay settle upon *"changes* in the volume of trade as an imperfect proxy for *changes* in trade policy" (p. 3). Their statistical results linking growth to the trade ratio have been discussed above. However, their attribution of changes in trade ratio to changes in trade policy warrants further scrutiny.

Birdsall and Hamoudi (2002) cast considerable doubt on Dollar and Kraay's interpretation of the trade ratio as a trade policy variable. They argue that the change in this measure is biased by commodity price trends. In the early 1980s when commodity prices were high, developing countries borrowed and expanded imports. When prices collapsed, they were forced to cut back imports, shrinking the numerator of the trade ratio. Birdsall and Hamoudi conclude that using the trade/GDP ratio systematically classifies commodity-dependent exporting countries as "less open" in trade policies. Arguing that these are the same countries that have had low growth in the past two decades, they judge that Dollar and Kraay overstate the importance of trade policy in growth. When they add a commodity dependence dummy variable to the Dollar-Kraay growth equations, they reduce the size of the growth effect of openness by at least half.

Perhaps the most spirited econometric debate in this area, however, is that between the critics Rodriguez and Rodrik (2000) and the authors of two leading statistical analyses showing how open trade policy contributes to growth: Sachs and Warner (1995) and Edwards (1998). Consider first Sachs and Warner's results. They examine growth performance as a function of trade policy and other variables (investment rate, government spending as a percent of GDP, education, and number of revolutions and coups) for 79 countries during the period 1970–89. Their variable for trade policy is a binary dummy variable that is set to "closed" (zero) if any one of five conditions is met. First, the average tariff on capital and intermediate goods is more than 40 percent. Second, NTBs cover more than 40 percent of imports of capital goods and intermediates. Third, the country has a socialist economic system. Fourth, there is a state monopoly on the principal exports. Fifth, the black market premium on the official exchange rate exceeded 20 percent in the 1970s or 1980s.

The authors first conduct regressions relating growth in real per capita income during the period 1970–89 to initial per capita income, a binary variable for whether the economy was "open" during the full period, the investment rate, the relative price of investment goods, government consumption spending relative to GDP, and a series of variables for political stability. These regressions find a statistically significant coefficient on openness, which indicates that over the two decades examined real per capita income grew at 2.2 percentage points faster in "open" economies than in "closed" economies. A second set of regressions examines whether growth accelerated after a shift to "open" status for 38 noncommunist countries that opened after 1975 and sustained their open status through 1993. These results also show a statistically significant impact of opening, indicating an increase in growth from the country's past rate by about 1.2 percentage points.

In an important critical review, Rodriguez and Rodrik examine the Sachs and Warner study and three others. They judge that the studies have "serious shortcomings," leading them to conclude that there is "little evidence that open trade policies—in the sense of lower tariff and nontariff barriers to trade—are significantly associated with economic growth" (Rodriguez and Rodrik 2000, i).[15] Rodriguez and Rodrik rerun

---

15. The four studies are Sachs and Warner (1995), Edwards (1998), Dollar (1992), and Ben-David (1993). The early Dollar study sought to use purchasing power parity data to gauge protection by departures of domestic tradable prices from international levels, but this has a number of problems, including reliance on the empirically weak "law of one price." The Ben-David study focuses on whether trade liberalization generated convergence among European industrialized countries, and it is of less direct relevance to the purposes of this chapter than the other studies considered here. Slaughter (2001) also examines the impact of trade liberalization on income convergence, but three of his tests similarly involve European integration events. His fourth test, the Kennedy Round, involves using "all countries in the world not part of the Kennedy Round" as the control group. This may be necessary for the control group technique, but it means that a relatively unrepresentative collection of countries will serve as the control, given the widespread coverage of countries that did participate. Moreover, the convergence issue is distinct from the more direct question of whether liberalization affects growth.

the Sachs and Warner regressions separating the Sachs and Warner trade policy index into its five components (black market premium, BMP; state monopoly, MON; socialist, SOC; nontariff barriers, NTB; and tariffs, TAR). Only two of them, BMP and MON, turn out to be significant—although all three of the others retain the right sign. They next reaggregate into two components: BM comprising BMP and MON, and SQT as an index comprising the other three. If SQT is run separately, it has the right sign (for the Rodriguez and Rodrik reformulation) and is highly significant. The same is true of BM. If both are entered jointly, however, BM remains significant but SQT does not. Rodriguez and Rodrik conclude that SQT and thus the most unambiguous trade policy measures—tariffs and quotas— do not stand up to scrutiny as influencing growth.

Rodriguez and Rodrik then dismiss the state monopoly variable as failing to include such countries as Mauritius and Indonesia and instead acting as an Africa dummy. They then ask whether the BMP is in fact a measure of protection. They note that if all imports are purchased with foreign currency bought on the black market while all exporters must turn in earnings at the official rate, the BMP "works exactly like a trade restriction (by raising [the price of imports relative to the price of exports])." If, instead, exporters can sell on the black market, the BMP does not act like a trade restriction. Rodriguez and Rodrik do not state which is more likely, but surely mandatory exchange surrender by exporters is the rule rather than the exception in most regimes with a large BMP.

Nonetheless, Rodriguez and Rodrik judge that the BMP more fundamentally reflects prolonged macroeconomic and sociopolitical imbalances, and it is more likely that these factors are driving the low growth rate rather than the BMP's trade distortions. When Rodriguez and Rodrik insert variables for macroeconomic and political distress, they stress that the BMP loses significance. Well, yes and no. In two of six models, the BMP retains its original size (about –1) and significance. In three of the others, its sign remains the same, its size declines somewhat (to about –0.6 to –0.7), and its $t$-statistic drops below the conventional cutoff but is still not de minimis at about 1.6 (i.e., close to the 10 percent significance level). In only one of the six augmented models do the coefficient and its $t$-statistic collapse substantially further. So is the BMP really unimportant? It would seem of interest, in particular, that in the equations including either a terms-of-trade shock variable or a war variable the BMP coefficient remains essentially unchanged and significant.

Warner (2003) has provided a trenchant defense of the Sachs and Warner results. He argues persuasively that it is necessary to aggregate various protectionist variables rather than test them one by one, because different countries may be applying different means of protection and it is not the marginal effect of a single instrument but their joint effect that is of interest. Or, as Berg and Krueger (2003) put it in their support of Sachs and Warner, "the motivation for such a multivariate indicator in the first place" is to capture "the frequent substitution of one for the other method of protection" (p. 10).

Warner then supports the black market premium as a gauge of protection. He cites the case of Algeria, where the premium was in the range of 250 to 400 percent in the late 1980s, a period when Algeria had tight import restrictions despite an average tariff of only 13 percent. Inflation was a moderate 8.6 percent in the 1980s, so the black market premium hardly appears to be a symptom of macroeconomic disturbance in this example. He then shows a scatter diagram for 1,400 country years in the period 1971–92 showing no relation between the BMP and inflation. He argues that it is much more common historically for a high BMP to result from exchange controls, and further argues that these have tended to stem from rationing foreign exchange for imports rather than from dual exchange rates penalizing capital transactions.

Warner then notes that the marketing board monopoly variable is not a simple dummy for Africa, because only 28 of the 41 African countries in Sachs and Warner's sample trigger the protection dummy on this basis. To Rodriguez and Rodrik's point that Mauritius had a marketing board, Warner replies that it did not have a monopoly on selling foreign exchange for imports. He cites Mozambique as an example of a country with disastrous growth (–3 percent annually) having high protection through the marketing board according to country-study accounts, which will bias results if it is reported as open because of its moderate tariff (10 percent).

Warner's tour de force, however, is in his statistical results obtained even after bending over backward by removing several of the protection cases that tend to violate Rodriguez and Rodrik conditions. He drops 13 countries that were only classified closed because of the black market premium. He then further drops all African countries that were designated closed solely on the basis of their marketing board monopolies. The results still confirm the original Sachs and Warner statistical significance of a negative impact of a closed trade regime on growth.[16]

Reviewing the debate, Berg and Krueger (2003) judge that the Sachs and Warner index "represents a fairly successful effort to measure the overall importance of trade policy restrictions, though it does not differentiate degrees of restrictiveness" (p. 9). They consider Rodriguez and Rod-

---

16. Warner (2003) further queries the robustness of Rodriguez and Rodrik's estimates. Rodriguez and Rodrik state that there is no simple inverse relation between growth and protection. But they conduct a test using tariff revenue divided by imports, rather than the widely available Barro and Lee (1994) data on average tariff rates. Warner shows that the latter data do show a negative relationship of growth to protection, and this relationship is highly significant if a single outlier—India—is removed. He adds that by using tariff revenue data for the late 1990s, Rodriguez and Rodrik are missing the key period for testing trade regimes: the 1970s and early 1980s, before the wave of liberalization in developing countries removed much of the variation in protection.

rik's critique of the black market premium as overdone, because a premium acts like a tariff by driving a wedge between the exchange rate exporters receive and the rate paid by importers. They are comfortable, moreover, in attributing macroeconomic policy disarray to protection because such disequilibria are precisely the type of consequences seen associated with protection in the past. This is consistent with their more general position that although the influence of trade policy is admittedly difficult to disentangle from that of overall policy quality, it is not necessary to do so for the purposes of arriving at advice favoring open trade policies.

Other researchers have obtained positive growth effects using the Sachs and Warner index. Using data for 84 countries from 1960 to 2000, Bosworth and Collins (2003) estimate regressions of per capita growth on initial income per capita (finding a negative coefficient and thus conditional convergence), human capital as proxied by life expectancy in the initial year, change in terms of trade, institutional quality, geography (number of frost days and tropical area), change in inflation, budget balance, and Sachs and Warner openness. Their coefficient on the Sachs and Warner variable indicates a statistically significant increase of 0.82 percentage point in per capita growth for open versus closed economies.[17] Additional tests indicate that this works through the influence of openness on capital deepening, where the Sachs and Warner variable is significant, rather than a shift in total factor productivity, for which it is not.

Similarly, Greenaway, Morgan, and Wright (1998) apply the Sachs and Warner index at 0 prior to the year of opening and 1 thereafter. In GMM regressions after first differencing, they relate per capita GDP growth in 69 countries during the period 1975–93 to per capita income in 1965, secondary school enrollment in 1965, change in terms of trade, population growth, the ratio of investment to GDP, and the Sachs and Warner trade policy variable. They find a significant coefficient on the last indicating that a shift to openness boosts the rate of per capita GDP growth by a sustained 2.7 percent annually. The authors conduct similar panel regressions using two alternative binary measures of when liberalization occurred (both based on work conducted at the World Bank). They obtain significant liberalization effects with both. However, the cumulative impact on per capita income level is modest (about 2 percent) and far smaller than that from the Sachs and Warner variable (46 percent). They infer that the Sachs and Warner measure is a broader gauge of openness, whereas their other two variables are narrower measures of liberalization and tend to

---

17. In their text, the authors seem to prefer an interpretation to the effect that the Sachs and Warner variable loses significance when the number of "other conditioning variables" is increased. However, the main other conditioning variables are already present in one key set of results (their table 10), where Sachs and Warner is significant. The addition of regional dummies removes significance (their table 8), but in general, the information from an economic variable should be preferred to that from a regional dummy.

capture "first steps rather than final steps," thereby likely understating the eventual effect.

Harrison and Hanson (1999) carried out the same exercise as Rodriguez and Rodrik (2000) in reestimating growth equations with the individual components of Sachs and Warner rather than its aggregate dummy-variable form. When they include the full set of control variables used by Sachs and Warner and level of the black market premium, they do find tariffs, the marketing board dummy, and the socialist dummy significant individually. However, when they use a dummy variable for the black market premium, the tariff variable loses significance. They conclude that the Sachs and Warner variable "fails to establish a robust link" between more open trade policy and growth. They then consider that the problem may stem from Sachs and Warner's use of end-period tariff and quota data rather than average period rates. They create an alternative measure using tariff revenues relative to imports. Using this variable to measure tariffs, they find that it does have a statistically significant negative effect on growth. A 10-percentage-point rise in tariffs reduces average growth in GDP per capita by 0.5 to 0.6 percent. However, when they add dummy variables for the four East Asian tigers, Latin America, and India, the significance of this openness variable disappears. They infer that there is "limited validity of pure cross-section estimation" (p. 134). However, it would seem questionable to prefer the indirect measure of regional dummies to the direct measure of the openness variable. An alternative interpretation would be to accept the Harrison-Hanson result using duty collections as providing significant evidence of the adverse impact of protection on growth.

Overall, despite the Rodriguez and Rodrik critique, the Sachs and Warner results seem to represent a relatively durable benchmark study showing that protection does adversely affect growth. Consider next Edwards (1998), who makes another important attempt to examine the strength of the empirical relationship between trade policy and growth. He first uses estimates of capital and labor stocks for 93 developing and industrial countries during the period 1960–90 to estimate growth in total factor productivity (TFP), which is a residual in a regression of real GDP growth on growth in capital and labor (with factor-share coefficients constrained to sum to unity). The median rate of TFP growth was 1.1 percent, or 1.0 percent in a version adding a human capital variable.

Edwards then tests the relationship between TFP growth and trade policy openness, using nine alternative measures of the latter. These include the Sachs and Warner variable (discussed above), the "outward orientation index" of the World Bank, Leamer's (1988) index of openness (the country's average residual from disaggregated trade flow regressions), the average black market premium, the average tariff in 1982, the average coverage of NTBs (both from Barro and Lee 1994), the Heritage Foundation Index of Distortions in International Trade, the Collected Trade Taxes ratio for the period 1980–85, and a regression-based index of import distortions in 1985 prepared by Wolf (1993). For each measure, the benchmark value for each country is typically for the early 1980s.

Edwards then conducts cross-country regressions of TFP growth on each of the alternative trade policy indicators, in samples ranging from 32 observations for the World Bank index to 75 for the black market premium. He uses weighted least squares, weighting by GDP per capita. A second round of regressions adds the initial per capita income and initial level of human capital as control variables. In 17 of the 18 resulting regressions, the trade policy openness variable has the right sign, and in 13 of these 17 it is statistically significant. He considers the results as "quite remarkable" evidence of a "tremendous consistency that there is a significantly positive relationship between openness and productivity growth" (p. 391). Many readers are likely to agree with him, although one might worry about his having only a single point estimate of policy openness for each country for the full time span.

Complementing their critique of Sachs and Warner, Rodriguez and Rodrik also criticize Edwards (1998). Their principal critique is that his use of weighted least squares gives undue weight to countries with a higher per capita income. They acknowledge that heteroskedasticity is likely to be present, but they prefer an alternative (White's) form of correction. When they apply this alternative, only four of the nine least-squares models show a significant trade policy variable. They then go on to find fault with individual components of Edwards's variables (property rights should be included) and data (India's collected import taxes are too high to be believable).

How can we be sure, however, that there is not still another weighting system to address heteroskedasticity that will not increase rather than reduce the significance of Edwards's results? How many combinations and permutations would Rodriguez and Rodrik really need to run to arrive at "confidence interval" robustness (see the discussion of Sala i Martin 1997) with these different approaches? In particular, my own sense is that there should be far more effort in the cross-country regression literature toward country weighting, considering that otherwise the large number of small economies may give a false impression of how economies really work for the great majority of the world's population. So there are surely alternative dimensions of weighting that neither Rodriguez and Rodrik nor Edwards have tried. Should we reject Edwards's findings on grounds that Rodriguez and Rodrik find weaker results with an alternative technique? Or for that matter, should we look at Rodriguez and Rodrik's tests as showing the glass half empty or half full, with five of Edwards's eight significant and correct signs still significant and correct in one of Rodriguez and Rodrik's corrections for heteroskedasticity (using the log of per capita GDP weighting rather than per capita GDP weighting) and in four of the other alternative (White's)?

More generally, an underlying problem is that there do not seem to be standardized rules of the game for confirming or rejecting earlier statistical results. In particular, adding additional variables can remove the statistical significance of the trade policy variable, but with additional variables is the comparison between the two sets of results a fair one? As Sala-i-Martin (1997, 179) points out, "one is bound to find one regression for which the estimated coefficient changes signs if enough regressions are run." He cites the earlier results of Levine and Renelt (1992), indicating that few or none of the large stable of explanatory variables in international growth equations stand up to Leamer's (1983) extreme-bounds test of robustness. Sala-i-Martin points out that by this test, if a single regression can be found in which the sign of a coefficient changes or even becomes insignificant, the variable is not robust. He argues persuasively that this is simply too extreme a test of robustness.

Sala-i-Martin offers an alternative approach that identifies a weighted mean and variance of each parameter estimate from the full set of alternative models, weighting by likelihood. He proposes that a variable be judged significantly correlated with growth in a "robust" way if the cumulative density function of its coefficient around this mean, within 1 standard deviation, is 0.95 or higher. He then suggests that about 60 variables are reasonable candidates for growth correlations, but that choosing one variable at a time and letting all the others compete for entry in a total of seven right-hand-side variables would require 3.2 billion regressions. After he narrows the field by selecting three core variables to appear in all the regressions, he still has 2 million regressions to run (hence his title). When he does so, he finds that by the Leamer extreme-bounds test only 1 variable passes robustness, but by his confidence-interval approach 22 out of 59 variables are robustly "significant."[18]

The main lesson of Sala-i-Martin's exercise should be to make us wary of throwing out the baby with the bathwater of yet another regression that happens to turn insignificant a key variable previously found to be significant. This in turn suggests that there should be a relatively high hurdle for overturning a significant result that confirms a relatively well-established theory, and the simple presentation of another regression in which the variable is insignificant (and especially if the sign remains un-

18. For a recent examination of the Rodriguez and Rodrik-Sachs and Warner controversy that adopts the spirit of Sala-i-Martin's warning, see Jones (2000). He suggests that a "best estimate" approach to robustness is preferable to an approach in which a single reversal destroys the diagnosis. He examines approximately 100 specifications, selects the 13 he considers most appropriate, and averages the relevant coefficients and probability values. He notes that adding a quality of institutions variable often removes significance of the trade policy variable, but he suggests that there are problems with this variable (Knack-Keefer) as well. He concludes that for all but the worst specifications, the best estimate of the effect of a large adverse change in trade policy (e.g., a move from 1 to 0 on Sachs and Warner) is a 40 to 70 percent decline in steady state income, and the decline is 13 to 24 percent in his "worst" specifications.

changed) should probably not be sufficient to surmount this hurdle, especially if the number of variables has been increased.[19]

As an illustration of this problem, consider Rodriguez and Rodrik's critique of Sachs and Warner. First, they run the Sachs and Warner test separately on each of the five subcomponents of the Sachs and Warner trade policy index, and they find that only two are significant. This procedure, however, does not deal with the economic problem that the original index is designed to capture the combined effect of alternative substitute approaches to protection (as discussed above). Then they replace the Sachs and Warner trade policy variable with two intermediate indexes comprising parts of the five subcomponents. Both subaggregates are significant when run individually, but one loses significance when they enter jointly. But this test increases the total number of variables, raising the question of whether robustness is really disproven in the sense of Sala-i-Martin's confidence-interval approach. The general problem is the risk of the unwarranted rejection of a meaningful econometric result by changing the number or composition of variables.

Wacziarg and Welch (2003) provide an important extension of the Sachs and Warner analysis by shifting the focus from cross-section to time-series and panel analysis. They replicate and update the Sachs and Warner measure of openness, and as a first step confirm the Sachs and Warner cross-sectional results for the 1950–90 period. However, they find that for the period 1991–98 liberalization's impact on growth disappears. Nonetheless, this could simply be because the growth effect of liberalization is transitional (standard neoclassical growth model) rather than permanent (endogenous growth model), and by the 1990s many of the liberalizing countries had already maintained liberalized regimes for several years. Moreover, far from concluding that Sachs and Warner overestimated the impact of liberalization (even though Wacziarg and Welch agree with Rodriguez and Rodrik about the dominant subcomponents of the Sachs and Warner protection measure), Wacziarg and Welch go on to estimate large liberalization effects on the basis of the time-series performance of individual country growth before and after liberalization.

Wacziarg and Welch set the date of trade regime opening for each country, and they find that for 133 countries during the period 1950–98, 32 percent of the country years had liberalized trade regimes. As noted above, they estimate that growth for postliberalization country periods was on average 1.4 percent higher than in preliberalization periods. The thrust of the study is to provide strong reinforcement for the view that trade liberalization has a positive impact on growth, even though the summary growth impact is somewhat lower than the original Sachs and Warner es-

---

19. A caveat to this caveat is the standard concern that researchers may tend to conduct their search until they find the "right" result.

timate of a difference in annual growth of 2.2 percentage points between open and closed economies (as discussed above).[20]

Overall, it would seem that the weight of the empirical evidence is on the side of those who judge that more open trade policies lead to better growth performance.[21] The Rodriguez and Rodrik analysis has served an important role in sharpening the debate (e.g., see Baldwin 2003), but it would not appear to warrant their outright rejection of meaningful evidence on the link. Perhaps more important, no one has provided persuasive statistical evidence showing support of better growth results using protective regimes.[22] The most compelling evidence on the broad alternative of using high protection to foster import-substituting industrialization remains the spectacular failure of the later stages of this strategy in Latin America by the 1970s, which led to a wave of unilateral liberalization by the late 1980s.

## The Dynamic Productivity Effects of Trade Liberalization on Global Poverty

It is possible to synthesize the dynamic productivity effects of trade surveyed above with the impact of global trade's liberalization on the trade of developing countries to obtain the implied long-term effects on growth and poverty. The central elasticity of long-term output per capita with respect to the ratio of trade to GDP in table 5.1 turns out to be 0.5. For ex-

---

20. Note, however, that the Wacziarg and Welch estimate of 1.4 percent is quite close to the comparable concept estimated by Sachs and Warner: 1.2 percent increase in growth from the preliberalization to postliberalization period, estimated for a smaller set of countries and years.

21. A recent study by Yanikkaya (2003) finds to the contrary that there is a positive relationship between per capita growth and protection, for 80 countries in the period 1970–97. It is unclear how much weight to give these results, however. His estimates finding a positive coefficient of growth on tariff collections relative to import values contradict negative relationships estimated for the same variable in the studies by Edwards (1998), Harrison and Hanson (1999), and Jones (2000). Moreover, this measure is subject to the Sachs and Warner critique that it fails to capture nontariff restrictions, and to the problems that it will understate protection where corruption diverts duties payable and where the tariff is so high that it suppresses imports and revenue. Alternative measures of protection suggested by Yanikkaya either seem questionable (bilateral payments arrangement) or have the wrong sign for his unconventional finding that protection spurs growth (incidence of restrictions on current account payments).

22. Noland and Pack (2003) find, moreover, that even outward-oriented (i.e., export-oriented) strategies that rely on a combination of interventions seeking to encourage exports and at least tacitly curb imports, identified with such cases as Japan and South Korea, do not stand up to empirical scrutiny as supporting success of the "industrial policy" strategy, which some would categorize as within the family of protection even if the result is to foster "openness" as measured by the ratio of exports to GDP.

ample, if a country's exports plus imports rise from 40 to 40.4 percent of GDP (an increase of 1 percent in the ratio), the cumulative dynamic productivity effect over the long term (10–20 years) will be an increase in the level of per capita GDP by 0.5 percent.

Chapter 4 has already considered the quasi-dynamic gains from trade by examining the "steady state" results on output if capital investment is allowed to respond to the increased trade opportunities to the point where the return on investment is driven back down to its preliberalization level. This chapter seeks instead a concept that is equivalent to technical change without additional capital. As discussed above, most of the trade-productivity studies tend to find this the dominant source, rather than capital deepening. However, to allow for the likely inclusion of some capital-deepening contribution to the overall productivity elasticity average identified above, it is appropriate for the purposes of the calculations below to apply a somewhat more moderate central estimate. The parameter used is 0.4, which means that one-fifth of the productivity impact in the field of estimates comes from capital deepening and four-fifths comes from TFP increase.

Table 5.2 first repeats the estimates of the number of poor and the "poverty elasticity" applicable to each of the countries in the Poverty Effects version of the Harrison-Rutherford-Tarr, or PEHRT, model, developed in chapter 4. It next reports the percent increase in real aggregate (Armington) imports estimated from that model for the static free trade scenario (corresponding to table 4.1). These estimates are aggregated from the individual product level, weighting by base period shares of the products in total imports.

The average increase in real imports for all developing countries is 3.0 percent, weighting by base-period imports, and 5.4 percent weighting by poverty. The rise in trade is above average in several countries with large poor populations, including Bangladesh, China, India, Indonesia, and Pakistan.

The next step is to apply the elasticity of 0.4 to the percent increase in trade, to obtain the percent increase in long-term per capita output. This percentage is then multiplied by the poverty elasticity, and the product is multiplied by the number of people in poverty to obtain the long term change in poverty for each country. The result is that an estimated 202 million people would be lifted out of poverty over the long term through the dynamic productivity effects of free trade. This is in addition to the central estimate of a 114 million reduction in poverty from the real income effects (mainly in unskilled wages) arising from the static effects of free trade (table 4.5). Thus, *a total of 316 million people would be lifted out of poverty* over the next decade or two through the static and dynamic productivity gains from free trade, even without taking account of further poverty reduction from induced capital investment, and even using a conservative estimate of agricultural liberalization effects (e.g., the chap-

**Table 5.2    Poverty impact of dynamic productivity gains from free trade**

| Region and economy | Number of poor (millions) | Poverty elasticity | Increase in trade (percent) | Long-term productivity gain (percent) | Change in poverty (millions) |
|---|---|---|---|---|---|
| **Asia** | | | | | |
| Bangladesh | 99.3 | 3.5 | 25.6 | 10.24 | −35.6 |
| China | 673.2 | 3.5 | 5.0 | 2.00 | −47.1 |
| India | 859.9 | 3.5 | 6.2 | 2.48 | −74.6 |
| Indonesia | 136.8 | 3.5 | 4.6 | 1.84 | −8.8 |
| South Korea | 0.9 | 3.5 | 3.1 | 1.24 | 0.0 |
| Malaysia | 5.6 | 3.2 | 5.9 | 2.36 | −0.4 |
| Pakistan | 114.2 | 3.5 | 14.3 | 5.72 | −22.9 |
| Philippines | 29.2 | 3.0 | 8.4 | 3.36 | −2.9 |
| Thailand | 17.0 | 3.5 | 3.0 | 1.20 | −0.7 |
| Hong Kong, Taiwan, and Singapore | 0.0 | 2.0 | 2.1 | 0.84 | 0.0 |
| Other | 84.8 | 2.0 | 4.2 | 1.68 | −2.8 |
| *Subtotal* | 2,020.9 | | | | −196.0 |
| **Latin America** | | | | | |
| Argentina | 5.4 | 3.1 | 2.2 | 0.88 | −0.1 |
| Brazil | 29.2 | 1.0 | −0.3 | −0.12 | 0.0 |
| Central America and Caribbean | 26.6 | 2.0 | 5.4 | 2.16 | −1.1 |
| Mexico | 41.1 | 2.0 | 0.7 | 0.28 | −0.2 |
| Other | 45.9 | 2.0 | −0.4 | −0.16 | 0.1 |
| *Subtotal* | 148.2 | | | | −1.3 |
| **Europe** | | | | | |
| Central and Eastern Europe | 92.2 | 2.0 | 1.0 | 0.40 | −0.7 |
| **Middle East, North Africa** | | | | | |
| Turkey | 11.6 | 3.5 | 3.7 | 1.48 | −0.6 |
| Other | 76.4 | 2.0 | 3.5 | 1.40 | −2.1 |
| *Subtotal* | 88.0 | | | | −2.7 |
| **Sub-Saharan Africa** | | | | | |
| Mozambique | 13.6 | 1.4 | 4.1 | 1.64 | −0.3 |
| South Africa | 15.1 | 1.2 | −0.8 | −0.32 | 0.1 |
| Tanzania | 19.7 | 1.0 | 0.5 | 0.20 | 0.0 |
| Uganda | 16.6 | 2.3 | 0.5 | 0.20 | −0.1 |
| Other | 328.4 | 2.0 | 0.3 | 0.12 | −0.8 |
| *Subtotal* | 393.2 | | | | −1.2 |
| **Total** | 2,742.5 | | | | −201.9 |

*Source:* Author's calculations.

ter 4 estimates rather than the chapter 3 estimates). This is surprisingly close to the estimate by the World Bank (2002a, 174) that free trade would reduce global poverty by 320 million by 2015 from its baseline level. The World Bank authors use a different CGE model and somewhat different methodology to arrive at the poverty estimates.

# The Combined Static, Dynamic, and Induced-Investment Effects

Finally, the estimates in chapters 3 and 4 and in the present chapter can be combined to obtain an overview of the scale and composition of potential poverty reduction resulting from global trade liberalization. Appendix 3C used a stylized-parameter model combined with country detail on the share of the poor located in the rural sector to arrive at an estimate of the impact of free trade in agriculture on global poverty. This estimate is considerably higher than the implied agricultural-sector contribution to chapter 4's PEHRT model estimate of the poverty reduction resulting from the static effects of free trade. We can thus obtain a "central" static effect from the PEHRT results, and a "high" static effect replacing the agricultural liberalization component of these results with chapter 3's stylized-parameter estimates for the impact of agricultural liberalization. To do so, it is necessary to subtract from the PEHRT static poverty-impact estimates (table 4.5) the fraction broadly associated with agricultural liberalization, as inferred from the ratio of agricultural-sector welfare gains to total gains (from table 4.1).[23] This leaves the nonagricultural static poverty effects, which are then added to chapter 3's agricultural effects to obtain the "high" estimate of the static poverty effects in table 5.3.

The other major step in consolidating the various estimates is to decide how to treat the quasi-dynamic gains in the "steady state" results requiring increased capital investment. As noted in chapter 4, these net welfare and poverty reduction effects are large, even after fully deducting capital costs at a relatively high imputed real interest rate (7 percent). However, they would require additional capital amounting to about 40 percent of base-period GDP in developing countries. Nonetheless, because the consolidated estimates of this chapter seek to gauge the long-term effects over a horizon of perhaps 15 years, at least a substantial part of the increased capital stock would seem feasible.

The consolidated long-term estimates include *one half* of the incremental welfare and poverty effects in chapter 4's steady state (SS) results above its static results.[24] This implies the mobilization of about 20 percent of base-period GDP (and 15 percent of average real GDP after accounting for reasonable growth of 4 percent annually) in additional capital stock over a period of 15 years. The increase to the investment rate would be only 1 percentage point of GDP (e.g., from 20 to 21 percent), and a significant

---

23. More precisely, the contribution to welfare gains from agricultural liberalization is divided by the total welfare gains minus the interaction effect, to obtain the proportionate contribution of agricultural liberalization to welfare gains. It is assumed that the same proportion applies to poverty effects.

24. For the purposes of table 5.3, this is based on the central (lower) case of the two alternative steady state estimates in table 4.7.

## Table 5.3 Combined long-term static and dynamic effects of free trade on poverty (millions, change from baseline)

| Region and economy | Static Central | Static High[a] | Dynamic Productivity effect | Dynamic One-half additional net steady-state effect[b] | Total Central | Total High |
|---|---|---|---|---|---|---|
| **Asia** | | | | | | |
| Bangladesh | −4.1 | −13.3 | −35.6 | −3.6 | −43.3 | −52.6 |
| China | −24.7 | −87.2 | −47.1 | 0.0 | −71.8 | −134.3 |
| India | −28.3 | −74.8 | −74.6 | −109.1 | −212.1 | −258.5 |
| Indonesia | −6.1 | −15.1 | −8.8 | −7.4 | −22.3 | −31.3 |
| South Korea | 0.0 | 0.1 | 0.0 | 0.0 | −0.1 | 0.0 |
| Malaysia | −0.2 | −0.2 | −0.4 | −0.6 | −1.1 | −1.1 |
| Pakistan | −7.9 | −13.0 | −22.9 | −46.1 | −76.9 | −82.0 |
| Philippines | −2.3 | −2.0 | −2.9 | −1.4 | −6.6 | −6.4 |
| Thailand | −4.1 | −4.0 | −0.7 | −9.2 | −14.0 | −13.9 |
| Hong Kong, Taiwan, and Singapore | 0.0 | 0.0 | 0.0 | 0.0 | 0.0 | 0.0 |
| Other | −2.1 | −8.8 | −2.8 | −5.9 | −10.8 | −17.5 |
| *Subtotal* | −79.7 | −218.3 | −196.0 | −183.3 | −459.0 | −597.6 |
| **Latin America** | | | | | | |
| Argentina | −0.7 | 0.1 | −0.1 | −0.1 | −0.9 | −0.1 |
| Brazil | −1.0 | −0.4 | 0.0 | −0.3 | −1.3 | −0.7 |
| Central America and Caribbean | −3.2 | −2.9 | −1.1 | −1.6 | −5.9 | −5.6 |
| Mexico | −0.4 | 0.4 | −0.2 | −0.1 | −0.7 | 0.1 |
| Other | −2.7 | −2.2 | 0.1 | −3.3 | −5.8 | −5.4 |
| *Subtotal* | −7.9 | −5.0 | −1.3 | −5.3 | −14.6 | −11.7 |
| **Europe** | | | | | | |
| Central and Eastern Europe | −2.4 | −1.0 | −0.7 | −0.2 | −3.3 | −1.9 |
| **Middle East and North Africa** | | | | | | |
| Turkey | −1.3 | 0.0 | −0.6 | −1.1 | −3.0 | −1.8 |
| Other | −3.8 | −4.4 | −2.1 | −6.4 | −12.3 | −12.9 |
| *Subtotal* | −5.1 | −4.4 | −2.7 | −7.5 | −15.4 | −14.7 |
| **Sub-Saharan Africa** | | | | | | |
| Mozambique | −0.8 | −0.4 | −0.3 | −0.8 | −1.9 | −1.5 |
| South Africa | −0.6 | −1.1 | 0.1 | −0.1 | −0.6 | −1.2 |
| Tanzania | −1.4 | −3.1 | 0.0 | −0.5 | −2.0 | −3.6 |
| Uganda | −0.7 | −2.5 | −0.1 | −0.8 | −1.5 | −3.4 |
| Other | −15.6 | −24.8 | −0.8 | −24.6 | −41.0 | −50.1 |
| *Subtotal* | −19.1 | −31.9 | −1.2 | −26.8 | −47.0 | −59.8 |
| **Total** | −114.3 | −260.7 | −201.9 | −223.1 | −539.3 | −685.7 |

a. Adjusts for chapter 3's agricultural-sector estimates; see the text.
b. One-half increment of steady state (induced capital investment) effects above static.

*Source:* Author's calculations.

portion of this increment could be financed by external capital flows in a benign global economic environment.[25] Of particular importance, the inclusion of only half of the net SS welfare and poverty effects has the additional advantage of making some downward allowance for the possibility that the model calibration overstates the extent of induced investment, as discussed in chapter 4.

The resulting consolidated estimate is that over the long horizon of about 15 years, *global free trade could reduce global poverty by a central estimate of 540 million people, and perhaps as many as 685 million*, from the baseline it would otherwise reach. As noted in chapter 3, the World Bank (2002a) has estimated that even without trade liberalization, global poverty should moderate from 2.9 billion today to 2.13 billion in 2015. So the estimates here suggest that *free trade would reduce global poverty by about one-fourth or more from its baseline levels by 2015 and after*.

The bulk of this poverty reduction would occur in Asia. This partly reflects the fact that a large fraction of the world's poor are in Asia: approximately 74 percent (table 5.2). However, an even higher portion of the number of people lifted out of poverty from free trade, almost 85 percent, would be in Asia. This would correspond to 23 percent of today's number of poor people in Asia (central estimate), and an even larger fraction against the baseline number by 2015. In comparison, the consolidated poverty reduction estimates in table 5.3 for Latin America are relatively modest at about 15 million, or only about 10 percent of the number of poor people in this region today. The corresponding proportionate reductions in the number of the poor would be 3.6 percent in Eastern Europe, 17.5 percent in the Middle East and North Africa, and 12 percent in sub-Saharan Africa (again, compared with today's number of poor rather than the somewhat lower 2015 baseline numbers and using the lower "central" estimate).

The long term poverty reduction estimates (in millions of persons) here are close to those in World Bank (2002a, 175) for the Middle East and North Africa and for Latin America.[26] However, the estimates here are far larger for Asia, and smaller for sub-Saharan Africa and Eastern Europe. The World Bank estimate for 2015 is that free trade would reduce the number of poor by 65 million in East Asia and the Pacific and 118 million in South Asia, or 183 million for the region. In contrast, the central estimate in table 5.3 is 460 million for all of Asia, more than twice as large. Conversely, the central estimate here for sub-Saharan Africa is 47 million, less than half the World Bank estimate of 107 million; and the estimate for the Middle East and North Africa is also smaller (at 3.3 vs. 9 million).

---

25. That is, 20 percent of average GDP over 15 years amounts to 1.33 percent of GDP annually.

26. Specifically, the numbers are 15 million here vs. 19 million as estimated by the World Bank for the Middle East and North Africa, and 15 million vs. 17 million for Latin America.

A major reason for the difference in Asia especially is that the present study applies an estimated poverty elasticity specific to each country or region. For most of Asia, this elasticity is high, frequently constrained to the ceiling value of 3.5 (table 5.2). In contrast, the World Bank uses a standard poverty elasticity of 2.0. The theoretical basis for a higher elasticity is set forth in appendix 1B above. It is shown there that in the lognormal distribution of income, the poverty elasticity depends positively on the ratio of mean income to poverty-line income, and negatively on the degree of income concentration (Gini coefficient). Because mean income is relatively high in comparison with the poverty line (e.g., about 3 to 1 in India and Indonesia, almost 10 to 1 in China, and about 2 or 2.5 to 1 even in Bangladesh and Pakistan), and because income concentrations in the region tend to be moderate to intermediate (Gini coefficients of about 0.3 to 0.4), the predicted poverty elasticities tend to be relatively high.[27]

Similarly, one reason the sub-Saharan African estimates here are lower than those of the World Bank is that the low level of mean income relative to poverty income in this region results in a relatively low poverty elasticity where it is estimated directly (averaging around 1.2), although for the large bloc of "other" countries in the region, the same elasticity is used as that by the World Bank (2.0).

The more fundamental difference between the consolidated estimates here and those of the World Bank, however, is the inclusion here of a conceptually additive effect not present in the World Bank model. The estimates here comprise three components: static effects, dynamic productivity effects, and dynamic capital investment effects. The World Bank model captures only the first two effects. The estimates of the first two effects in the present study are indeed surprisingly close to those of the World Bank, as reviewed above. However, gains from induced capital investment in the Steady State model of Harrison, Rutherford, and Tarr (1996, 1997a) used in chapter 4 are not present in the WBGEP model.

Moreover, as elaborated above, the dynamic productivity gain used in the calculations of this chapter has been conservatively gauged to refer only to total productivity gains (analogous to the World Bank's model) rather than incorporating capital deepening, treated separately here through the SS effects. It should be emphasized again that for the latter, a conservative approach is taken by incorporating only half of the PEHRT model estimates, after considering plausible levels of additional investment and making some allowance for possible calibration overstatement. The overall effect, however, is that the central estimate of long-term poverty reduction from global free trade in this study is nearly two-thirds larger than that by the World Bank, at 540 million people instead of 320 million (table 5.3).

---

27. See appendix table 1A.1. The poverty line used here is $2 per day.

Finally, it is important to consider the welfare gain estimates that correspond to the consolidated poverty-impact estimates. As indicated in chapter 4, global free trade would confer static welfare gains estimated at $87 billion annually for developing countries, at 1997 prices (table 4.1). Welfare gains under the Steady State model would be $161.6 billion annually (table 4.5). Half the increment above the static effects would be $37 billion annually. The welfare gains from the long-term productivity effect can be calculated by applying the percentage productivity gains estimated for each country (table 5.2) to the 1997 base figure for GDP (Dimaranan and McDougall 2002, 2-8, 2-9). When this is done, the welfare gains from the long-term productivity effect amount to $79 billion annually. Summing the three components of total long-term gains (static, half the incremental steady state or induced-investment gains, and productivity-effect gains), the combined long-term welfare gains to developing countries from global free trade would amount to $203 billion annually at 1997 prices and economic scale, or 3.2 percent of GDP.

Global concessional assistance from industrial countries to developing countries amounts to about $50 billion annually. The calculations here suggest that the move to global free trade would confer gains on developing countries that are about four times as large. As set forth in chapter 4, at least half of the developing countries' gains from global free trade would stem from the removal of protection in industrial country markets. On this basis, it can be concluded that if industrial-countries eliminated protection, the resulting welfare gains to developing countries would amount to $100 billion or more annually, or twice the annual benefits currently being conveyed from industrial to developing countries through concessional assistance. The distribution of the trade gains would be much more oriented toward middle-income countries than the existing flows of concessional assistance, however, which tend to go to low income countries.

## Caveats

Globalization skeptics and development pessimists may find these estimates too large. It is useful to consider some of their likely concerns.

### Inequality Impact in the 1990s?

Some appear to consider it a stylized fact that the opening of trade regimes in developing countries in the 1990s was generally associated with a widening rather than narrowing of inequality, contradicting expectations based on the Heckscher-Ohlin model and its prediction that open trade should boost the relative price of the abundant factor, unskilled labor in the case of developing countries. If so, might further globalization through a move toward multilateral free trade yield results far less favorable for the global poor than those estimated in this study?

The first point to be made is that the liberalization initiatives of developing countries in recent years have mainly been unilateral, whereas the estimates of this study refer to the potential effects of multilateral liberalization, and in particular to the thoroughgoing liberalization of industrial-country markets for goods exported by developing countries. Typically, studies that find a globalization-inequality link attempt to identify a unilateral liberalization episode and then examine whether it was associated with narrowing or widening income inequality.

Whatever else one should expect from such episodes, it is certain that their terms-of-trade effects will be less favorable for the liberalizing countries than will be the case in multilateral liberalization. Even if the record of the past decade or two were unambiguous in concluding that liberalization by developing countries had contributed to widening inequality and even increased poverty, it would by no means follow that multilateral liberalization would do the same, because there would be additional terms-of-trade benefits.

Surely it is far from clear, however, that the liberalization episodes in recent years aggravated inequality and especially poverty. There was simply too much else going on for a simple coexistence of liberalization and widening inequality to be attributed to the adverse effects of liberalization. In particular, the debt crisis in Latin America in the 1980s and the round of financial crises in the second half of the 1990s must have had much greater impacts on poverty. Moreover, whether inequality in fact worsened is often unclear given data uncertainties.

Wood (1997) has provided a useful review of this issue. He asks why the East Asian experience in the 1960s and 1970s, in which more openness to trade tended to narrow the wage gap between skilled and unskilled workers, appears to have been contradicted by the Latin American experience since the 1980s, in which greater openness has been "accompanied by rising rather than falling wage inequality" (p. 33). He judges that the difference primarily reflects the differences between the 1960s and the 1980s, especially the entry of China into the world market, and perhaps the increase in the latter period of technical change biased against unskilled workers.

Wood first makes the point that when there are more than two countries, two goods, and two factors, the Heckscher-Ohlin prediction becomes ambiguous. For countries with intermediate skill endowments, exports are of goods with medium skill requirements while imports are of goods at both ends of the skill spectrum, so increased trade could either decrease or increase relative unskilled wages. The basic idea here is that Latin America is less abundant in unskilled labor than China, in particular, so it is in this intermediate position.

Wood relies primarily on a series of Latin American studies by Robbins and various coauthors (e.g., Robbins 1996) for the stylized fact that a trade regime change was associated with widening wage differentials.[28] For seven episodes, wage differentials widened in five, narrowed in one, and fluctuated in one. However, the first episode for Argentina ends in 1982, when surely the dominant influence was the country's entry into an acute debt crisis. The episode of widening for Chile is in the 1970s, too early for the general pattern (predating the entry of China). One episode (Chile, 1984–92) is solely "devaluation," which surely is not a test of trade liberalization. Two of the other episodes intermix devaluation with liberalization. Of the seven episodes, only one (Uruguay, 1990–95) is a pure test of liberalization. This is a slim basis indeed for enshrining as a stylized fact that trade liberalization in Latin America systematically increased wage inequality.

The other case usually cited in this direction is that of Mexico, where skill differentials in wages widened after the mid-1980s. Both Feenstra and Hanson (1995) and Revenga and Montenegro (1998) have attributed this outcome to the impact of trade liberalization, and they have searched for explanations of why this result contradicted Heckscher-Ohlin expectations. However, I have emphasized that a far more direct explanation of the widening real wage dispersion was the macroeconomic stabilization package adopted in late 1987. The Solidarity Pact imposed a wage and price freeze along with an exchange rate freeze, reversing the previous practice of indexing wages. The real minimum wage fell sharply as inflation declined only with a lag, and despite the small fraction of the labor force directly receiving the minimum wage, it is likely that low-end wages were eroded relative to skilled wages as a result. The data show no change in the skilled-wage differential during the period 1984–87, but a rise of about one-third in 1988–90, implicating the stabilization program rather than trade opening (Cline 1998, 335).

A prominent feature of Mexico's opening to trade, moreover, was the sharp increase in employment of unskilled workers in the *maquiladora* sector. This suggests a positive rather than negative demand effect for unskilled wages from the opening to trade.

Wood notes that protection was initially high in labor-intensive sectors such as clothing and footwear in Latin America, so that liberalization could have been expected to affect unskilled workers more adversely than skilled. He emphasizes, however, that Bangladesh, China, India, Indone-

---

28. Ironically, in Robbins's underlying data, the skilled-wage differential is actually declining in each of the episodes (Robbins 1996, table 5). The interpretation of rising differential associated with liberalization depends on his imputation of the net effect after calculating the amount of decline in the relative wage that would have been expected in view of the rise in the relative supply of skilled labor, a pervasive pattern. This approach is vulnerable to overstatement of the decline that could be expected from rising relative skills supply (e.g., by understating the elasticity of substitution between the two types), leaving a residual that has the wrong sign when related to the labor demand shift resulting from liberalization.

sia, and Pakistan had all been largely closed to trade in the 1960s and 1970s but were opening to trade by the mid-1980s, led by Indonesia and China. This was likely to have changed the comparative advantage of middle-income countries toward goods of intermediate skill intensity.

On this basis, whereas the opening of trade by middle-income countries in the 1960s would have tended to reduce wage inequality, by the 1980s it would have been likely to do the opposite. Wood also cites rising skill-intensive technical change in the 1980s and after as an alternative plausible explanation for rising skill differentials in wages, perhaps in an interactive effect in which such technologies became more available as trade regimes were opened. With technical change, Wood emphasizes, the real wage of unskilled workers could rise even if their relative wage fell.

Overall, the historical experience of Latin America in the past two decades would seem an unconvincing basis on which to reject the estimates of potential poverty reduction using the CGE modeling approach of the present study. The stylized facts are largely on relative wages rather than their implications for poverty, and they are at best sketchy in support of any general proposition that liberalization, rather than other influences including financial crises and skill-biased technical change, was the driving force in any widening of wage differentials.

Moreover, with respect to the influence of the entry of China and other large low-income countries into international trade, the CGE approach is ideally suited to taking this effect into account, because it captures the fact that these countries have an even greater relative abundance of unskilled labor than do Latin American countries. Finally, as noted, global liberalization opening foreign markets should be expected to have more positive effects in reducing poverty than unilateral liberalization because of terms-of-trade implications.

## Governance and Institutions

A second strand of concern about the potential for poverty reduction through global free trade is likely to be that of the development pessimists, who emphasize that a succession of past panaceas have failed to secure development in much of sub-Saharan Africa because of governance and institutional obstacles. It is certainly true that the calculations of this study represent potential effects under assumptions of a reasonable supply response to new opportunities. It might be possible to recalibrate the model by imposing lower supply elasticities, for example, for countries considered to have governance and institutional problems.

It is certainly true that global trade liberalization is no more a panacea for, especially, countries with chronic governance problems than any of the precursor candidates for solving the problem of economic development. In practice, however, the principal effect of any adjustments for these obstacles would likely be to reduce the projected reduction of poverty in sub-Saharan Africa and perhaps such countries as Pakistan. In sharp contrast, both China and India, which bulk large in the total poverty reduction estimates, have amply demonstrated the governance and institutional capacities to achieve high and sustained growth. In particular, if the central total estimates of poverty reduction in table 5.3 are cut in half for all of sub-Saharan Africa and Pakistan, and cut by one-third for Indonesia and Bangladesh, the effect is to reduce the global estimate for long-run poverty reduction from 540 million to 455 million. This leaves the qualitative conclusion of a major impact unchanged.

## Transmission Mechanisms

A reasonable question concerns identifying the mechanisms by which open trade stimulates growth. Even if the statistical results linking productivity growth to trade (table 5.1) are accepted, it may fairly be asked what are the mechanisms underlying the relationship, so that there can be greater confidence in the conclusion that they might apply going forward for developing countries and hence be relied upon as a basis for estimating the poverty effects of global trade liberalization.

More than two centuries ago, Adam Smith set forth two of the key mechanisms: gains in efficiency from specialization and economies of scale. Few would doubt that the traditional static specialization gains remain valid, including for developing countries. Most developing countries will obtain wide-bodied aircraft more cheaply by importing them from Boeing or Airbus with earnings from exports of agricultural goods or labor-intensive manufactures than by attempting to build them domestically. Most developing countries, moreover, are even more acutely dependent on the world market for economies of scale than are the larger industrial countries. Costa Rica has large exports of computer chips from its Intel plant, but it would not have the scale to produce chips efficiently if it did not have access to the external market.

Similarly, the antimonopoly mechanism for a beneficial impact of open trade is likely to be even more important for developing countries than for industrial countries, again because the domestic market will tend to be smaller and hence more susceptible to monopolization. As for the concern about a conflict between static and dynamic comparative advantage (the infant-industry argument), and in particular concern about developing countries' being locked into monoculture—excessive dependence on a handful of traditional tropical or mineral exports—it is perhaps instructive to recall examples such as that of Chile, which moved from high protection in the 1950s and 1960s to open trade by the late 1970s yet did not remain condemned to a monoculture. Copper as a share of exports fell from 52 percent in 1980 to 44 percent by 1990 and 30 percent in 2000

(UNCTAD 2003, 116), while new product lines such as grapes and other fruits and vegetables became major sources of export growth.

Thinking about the mechanisms relating trade to growth is especially important for interpreting the dynamic productivity effects emphasized in this chapter. It might be asked, how can contact with the world market enhance total factor productivity in an agricultural product such as cotton (West Africa) or soybeans (Brazil)? It should be kept in mind that agriculture is a sector in which technical change has been extremely important, as shown by the Green Revolution in Asia based on new seed varieties and improved practices. Today's version of this same point concerns the spread of genetically modified crops in countries such as Brazil. It is far more likely that such advances will be made by countries in close contact with global markets than by countries isolated from them.

The productivity-impact point applies more broadly. One of the more robust stylized facts about trade and growth is summed up by Paul Krugman as follows:

> The raw fact is that every successful example of economic development this past century—every case of a poor nation that worked its way up to a more or less decent, or at least dramatically better, standard of living—has taken place via globalization; that is, by producing for the world market rather than trying for self-sufficiency. (Krugman 2003, 368)

Grossman and Helpman (1994, 40) spell out several ways in which integration with the world economy can help boost productivity growth:

> First, residents of a country that is integrated into world markets are likely to enjoy access to a larger technical knowledge base than those living in relative isolation. Trade itself may help the process of technological dissemination, if foreign exporters suggest ways that their wares can be used more productively or foreign importers indicate how local products can be made more attractive to consumers in their country. . . . Second, exposure to international competition may mitigate redundancy in industrial research. Whereas a firm that develops a product for a protected domestic market need only make use of technologies that are new to the local economy, one that hopes to compete in the international market-place will be forced to generate ideas that are truly innovative on a global scale. . . . [Third,] by expanding the size of the potential customer base, international integration may bolster incentives for industrial research.[29]

---

29. Note that Grossman and Helpman (1991) are sometimes misinterpreted as showing that protection can be beneficial to a country that otherwise would specialize in labor- and natural-resource-intensive sectors at the expense of human-capital-intensive sectors with high research and development. Given the role of research and development (R&D) in their model, this can indeed lead to slower long-run growth. But they emphasize that "output growth rates do not measure economic welfare." Instead, "a country that lacks the size and technological experience to support a world class R&D effort, or one that has the endowments appropriate to activities like agriculture and mining, typically will gain from specializing in the production of goods that do not require the latest technologies . . . [thereby being] better off trading . . . for manufactured goods than it would if it tried to develop the latest high-technology goods itself" (Grossman and Helpman 1994, 41).

Overall, there is no evident reason why the transmission mechanisms from more open trade to the dynamic gain of factor productivity growth should be any less applicable to developing countries than to industrial countries. Certainly for the two countries with the largest poverty populations in the world, China and India, the experience of the past two decades has been resoundingly consistent with the diagnosis that opening to the world economy fosters more rapid productivity growth.

## Underestimation from the Exclusion of Services

Finally, those who are concerned that the central estimates of this study may overstate the potential for reduction in global poverty through free trade should take comfort in the fact that the estimates exclude the liberalization of trade in services. As noted in chapter 3, the World Bank (2002a) has estimated that removing global protection in services trade would generate welfare gains for developing countries that are more than four times as large as the gains from removing protection in merchandise trade. For the reasons set forth in chapter 3, I suspect that such estimates are exaggerated. Nonetheless, they strongly suggest that significant additional gains, and hence additional poverty reduction, are possible if trade is liberalized in services as well as goods.

# 6

# Conclusion

This study has examined the potential for global trade liberalization to contribute to the reduction of world poverty. This chapter first recapitulates the principal findings and then considers the implications for multilateral trade negotiations in the Doha Round.

## Principal Findings

The findings of this study are of two types. First, in chapters 1 through 3, empirical profiles are drawn of the location and tendencies of global poverty, the past experience of regimes for preferential market access, and the extent of remaining industrial-country protection against imports from developing countries. Second, in chapters 4 and 5, simulation experiments are conducted using a computable general equilibrium (CGE) model to evaluate the potential for future trade liberalization to reduce global poverty. Overall, the results suggest that this potential is large. Throughout, the existing literature is critically surveyed to provide a base on which the new diagnoses and estimates seek to build.

### Trends in Global Poverty

It is difficult to imagine surviving in the United States today on $2 per day, which amounts to only one-sixth of the income level for the official US poverty line. Yet half of the world's population lives at this level of real income or below, even after taking account of the lower cost of living in developing countries.[1] Half of these in turn have incomes of only $1 per day or less. One-fourth of the world's population thus lives on less than one-tenth of what would be considered the minimum acceptable in the United States and other rich countries.

Much of public discourse and a considerable body of expert literature lament, moreover, that globally the rich are getting richer while the poor are getting poorer, and that there is a "divergence" instead of "convergence" of income levels in rich and poor countries. Fortunately this perception is inaccurate with respect to populations, as opposed to "countries." In the past four decades, the per capita income of countries that accounted for the world's poorest 60 percent in 1960 *doubled* relative to the per capita income of countries that accounted for the world's richest 20 percent at that time (appendix 1C). Countries that started out in the poor group but have grown more rapidly than the rich countries include China and South Korea (about 6 percent annual per capita growth vs. 2.2 percent for rich countries); Thailand and Pakistan (about 4½ percent); Indonesia and Egypt (3 percent); and, although just barely, India and Sri Lanka (2½ percent).

The frequent contrary diagnosis that there has been an income divergence is an optical illusion based on the statistical treatment of each country as equally important regardless of its population size. Growth records have indeed been dismal in a sizable number of smaller countries, especially in sub-Saharan Africa (SSA). This means, however, that there is a hard core of countries that have experienced prolonged stagnation or decline, even though most of the world's poor live in countries that have been growing faster than industrial countries.

This diagnosis fits well with the two-track strategy for global trade policy developed in this study: immediately intensified special-access regimes for the at-risk countries, coupled with the phase-in of general liberalization of markets for goods from the other developing countries. Using the designation as heavily indebted poor country (HIPC), least developed country (LDC), or location in sub-Saharan Africa as the definition, at-risk countries account for 1 billion people (one-sixth of global population) and 715 million living in poverty at the $2 threshold (one-fourth of the global poor). These countries account for only 6.9 percent of total US, EU, and Japanese imports from all developing countries, so it should be feasible to intensify their special market access with minimal adjustment cost in industrial countries and minimal trade diversion from other developing countries.

The two-track strategy tends to be reinforced by the concept of the "poverty intensity of trade," which was developed in chapter 1. In this

---

1. The threshold is in purchasing power parity dollars. At market exchange rates, this threshold would be considerably less than $2 per day.

measure, imports from trading partners are weighted by the poverty incidence in the country in question. Imports from a country where everyone is poor would have a poverty intensity of 100 percent; imports from a rich country with no poverty, zero percent. The weighting can be by headcount poverty incidence or by share of the poor in national income.

It turns out that US imports from all developing countries have a weighted poverty intensity of 38 percent on the headcount basis and 8 percent on the income-share basis. The measures are approximately the same for Canada and Japan, though slightly lower for the European Union (26 and 7 percent, respectively). When the poverty intensity is calculated for imports from the at-risk countries, however, the result is much higher. For the United States, the poverty intensity of imports from least developed countries, highly indebted poor countries, and sub-Saharan Africa is an average of 68 percent on the headcount basis and 46 percent on the income-share basis, far higher than for US imports from all developing countries.

If we assume that the benefits conveyed by trade are roughly proportional to existing shares in income, these estimates suggest that whereas less than one-tenth of benefits of US trade with developing countries overall will tend to reach the poor, almost half of such benefits will reach the poor in the at-risk countries. This way of looking at the question leads quickly to the view that deepening the existing special access arrangements for these countries may be one important way in which trade policy can be used as an instrument to address global poverty.

The poverty-intensity concept can also be applied by sector rather than by country. In this case, the shares of imports for each sector coming from each developing country are weighted by that country's poverty incidence. For US imports in 2001, the resulting poverty intensity weighted by the income share of the poor is the highest for pearls and precious stones (21 percent), followed by petroleum and cocoa (both 17 percent), textiles and apparel (both 12 percent), and footwear and toys (both 10 percent). When the measurement is made on the basis of principal developing-country exports to the world (rather than just the US market), the poverty intensities are about the same, and additional detail shows a high poverty intensity of cotton textile fibers (23 percent) and jute textile fibers (36 percent).

This way of looking at the issue sheds additional light on the priorities for market access if poverty reduction is a goal. For example, some agricultural goods turn out to have a lower poverty intensity (wheat, at about 2 percent, maize at 6 percent, and sugar at 7 percent) than others (rice at 13 percent, coffee at 15 percent, in addition to even higher rates for cocoa, cotton, and jute). For example, the high poverty intensity of cotton exports is consistent with the surprisingly high profile of this product at the World Trade Organization's (WTO's) ministerial negotiations in Cancún in September 2003.

Returning to the broader profile of global poverty, the country concentration of the global poor means that the prospects for poverty alleviation will depend critically on the growth performance in a handful of large countries. India accounts for about 860 million poor people at the $2 level and China for about 670 million, using the official figures. A simple statistical regression based on real per capita income and income concentration (appendix 1A) suggests that by international patterns the expected number of poor people would only be about 485 million in each country.[2] Even at the lower numbers, however, India and China alone would account for two-fifths of the world's poor. So continuation of growth near the rapid rates experienced by both countries in the past decade (9.2 percent annually per capita in the period 1990–2000 for China, 4.2 percent for India [World Bank 2002d]) would make a major contribution toward reducing global poverty.

Four other countries also account for poverty populations of 100 million or more each: Bangladesh, Indonesia, Nigeria, and Pakistan. Another 25 countries have poverty populations of at least 10 million each, either because they are high-population countries with intermediate poverty rates (e.g., Brazil, Mexico, and Russia) or intermediate-population countries with high poverty rates (e.g., Nepal and Uganda).

The fundamental source of poverty reduction is economic growth. The World Bank (2001) estimates that on average, international experience suggests that the "poverty elasticity" of growth is about 2. That is, a rise in per capita income by 1 percent reduces the number of people in poverty by about 2 percent. Appendix 1B shows that in a prominent mathematical function used to describe income distribution (the lognormal distribution), there is a positive relationship of the poverty elasticity to the ratio of average per capita income to the poverty threshold income; and a negative relationship to the degree of concentration of income. As a result, the expected poverty elasticity can be in the range of 3 or higher for a country with an intermediate per capita income (e.g., $3,000) and intermediate income concentration (e.g., a Gini coefficient of 0.45). Conversely, it will tend to be lower at about 1 to 1.5 for a country with either a low per capita income (e.g., $900) or a high degree of income concentration (e.g., a Gini of 0.6).

There is a paradox, however, between the slow pace of measured global poverty reduction in recent years and the faster reduction that might have been expected in applying poverty elasticity to per capita income growth.[3]

---

2. This calculation is consistent with the view that in India especially, the usual measure overstates the incidence of poverty (Bhalla 2002).

3. In addition to this paradox over time, there is a "cross-section" paradox. For countries with a per capita income above about $1,000, the incidence of poverty that would be predicted using the lognormal distribution is much lower than the poverty actually observed (except for countries with very high income inequality). This suggests that as per capita income rises, poverty is more persistent than this standard distributional form would anticipate.

At a $1 per day threshold, the World Bank (2001) estimates that global poverty fell from 28.3 percent in 1987 to 24 percent in 1998. Yet the real per capita income of developing countries rose at an average 2 percent in this period, and applying a poverty elasticity of 2, global poverty should have fallen from 28.4 to 18.4 percent.

Bhalla (2002) has argued that the paradox is explained by bad data. He uses national accounts data to correct the estimates of average income from sample surveys, and he applies the distribution from the surveys. His result is a much more rapid reduction in global poverty than usually measured. Although it is true that there seems to be a general pattern of a falling ratio of sample income averages to national accounts average incomes, a plausible alternative interpretation is that underreporting of income is mainly in the higher income brackets, so it will be misleading to apply the sample distribution of income. If so, the pace of poverty reduction is likely slower than suggested by Bhalla, although probably faster than recorded in the World Bank estimates.

Part of the explanation of the paradox seems to be that in the 1990s within-country income distributions started to become more concentrated, in contrast to previous long periods of little if any change (Cornia and Kiiski 2001). New tests in chapter 1 tend to confirm a shift from no trend in the first three decades after 1950 to a trend toward increased concentration in the period 1980–2000, and this shift is especially pronounced if country observations are weighted by population. Large countries with rising concentrations in the past decade include Brazil, China, Indonesia, Mexico, and Nigeria (figure 1.1).

Even after taking account of the qualifications (differing poverty elasticities, muted effects because of rising income concentration), growth remains central to the reduction of poverty. The role of trade in reducing poverty then turns primarily on the role of trade in achieving sustained economic growth. There is a clear positive relationship between the growth of exports and the growth rate achieved in the overall economy (figure 1.3), and a simple regression shows a highly significant coefficient of 0.15 (each additional percentage point of export growth is associated with 0.15 percent additional GDP growth). Even acknowledging the question of the direction of causality, the strong suggestion is that global trade liberalization can help spur growth in developing countries and hence poverty reduction by boosting exports. It is within this broad framework that the more specific analyses of chapters 2 through 5 are set.

## Preferential Regimes

Chapter 2 reviews international experience with preferential market access for developing countries. It broadly finds that whereas the Generalized System of Preferences (GSP) has had meager results, the deeper special-access regimes oriented toward low-income countries have tended to achieve more significant results. The GSP systems differ in approach. The United States treats countries and/or sectors as either eligible or ineligible for zero-duty access, whereas the European Union uses graduated margins of preference that are deeper for poorer countries. In both cases, the overall effect is to provide relatively limited preferential benefits under the GSP.

There is a gauntlet of hurdles that must be run to obtain meaningful tariff relief through the GSP in most programs. The first is country eligibility. GSP-eligible economies account for only one-fourth of US imports from all developing countries, primarily because China, Hong Kong, Singapore, and Taiwan are not eligible and Mexico has access through the North American Free Trade Agreement (NAFTA). For the European Union, eligible countries account for only two-thirds of imports from developing countries. The second hurdle is whether the product is dutiable on a most-favored-nation (MFN) basis (the preference is meaningless for zero-duty items). The third is product eligibility. The US system in particular removes the product from eligibility for a country that has passed certain competitiveness thresholds (e.g., a $100 million ceiling), and moreover tends to exclude sensitive product categories, leaving less than 40 percent of dutiable goods from GSP-eligible countries qualified for GSP treatment. Even among qualified products from qualified countries, such factors as the uncertainty associated with periodic GSP expirations have narrowed GSP use below the total potential.

The resulting value of imports granted GSP benefits in 1997 was only 15 percent of total imports from developing countries for the European Union, only 3.6 percent for the United States, and only 9 percent for Japan (table 2.1). Revenue forgone amounted to 2.5 percent of the value of GSP-benefited imports for the European Union, 1.6 percent for the United States, and 2.1 percent for Japan. These savings on tariffs were a near-vanishing 0.4 percent of the value of total imports from developing countries for the European Union, 0.06 percent for the United States, and 0.2 percent for Japan. For the small base of ultimately eligible and preference-using goods, there was a nontrivial cut in the average tariff applicable in the European Union from 6 to 3.4 percent, and only 0.2 percent for the least developed countries. The cuts were smaller for the United States and Japan, especially for LDC suppliers.

In contrast to the broad GSP systems, the special programs instituted in favor of developing countries with special cultural ties, or for geopolitical or antidrug purposes or, more recently, for the poorest countries, have tended to have greater potential impact. These include the EU's Lomé, Cotonou, and Everything But Arms (EBA) initiatives, and the US Caribbean Basin Initiative (CBI), Andean Trade Preference Act (ATPA), and African Growth and Opportunity Act (AGOA) arrangements.

Studies of the effects of these more intense special-access regimes have arrived at mixed conclusions. Grilli (1994) judged that the Lomé Convention begun in 1975 had shown minimal impact. He noted that the share of Lomé countries in EU trade had fallen by half rather than rising, and that potential gains were limited because the majority of trade was already duty free and rules of origin constrained effective use. In contrast, Nilsson (2002), using a gravity model, calculated that Lomé country exports to the European Union by 1992 were about 40 percent higher than their baseline would have indicated without the preferential arrangement. As for EBA, Bora, Cernat, and Turrini (2002) use a CGE model to estimate sizable LDC gains (about $400 million annually) that come however at the expense of the European Union (from terms-of-trade loss) and non-LDC developing countries. Page and Hewitt (2002) worry about EBA trade diversion from such non-LDC countries as India and Kenya.

The Caribbean Basin Initiative has been associated with accelerated export growth (nonoil exports from the region rose more than fourfold from 1984 to 2000) and a strong rise in foreign direct investment (from 1 to 5 percent of GDP for Caribbean countries, and from 0.8 to 1.7 percent for Central America). Production-sharing agreements have had a strong impact on both growth and investment (USITC 2001). In the Andean Trade Preference Act, there has been rapid export growth in benefiting products such as flowers and tuna, and a gravity model estimated by Hufbauer and Kotschwar (1998) shows strong positive export effects from the arrangement.

Evaluating the impact of these special regimes is difficult, in part because these at-risk countries tend to have lower export and growth performance than developing countries on average for numerous reasons having to do with income levels, governance, and economic policies. Relatively weak performance can then give the misleading impression that the special-access arrangement provides little help. In an attempt to control for some of these influences, chapter 2 includes a regression analysis relating real export growth rates to a series of economic variables as well as the special-regime variable. The estimate finds that after removing the influences of growth in the world market, lagged income growth, lagged level of per capita income, share of manufactures in exports, lagged real exchange rate, and a regional adverse effect for sub-Saharan Africa, there were relatively strong positive export effects from the special regimes. The Lomé arrangement boosted export growth by about 9 percent above rates otherwise expected, and the Caribbean Basin Initiative about 7 percent. Although the size and significance of these effects falls if the highest and lowest 1 percent of observations are removed, the results are nonetheless suggestive of a substantial positive impact.

As for the African Growth and Opportunity Act, there are also early signs of impact. US imports of textiles and apparel from AGOA rose about 80 percent from 1999 to 2002, and vehicles and parts imports rose 370 percent. Overall nonoil imports rose 25 percent from 1998–99 to 2001–02. In 2001, 43 percent of US imports from AGOA-beneficiary countries received AGOA duty-free treatment. Another 29 percent entered duty free in zero-MFN-tariff categories, and a further 3 percent entered free under the GSP. Altogether, three-fourths of imports from these countries entered duty free.

AGOA nonetheless provides a good illustration of how there remains considerable deepening that can be done in the special-access regimes. Duty-free treatment could be extended to all goods currently not covered. To improve certainty, AGOA eligibility could be shifted from annual to 5-year review; AGOA's life span could be extended from 2008 to 2013 and made automatically renewable for 10 years in the absence of new legislation to the contrary. The 2004 expiration date for duty-free access for apparel made in the 30 poorer countries from non-US fabric could similarly be extended until 2013. The African Growth and Opportunity Act (and the other special-access regimes) could achieve investment and trade synergy by being granted a 10-year home-country tax holiday on earnings from direct investment, and access to political risk insurance could be expanded (through the Overseas Private Investment Corporation in the case of the United States).

In short, there is some evidence that although the wider GSP regimes have had minimal influence, the deeper special-access regimes have had a greater impact. Moreover, there are dimensions in which these regimes could be substantially enhanced. There is thus meaningful room for action on this track of international trade policy oriented toward reducing poverty: the deepening of special-access regimes for at-risk countries. Such action could be helpful, as discussed below, to provide a carrot to these countries that can allay their fears that multilateral liberalization will adversely affect them by eroding the size of their preferences. Without such reassurance, many of them could be tempted to seek to block broader progress in the Doha Round.

## Industrial-Country Protection

Successive rounds of postwar multilateral trade negotiations have reduced tariffs in industrial countries to relatively low levels for most manufactures and nonagricultural raw materials. However, tariffs in agriculture remain high (including especially the ad valorem equivalent of specific tariffs as well as the influence of above-quota tariff-rate quota tariffs). Tariffs are also relatively high in textiles and apparel. As a result, considerable scope remains for increased export opportunities for developing countries through the further liberalization of industrial-country markets.

The profile of tariff protection is surprisingly similar for industrial and developing countries. Both groups apply the highest protection to agricultural goods. Using tariff data compiled in the Global Trade Analysis Project (GTAP) database, and weighting product sectors by their shares in global output, agricultural tariffs range from a low of 4 to 6 percent in Australia and New Zealand to highs of 119 percent in Switzerland and 154 percent in Norway, among industrial countries. Weighting by GDP and trade turnover, the average agricultural tariff for industrial countries stands at 36 percent. The corresponding average for developing countries is not much lower, at 30 percent (table 4.4).

Similarly, textiles and apparel bear the highest protection among manufactures in both areas. For industrial countries, the average tariff is about 12 percent; for developing countries, 18 percent. In contrast, all other manufactures tend to have low tariffs in industrial countries, averaging 3 percent. Other manufactures still face relatively high tariffs in developing countries, however, at a weighted average of about 12 percent. Finally, both groups of countries grant practically duty-free entry to oil and other nonagricultural raw materials.

The high tariffs in agriculture in several industrial countries are in addition to the protective effect of subsidies. Chapter 3 develops a method for converting subsidies into a tariff equivalent that has the same effect in suppressing imports. It turns out that US and EU agricultural subsidies are both about equivalent to a 10 percent tariff in terms of dislocating demand away from imports. The size of the subsidies is higher in the European Union, but this is offset by the fact that there is a larger base of imports in the European Union so the proportional tariff equivalent effect of discouraging imports ends up being about the same as that in the United States.

The combined effect of tariffs and subsidies in agriculture is an overall tariff equivalent of about 20 percent in the United States, 46 percent in the European Union, 52 percent in Canada, and 82 percent in Japan (table 3.9). There is an important message in the composition of these estimates. For the European Union and Japan, the bulk of agricultural protection stems from tariffs and tariff-rate quotas, not from subsidies. In particular, the tariff component of EU protection is a tariff equivalent of about 33 percent, while the subsidy component is a tariff equivalent of only 10 percent. The composition is even more skewed for Japan, where tariffs amount to a tariff equivalent of 76 percent and subsidies only 3 percent.[4] This is an important finding, because it suggests that much of the rhetoric in the international debate has overemphasized agricultural subsidies and given insufficient attention to reducing agricultural tariffs and tariff-rate quotas.

In particular, the widely quoted figure of about $300 billion or more in agricultural "subsidies" in industrial countries is a misnomer. This estimate is the Organization for Economic Cooperation and Development's (OECD's) Total Support Estimate, which includes the effect not only of

---

4. Note that the combined effect of the tariff and the subsidy tariff equivalent equals their chained effect, which is significantly more than their simple sum.

**Table 6.1  Aggregate Measure of Protection (AMP) against developing countries** (percent tariff equivalent)

| Sector | United States | European Union | Japan |
|---|---|---|---|
| Agriculture | 19.9 | 46.4 | 82.1 |
| Textiles, apparel | 10.9 | 11.6 | 9.2 |
| Other manufactures | 2.1 | 3.2 | 1.5 |
| Oil, other | 0.9 | 0.6 | 0.3 |
| All (AMP) | 4.0 | 9.5 | 15.6 |

*Source:* Table 3.10.

both subsidies and tariffs but also of indirect services such as agricultural research. Even for the narrower Producer Support Estimate, amounting to $235 billion annually, subsidies make up only about a third of the total. The greater weight of tariffs somehow seems to have been lost in the Doha negotiations as well as in most international calls for agricultural liberalization, which instead treat the $300 billion figure loosely as if it were all subsidies appropriated by OECD legislatures (which, by implication in some pronouncements, could be spent on development assistance instead). The danger in this misperception is that developing countries will use up too much of their Doha Round negotiating capital calling for the elimination of industrial-country subsidies in agriculture rather than allocating more of it to the more important reduction of industrial countries' agricultural tariffs and increased in-quota market access to products with tariff-rate quotas.

When agricultural protection is averaged with protection in other sectors (including the tariff equivalent of quotas in textiles and apparel), weighting by "adjusted" imports from developing countries (using a measure that compensates for the possible bias toward low imports in products with high protection), the resulting Aggregate Measure of Protection (AMP) against developing countries amounts to a total tariff equivalent of 4 percent in the United States, 10 percent in the European Union, 16 percent in Japan, and 11 percent in Canada (table 6.1). This protection remains substantial, and the AMP gauge suggests that considerable scope remains for increased developing-country exports to industrial countries as a consequence of removing protection in industrial countries.

These protection measures are for MFN tariffs, and it is often argued that for the European Union, the incorporation of preferences for low-income countries substantially reduces the overall protection level against developing countries. This is not a convincing argument, because total EU imports from all at-risk countries in the HIPC, LDC, and SSA groupings amount to only 8.5 percent of EU imports from all developing countries (chapter 2). So even if all of these countries enjoyed free entry (and not all of them are Lomé countries, nor are all products eligible for free Lomé entry), the effect would be to reduce the average protection rate by only about one-twelfth (e.g., from about 10 to 9 percent). Lomé and EBA imports are simply too small, compared with total EU imports from developing countries, to make a meaningful difference in the aggregate measure of EU protection against developing countries.

The telescoping of all protection into a single number for each of the four broad sectors, and further consolidation into a single overall number, helps sharpen an understanding of why agricultural liberalization features so heavily in the Doha Round trade negotiations as an objective of developing countries. Industrial countries' protection in agriculture is far higher than in the other sectors (including textiles and apparel). A Doha agreement that carves out agriculture would remove from the table the sector with the highest protection against developing countries, in a product sector in which most developing countries tend to have a comparative advantage.

Within manufactures, there has been considerable concern about the impact of tariff peaks on developing-country exports. An analysis of tariff peaks in chapter 3 finds, however, that only 2.1 percent of tariff categories for manufactures have tariffs of 15 percent or higher in the United States, only 0.5 percent in the European Union, and only 0.9 percent in Japan. This suggests that removal of protection in tariff peaks at the usual threshold of 15 percent may also have limited potential. The scope for liberalization is greater if the threshold considered is 10 percent, because an additional bloc of about 6 percent of categories is in this bracket for the United States, about 7 percent for the European Union, and about 3 percent in Japan. A back-of-the-envelope calculation suggests, moreover, that about one half of total developing-country export gains to be expected from complete elimination of industrial-country tariffs on manufactures could be achieved solely through the elimination of tariffs of 10 percent and higher. This suggests considerable utility to setting a ceiling of 10 percent for all manufacturing tariffs in industrial-countries by an early date, as an important step toward free trade.

Because of the high protection in industrial-country agriculture, and because of special questions about the poverty impact of agricultural liberalization given the high share of food in low-income budgets, appendix 3C develops a simple model of the impact of completely liberalizing agriculture on global poverty. There are two basic influences in this calculation. The first is that free trade in agriculture would tend to boost world prices of agricultural goods. The reason is that removing industrial-country protection would boost demand from developing-country suppliers, and removing subsidies would reduce the amount produced in industrial countries. With greater demand and less supply, world agricultural prices would rise.

The second key influence is whether the global poor tend primarily to be producers or consumers of food. Here the critical condition for higher world agricultural prices to reduce rather than increase global poverty is essentially that the share of the global poor located in the rural sector exceeds the share of food in the consumption basket of the poor. Because about three-fourths of the world's poor are in the rural sector while a plausible estimate for food share in consumption is only about 40 to 50 percent, on balance agricultural liberalization should be expected to reduce global poverty. On the basis of existing estimates that agricultural free trade would boost world agricultural prices by about 10 percent, chapter 3 estimates that about 200 million people would be lifted out of poverty globally as a consequence of removing protection from agriculture. There would be some increase in urban poverty, but this would be far outweighed by decreases in the number of rural poor people.

There have been concerns, nonetheless, that numerous poor countries in particular are net food importers, and that they would suffer an adverse effect from higher global food prices as a result of agricultural free trade globally. Chapter 3 uses the GTAP country data to examine this question and finds that at this level of aggregation, the food deficit problem should not be severe. It turns out that key countries with large poverty populations are net food exporters rather than importers, including China, India, Indonesia, and sub-Saharan Africa as a group (with the notable exception of Botswana). Although Bangladesh and Pakistan are net food importers, their imports are relatively small (about $6 per capita annually). The principal cases of large net food imports are for the Middle East and North Africa.

There is nonetheless concern that the least developed countries in particular tend to be net food importers. For these countries, however, there is a conceptual problem in simply looking at the food trade balance. Because these countries tend to receive large foreign assistance relative to GDP, they tend to be large net importers of everything, not just food. Consider, however, whether they will be made better off or worse off by higher food prices as a consequence of global trade liberalization. The main point to recognize is that there will be reductions in prices of other goods that can more than offset increases in food prices. Otherwise global free trade would reduce global welfare rather than increase it. If the typical LDC has a comparative advantage in agriculture and food rather than in manufactures, then the terms-of-trade gains it enjoys from lower prices of manufactured imports should more than offset the higher prices it pays for food imports after global liberalization.

It turns out that most of the least developed countries do indeed have a comparative advantage in food and agriculture, even though almost all of them have food trade deficits and a majority have agricultural trade deficits (table 3A.4). The ratios of their exports to imports for food and agriculture are typically higher than the ratios of their exports of nonfood products (or nonagricultural products) to imports of nonfood products (nonagricultural products). By this test, fewer than half of least developed countries have a comparative disadvantage in food, accounting for only 44 percent of the poor in least developed countries if Bangladesh is included and only 29 percent if it is excluded.[5] The least developed countries as a group should thus favor global agricultural liberalization, even though special aid or other measures may be appropriate for the minority that do have a comparative disadvantage in food.

## CGE Estimates of Trade Liberalization Effects

Chapter 4 develops the Poverty Effects version of the Harrison-Rutherford-Tarr model, or PEHRT model, and applies it to estimate the impact of trade liberalization on trade, real incomes or "welfare," and global poverty. The underlying model (Harrison, Rutherford, and Tarr 1996, 1997a) is one of the leading computable general equilibrium models for analyzing trade. It is applied in this study to the GTAP5 trade and tariff database for 1997–98. The PEHRT version chooses the country aggregation to give special emphasis to countries relevant for global poverty.

The CGE approach takes into account both the direct and indirect effects of trade liberalization. In contrast to the simplest traditional "partial equilibrium" model—which calculates trade welfare gains as the rise in domestic "consumer surplus" net of loss of domestic "producer surplus" and government tariff revenue when imports are liberalized—the general equilibrium approach also calculates changes in terms of trade and hence benefits accruing from improved markets on the export side. It also calculates changes in factor prices and enforces consistency in such areas as unchanged trade and fiscal balances. The changes in factor prices are of special relevance in examining the impact on poverty, because the factor price estimates for unskilled labor provide a close approximation to incomes of poor households.

The structure of the HRT model involves limited substitutability between factors in production, between alternative foreign products in demand for imports, and between imports as a group and the home variety of the product in question.[6] The basic strategy of the trade liberalization experiments is to shock the model by changing (or eliminating) tariffs and export subsidies (as in agriculture) or taxes (as in textiles), and then to allow the model to identify the new "equilibrium" levels of production, imports, exports, and factor allocation in each sector and country. There will be a corresponding new total level of "welfare" (roughly synonymous with real income), which will be higher than in the original pro-

---

5. The corresponding figures for agriculture are 48 and 34 percent, respectively.

6. A tiered nesting of constant elasticity of substitution functions is used for this purpose. On the export side, there is a corresponding constant elasticity of transformation specification relating domestic production to exports.

tected equilibrium because of the increased efficiency in resource allocation made possible by removing distortions from protection. The additional feature of the PEHRT model is the application of the relevant factor price changes to the base levels of poverty and the "poverty elasticity" of each country to arrive at an implied change in poverty resulting from the trade policy shock.

The trade and welfare results of the simulations are of interest in their own right. In the basic "static" version of the model, complete elimination of protection would raise global welfare by about $230 billion annually, of which developing countries would obtain $87 billion, or 1.35 percent of their GDP. Tests decomposing the sectoral contribution of these gains confirm that agricultural liberalization is the most important, accounting for 58 percent of gains for industrial countries and 50 percent of gains for developing countries. This is consistent with the analysis identifying agriculture as the most highly protected sector, and it is a testimony to the importance of this protection considering that the trade base of agriculture is considerably smaller. In the GTAP5 database, agriculture accounts for only 9.4 percent of world merchandise trade (Dimaranan and McDougall 2002, 3-4).

In essence, the ratio of protection in agriculture to that in all other sectors is about 10 to 1 or even higher, whereas the ratio of trade in agriculture to trade in all other goods is about 1 to 10, so agriculture and nonagriculture wind up being about equally important as sources for gains from global free trade.[7] The sectoral share of textiles and apparel in welfare gains is also disproportionately large as a consequence of relatively high protection. The two products account for 11 percent of global gains, even though they represent only 6.6 percent of global trade.

The basic free trade simulation finds that all developing countries except Mexico experience positive welfare gains.[8] Mexico's loss is under-

---

7. It can be estimated from table 3.10 that average protection for all goods excluding agriculture is 3.3 percent for the United States, 4.0 percent for the European Union, and 2.0 percent for Japan. The corresponding ratios of the level of protection in agriculture to those in nonagricultural sectors are 6.0, 11.6, and 41.1, respectively. Note, however, that these are protection levels facing developing countries, which tend to be somewhat higher than those facing industrial-country trading partners. Note further that in a traditional partial equilibrium framework, the estimated share of agriculture in welfare gains would tend to be even higher, because in that framework the welfare gain rises with the square of the tariff. In contrast, the CGE models tend to show much closer to linear welfare effects, presumably because of terms-of-trade gains on the export side.

8. Malaysia, however, has a zero net welfare effect. Note that the general pattern of positive gains differs from the estimates for Uruguay Round effects in Harrison, Rutherford, and Tarr (1996). They found losses in sub-Saharan Africa, the Middle East and North Africa, Eastern Europe, and Hong Kong. They attributed the results to losses in terms of trade for food importers with reduction of industrial-country farm subsidies, and to losses of quota rents for textile and apparel exporters. In the subsequent GTAP5 database, however, the estimate of textile quota rents is much lower. The elimination of all protection in the free trade simulation here, moreover, provides larger welfare gains than the much more limited Uruguay Round cuts.

standable, because 82.5 percent of its trade turnover is with its free trade NAFTA partners, Canada and the United States, and global trade liberalization would mainly have the effect of eroding Mexico's preferential access to these markets (IMF 2002a). Because the protection database does not capture the influence of other preferences, a special test is run to approximate the influence of preference erosion: US and EU protection is frozen against the seven relevant poor regions in an otherwise free trade simulation. Even though this test should overstate preference erosion because this trade is not fully protection free in the US and EU markets, the inclusion of the preference erosion effect reduces gains of the seven poor regions from global free trade but does not turn them into losses.[9]

In an alternative "asymmetric" liberalization scenario, only the industrial countries remove their protection. This case generates considerably lower global welfare gains ($125 billion). Annual welfare gains for the developing countries would also fall but would nonetheless still be relatively large, at $57 billion, or 65 percent of the potential if they also eliminated their protection. These results bring new evidence to what seems to be an emerging debate on the extent to which the developing countries are or are not primarily responsible themselves for the present losses from global protection.

In contrast, the World Bank (2002a) estimates that 59 percent of the free trade potential welfare gains would come from the developing countries' own liberalization. As noted in chapter 4, *The Economist* (October 6, 2003, 60) has emphasized that in a subsequent World Bank study applying more plausible protection cuts than total free trade, the developing countries' own liberalization of agriculture generates 80 percent of welfare gains in that sector. The magazine's message was that the developing countries had shot themselves in the foot at Cancún, because it was not industrial countries' agricultural protection that mattered but their own.

The PEHRT results contradict this view of the world, because the results of this study suggest that more than half of potential developing countries' gains from global free trade come from liberalizing industrial countries' markets rather than their own.[10] A recent CGE study by the

---

9. The test reduces free trade welfare gains for seven poor regions from $8.6 billion to $2.2 billion annually. Only Bangladesh experiences a loss (of about 0.4 percent of GDP), suggesting the need for special international assistance for Bangladesh to accompany global trade liberalization.

10. As discussed in chapter 4, this "source attribution" question is ambiguous. One obtains one number in an experiment in which only industrial countries liberalize, and another number in an experiment in which only developing countries liberalize. The two extremes are that developing countries' own liberalization (including for imports from each other) accounts for between 35 percent of the total global free trade potential (the asymmetric case in chapter 4) and 48 percent (a variant in which only developing countries liberalize). In the former case, the developing-country gains include "free rider" terms-of-trade gains; in the latter case, there are terms-of-trade losses because it is the industrial countries that are the free riders.

OECD finds an even more extreme result in the same direction (OECD 2003c). That study estimates that 79 percent of potential developing-country welfare gains from global free trade come from the elimination of protection in industrial countries.

These three different results reflect differences in the CGE models. A principal influence is the extent of "terms-of-trade" effects. Although the OECD model may overstate these effects significantly, the World Bank model may understate them somewhat. More important for the World Bank's results, its calculations refer to a world in 2015, when the relative size of the highly protected developing-country market for manufactures is much larger, and the relative size of the highly protected industrial-country market for agricultural goods is much smaller, than today. The World Bank estimates thus tend to understate the relative importance to developing countries of today's liberalization by industrial countries.

In short, the tests in this study reinforce the view that the developing countries' potential gains from global free trade stem heavily—at least one-half and perhaps two-thirds—from increased access to industrial-country markets, rather than primarily from liberalizing their own imports. These findings tend to suggest that the standoff at Cancún, in which a group of 21 developing countries essentially refused the industrial countries' proposal for agricultural liberalization as insufficient, was strategically sound rather than a blunder as diagnosed by *The Economist*. There was simply too much at stake in liberalizing their access to industrial-country markets for the developing countries to accept a minimalist outcome, even if it meant risking no outcome at all.[11]

The HRT model includes a version that seeks to capture the longer-term dynamic effects of trade liberalization in addition to the static effects. This is a traditional challenge in analysis of trade reform. Economists have well-established methods for estimating the "static" welfare effects of trade liberalization, but there is no corresponding consensus on how to estimate the dynamic effects, even though most economists would agree that the dynamic gains tend to be considerably more important than the static gains. Harrison, Rutherford, and Tarr (1996) propose the following approach for dynamic effects. In their CGE model, trade liberalization tends to boost the rate of return to investment, as new opportunities opened up by more open markets increase profitability and as the price of imported capital equipment tends to fall from reduced protection.[12] The

---

11. This line of analysis is further reinforced by a simulation in chapter 4, in which developing countries cut their protection by half except that they grant free entry to other developing countries' goods, while industrial countries eliminate all protection. This outcome is actually slightly better than total free trade for the developing countries, because there is some degree of "optimum tariff" implied for even smaller developing countries in a model structure in which each country has a specialized variety of the product.

12. Chapter 4 discusses the relationship of this pattern to the Heckscher-Ohlin and Stolper-Samuelson models.

static version of the model reallocates factors but leaves their total availability unchanged. The long-term Steady State version of the model instead allows the stock of capital to rise until the rate of return on investment is driven back down to the preliberalization level. This provides one gauge of the longer-term dynamic effects from liberalization.

In the Steady State version of the PEHRT model in chapter 4, potential welfare gains (after deducting the cost of additional capital) are considerably larger than in the static version, reaching $343 billion annually globally. The developing-country share in this total is larger than in the static case, amounting to $162 billion, or 2.5 percent of their combined GDP.

## Poverty Impact

The next step in arriving at poverty-impact estimates is to consider the changes in factor prices from trade liberalization. Global free trade is found to raise the median real wage for unskilled labor in developing countries by 5 percent. The most dramatic factor price changes are for land. The real price of land rises by more than 100 percent in Australia New Zealand and Canada, but it falls by 50 to 70 percent in industrial Europe and Japan. These results are consistent with a strong comparative advantage in agriculture for the main agricultural exporters, and they are vivid illustrations of why strong opposition to agricultural liberalization can be expected in Europe and Japan.

The sparse data available for factor shares of income received by poverty-level households suggest that unskilled labor represents about 90 percent, and that transfers account for the remaining 10 percent. The model results provide the estimate for each country for the change in the real unskilled wage, and the overall percent increase in welfare for the country is used to estimate the rise in transfers. On this basis, there is an estimate for each country of the percent rise in real income of poverty-level households. This change is applied to the poverty elasticity estimated for each country to arrive at the percent reduction expected in the number of households in poverty. Application of this percent change to the base number of total population in poverty provides an estimate of the number of people who would be lifted out of poverty by global free trade, for each of the countries or regions in the model.

When this method is applied to the static PEHRT model, the resulting estimate is that the number of poor people globally would fall by about 110 million, of which about 27 million would be in China and another 28 million in India, and 16 million in sub-Saharan Africa.[13] This estimate would appear to be on the low side, considering that the simple back-of-the-envelope model in chapter 3 arrives at an estimate of 200 million just

---

13. The estimates for China and India use the World Bank poverty estimates, not the potentially lower figures discussed above.

from agricultural liberalization. One possible explanation is that the simple agricultural model distinguishes between the rural and urban sectors, whereas the PEHRT model assumes a countrywide uniform impact on unskilled labor.

When the poverty-impact approach based on factor price increases is applied to the Steady State model, the result is a central estimate of 535 million for global poverty reduction. Although from some standpoints this may be an overestimate, as discussed in chapter 4, from others it is not, because it does not incorporate the dynamic total factor productivity gains from free trade.

The next step is to incorporate dynamic growth effects. Chapter 5 surveys the existing literature relating trade to growth. It first compiles the numerous statistical estimates showing that higher trade relative to GDP is associated with higher productivity. Economists since Adam Smith more than two centuries ago have generally considered that countries more integrated with the world economy are likely to achieve more rapid growth. The specific mechanisms include achieving economies of scale through specialization; stimulus to technological change as a consequence of the competitive prod of imports and from greater exposure to world-standard technologies; and higher production at more cost-efficient levels because of the breaking of domestic monopoly power through the influence of import competition. Numerous recent studies have used statistical methods that circumvent the problem of circular causation from trade to productivity and from productivity to trade, for example, by applying "gravity models" that first normalize by considering countries' geographical location relative to major markets.

The survey of these studies in chapter 5 arrives at the following overall relationship between trade and productivity (the trade-productivity elasticity): A 1 percent rise in the ratio of trade relative to GDP is associated with a 0.5 percent rise in GDP per capita over a period of one to two decades. For example, if exports plus imports were to rise from 50 percent of GDP to 55 percent (a 10 percent rise in the ratio), GDP would be expected to rise by 5 percent above the baseline over about 15 years.

Before applying this relationship, chapter 5 pauses to review the heated debate on the empirical relationship of trade policy to economic growth. Prominent studies finding a strong relationship between open trade policy and growth include Sachs and Warner (1995) and Edwards (1993, 1998). The most prominent critique of these and similar studies is that by Rodriguez and Rodrik (2000). The survey in chapter 5 suggests that the critique may have gone too far by discarding results through variations in specification that turn statistical findings less significant, whereas this approach may be biased toward rejecting most statistical results (Sala-i-Martin 1997). In any event, much of this particular debate turns on whether trade *policy* has accurately been measured and affects growth, whereas the broader set of statistical results states (less ambitiously) that trade *levels* affect productivity (even if higher trade is the result of the good fortune of being located next to a big market).

Chapter 5 then proceeds with the dynamic calculation by applying the rise in trade relative to GDP from free trade, as predicted by the static PEHRT model, to a conservative estimate of the trade-productivity elasticity of 0.4. This somewhat lower number is used to avoid intermixing pure overall (total factor) productivity gains with gains from increased investment, which may be responsible for part of the measured effects in some of the studies surveyed. The PEHRT results for free trade predict a specific increase in trade for each country in the model, which tends to be in the range of 5 percent (the estimate is 5 percent for China and 6 percent for India), although there is relatively wide variability. The percent increases in trade are then applied to the trade-productivity elasticity of 0.4 to estimate the long-term rise in productivity as the dynamic effect of free trade. Thus, in the representative case of a 5 percent trade increase, and applying the parameter of 0.4, over a horizon of some 15 years real GDP per capita could be expected to rise to a level 2 percent higher (5 percent × 0.4) than in the nonliberalization baseline. When this increase in income is applied to each country's poverty elasticity, and the resulting percent change is applied to the base level of poverty, there is a second, dynamic tranche of global poverty reduction that can be added to the initial static effect. This dynamic productivity effect amounts to 200 million people lifted out of poverty globally, over perhaps 15 years.

The final step in calculating the poverty impact of trade liberalization is to incorporate the second major component of dynamic effects: induced investment. The Steady State version of the PEHRT model provides benchmark estimates of the change in real factor prices when the capital stock is allowed to increase by enough to drive the postliberalization return to investment back down to the preliberalization level.

A relatively conservative incorporation of this effect is, first, to consider only the net welfare effects after deducting for the cost of additional capital, and second, to allow only one-half of the potential induced-investment impact to be included in the summary poverty estimates. The resulting increase in capital could be accomplished by an increment of only 1 percent of GDP in developing-country investment rates over a 15-year horizon (e.g., from 20 to 21 percent of GDP). This amount is plausible, especially considering that a substantial portion of the increased capital could come from capital inflows from industrial countries, in a world with well-functioning international capital markets.

As discussed in chapter 4, it can be asked whether this tranche of dynamic effects should be considered a legitimate part of trade liberalization benefits and impact on poverty. It might be argued that countries are already at their ideal equilibrium between investment and consumption, and that incorporating an increased-investment effect fails to address the costs of the resulting reduction in consumption. However, the same argument could be made against attributing any welfare gain or poverty reduction effects to a technological breakthrough (e.g., the invention of the steam locomotive), because a new wave of technology also requires induced investment. The point is that, like a technological innovation, a move to global free trade provides a favorable shock to the previous investment-consumption equilibrium that increases the desired amount of investment. As long as the opportunity cost of the new investment is taken into account (and the 7 percent real interest rate used in chapter 4 is an ample allowance for this), it is surely appropriate to include the poverty reduction effects of major investment changes induced by trade policy changes. Even so, to be on the conservative side, only one-half of the incremental poverty reduction from the net steady state welfare estimates are included in the consolidated estimates of this study. This tranche yields a global impact of 223 million persons lifted out of poverty over a time horizon of 15 years as the consequence of free trade (table 5.3). This figure is additional to that portion of the total steady state effects included in the basic static gains estimates.

Table 6.2 summarizes the poverty-impact estimates of this study, showing detail for each of the developing countries and regions in the PEHRT model. The total including static, dynamic productivity, and dynamic induced-investment effects is a reduction by about 540 million in the number of poor people globally. This total represents about one-fifth of the global number of poor today (at the $2 level) and about one-fourth of the number of poor projected by the World Bank in the baseline for 2015.

To recapitulate, the overall long-term estimate of about 540 million people potentially removed from poverty as a consequence of adoption of global free trade is composed of three roughly comparable parts. The static effects are a lower bound of 110 million and an upper bound of 260 million (table 5.3), with the higher figure based on an application of the simple rural-urban model for agricultural impacts (chapter 3) added to the PEHRT model estimates for nonagricultural sectors. The second component is the dynamic productivity effect, accounting for 202 million. The third component is (one-half of) the dynamic induced-investment effect, representing another 223 million people lifted out of poverty. The summary figure of 540 million applies the lower ("central") static effect. Figure 6.1 summarizes these effects, using however the average between the central and high estimates for the static effects to give a better sense of the potential static impact.

The World Bank (2002a) has similarly estimated potential poverty reduction attainable by 2015 through global free trade. It places the figure at 320 million. More recently, the World Bank (2003) has estimated that a more plausible but still relatively deep liberalization of global trade in the Doha Round could reduce global poverty by 144 million by 2015.

The estimates of this study suggest that the World Bank estimates are on the conservative side. In terms of figure 6.1, the first two components

## Table 6.2 Long-term poverty reduction impact of global free trade: Central estimate

| Region and economy | Millions of poor people | Poverty elasticity | Poverty reduction Millions of people | Poverty reduction Percent of base year |
|---|---|---|---|---|
| **Asia** | | | | |
| Bangladesh | 99.3 | 3.5 | 43.3 | 43.6 |
| China | 673.2 | 3.5 | 71.8 | 10.7 |
| India | 859.9 | 3.5 | 212.1 | 24.7 |
| Indonesia | 136.8 | 3.5 | 22.3 | 16.3 |
| South Korea | 0.9 | 3.5 | 0.1 | 5.6 |
| Malaysia | 5.6 | 3.2 | 1.1 | 20.3 |
| Pakistan | 114.2 | 3.5 | 76.9 | 67.3 |
| Philippines | 29.2 | 3.0 | 6.6 | 22.7 |
| Thailand | 17.0 | 3.5 | 14.0 | 82.3 |
| Hong Kong, Taiwan, and Singapore | 0.0 | 2.0 | 0.0 | n.a. |
| Other | 84.8 | 2.0 | 10.8 | 12.7 |
| *Subtotal* | 2,020.9 | | 459.0 | 22.7 |
| | | | | |
| **Latin America** | | | | |
| Argentina | 5.4 | 3.1 | 0.9 | 17.1 |
| Brazil | 29.2 | 1.0 | 1.3 | 4.3 |
| Central America and Caribbean | 26.6 | 2.0 | 5.9 | 22.1 |
| Mexico | 41.1 | 2.0 | 0.7 | 1.8 |
| Other | 45.9 | 2.0 | 5.8 | 12.7 |
| *Subtotal* | 148.2 | | 14.6 | 9.9 |
| | | | | |
| **Europe** | | | | |
| Central and Eastern Europe | 92.2 | 2.0 | 3.3 | 3.6 |
| | | | | |
| **Middle East and North Africa** | | | | |
| Turkey | 11.6 | 3.5 | 3.0 | 26.3 |
| Other | 70.4 | 2.0 | 12.3 | 16.1 |
| *Subtotal* | 88.0 | | 15.4 | 17.4 |
| | | | | |
| **Sub-Saharan Africa** | | | | |
| Mozambique | 13.6 | 1.4 | 1.9 | 14.2 |
| South Africa | 15.1 | 1.2 | 0.6 | 4.3 |
| Tanzania | 19.7 | 1.0 | 2.0 | 10.0 |
| Uganda | 16.6 | 2.3 | 1.5 | 9.1 |
| Other | 328.4 | 2.0 | 41.0 | 12.5 |
| *Subtotal* | 393.2 | | 47.0 | 12.0 |
| | | | | |
| **Total** | **2,742.5** | | **539.3** | **19.7** |

n.a. = not applicable

*Source:* Tables 5.2 and 5.3.

**Figure 6.1   Long-term impact of global free trade on poverty reduction**

millions of people

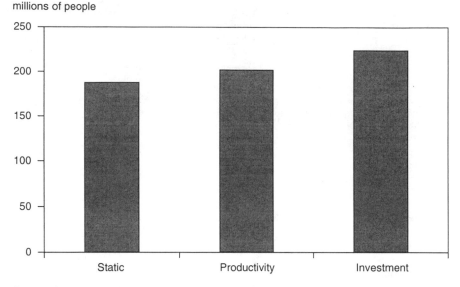

*Source:* Author's calculations.

(static effects and long-term productivity effects) are included in the World Bank model. The sum of these two effects in fact, using the lower-bound static estimate from the PEHRT model, yields an estimate extremely close to the World Bank estimate: 316 million in this study (table 5.3), compared with 320 million in the World Bank study.

The key difference in the estimates here is that the total includes a long-term induced-investment effect, whereas the World Bank estimates do not. In terms of figure 6.1, the World Bank estimates omit the third column. Inclusion of this effect raises by about two-thirds the central estimate of the total number of poor people lifted out of poverty globally as a consequence of global free trade.

There are important differences in the country distribution of estimated poverty reduction, however, and these differences are present even in the first two effects. A major reason for the differences is that the World Bank applies a standard poverty elasticity of 2, whereas this study applies country-specific poverty elasticities. Because these elasticities tend to be higher in Asia than in Latin America and Africa, a greater share of poverty reduction in the present study is found in Asia, and lesser shares in sub-Saharan Africa, than in the World Bank estimates. The poverty elasticities tend to be high in Asia because income concentration is moderate and the ratio of mean to poverty-level income is substantial. The elasticities are low in Latin America because income is highly concentrated, and they are relatively low in Africa because the ratio of mean income to poverty income is considerably lower than in Asia (reflecting the lower overall per capita income).

The central finding of this study, however, is qualitatively similar to that of the earlier World Bank studies: There could be relatively large reductions in global poverty if all nations could agree to remove trade barriers. The global-poverty stakes in the Doha Round are thus high. Moreover, the central estimate of 540 million lifted out of poverty over 15 years from global free trade is more likely to be understated than overstated, because it is based on estimates for goods only. Various estimates suggest that the additional gains (and by implication poverty reduction) from liberalizing trade in services could be large.

Chapter 5 also estimates the annual welfare gains from the combined static, dynamic productivity, and incremental dynamic induced-investment effects (with the latter again estimated conservatively at one-half the Steady State model estimates). The result is that overall long-term welfare gains to developing countries from global free trade would amount to an estimated $203 billion annually (at 1997 prices and economic scale), or 3.2 percent of developing-country GDP. Considering that, as discussed above, at least half of these gains would stem from the removal of protection in industrial countries, the implication is that by eliminating protection industrial countries could convey to developing countries benefits that are about twice as large as the $50 billion currently provided by rich countries to poor countries in the form of concessional assistance. Moreover, the large benefit through open trade would carry with it a net welfare benefit to industrial-country consumers, rather than a cost to taxpayers as is borne in concessional assistance.

## The Doha Round after Cancún

The overall policy implication of this study is that nations should seek through multilateral trade negotiations to eliminate protection, as a means of spurring global growth and reducing global poverty. This is the first and potentially most important track for trade policy insofar as it seeks to reduce poverty. In addition, as discussed above, in a second policy track negotiators should seek to extend free entry immediately to at-risk countries, broadly those in the LDC, HIPC, and SSA groupings. Because it will take a number of years for the trade liberalization agreed on in the Doha Round to be fully implemented, immediate free entry for at-risk countries would provide a major head start for these countries.

As for the protection imposed by developing countries themselves, the findings of this study suggest that this protection should also be removed if developing countries are to obtain the full benefits of global free trade. However, various scenarios examined in chapter 4 (and in particular the differential free trade variant) suggest that there is scope for developing countries to obtain much of the total free trade benefits while applying intermediate liberalization of their own markets as industrial countries adopt full liberalization, such as a cut of all developing-country protection by half rather than complete removal. This finding tends to coincide with the political reality that many developing countries will seek an agreement calling for either lesser proportional cuts in protection for developing countries than for industrial countries, or a longer phase-in of cuts, or both.

This position broadly reflects a continued sense on the part of many developing-country policymakers (as well as what is probably a minority of economists) that it is desirable to retain at least the option to pursue some degree of infant-industry protection (presumably less extreme than in the 1970s), even though many of the more successful developing countries have unilaterally reduced protection in the past two decades. The best judgment is probably that it would be best for the developing countries to join with the industrial countries in fully removing protection, but that a relatively close second-best outcome (for the developing countries) would be achieved if they were to liberalize their own markets somewhat less than by a move to total free entry. For example, cuts in developing-country protection by perhaps two-thirds instead of 100 percent would probably generate benefits for them that would be close to the free trade total (because they would pick up some terms-of-trade gains as industrial countries fully liberalize). Even so, such a less than full liberalization scenario would likely jeopardize important developing-country gains unless the developing-countries completely removed protection against imports from other developing countries.[14]

In September 2003, the Cancún ministerial meeting of the WTO multilateral trade negotiations in the Doha Round broke down. The proximate trigger was that a group of 21 developing countries led by Brazil, India, and China rejected the demand by EU negotiators that the new "Singapore issues" (investment, competition, government procurement, and trade facilitation) be included in any agreement. Several African nations in particular were reluctant to include these issues, in part because of concerns about the administrative costs of dealing with these areas. In the face of this rejection, the Mexican official in charge of the negotiations declared them suspended.

The underlying cause of the breakdown was almost certainly disagreement over agriculture, however, and in particular discontent with a compromise US-EU agreement reached shortly before Cancún that seemed to remove the bulk of agricultural liberalization from the table. This accord in turn represented a major retreat by the United States on agricultural lib-

---

14. This is a critical feature of the surprisingly favorable "differential liberalization" scenario examined in chapter 4.

eralization. The United States, as an important agricultural exporter, had previously been in the vanguard calling for the liberalization of the sector, along with the Cairns Group composed mostly of developing-country exporters but also Australia and New Zealand, key agricultural exporting nations. Just why the US negotiators adopted a much less ambitious compromise with the European Union is unclear; the change may have been tactical and premised on a return to more ambitious goals in actual negotiations at Cancún, and/or it may have been driven by changing domestic US political considerations with an increase in the importance of maintaining farm subsidies.[15]

There are two competing interpretations of the overall effect of the Cancún breakdown. As discussed above, one popular interpretation (*The Economist*, October 6, 2003) is that the developing countries shot themselves in the foot. By being overly concerned that the Doha Round should be the "Development Round" it was declared to be at its launching in 2001, the developing countries mistakenly sought liberalization mainly by industrial countries while seeking to avoid liberalizing their own markets. As noted above, this view has been buttressed by press references to the World Bank study finding that as much as 80 percent of agricultural liberalization benefits for developing countries would come from their own liberalization rather than that of industrial countries.

The second interpretation, which is much more consistent with the findings of the present study, is that the Group of 21 (G-21) undertook an understandable strategic confrontation at Cancún, because otherwise the likelihood was extremely high that trade liberalization, especially in agriculture, would turn out to be a mouse, too small to warrant the name. The findings of this study in this regard are, first, that agriculture is by far the most important sector to liberalize, and second, that at least half the potential gains for developing countries from the global liberalization of overall trade, and possibly as much as two-thirds, comes from removing protection against their goods in industrial-country markets. In this framework, making a strategic forcing move meant that the G-21 was seeking to increase the probability of a meaningful overall liberalization, even if doing so reduced the probability of an early conclusion of negotiations.

There are nuances within these two polar views. For example, some Brazilian authorities complained after the breakdown that the agricultural negotiations had in fact begun to make some headway. Of particular importance, there are questions about why the Mexican official who was formally in charge of the Cancún meetings called a halt to the negotiations, and even logistical questions about why arrangements had not been

---

15. It cannot be ruled out that US officials considered solidarity with the European Union particularly important at the time, given upcoming United Nations deliberations on arrangements in postwar Iraq.

prepared for the negotiations to continue longer. Fundamentally, however, Cancún can be interpreted as a forceful move by the developing countries in a game in which they are seeking to achieve much more meaningful results than would otherwise have been available.

The structure of decision making in the WTO is an important underlying reason why the developing countries appear to be in a stronger position than in the past to influence the negotiations. Through much of the postwar period key decisions in the General Agreement on Tariffs and Trade (GATT) were typically first resolved by the Quad nations (United States, European Union, Japan, and Canada) and then presented to the rest of the GATT membership for endorsement largely as a fait accompli. Nonetheless, by the time of the Tokyo Round of the 1970s, there was an increasing sense among the Quad that the need for normal consensus approval was unduly limiting the scope of agreements, and there was a move toward "GATT-plus" side deals with obligations only for signatories but with benefits available on an MFN basis. The Tokyo Round codes on such nontariff barriers as discrimination in government procurement were major "plurilateral" agreements of this nature.

By the time of the Uruguay Round in the late 1980s and early 1990s, the major trading nations that had subscribed to the plurilateral codes were increasingly concerned that other countries, especially the larger middle-income economies, were free riding on these codes, enjoying their market-opening benefits but not undertaking their obligations in their own markets. The round thus sought a "single undertaking" package accepted by all members. The Uruguay Round adopted the more structured WTO, with its dispute settlement mechanisms, as successor to the looser GATT, so there was a strong incentive for each country to accept the overall package. Any country's nonacceptance would have meant its exclusion from membership in the new WTO.

Yet the WTO's continuation of the tradition of consensus decisions, coupled with its approach of negotiating a single undertaking, means that smaller members have the potential to exert blocking influence. Moreover, now that WTO membership is in place, any downside risk to a country seeking to block agreements is much lower. Although technically, certain "interpretations" and "waivers" can be passed by three-fourths majority vote (Jackson 1998, 44), in practice key negotiators would typically seek to obtain consensus rather than overrule a minority. A Doha Round agreement to grant immediate free entry to least developed countries, heavily indebted poor countries, and sub-Saharan Africa, as suggested in this study, might require a vote on the waiver of most-favored nation, although it also might be achieved without a waiver through the "enabling clause" adopted in the Tokyo Round to facilitate special access for developing countries. Similarly, major new extensions of WTO obligations into new issue areas such as antimonopoly (competition) rules might need amendment by two-thirds majority, but it also might be possible to achieve them on a "plurilateral" basis for those countries willing to liberalize in these areas.

A sufficiently numerous grouping of small countries could presumably block new interpretations, waivers, and amendments. However, it is likely that the Quad and other leading trading nations would seek to assemble a large enough coalition of countries supporting any major initiative that an outright opposing vote would be avoided in a consensus test. To do so, however, the Quad and other nations would likely need to take more fully into account than in the past the views of a sizable bloc such as the G-21 developing countries that played a key role at the Cancún ministerial meeting. The principal exception to the resulting blocking potential by smaller countries would appear to be in initiatives that clearly involve reduction in the initiating countries' own protection, rather than extension of trading rules to countries other than those proposing the new initiative. There is a strong tradition from the GATT that any country seeking to liberalize its own market is allowed to do so. A coordinated initiative of "own-liberalization" by the Quad, for example, could probably not be blocked by even a fairly numerous group of other countries.[16]

Overall, the effect of the "single undertaking" structure of the WTO and the consensus decision-approval process is to strengthen the hand of the weaker parties by giving them a potential veto power. Arbitrary veto would be unlikely, because it would tend to shame the group of countries blocking progress by the rest. When such a veto can be exercised by invoking the moral high ground, however, nations will be more willing to make the veto. At Cancún, the moral high ground was indeed with the G-21 countries, because they were simply asking the industrial countries to make good on their pledges of liberalizing agriculture, and correspondingly to make good on their pledge that the Doha Round would in fact be a development round. There was even an icon encapsulating the moral high ground: The developing-country group sought some form of compensation for a handful of West African nations that had been adversely affected by US cotton subsidies. Some of the African countries more generally appear to have had mixed views about the new Singapore issues, but when they found that the industrial countries were unprepared to act even on such a small issue of interest to Africa, they rejected the European Union call for inclusion of the new issues.

The Doha Round can be revived. The operational deadline is in 2007, when US presidential authority to negotiate a "fast-track" trade deal expires. Progress is likely to be slow prior to the US presidential elections in 2004, but thereafter it should be possible to move ahead rapidly.

---

16. Thus, a 1949 GATT decision indicated that any country's reduction of its tariffs below previously bound rates "does not require unanimous consent of the contracting parties" (Jackson 1998, 42).

The shape of a potential Doha deal could be along the following lines. Industrial countries would commit to a deep reduction in tariffs and tariff-rate quotas in agriculture. They would commit to decouple forcefully any domestic subsidies from exports and production. The developing countries for their part would accept the notion of decoupling rather than seeking to eliminate industrial-country farm subsidies entirely. The prime example of a decoupled subsidy is one that rewards the farmer for removing land from production, rather than for producing. Such "set-aside" conservation-oriented subsidies featured prominently in earlier periods of US farm support, and they could easily once again become the centerpiece of farm programs.

At the same time, industrial countries could commit to a systematic "sunshine" program of publishing annual statistical reports on the amounts of subsidies received by farm size group. For example, it could be reported that the top 10 percent of farms receiving subsidies obtain $x$ percent of total subsidy amounts, at an average of $y$ dollar amounts per farm. One nongovernmental organization compiling such statistics reports that in 2002, the top 10 percent of recipients received 65 percent of total farm subsidies (Environmental Working Group 2003). In 2001, the largest farm recipient of subsidies in California received $1.8 million, and even the 100th largest recipient received $430,000. Farm subsidies have tended to be justified on the grounds that they help sustain the small family farm, but the reality is that they are concentrated among larger farms. Sunshine laws would help reveal this reality and weaken the lobbying power of these groups. But again, if the United States electorate and its counterparts in Europe decide that they wish to make transfer payments of tens of billions of dollars annually to wealthy farmers, that is their business. They should do so in a way that does not impose a burden on the farmers in poor countries, however. They should decouple.

The second part of a Doha deal will have to be substantial liberalization by middle-income countries. As noted, the average tariff on textiles and apparel in developing countries is 18 percent, and on other manufactures, 12 percent. The developing countries could fruitfully agree to set a ceiling of 10 percent on all manufactured-goods tariffs, and to achieve an overall cut of 60 percent in their tariff protection (e.g., from an average 12 percent in nontextile manufactures to 4.8 percent). Without a commitment to such cuts, there will simply not be enough attraction in the potential gains from a WTO deal to mobilize support from business groups in industrial countries. Yet without pressure from such potential supporters, there will be a political vacuum that will be occupied by the vested interests seeking to maintain high protection in agriculture and in selected areas of manufactures. The timing of developing-country liberalization could be stretched out longer than the phase-in allowed for industrial-country liberalization, but developing countries will not be able simply to cut an attractive global liberalization deal without putting their own protection on the table. This is especially so if the new Singapore issues are to be excluded.

The third component of a Doha deal involves the "second track" suggested above: immediate, meaningful free entry for the at-risk countries. These are the countries that will be most tempted to play the role of the spoiler in the Doha Round. Their negotiators are especially concerned that any multilateral liberalization will "erode preferences" they currently receive in the Lomé, EBA, AGOA, and other arrangements. Given the heightened potential for veto strategies in the new WTO single-undertaking approach, it should be clear that this group (e.g., the least developed countries) will have to see some positive benefit in an agreement for themselves if they are to exercise self-restraint and withhold their potential veto.

There is already some talk of a special facility within the IMF to provide lending for adjustment to LDC preference erosion resulting from the Doha Round. This carrot seems unlikely to be particularly appealing. IMF funds are loans, not grants. The two-track strategy suggested in this study would be a more persuasive carrot. Removing the obstacles (including excessively stringent rules-of-origin requirements) that currently keep the special-access regimes from providing truly free entry would be an important enhancement for the LDCs and other at-risk countries. While the preference involved in immediate fully free entry would eventually indeed be eroded by the phase-in of multilateral liberalization (especially in the ideal case of complete multilateral free trade), for a substantial time horizon on the order of a decade, this track would enhance rather than undermine existing preferential treatment. Complementing this free entry with an international initiative for a 10-year tax holiday on foreign direct investment going into these countries would be a further powerful enhancement. The parallel track of immediate free entry for at-risk countries could therefore hold the potential to avoid Doha Round blockage by LDCs that otherwise might find it attractive to exercise their new veto power, likely while invoking the moral argument that they will suffer preference erosion if a multilateral deal goes ahead. Perhaps more important, it would provide additional benefits to the countries where poverty is the most intense.

A final issue of negotiating strategy concerns the advent of bilateral and regional free trade agreements (FTAs). One consequence of the Cancún breakdown may be at least temporarily to cause US and perhaps EU negotiators to pursue such agreements.[17] It can be argued that in the past, FTA negotiations have served as sources of "competitive liberalization" that contributed to pressure for multilateral liberalization. This was the case for NAFTA negotiations begun in the early 1980s, which placed pressure on the European Union to move sufficiently on agricultural protec-

---

17. Jeffrey Schott, "Unlocking the Benefits of World Trade," *The Economist*, November 1, 2003, 65–67.

tion so that the Uruguay Round of multilateral liberalization could be mobilized. However, increasingly this strategy may be reaching diminishing returns. The growing list of small countries in the queue for US bilateral agreements, for example, suggests the risk of cluttering the negotiating agenda with agreements whose aggregate economic potential is meager at best. Moreover, a developing country's bargaining leverage is much less in a bilateral negotiation with the United States or the European Union than as part of a group of developing countries negotiating within the WTO.

More problematically, free trade agreements could follow a pattern of liberalizing only the sectors that are easy while exempting agriculture, textiles, and other sensitive sectors. If so, the result after a period of time would be to remove most sectors from what is left to be negotiated, making it difficult to arrive at a "big package" with enough appeal to exert leverage capable of breaking protectionist pressures in the sensitive sectors. Instead of competitive free trade agreements, it would seem that a revival of multilateral negotiations in the Doha Round holds the most promise for major trade liberalization.

In sum, it is crucial to reinvigorate the Doha Round, and to use it to pursue thoroughgoing trade liberalization. To do so will require a firm commitment by political leaders, however, especially in the United States and the European Union but also in the key middle-income countries. The analysis of this study suggests that the stakes of the global poor in the mobilization of this international political leadership are high indeed.

# References

ABARE (Australian Bureau of Agricultural Resources Economics). 2000. Developing Countries: Impact of Agricultural Trade Liberalization. *ABARE Current Issues*, 1–5 (July).

ABARE (Australian Bureau of Agricultural Resources Economics) and Sparks Commodities. 1999. Policies Affecting Market Expansion of Sugar: Sugar Industries and Policies in APEC. ABARE and Sparks Commodities, Melbourne. Photocopy.

Aitchison, J., and J. A. C. Brown. 1963. *The Lognormal Distribution.* Cambridge: Cambridge University Press.

Alcalá, Francisco, and Antonio Ciccone. 2001. *Trade and Productivity.* Center for Economic Policy Research Discussion Paper 3095. London: Center for Economic Policy Research.

Anderson, J. E., and J. P. Neary. 1996. A New Approach to Evaluating Trade Policy. *Review of Economic Studies* 63, no. 1 (January): 107–25.

Anderson, Kym, Betina Dimaranan, Joe François, Tom Hertel, Bernard Hoekman, and Will Martin. 2001. *The Cost of Rich (and Poor) Country Protection to Developing Countries.* Center for International Economic Studies Discussion Paper 0136. Adelaide, Australia: Adelaide University.

Anderson, Kym, Joe François, Tom Hertel, Bernard Hoekman, and Will Martin. 2000. Potential Gains from Trade Reform in the New Millennium. Paper prepared for the Third Annual Conference on Global Economic Analysis, Monash University, Melbourne, June 27–30.

Andriamananjara, Soamiely, and Russell Hillberry. 2001. *Regionalism, Trade and Growth: The Case of the EU–South Africa Free Trade Arrangement.* Office of Economics Working Paper 2001-07-A. Washington: US International Trade Commission.

Balassa, Bela. 1971. *The Structure of Protection in Industrial Countries: An Evaluation.* Baltimore: Johns Hopkins University Press.

Baldwin, Robert E. 2003. *Openness and Growth: What's the Empirical Relationship?* NBER Working Paper 9578. Cambridge, MA: National Bureau of Economic Research.

Barro, Robert J., and Jong-Wha Lee. 1994. Sources of Economic Growth. *Carnegie-Rochester Conference Series on Public Policy* 40 (June): 1–46.

Beghin, John C., David Roland-Holst, and Dominique van der Mensbrugghe. 2002. Global Agricultural Trade and the Doha Round: What Are the Implications for North and

South? Working Paper 02-WP 308, Center for Agricultural and Rural Development, Iowa State University, Ames. Photocopy (June).

Beierle, Thomas C. 2002. *From Uruguay to Doha: Agricultural Trade Negotiations at the World Trade Organization*. Discussion Paper 02-3. Washington: Resources for the Future.

Beierle, Thomas C., and Eugenio Diaz-Bonilla. 2003. The Impact of Agricultural Trade Liberalization on the Rural Poor: An Overview. Resources for the Future and International Food Policy Research Institute, Washington. Photocopy (October).

Ben-David, Dan. 1993. Equalizing Exchange: Trade Liberalization and Income Convergence. *Quarterly Journal of Economics* 108, no. 3: 653–79.

Berg, Andrew, and Anne Krueger. 2003. *Trade, Growth, and Poverty: A Selective Survey*. IMF Working Paper WP/03/30. Washington: International Monetary Fund. www.imf.org/external/pubs/cat/longres.cfm?sk=16281.0.

Bergsten, C. Fred. 2002. A Renaissance for U.S. Trade Policy? *Foreign Affairs* 81, no. 6: 86–98.

Bhalla, Surgit S. 2002. *Imagine There's No Country: Poverty, Inequality, and Growth in the Era of Globalization*. Washington: Institute for International Economics.

Bhalla, Surjit S. 2003. Crying Wolf on Poverty: Or How the Millennium Development Goal for Poverty Has Already Been Reached. April 29. www.iie.com.

Birdsall, Nancy, and Amar Hamoudi. 2002. *Commodity Dependence, Trade, and Growth: When "Openness" Is Not Enough*. Center for Global Development Working Paper 7. Washington: Center for Global Development. www.cgdev.org.

Bjørnskov, Christian, and Ekaterina Krivonos. 2001. *From Lomé to Cotonou: The New EU-ACP Agreement*. SJFI Working Paper 14/2001. Copenhagen: Danish Institute of Agricultural and Fisheries Economics. www.sfji.dk.

Bora, Bijit, Lucian Cernat, and Alessandro Turrini. 2002. *Duty and Quota-Free Access for LDCs: Further Evidence from CGE Modelling*. Policy Issues in International Trade and Commodities Study Series 14. Geneva: UN Conference on Trade and Development.

Bosworth, Barry P., and Susan M. Collins. 2003. The Empirics of Growth: An Update. Brookings Institution, Washington. Photocopy (September).

Bouet, Antoine, Lionel Fontagne, Mondher Mimouni, and Xavier Pichot. 2001. *Market Access Maps: A Bilateral and Disaggregated Measure of Market Access*. Paris: Centre d'Etudes Prospectives et d'Informations Internationales.

Bourguignon, François. 2002. The Growth Elasticity of Poverty Reduction: Explaining Heterogeneity across Countries and Time Periods. World Bank, Washington. Photocopy (February). http://faculty.washington.edu/~te/papers/inequality/bour.pdf.

Brooke, Anthony, David Kendrick, Alexander Meeraus, and Ramesh Raman. 2003. *GAMS: A User's Guide*. Washington: GAMS Development Corporation.

Brown, Drusilla K., Alan V. Deardorff, and Robert M. Stern. 2001. *CGE Modeling and Analysis of Multilateral and Regional Negotiating Options*. Research Seminar in International Economics Discussion Paper 468. Ann Arbor, MI: University of Michigan.

Burnside, Craig, and David Dollar. 1997. *Aid, Policies and Growth*. World Bank Working Paper 1777. Washington: World Bank.

Burt, Martha, Laudan Aron, Edgar Lee, and Jesse Valente. 2001. *Helping America's Homeless: Emergency Shelter or Affordable Housing?* Washington: Urban Institute Press.

CCFA (Commission on Capital Flows to Africa). 2003. *A Ten-Year Strategy for Increasing Capital Flows to Africa*. Washington: Institute for International Economics.

Choudhri, Ehasan U., and Dalia S. Hakura. 2000. International Trade and Productivity Growth: Exploring the Sectoral Effects for Developing Countries. *IMF Staff Papers* 47, no. 1: 30–53.

Cline, William R. 1972. *Potential Effects of Income Redistribution on Economic Growth: Latin American Cases*. New York: Praeger.

Cline, William R. 1990. The *Future of World Trade in Textiles and Apparel*, revised edition. Washington: Institute for International Economics.

Cline, William R. 1995. Evaluating the Uruguay Round. *The World Economy* 18, no. 1 (January): 1–23.

Cline, William R. 1997. *Trade and Income Distribution*. Washington: Institute for International Economics.

Cline, William R. 1998. Comment on Revenga and Montenegro. In *Imports, Exports, and the American Worker*, ed. Susan M. Collins. Washington: Brookings Institution Press.

Cline, William R. 2002a. *Financial Crises and Poverty in Emerging Market Economies*. Center for Global Development Working Paper 8. Washington: Center for Global Development. www.cgdev.org.

Cline, William R. 2002b. *An Index of Industrial Country Trade Policy toward Developing Countries*. Center for Global Development Working Paper 14. Washington: Center for Global Development. www.cgdev.org.

Cline, William R. 2003a. *Trading Up: Strengthening AGOA's Development Potential*. CGD Brief. Washington: Center for Global Development. www.cgdev.org.

Cline, William R. 2003b. *Trading Up: Trade Policy and Global Poverty*. CGD Brief. Washington: Center for Global Development. www.cgdev.org.

Collier, Paul, and David Dollar. 2001. Can the World Cut Poverty in Half? How Policy Reform and Effective Aid Can Meet International Development Goals. *World Development* 29, no. 11: 1787–802.

Collins, Susan M., ed. 1998. *Imports, Exports, and the American Worker*. Washington: Brookings Institution Press.

Cornia, Giovanni Andrea, and Sampsa Kiiski. 2001. *Trends in Income Distribution in the Post–World War II Period: Evidence and Interpretation*. World Institute for Development Economics Research Discussion Paper 2001/89. Tokyo: United Nations University.

Deardorff, Alan V. 2000. *Market Access for Developing Countries*. Research Seminar in International Economics Discussion Paper 461. Ann Arbor, MI: University of Michigan.

Deaton, Angus. 2003. Measuring Poverty in a Growing World (or Measuring Growth in a Poor World). Review of Economics and Statistics Lecture. Woodrow Wilson School, Princeton University, Princeton, NJ. Photocopy (15 April). www.wws.princeton.edu/faculty/deaton.html.

de Gorter, Harry, Merlinda Ingco, and Laura Ignacio. 2003. *Domestic Support for Agriculture: Agricultural Policy Reform and Developing Countries*. Trade Note 7. Washington: World Bank. www.worldbank.org.

Deininger, Klaus, and Lyn Squire. 1996. A New Data Set Measuring Income Inequality. *World Bank Economic Review* 10, no. 3: 565–91.

De Melo, Jaime, and David Tarr. 1992. *A General Equilibrium Analysis of US Foreign Trade Policy*. Cambridge, MA: MIT Press.

Dessus, Sebastien, Kiichiro Fukasaku, and Raed Safadi. 1999. *Multilateral Tariff Liberalisation and the Developing Countries*. OECD Development Center Policy Brief 18. Paris: Organization for Economic Cooperation and Development. www.oecd.org/dev/englis/publication/Policy-B.htm.

DFAT (Australian Department of Foreign Affairs and Trade). 1999. *Global Trade Reform: Maintaining Momentum*. Canberra: DFAT. www.dfat.gov.au/trade/negotiations/gtr_2000.pdf.

Dimaranan, Betina V., and Robert A. McDougall, eds. 2002. *Global Trade, Assistance, and Production: The GTAP5 Data Base*. West Lafayette, IN: Center for Global Trade Analysis, Purdue University.

Dimaranan, Betina V., Robert A. McDougall, and Thomas Hertel. 2002. Behavioral Parameters. In *Global Trade, Assistance, and Production: The GTAP5 Data Base*, ed. Betina V. Dimaranan and Robert A. McDougall. West Lafayette, IN: Center for Global Trade Analysis, Purdue University.

Dixit, Avinash, and Joseph Stiglitz. 1977. Monopolistic Competition and Optimum Product Diversity. *American Economic Review* 72, no. 3 (June): 297–308.

Dollar, David. 1992. Outward-Oriented Developing Economies Really Do Grow More Rapidly: Evidence from 95 LDCs, 1976–85. *Economic Development and Cultural Change* 40, no. 3: 523–44.

Dollar, David, and Aart Kraay. 2001a. Growth Is Good for the Poor. World Bank, Washington. Photocopy (April).

Dollar, David, and Aart Kraay. 2001b. Trade, Growth, and Poverty. Washington: World Bank. Photocopy (June).

Dornbusch, Rudiger. 1992. The Case for Trade Liberalization in Developing Countries. *Journal of Economic Perspectives* 6, no. 1 (winter): 69–85.

Easterly, William. 2003. *National Policies and Economic Growth: A Reappraisal.* Center for Global Development Working Paper 27. Washington: Center for Global Development. www.cgdev.org.

Easterly, William, and Ross Levine. 2001. It's Not Factor Accumulation: Stylized Facts and Growth Models. *World Bank Economic Review* 15, no. 2: 177–219.

Edwards, Sebastian. 1993. Openness, Trade Liberalization, and Growth in Developing Countries. *Journal of Economic Literature* 31: 1358–93.

Edwards, Sebastian. 1998. Openness, Productivity and Growth: What Do We Really Know? *Economic Journal* 108: 383–98.

Elbehri, Aziz, Thomas Hertel, Merlinda Ingco, and K. R. Pearson. 2000. Partial Liberalization of the World Sugar Market: A General Equilibrium Analysis of Tariff-Rate Quota Regimes. Paper prepared for the Third Annual Conference on Global Economic Analysis, Melbourne, June 27–30.

Embassy of Brazil. 2001. U.S. Barriers to Brazilian Goods and Services. Embassy of Brazil, Washington. Photocopy (October).

Environmental Working Group. 2003. Farm Subsidy Database 2.0 www.ewg.org.

Ethier, W. J. 1982. National and International Returns to Scale in the Modern Theory of International Trade. *American Economic Review* 72, no. 3: 389–405.

European Commission. 1996. Green Paper on Relations between the European Union and the ACP Countries on the Eve of the 21st Century: Challenges and Options for a New Partnership. European Commission, Brussels. Photocopy (November).

European Commission. 2000. EU Trade Concession to Least Developed Countries: Everything but Arms Proposal—Possible Impacts on the Agricultural Sector. European Commission, Brussels. Photocopy (November). http://europa.eu.int/comm/trade/pdf/eba_ias.pdf.

European Commission. 2002a. *Comments from the Commission on "Rigged Rules and Double Standards."* Brussels: European Commission. http://europa.eu.int/comm/trade/pdf/oxfamreply.pdf.

European Commission. 2002b. *Eurostat.* http://europa.eu.int/comm/eurostat, July.

European Union. 2001. *Commission of the European Communities, 30th Financial Report on the European Agricultural Guidance and Guarantee Fund: EAGF Guarantee Section.* Brussels: European Commission.

Feenstra, Robert, and Gordon Hanson. 1995. Foreign Investment, Outsourcing, and Relative Wages. In *Political Economy of Trade Policy: Essays in Honor of Jagdish Bhagwati,* ed. Robert Feenstra, Gene Grossman, and Douglas Irwin. Cambridge, MA: MIT Press.

Finger, J. Michael, Francis Ng, and Sonam Wangchuk. 2001. Antidumping as Safeguard Policy. World Bank, Washington. Photocopy (December).

Finger, J. Michael, and Julio J. Nogues. 2002. The Unbalanced Uruguay Round Outcome: The New Areas in Future WTO Negotiations. *The World Economy* 25, no. 3 (March): 321–40.

Finger, J. Michael, and Ludger Schuknecht. 1999. Market Access Advances and Retreats: The Uruguay Round and Beyond. World Bank, Washington. Photocopy (September).

Fink, Carsten, Aaditya Mattoo, and Ileana Cristina Neagu. 2001. *Trade in International Maritime Services: How Much Does Policy Matter?* World Bank Working Paper 2522. Washington: World Bank.

Foster, J. E., J. Greer, and E. Thorbecke. 1984. A Class of Decomposable Poverty Measures. *Econometrica* 52: 761–66.

François, Joseph. 2000. Assessing the Results of General Equilibrium Studies of Multilateral Trade Negotiations, *Policy Issues in International Trade and Commodities: Study Series No. 3* (New York: United Nations Conference on Trade and Development).

François, Joseph, and Dean Spinanger. 2002. ATC Export Tax Equivalents. In *Global Trade, Assistance, and Production: The GTAP5 Data Base*, ed. Betina V. Dimaranan and Robert A. McDougall. West Lafayette, IN: Center for Global Trade Analysis, Purdue University.

Frankel, Jeffrey A., and David Romer. 1999. Does Trade Cause Growth? *American Economic Review* 89, no. 3: 379–99.

Frankel, Jeffrey A., and Andrew K. Rose. 2000. *Estimating the Effect of Currency Unions on Trade and Growth*. NBER Working Paper 7857. Cambridge, MA: National Bureau of Economic Research.

Galbraith, James K., and Hyunsub Kum. 2002. *Inequality and Economic Growth: Data Comparisons and Econometric Tests*. University of Texas Inequality Project Working Paper 21. Austin, TX: University of Texas.

Gallezot, Jacques. 2002. L'Accès Effectif au Marché Agricole de l'UE. INRA-INAPG, Paris. Photocopy (July).

Gelhar, Mark, Denice Gray, Thomas W. Hertel, Karen M. Huff, Elena Ianchovichina, Bradley J. McDonald, Robert McDougall, Marinos E. Tsigas, and Randall Wigle. 1997. Overview of the GTAP Data Base. In *Global Trade Analysis: Modeling and Applications*, ed. Thomas W. Hertel. Cambridge: Cambridge University Press.

Gibson, Paul, John Wainio, and Daniel Whitley. 2002. Agricultural Tariff Data. In *Global Trade, Assistance, and Production: The GTAP5 Data Base*, ed. Betina V. Dimaranan and Robert A. McDougall. West Lafayette, IN: Center for Global Trade Analysis, Purdue University.

Grilli, Enzo R. 1994. *The European Community and the Developing Countries*. New York: Cambridge University Press.

Greenaway, David, Wyn Morgan, and Peter Wright. 1998. Trade Reform, Adjustment and Growth: What Does the Evidence Tell Us? *Economic Journal* 108: 1547–61.

Grossman, Gene, and Elhanan Helpman. 1991. *Innovation and Growth in the Global Economy*, Cambridge, MA: MIT Press.

Grossman, Gene, and Elhanan Helpman. 1994. Endogenous Innovation in the Theory of Growth. *Journal of Economic Perspectives* 8, no. 1: 23–44.

Hall, Robert E., and Charles I. Jones. 1999. Why Do Some Countries Produce So Much More Output per Worker than Others? *Quarterly Journal of Economics* 114: 83–116.

Hamoudi, Amar. 2002. *How Much Go in AGOA? Growth and Opportunity in the African Growth and Opportunity Act*. CGD Brief Washington: Center for Global Development. www.cgdev.org.

Harrison, Ann, and Gordon Hanson. 1999. Who Gains from Trade Reform? Some Remaining Puzzles. *Journal of Development Economics* 59: 125–54.

Harrison, Glenn W., Thomas F. Rutherford, and David G. Tarr. 1996. Quantifying the Uruguay Round. In *The Uruguay Round and the Developing Countries*, ed. Will Martin and L. A. Winters. New York: Cambridge University Press.

Harrison, Glenn W., Thomas F. Rutherford, and David G. Tarr. 1997a. Quantifying the Uruguay Round. *Economic Journal*, no. 107: 1405–30.

Harrison, Glenn W., Thomas F. Rutherford, and David G. Tarr. 1997b. *Trade Policy Options for Chile: A Quantitative Evaluation*. Policy Research Working Paper 1783. Washington: World Bank.

Harrison, Glenn W., Thomas F. Rutherford, and David G. Tarr. 2003. Trade Liberalization, Poverty and Efficient Equity. *Journal of Development Economics* 71: 97–128.

Harrison, Glenn W., Thomas F. Rutherford, David G. Tarr, and Angelo Gurgel. 2002. Regional, Multilateral and Unilateral Trade Policies of MERCOSUR for Growth and Poverty Reduction in Brazil. World Bank, Washington. Photocopy (September).

Hertel, Thomas W., ed. 1997. *Global Trade Analysis: Modeling and Applications.* Cambridge: Cambridge University Press.

Hertel, Thomas W., David Hummels, Maros Ivanic, and Roman Keeney. 2003. *How Confident Can We Be in CGE-Based Assessments of Free Trade Agreements?* GTAP Working Paper 26. West Lafayette, IN: Center for Global Trade Analysis, Purdue University.

Hertel, Thomas W., Maros Ivanic, Paul V. Preckel, and John A. L. Cranfield. 2003a. The Earnings Effects of Multilateral Trade Liberalization: Implications for Poverty in Developing Countries. Purdue University, West Lafayette, IN. Photocopy (March).

Hertel, Thomas W., Maros Ivanic, Paul V. Preckel, and John A. L. Cranfield. 2003b. Trade Liberalization and the Structure of Poverty in Developing Countries. Purdue University, West Lafayette, IN. Photocopy (February).

Hertel, Thomas W., Maros Ivanic, Paul V. Preckel, John A. L. Cranfield, and Will Martin. 2003. Short- vs. Long-Run Implications of Trade Liberalization for Poverty in Three Developing Countries. *American Journal of Agricultural Economics* 85, no. 5: 1299–306.

Hertel, Thomas W., and Will Martin. 1999. Would Developing Countries Gain from Inclusion of Manufactures in the WTO Negotiations? Paper prepared for the Conference on WTO and the Millennium Round, Geneva, September 20–21.

Hertel, Thomas W., Paul V. Preckel, John A. L. Cranfield, and Maros Ivanic. 2002. Poverty Impacts of Multilateral Trade Liberalization. Purdue University, West Lafayette, IN. Photocopy (March).

Hertel, Thomas W., and Marinos E. Tsigas. 1997. Structure of GTAP. In *Global Trade Analysis: Modeling and Applications*, ed. Thomas W. Hertel. Cambridge: Cambridge University Press.

Hoekman, Bernard. 2000. The Next Round of Services Negotiations: Identifying Priorities and Options. *Federal Reserve Bank of St. Louis Review*, July–August: 31-48.

Hoekman, Bernard, Aaditya Mattoo, and Philip English, eds. 2002. *Development, Trade, and the WTO: A Handbook.* Washington: World Bank.

Hoekman, Bernard, Constantine Michalopoulos, Maurice Schiff, and David Tarr. 2001. *Trade Policy Reform and Poverty Alleviation.* Policy Research Working Paper 2733. Washington: World Bank.

Hoekman, Bernard, Francis Ng, and Marcelo Olarreaga. 2001. Tariff Peaks in the Quad and Least Developed Country Exports. World Bank, Washington. Photocopy (February).

Hoekman, Bernard, Francis Ng, and Marcelo Olarreaga. 2002a. Eliminating Excessive Tariffs on Exports of Least Developed Countries. *World Bank Economic Review* 16, no. 1: 1–21.

Hoekman, Bernard, Francis Ng, and Marcelo Olarreaga. 2002b. *Reducing Agricultural Tariffs versus Domestic Support: What's More Important for Developing Countries?* Policy Research Working Paper 2918. Washington: World Bank.

Hornbeck, J. F. 2001. *The Andean Trade Preference Act: Background and Issues for Reauthorization.* Report for Congress RL30790. Washington: Congressional Research Service.

Hufbauer, Gary Clyde, and Ben Goodrich. 2002. *Time for a Grand Bargain in Steel?* International Economic Policy Brief 02-1. Washington: Institute for International Economics.

Hufbauer, Gary Clyde, and Ben Goodrich. 2003. *Steel Policy: The Good, the Bad, and the Ugly.* International Economic Policy Brief 03-1. Washington: Institute for International Economics.

Hufbauer, Gary Clyde, and Barbara Kotschwar. 1998. The United States and the Andean Community: Prospects and Problems at the End of the Twentieth Century. In *The Andean Community and the U.S. Trade and Investment Relations in the 1990s*, ed. Miguel Rodrigues Mendoza, Patricia Correa, and Barbara Kotschwar. Washington: Organization of American States.

Hufbauer, Gary Clyde, and Yee Wong. 2002. Tax Relief for Investment in Africa. Institute for International Economics, Washington. Photocopy (October).

Ianchovichina, Elena, Aaditya Mattoo, and Marcelo Olarreaga. 2001. Unrestricted Market Access for Sub-Saharan Africa: How Much Is It Worth and Who Pays? World Bank, Washington. Photocopy (no date).

IIF (Institute of International Finance). 2003. *Capital Flows to Emerging Market Economies.* Washington: IIF. www.iif.com.

IMF (International Monetary Fund). 1990. *World Economic Outlook: A Survey by the Staff of the International Monetary Fund*, October. Washington: IMF.

IMF (International Monetary Fund). 2001a. *Direction of Trade Statistics Quarterly*, December. Washington: IMF.

IMF (International Monetary Fund). 2001b. *World Economic Outlook: The Information Technology Revolution*, October. Washington: IMF.

IMF (International Monetary Fund). 2002a. Direction of Trade Statistics, CD-ROM, April. Washington: IMF.

IMF (International Monetary Fund). 2002b. International Financial Statistics, CD-ROM, August. Washington: IMF.

IMF (International Monetary Fund). 2002c. *World Economic Outlook, April 2002*, May. Washington: IMF.

IMF (International Monetary Fund). 2002d. *World Economic Outlook: Trade and Finance*, September. Washington: IMF.

IMF (International Monetary Fund). 2003. International Financial Statistics, CD-ROM, September. Washington: IMF.

IMF (International Monetary Fund) and World Bank. 2001. Market Access for Developing Countries' Exports. IMF, Washington. Photocopy (April).

IMF (International Monetary Fund) and World Bank. 2002. Market Access for Developing Country Exports—Selected Issues. IMF, Washington. Photocopy (September).

Informs Online. 2002. Updated Study Shows Baseline Annual Diet Costs Less for Women than Men. Linthicum, MD: Institute for Operations Research and the Management Sciences. www.informs.org/Press/Gass06.html.

Ingco, Merlinda D. 1997. *Has Agricultural Trade Liberalization Improved Welfare in the Least-Developed Countries? Yes.* Policy Research Working Paper 1748. Washington: World Bank.

Irwin, Douglas A., and Marko Tervio. 2000. *Does Trade Raise Income? Evidence from the Twentieth Century.* NBER Working Paper 7745. Cambridge, MA: National Bureau of Economic Research.

Jackson, John H. 1998. *The World Trade Organization: Constitution and Jurisprudence.* London: Royal Institute of International Affairs.

Jones, Charles I. 2000. Comment on Rodriguez and Rodrik, Trade Policy and Economic Growth: A Skeptic's Guide to the Cross-National Evidence. Stanford University, Stanford, CA. Photocopy (June).

Krueger, Anne O. 1978. *Foreign Trade Regimes and Economic Development: Liberalization Attempts and Consequences.* Cambridge, MA: Ballinger.

Krueger, Anne O. 1997. *Trade Policy and Economic Development: How We Learn.* NBER Working Paper 5896. Cambridge, MA: National Bureau of Economic Research.

Krueger, Anne O. 1999. *The Developing Countries and the Next Round of Multilateral Trade Negotiations.* World Bank Working Paper 2118. Washington: World Bank.

Krugman, Paul. 2003. *The Great Unraveling: Losing Our Way in the New Century.* New York: Norton.

Kuznets, Simon. 1955. Economic Growth and Income Inequality. *American Economic Review* 45, no. 1: 1–28.

Laird, Sam, and Raed Safadi. 2001. The WTO and Development. World Trade Organization, Geneva. Photocopy (October). Available at www.unctad.org/en/docs/c1d2.en.pdf.

Lawrence, Robert Z., ed. 1998. *Brookings Trade Forum 1998.* Washington: Brookings Institution Press.

Leamer, Edward E. 1983. Let's Take the Con Out of Econometrics. *American Economic Review* 73, no. 1: 31–43.

Leamer, Edward E. 1988. Measures of Openness. In *Trade Policy Issues and Empirical Analysis*, ed. Robert E. Baldwin. National Bureau of Economic Research Conference Report Series. Chicago: University of Chicago Press.

Lerner, Abba P. 1936. The Symmetry Between Import and Export Taxes. *Economica* 3: 306–13.

Levine, Ross, and David Renelt. 1992. A Sensitivity Analysis of Cross-Country Growth Regressions. *American Economic Review* 82, no. 4: 942–63.

Lewis, Jeffrey D., Sherman Robinson, and Kren Thierfelder. 2002. *Free Trade Agreements and the SADC Economies*. Africa Region Working Paper 27. Washington: World Bank.

Lindsey, Brink. 1999. *The US Antidumping Law: Rhetoric versus Reality*. Trade Policy Analysis 7. Washington: Cato Institute. www.freetrade.org/pubs/pas/tpa-007es.html.

Little, Ian, Tibor Scitovsky, and Maurice Scott. 1970. *Industry and Trade in Some Developing Countries*. London: Oxford University Press.

Lofgren, Hans, Rebecca Lee Harris, and Sherman Robinson. 2001. *A Standard Computable General Equilibrium (CGE) Model in GAMS*. Trade and Macroeconomics Division Discussion Paper 75. Washington: International Food Policy Research Institute.

MacLaren, Donald. 1997. An Evaluation of the Cairns Group Strategies for Agriculture in the Uruguay Round. In *Global Trade Analysis: Modeling and Applications*, ed. Thomas W. Hertel. Cambridge: Cambridge University Press.

Martin, Will. 2001. Trade Policies, Developing Countries, and Globalization. World Bank, Washington. Photocopy (October).

Martin, Will, Dominique van der Mensbrugghe, and Vlad Manole. 2003. Is the Devil in the Details? Assessing the Welfare Implications of Agricultural and Non-Agricultural Trade Reforms. World Bank, Washington. Photocopy (May).

Martin, Will, and L. A. Winters, eds. 1996. *The Uruguay Round and the Developing Countries*. New York: Cambridge University Press.

Mattoo, Aaditya. 2000. Trade in Services: Economics and Law. World Bank, Washington. Photocopy (April).

Mattoo, Aaditya, Devesh Roy, and Arvind Subramanian. 2002. *The Africa Growth and Opportunity Act and Its Rules of Origin: Generosity Undermined?* IMF Working Paper WP/02/158. Washington: International Monetary Fund.

McDougall, Robert A., and Betina V., Dimaranan. No date. Guide to the GTAP Data Base. www.gtap.agecon.purdue.edu/databases/v5/v5_doco.asp.

Meeraus, Alexander. 1983. An Algebraic Approach to Modelling. *Journal of Economic Dynamics and Control* 5: 81–108.

Michalopoulos, Constantine. 1999. Trade Policy and Market Access Issues for Developing Countries: Implications for the Millennium Round. World Bank, Washington. Photocopy (October).

Mistiaen, Johan A., and Martin Ravallion. 2003. Survey Compliance and the Distribution of Income. World Bank, Washington. Photocopy (July). http://econ.worldbank.org/files/23189_wps2956.pdf.

Moran, Theodore H. 2003. *Reforming OPIC for the 21st Century*. POLICY ANALYSES IN INTERNATIONAL ECONOMICS 69. Washington: Institute for International Economics.

Ng, Francis, and Alexander Yeats. 1996. *Open Economies Work Better! Did Africa's Protectionist Policies Cause Its Marginalization in World Trade?* World Bank Working Paper 1636. Washington: World Bank.

Nilsson, Lars. 2002. Trading Relations: Is the Roadmap from Lomé to Cotonou Correct? *Applied Economics* 34: 439–52.

Noland, Marcus, and Howard Pack. 2003. *Industrial Policy in an Era of Globalization: Lessons from Asia*. Washington: Institute for International Economics.

OECD (Organization for Economic Cooperation and Development). 1997. Market Access for the Least Developed Countries: Where Are the Obstacles? OECD, Paris. Photocopy (October).

OECD (Organization for Economic Cooperation and Development). 2000. Tariffs and Trade: OECD Query and Reporting System, CD-ROM. Paris: OECD.

OECD (Organization for Economic Cooperation and Development). 2002a. *Agricultural Policies in OECD Countries: Monitoring and Evaluation*. Paris: OECD.

OECD (Organization for Economic Cooperation and Development). 2002b. *Annual National Accounts of OECD Countries.* Paris: OECD. www.oecd.org/EN/document/O,,EN-document-424-15-no-1-30531-0,00.html.

OECD (Organization for Economic Cooperation and Development). 2002c. *International Trade in Goods Statistics.* Paris: OECD. www.oecd.org/EN/statistics/0,,EN-statistics-422-nodirectorate-no-1-no-24,00.html.

OECD (Organization for Economic Cooperation and Development). 2003a. *Agricultural Policies in OECD Countries: Monitoring and Evaluation.* Paris: OECD.

OECD (Organization for Economic Cooperation and Development). 2003b. *Agricultural Trade and Poverty: Making Policy Count.* Paris: OECD.

OECD (Organization for Economic Cooperation and Development). 2003c. *The Doha Development Agenda: Welfare Gains from Further Multilateral Trade Liberalisation with Respect to Tariffs.* Paris: OECD.

OECD (Organization for Economic Cooperation and Development). 2003d. *Methodology for the Measurement of Support and Use in Policy Evaluation.* Paris: OECD. www.oecd.org.

OECD (Organization for Economic Cooperation and Development). 2003e. OECD in Figures: Statistics on the Member Countries. *OECD Observer,* Supplement.

OECD (Organization for Economic Cooperation and Development). 2003f. *The Sources of Growth in OECD Countries.* Paris: OECD.

Oxfam. 2002. *Rigged Rules and Double Standards: Trade, Globalisation, and the Fight against Poverty.* Oxford: Oxfam. www.maketradefair.com.

Oxfam International. 2001. Rigged Trade and Not Much Aid: How Rich Countries Help to Keep the Least Developed Countries Poor. Oxfam, Washington. Photocopy (May).

Page, Sheila, and Adrian Hewitt. 2002. The New European Trade Preferences: Does "Everything But Arms" (EBA) Help the Poor? *Development Policy Review* 20, no. 1: 91–102.

Panagariya, Arvind, and Rupa Dutta-Gupta. 2002. The "Gains" from Preferential Trade Liberalization in the CGE Models: Where Do They Come From? University of Maryland, College Park. Photocopy.

Ravallion, Martin. 2001. Growth, Inequality and Poverty: Looking Beyond Averages. *World Development* 29, no. 11: 1803–15.

Ravallion, Martin. 2002. Have We Already Met the Millennium Development Goals for Poverty? Surjit Bhalla's *Imagine There's No Country. Economic and Political Weekly,* November 16–22.

Reimer, Jeffrey J. 2002. *Estimating the Poverty Impacts of Trade Liberalization.* Policy Research Working Paper 2790. Washington: World Bank.

Resal. 1999. The "Everything But Arms" Initiative: What Are Its Consequences for the Resal Countries? Technical Note, Solagral, Nogent sur Marne, France. Photocopy (June).

Revenga, Ana L., and Claudio E. Montenegro. 1998. North American Integration and Factor Price Equalization: Is There Evidence of Wage Convergence Between Mexico and the United States? In *Imports, Exports, and the American Worker,* ed. Susan M. Collins. Washington: Brookings Institution Press.

Robbins, Donald. 1996. HOS Hits Facts: Facts Win—Evidence on Trade and Wages in the Developing World. Development Discussion Paper 557, Harvard Institute for International Development, Cambridge, MA. Photocopy (October).

Robinson, Sherman. 1989. Multisectoral Models. In *Handbook of Development Economics,* vol. 2, ed. Hollis Chenery and T. N. Srinivasan. Amsterdam: North Holland.

Robinson, Sherman, Zhi Wang, and Will Martin. 2002. Capturing the Implications of Services Trade Liberalization. International Food Policy Research Institute, Washington. Photocopy.

Rodriguez, Francisco, and Dani Rodrik. 2000. Trade Policy and Economic Growth: A Skeptic's Guide to the Cross-National Evidence. Harvard University, Cambridge, MA. Photocopy (May). (An earlier version is available as NBER Working Paper 7081. Cambridge, MA: National Bureau of Economic Research, 1999.)

Rodrik, Dani. 1992. The Limits of Trade Policy Reform in Developing Countries. *Journal of Economic Perspectives* 6, no. 1: 87–105.

Rodrik, Dani. 2001. *The Global Governance of Trade as If Development Really Mattered*. New York: United Nations Development Program.

Rodrik, Dani, Arvind Subramanian, and Francesco Trebbi. 2002. Institutions Rule: The Primacy of Institutions over Geography and Integration in Economic Development. Harvard University, Cambridge, MA. Photocopy (October).

Romer, Paul. 1994. The Origins of Endogenous Growth Theory. *Journal of Economic Perspectives* 8, no. 1: 3–21.

Rozanski, Jerzy, Aki Kuwahara, and Azita Amajadi. 2002. Merchandise Tariff Data. In *Global Trade, Assistance, and Production: The GTAP5 Data Base*, ed. Betina V. Dimaranan and Robert A. McDougall. West Lafayette, IN: Center for Global Trade Analysis, Purdue University.

Rutherford, Thomas F. 1998. Economic Equilibrium Modeling with GAMS: An Introduction to GAMS/MCP and GAMS/MPSGE. In *GAMS MPSGE Guide*. Washington: GAMS Development Corporation.

Rutherford, Thomas F., and David G. Tarr. 1998. *Trade Liberalization, Product Variety and Growth in a Small Open Economy: A Quantitative Assessment*. Policy Research Working Paper 1970. Washington: World Bank.

Rutherford, Thomas F., and David G. Tarr. 2002. Trade Liberalization, Product Variety and Growth in a Small Open Economy: A Quantitative Assessment. *Journal of International Economics* 56: 247–72.

Sala-i-Martin, Xavier X. 1997. I Just Ran Two Million Regressions. *American Economic Review* 87, no. 2: 178–83.

Sachs, Jeffrey, and Andrew Warner. 1995. Economic Reform and the Process of Global Integration. *Brookings Papers on Economic Activity* 1: 1–118.

Slaughter, Matthew J. 2001. Trade Liberalization and Per Capita Income Convergence: A Difference-in-difference Analysis. *Journal of International Economics* 55: 203–28.

Stevens, Christopher, and Jane Kennan. 2001. The Impact of the EU's "Everything but Arms" Proposal: A Report to Oxfam. Institute of Development Studies, Brighton, UK. Photocopy (January).

Stolper, Wolfgang, and Paul A. Samuelson. 1941. Protection and Real Wages. *Review of Economic Studies* 9, no. 1: 58–73.

Thierfelder, Karen, and Sherman Robinson. 2002. *Trade and Tradability: Exports, Imports, and Factor Markets in the Salter-Swan Model*. TMD Discussion Paper 93. Washington: International Food Policy Research Institute.

Thissen, Mark. 1998. Two Decades of CGE Modelling: Lessons from Models for Egypt. SOM Research Report 99C02, University of Groningen, Groningen, Netherlands. Photocopy (December).

UNCTAD (UN Conference on Trade and Development). 1964. Towards a New Trade Policy for Development. E/CONF.46/3. Geneva: UNCTAD.

UNCTAD (UN Conference on Trade and Development). 1999. *Quantifying the Benefits Obtained by Developing Countries from the Generalized System of Preferences*. Geneva: UNCTAD.

UNCTAD (UN Conference on Trade and Development). 2002a. *The Least Developed Countries Report 2002: Escaping the Poverty Trap*. Geneva: UNCTAD.

UNCTAD (UN Conference on Trade and Development). 2002b. *Statistical Profiles of LDCs, 2001*. Geneva: UNCTAD. www.unctad.org/en/pub/ldcprofiles2001.en.htm.

UNCTAD (UN Conference on Trade and Development). 2003. *Trade and Development Report 2003: Capital Accumulation, Growth and Structural Change*. Geneva: UNCTAD.

UNCTAD (UN Conference on Trade and Development) and Commonwealth Secretariat. 2001. *Duty and Quota Free Market Access for LDCs: An Analysis of Quad Initiatives*. Geneva: UNCTAD.

UNDP (UN Development Program). 2001. *Human Development Report 2001: Making New Technologies Work for Human Development.* New York: UNDP.

United Nations. 2000. *World Investment Report 2000: Cross-Border Mergers and Acquisitions and Development.* New York: United Nations Conference on Trade and Development.

United Nations. 2001. World Population Prospects: Population Database. New York: United Nations Population Division. http://esa.un.org/unpp/.

United Nations. 2002. United Nations Statistical Division, Comtrade Database.

US Census. 2002. *Foreign Trade Statistics.* Washington: US Census Bureau. www.census.gov/foreign-trade/www/.

US Department of Commerce. 2002. *About AGOA.* Washington: US Department of Commerce. www.agoa.gov/.

USITC (US International Trade Commission). 1997. *The Dynamic Effects of Trade Liberalization: An Empirical Analysis.* Investigation 332-375, Publication 3069. Washington: USITC.

USITC (US International Trade Commission). 2001. *The Impact of the Caribbean Basin Economic Recovery Act: Fifteenth Report, 1999–2000.* Investigation 332-227, Publication 3447. Washington: USITC.

USITC (US International Trade Commission). 2002. *Harmonized Tariff Schedule of the United States (2002)(Rev. 2).* Publication 3477. Washington: US Government Printing Office.

USITC (US International Trade Commission). 2003. USITC *Interactive* Tariff and Trade Data Web. http://dataweb.usitc.gov/.

USTR (Office of the US Trade Representative). 1999. *U.S. Generalized System of Preferences: Guidebook.* Washington: USTR. www.ustr.gov.

USTR (Office of the US Trade Representative). 2001a. *Fourth Report to Congress on the Operation of the Caribbean Basin Economic Recovery Act.* Washington: USTR. www.ustr.gov.

USTR (Office of the US Trade Representative). 2001b. *Third Report to the Congress on the Operation of the Andean Trade Preference Act.* Washington: USTR.

USTR (Office of the US Trade Representative). 2002. *Steel: President Bush Takes Action on Steel.* Washington: USTR. www.ustr.gov/sectors/industry/steel.html.

USTR (Office of the US Trade Representative). 2003. *Comprehensive Report on U.S. Trade and Investment Policy Toward Sub-Saharan Africa and Implementation of the African Growth and Opportunity Act.* Washington: USTR. www.ustr.gov/reports/2003agoa.pdf.

Van der Mensbrugghe, Dominique. 2003. Linkage Technical Reference Document. Development Prospects Group, World Bank, Washington. Photocopy (March)

Van der Mensbrugghe, Dominique 2004. Model Comparison: GEP 04 and William Cline (IIE). World Bank, Washington. Photocopy (February).

Van Meijl, J. C. M., and F. W. van Tongeren. 2001. Multilateral Trade Liberalisation and Developing Countries: A North-South Perspective on Agriculture and Processing Sectors. Agricultural Economics Research Institute, The Hague. Photocopy (July).

Venables, Anthony J. 1999. Regional Integration Agreements: A Force for Convergence or Divergence? London School of Economics, London. Photocopy (June).

Waczlarg, Romain, and Karen Horn Welch. 2003. Trade Liberalization and Growth: New Evidence. Graduate School of Business, Stanford University, Stanford, CA. Photocopy (November).

Warner, Andrew. 2003. *Once More into the Breach: Economic Growth and Integration.* Working Paper 34. Washington. Center for Global Development.

WIDER (World Institute for Development Economics Research, United Nations University). 2000. World Income Inequality Database, version 1.0. Tokyo: WIDER.

Winters, Alan L. 2001. Harnessing Trade for Development. Paper prepared for Conference on Making Globalization Work for the Poor—the European Contribution, Kramfors, Sweden, June 20–21.

Wolf, Holger. 1993. Trade Orientation: Measurement and Consequences. *Estudios de Economía* 20, no. 2: 52–72.

Wolfensohn, James D. 2002. A Time to Act. Address to the Board of Governors, World Bank Annual Meeting, Washington, September 29.

Wood, Adrian. 1997. Openness and Wage Inequality in Developing Countries: The Latin American Challenge to East Asian Conventional Wisdom. *World Bank Economic Review* 11, no. 1: 33–57.

Wooldridge, Jeffrey M. 2001. Applications of Generalized Method of Moments Estimation. *Journal of Economic Perspectives* 15, no. 4: 87–100.

World Bank. 1982. *World Development Report 1982.* New York: Oxford University Press.

World Bank. 2001. *World Development Report 2000/2001: Attacking Poverty.* New York: Oxford University Press.

World Bank. 2002a. *Global Economic Prospects and the Developing Countries 2002: Making Trade Work for the World's Poor.* Washington: World Bank.

World Bank. 2002b. Market Access and the World's Poor. In *Global Economic Prospects and the Developing Countries 2002: Making Trade Work for the World's Poor.* Washington: World Bank.

World Bank. 2002c. *Trade and Production 1976–1999.* Washington: World Bank. www. worldbank.org/wbiep/trade/TradeandProduction.html.

World Bank. 2002d. World Development Indicators 2002, CD-ROM. Washington: World Bank.

World Bank. 2002e. *World Development Report 2002: Building Institutions for Markets.* New York: Oxford University Press.

World Bank. 2003. *Global Economic Prospects 2004: Realizing the Development Prospects of the Doha Agenda.* Washington: World Bank.

WTO (World Trade Organization). 2001. *International Trade Statistics 2001.* Geneva: WTO. www.wto.org.

WTO (World Trade Organization). 2002. *Market Access: Unfinished Business, Post-Uruguay Round Inventory and Issues.* Geneva: WTO.

Yang, Yongzheng, Will Martin, and Koji Yanagishima. 1997. Evaluating the Benefits of Abolishing the MFA in the Uruguay Round Package. In *Global Trade Analysis: Modeling and Applications*, ed. Thomas W. Hertel. Cambridge: Cambridge University Press.

Yanikkaya, Halit. 2003. Trade Openness and Economic Growth: A Cross-Country Empirical Investigation. *Journal of Development Economics* 72, no. 1: 57–89.

Yeats, Alexander J., Azita Amjadi, Ulrich Reincke, and Francis Ng. 1996. What Caused Sub-Saharan Africa's Marginalization in World Trade? *Finance and Development*, December: 38–41.

# Index

manufactures, welfare gains, 179, 180*t*
manufacturing share coefficient, 97
marketing board monopoly variable, 242
metal industries
  NTBs, 137, 137*t*
Mexico, 24, 72, 73, 85, 99, 107, 182, 183, 206*n*, 221,
    236, 257, 268, 276–77
  food trade balance, 132, 133*t*
  underpredicted poverty, 37
  World Bank estimates, 17
MFN. *See* most-favored nation tariffs
Middle East
  combined effects on poverty reduction, 252*t*,
    253–54
  dynamic productivity effects on poverty, 250*t*
  poverty-impact estimates, 283*t*
middle-income countries
  liberalization, tariff protection, 290
Moldavia, 138
most-favored nation (MFN) tariffs
  duty-free, 94
  product weightings, 107
  rates, 176
"movement of individuals" services, 147
Mozambique, 218
  domestic growth, 242
  food trade balance, 132, 133*t*
Multi-Fiber Arrangement (MFA), 76, 114

NAFTA. *See* North American Free Trade
    Agreement
negative per-capita growth. *See* divergence
Nepal, 16
"new trade theory," 142
New Zealand, 271, 287
  agricultural shortfalls, 186
Nigeria, 10, 77
nonconvergence of economic growth, 40, 41
nontariff barriers (NTBs), 68
  in Quad, 137*t*
North Africa
  combined effects on poverty reduction, 252*t*,
    253–54
  dynamic productivity effects on poverty, 250*t*
  poverty-impact estimates, 283*t*
North American Free Trade Agreement (NAFTA),
    67, 85, 291
  US steel safeguarding, 138
Norway, 271
  GSP, 72, 73*n*
NTBs. *See* nontariff barriers
"numeraire," 204

OECD. *See* Organization for Economic
    Cooperation and Development
oil, petroleum, 77, 86*n*, 87, 87*n*
  AGOA, 92, 94
  AMP against developing countries, 127, 127*t*
  ATPA, 89

Japan, 128
  and poverty intensity, 24, 26
  trade measures, 92*n*
  US imports, 87
  Venezuela, 88
OPIC. *See* Overseas Private Investment
    Corporation
optimum tariffs, 190–91
Organization for Economic Cooperation and
    Development (OECD), 106
  agricultural exports, imports, 125, 125*n*
  HIOECD, 107, 107*n*
  productivity elasticity relative to trade/GDP
    ratio, 236, 237*t*
  PSE, 120
  subsidy estimates, 120
  trade exposure ratio, 235–36
  TSE, 120, 271–72
  welfare estimates, 195
  welfare source attributions, 195
  *vs.* World Bank model, 278
ordinary-least-squares regression
  impact of special trade arrangements, 95–97
output elasticity, trade/GDP ratio, 236–38, 237*t*
Overseas Private Investment Corporation (OPIC),
    99

Pakistan, 10, 61, 264
  food trade balance, 132, 133*t*
Pareto distribution, 32*n*
Paris Club, 14
peak tariffs, 108, 114*t*, 149, 273
  apparel, textiles, 112
pearls, 24
PEHRT (Poverty Effects-HRT) model, 172
  agricultural liberalization, 212, 277
  alternative shocks to, 184–91
  B25, 177, 224*t*
  description, use of, 5
  differing welfare source attribution, 195
  and erosion of trade preferences, 222
  factor price effects, 204–08
  features of, 221–22
  mapping to GTAP5, 223*t*, 225*t*
  P26, 177, 224*t*
  population in poverty, 279
  poverty elasticity, 250*t*
  poverty reduction, 212
  poverty-impact estimates, 213–14, 214*t*
  regions, 224*t*
  rural-urban poverty model, 211–12
  selected countries, 177
  SS model, 279, 281
  trade productivity, 281
  two-tier liberalization, 185–86
  *vs.* WBGEP, 197, 197*n*
per capita growth
  and per capita income, 60–61
Peru, 88, 89, 90

CGE model, 152
estimated impact of trade liberalization on
poverty, 143–44
estimates for China, India, 16–17
poverty estimates, 10, 28–29
accuracy of, 31
poverty reduction estimates, 143$n$, 144–45
poverty-impact estimates, 284–85
reporting estimates, 2–3
underestimates of poverty, 44
World Bank Global Economic Prospects
(WBGEP), 141–43
and asymmetric liberalization, 187
consumption structure, 196
differing welfare source attribution, 195
impact of free trade estimates, 234
productivity elasticity relative to trade/GDP
ratio, 236, 237$t$
trade ratio, 235
*vs.* consolidated estimates of others, 254
*vs.* OECD model, 278

*vs.* PEHRT, 197, 197$n$
welfare estimates, 144
World Bank's World Integrated Trade Solution
(WITS), 164, 176
World Institute for Development Economics
Research (WIDER), 33
World Trade Organization (WTO)
agricultural subsidy data, 176
Cancún meeting breakdown, 286–87
service trade modes, 146–47
structure of, 288–89
subsidy estimates, 119
US steel safeguarding, 138

Yanikkaya study, 248$n$
Yaoundé Convention, 78
yarn, 112, 113$n$

Zambia, 79, 83, 145
food trade balance, 132, 133$t$
Zimbabwe, food trade balance, 132, 133$t$

## BOOKS

## WORKS IN PROGRESS

## DISTRIBUTORS OUTSIDE THE UNITED STATES

**Australia, New Zealand,
and Papua New Guinea**
D.A. Information Services
648 Whitehorse Road
Mitcham, Victoria 3132, Australia
tel: 61-3-9210-7777
fax: 61-3-9210-7788
email: service@adadirect.com.au
http://www.dadirect.com.au

**United Kingdom and Europe**
(including Russia and Turkey)
The Eurospan Group
3 Henrietta Street, Covent Garden
London WC2E 8LU England
tel: 44-20-7240-0856
fax: 44-20-7379-0609
http:/ /www.eurospan.co.uk

**Japan and the Republic of Korea**
United Publishers Services, Ltd.
KenkyuSha Bldg.
9, Kanda Surugadai 2-Chome
Chiyoda-Ku, Tokyo 101 Japan
tel: 81-3-3291-4541
fax: 81-3-3292-8610
email: saito@ups.co.jp
**For trade accounts only.
Individuals will find IIE books in
leading Tokyo bookstores.**

**Thailand**
Asia Books
5 Sukhumvit Rd. Soi 61
Bangkok 10110 Thailand
tel: 662-714-07402 Ext: 221, 222, 223
fax: 662-391-2277
email: purchase@asiabooks.co.th
http://www.asiabooksonline.com

**Canada**
Renouf Bookstore
5369 Canotek Road, Unit 1
Ottawa, Ontario KIJ 9J3, Canada
tel: 613-745-2665
fax: 613-745-7660
http://www.renoufbooks.com

**India, Bangladesh, Nepal, and Sri Lanka**
Viva Books Pvt.
Mr. Vinod Vasishtha
4325/3, Ansari Rd.
Daryaganj, New Delhi-110002
India
tel: 91-11-327-9280
fax: 91-11-326-7224
email: vinod.viva@gndel.globalnet.
ems.vsnl.net.in

**Southeast Asia** (Brunei, Cambodia,
China, Malaysia, Hong Kong, Indonesia,
Laos, Myanmar, the Philippines, Singapore,
Taiwan, and Vietnam)
Hemisphere Publication Services
1 Kallang Pudding Rd. #0403
Golden Wheel Building
Singapore 349316
tel: 65-741-5166
fax: 65-742-9356

---

**Visit our Web site at:
www.iie.com
E-mail orders to:
orders@iie.com**